The Demise of Finance-dominated Capitalism

NEW DIRECTIONS IN MODERN ECONOMICS

Series Editor: Malcolm C. Sawyer, Professor of Economics, University of Leeds, UK

New Directions in Modern Economics presents a challenge to orthodox economic thinking. It focuses on new ideas emanating from radical traditions including post-Keynesian, Kaleckian, neo-Ricardian and Marxian. The books in the series do not adhere rigidly to any single school of thought but attempt to present a positive alternative to the conventional wisdom.

For a full list of Edward Elgar published titles, including the titles in this series, visit our website at www.e-elgar.com.

The Demise of Finance-dominated Capitalism

Explaining the Financial and Economic Crises

Edited by

Eckhard Hein

Institute for International Political Economy (IPE), Berlin School of Economics and Law, Germany

Daniel Detzer

Institute for International Political Economy (IPE), Berlin School of Economics and Law, Germany

Nina Dodig

Institute for International Political Economy (IPE), Berlin School of Economics and Law, Germany

NEW DIRECTIONS IN MODERN ECONOMICS

Edward Elgar
PUBLISHING

Cheltenham, UK • Northampton, MA, USA

Published by
Edward Elgar Publishing Limited
The Lypiatts
15 Lansdown Road
Cheltenham
Glos GL50 2JA
UK

Edward Elgar Publishing, Inc.
William Pratt House
9 Dewey Court
Northampton
Massachusetts 01060
USA

Paperback edition 2016

A catalogue record for this book
is available from the British Library

Library of Congress Control Number: 2014954937

This book is available electronically in the **Elgar**online
Economics subject collection
DOI 10.4337/9781784715076

ISBN   978 1 78471 506 9 (cased)
ISBN   978 1 78471 507 6 (eBook)
ISBN   978 1 78471 496 3 (paperback)

Typeset by Servis Filmsetting Ltd, Stockport, Cheshire
Printed and bound in Great Britain by TJ International Ltd, Padstow

Contents

v

Contributors

Ricardo Barradas is a Ph.D. Candidate in Economics at ISCTE – University Institute of Lisbon. He is a teaching assistant at the Higher School of Communication and Media Studies and Higher School of Accounting and Administration of Lisbon (Polytechnic Institute of Lisbon) and a research assistant at Dinâmia'CET – IUL. His main research interests are in the fields of financial markets, the financial system, monetary policy and other related areas. He has worked for four years in the Portuguese banking system as a financial markets analyst.

Natalia Budyldina is a Master in International Economics. She graduated from the Berlin School of Economics and Law, and currently she is working in the field of innovative business and consulting.

Carlos A. Carrasco is a FESSUD Research Fellow at the Department of Applied Economics V of the University of the Basque Country (UPV/ EHU). His current and past research fields include inflation targeting implementation and functioning, global and European imbalances, institutional dimensions of monetary policy, and economic integration in Mexico and the European Union. He has published in academic journals including *Journal of Economic Policy Reform, Journal of Post Keynesian Economics, Applied Economics, Panoeconomicus, Intereconomics: Review of European Economic Policy, Revista de Economía Mundial* and *Ola Financiera*.

Daniel Detzer obtained a BA in Economics and an MA in International Economics. He works as a FESSUD Research Fellow at the Department of Business and Economics of the Berlin School of Economics and Law. His current and past research fields include banking and financial systems, financial crises, financial regulation, macroeconomics and European imbalances. He also has four years of practical experience in finance, having worked for German and French banking institutions.

Nina Dodig has degrees in Economics of Tourism from the University of Perugia and in International Economics from the Berlin School of Economics and Law. She currently works as a Research Fellow on the project 'Financialisation, Economy, Society and Sustainable

Development' (FESSUD) and as a lecturer in macroeconomics at the Berlin School of Economics and Law. Her main research interests are in the field of finance and financial systems, financial crises, European economic policies and post-Keynesian macroeconomics.

Trevor Evans has degrees in Political Science from the University of Kent at Canterbury and Economics from the University of London. He worked for many years at the Centre for Economic and Social Research in Managua, Nicaragua, and has been Professor of Monetary Theory, Monetary Policy and International Monetary Relations at the Berlin School of Economics and Law since 2006.

Giampaolo Gabbi is Professor of Financial Markets at the University of Siena and Director of the Banking and Insurance Department of SDA Bocconi School of Management. He holds a Ph.D. in Banking and Corporate Management from the Bocconi University in Milan. He was a Lecturer at City University, London (2009–13). He has published many books and articles in refereed journals, including *Journal of International Financial Markets, Institutions and Money, Nature Scientific Report, Managerial Finance, European Journal of Finance*, and *Journal of Economic Dynamics and Control*.

Eckhard Hein is Professor of Economics at the Berlin School of Economics and Law, a member of the coordination committee of the Research Network Macroeconomics and Macroeconomic Policies (FMM), and managing co-editor of the *European Journal of Economics and Economic Policies: Intervention*. His research focuses on money, financial systems, distribution and growth, European economic policies and post-Keynesian macroeconomics. His latest books are *The Macroeconomics of Finance-Dominated Capitalism – and Its Crisis* (Edward Elgar, 2012) and *Distribution and Growth after Keynes: A Post-Keynesian Guide* (Edward Elgar, 2014). He is the coordinator of Work Package 3: 'Causes and Consequences of the Financial Crisis' of the FESSUD project.

Hansjörg Herr is Professor for Supranational Integration at the Berlin School of Economics and Law. His main research areas are in monetary macroeconomics, development economics (especially development in China) and European integration. He is one of the organizers of the Global Labour University.

Alesia Kalbaska holds a Ph.D. diploma from the University of Siena and is currently a Postdoctoral Research Fellow at its Department of Economics and Statistics. She has also been a visiting Ph.D. scholar at

Essex University, UK. She has published in the *Journal of Economic Behavior and Organization*.

Sérgio Lagoa is an Assistant Professor at Instituto Universitário de Lisboa (ISCTE – IUL) and a researcher at Dinâmia'CET – IUL. His research interests and publications are in macroeconomics, monetary economics and labour economics. He has recent publications in *Open Economies Review*, *Research in Economics*, *Economic and Industrial Democracy* and *Economics and Labour Relations Review*.

Emanuel Leão obtained a Ph.D. in Economics from the University of York. He is an Assistant Professor at ISCTE – University Institute of Lisbon and researcher at Dinâmia'CET – IUL. His research interests are in the areas of banking, financial markets, public finance and monetary policy. His main published articles have appeared in the *Journal of Economics* and *Economic Modelling*. He was head of department in 2005–07 and 2010–13, and he is currently Vice-Dean of the School of Social Sciences and Humanities of ISCTE – IUL.

Jo Michell is a Senior Lecturer in Economics at the University of the West of England, Bristol. He teaches macroeconomics, banking and finance, and history of economic thought. He completed his Ph.D. at SOAS, University of London in 2012. His research interests include post-Keynesian macroeconomics, banking and finance, growth and inequality, and the economic development of China. He serves on the committee of the UK-based Post-Keynesian Economics Study Group.

Özgür Orhangazi is an Associate Professor of Economics at Kadir Has University in Istanbul. He is the author of *Financialization and the US Economy* (2008) and numerous articles and book chapters on financialization, financial crises and alternative economic policies. He holds a Ph.D. from the University of Massachusetts Amherst (2006) and previously taught economics at Roosevelt University in Chicago (2006–11).

Felipe Serrano is a Full Professor in Applied Economics and Head of the Department of Applied Economics V of the University of the Basque Country (UPV/EHU). His research interests include pension economics, social security, economics of innovation, the labour market, institutional economics and macroeconomic policy. He has published in academic journals such as *Journal of Pension Economics and Finance*, *International Review of Applied Economics*, *International Labour Review*, *Journal of Economic Issues*, *Journal of Post Keynesian Economics*, *Industrial and Labor Relations Review*, *Panoeconomicus*, *International Journal of Public Policy* and *Journal of Innovation Economics*.

Alessandro Vercelli is a Professor of Political Economy and teaches 'Economics of sustainable development' at the University of Siena. He is a professorial research associate of the Department of Economics at SOAS, University of London, and life member of Clare Hall, Cambridge. He has been vice-president of the International Economic Association and a member of the Executive Committee of the Italian Economic Association. He obtained a Fulbright–SSRC award and was winner of the St Vincent Prize (1988) and the Casentino Prize (2011). He has been a distinguished visiting fellow at Queen Mary University of London, British Council senior visiting fellow, St Antony's College, Oxford (1996), and visiting scholar at universities including New York University, UCLA, STICERD at LSE, St Antony's College, Oxford, and the universities of Cambridge, Bielefeld, Nice, Valencia and Rio de Janeiro. He is the author and editor of several books and articles in the field of economic policy and sustainability published in international journals.

Acknowledgements

The chapters of this book are parts of the results of the project Financialisation, Economy, Society and Sustainable Development (FESSUD) (2011–16), which has received funding from the European Union Seventh Framework Programme (FP7/2007–13) under grant agreement no. 266800. The only exception is Chapter 5, which was first published in *The Perspective of the World Review*, 2011, Vol. 3 (1), 9–28. We are most grateful for the permission to reprint. We are heavily indebted to Jeffrey Althouse and Henriette Heinze, who have assisted us in the editing process. Finally, we would like to thank the staff of Edward Elgar Publishing for their reliable support throughout this project.

Eckhard Hein, Daniel Detzer and Nina Dodig
Berlin, September 2014

Introduction

Eckhard Hein, Daniel Detzer and Nina Dodig

This book explores and reviews the literature on the long-run transition towards finance-dominated capitalism, and the implications for macroeconomic and financial stability and, in particular, for the recent global financial and economic crises. In our view, the recent crises indicate the demise of finance-dominated capitalism. This does not mean that the dominance of finance will necessarily disappear – quite the opposite, in fact, as it seems presently. But, against the background of the analyses presented in this book, it is difficult to imagine that finance-dominated capitalism in the future will be able to generate sustainable high growth rates in the mature capitalist economies.

The advanced capitalist economies have gone through two distinct regimes or stages of development since the end of the Second World War. The 'golden age' period of the 1950s and 1960s was characterized by relatively high growth rates, low unemployment and low inflation. It was based on a 'social bargain' or 'social compromise' between capital and labour, increasingly involving government activities. (Nearly) full employment was attained by Keynesian macroeconomic policies and supported by a strong welfare state in most of the advanced economies. The erosion of the 'golden age' period culminated in the 'stagflation' of the 1970s, which triggered a neo-liberal economic reaction. Policy responses focused on the deregulation of markets, and of labour and financial markets particularly, on the one hand, and on achieving price stability instead of full employment, on the other hand. This neo-liberal 'counter-revolution' has provided the conditions for the emergence of 'financialization' or 'finance-dominated capitalism' since the early 1980s, starting in the USA and the UK and spreading over the developed and, subsequently, also the developing capitalist world. This stage of development has been characterized by the expansion of financial markets, the introduction of new financial instruments, and the increasing dominance of financial motives in economic activity. Over the last 30 or so years, finance has come to dominate industry, and non-financial corporations have been increasingly engaged in financial as opposed to productive activities. Alignment of manage-

1

ment with shareholder interests reflected the shifting focus towards pursuing short-term 'shareholder value' maximization instead of the long-run growth objectives of the firm. What followed was a period of distinctly lower rates of capital accumulation in advanced capitalist economies, accompanied by rising inequality of incomes and wealth, and redistribution in favour of capital and at the expense of labour. In order to sustain consumption or to follow rising consumption norms by higher income groups, in some countries households relied increasingly on credit to finance their consumption expenditures, creating the problems of private household over-indebtedness in these countries. In other countries, weak investment and weak income-financed consumption demand was (partly) compensated for by rising net exports and current account surpluses, contributing to regional and global imbalances and to the latent over-indebtedness of the counterpart current account deficit countries.

Against this background the subprime crisis that broke out in the United States in 2007 could subsequently turn into the global financial and economic crises, the most severe crisis of global capitalism since the Great Depression. Seven years later, the world economy is still suffering from the consequences. In our view the general causes of the global financial and economic crises can be found in the problems, inconsistencies and contradictions of finance-dominated capitalism.

Our book will therefore firstly provide an overview of the transition towards finance-dominated capitalism as described in different strands of the literature. The long-run tendencies of financialization and its consequences are then analysed from a macroeconomic perspective. Subsequently, theories of financial crisis as well as important past crises are reviewed. From Chapter 5 onwards, the book deals explicitly with the recent global financial and economic crises. There has been a wide range of specific causes advanced in the literature for the generation and transmission of the 2007–09 crisis. Chapter 5 gives an overview of five important factors, and Chapters 6–10 explore some of the key factors that are said to have contributed to the crisis in more detail. These are, respectively, redistribution of income, international imbalances, deregulation, securitization and contagion, and the failures in risk management. A sixth factor, overly lax monetary policies of the US Federal Reserve since the early 2000s, is already addressed more extensively in Chapter 5.

The book begins in Chapter 1 with a survey of some of the important literature on financial, economic and social systems, with an eye towards explaining the tendencies towards financialization. This introductory chapter by Eckhard Hein, Nina Dodig and Natalia Budyldina serves as a background for understanding the rise of finance-dominated capitalism following the end of the 'golden age' of capitalism. The authors focus on three important strands of the literature: the French Regulation School, the US-based Social Structures of Accumulation approach, and the contributions by several post-Keynesian authors, with a focus on the long-run views contained in Hyman Minsky's work, in particular. In their comparative assessment of these approaches, Hein, Dodig and Budyldina adopt the following four steps procedure. First, they sketch the basic structure of the approaches in order to single out how each of them views the interaction between social institutions and the economy, as well as the related dynamics regarding the development of the institutional structure and the associated stages or regimes of economic development. Second, they describe how these approaches view the structural breaks or the regime shifts in the long-run development of modern capitalism, which has triggered or at least has contributed to the emergence of a type of capitalism dominated by finance (financialization). Third, they outline how these different approaches view the main characteristics and features of financialization. Finally, they deal with the respective views on the consequences of financialization for long-run economic and social development, including the crisis of this stage of development.

In Chapter 2, Eckhard Hein and Nina Dodig review the empirical and theoretical literature on the effects of changes in the relationship between the financial sector and the non-financial sector of the economy associated with financialization on distribution, growth, instability and crises. The authors take a macroeconomic perspective and examine four channels of transmission of financialization to the macroeconomy: first, the effect on income distribution; second, the effects on investment in the capital stock; third, the effects on household debt and consumption; and, fourth, the effects on net exports and current account balances. For each of these channels Hein and Dodig briefly review some empirical and econometric literature supporting the presumed channels, and some theoretical and modelling literature examining the macroeconomic effects via these channels, and finally they present small Kaleckian models demonstrating the most important macroeconomic effects. The authors show that, against the background of redistribution of income at the expense of the labour income share and depressed investment in the capital stock, each a major feature of financialization, short- to medium-run dynamic 'profits without investment' regimes may emerge. These can be driven by flourishing debt-financed consumption demand or by rising export surpluses, compensating for low or falling investment in the capital stock. However, each type of these regimes, the 'debt-led consumption boom' type and the 'export-led mercantilist' type, contains internal contradictions: Rising household debt in the first regime and rising foreign debt of the counterpart current account deficit countries in the second regime may ultimately undermine the sustainability of these regimes and lead to financial and economic crises.

Chapter 3 by Daniel Detzer and Hansjörg Herr provides a review of the relevant contributions of different schools of economic thought to the theories of crises as cumulative processes. Detzer and Herr first examine the approaches that regard financial crises as a disturbing factor of a generally stable real economy. Contributions by Wicksell, Hayek, Schumpeter and Fisher, and the early writings by Keynes belong to this group. Thereafter, Detzer and Herr review those approaches in which the dichotomy between the monetary and the real sphere is lifted. Here, the later works by Keynes and the contributions by Minsky are particularly important. Finally, the authors take a closer look at behavioural finance approaches. Having reviewed the different approaches, Detzer and Herr assess the similarities amongst them and examine whether those approaches could be fruitfully combined. Based on this, they develop their own theoretical framework, methodologically based on a Wicksellian cumulative process, however, overcoming the neoclassical dichotomy. The chapter ends with some policy recommendations based on this theoretical framework.

In Chapter 4, Nina Dodig and Hansjörg Herr analyse several severe financial crises observed in the history of capitalism which led to a longer period of stagnation or low growth. Comparative case studies of the Great Depression, the Latin American debt crisis of the 1980s and the Japanese crisis of the 1990s and 2000s are presented. The following questions are asked: What triggered major financial crises? Which factors intensified financial crises? And, most importantly, which factors contributed most to preventing a rapid return to prosperity? The aim of the authors is thus to identify the stylized facts of previous crises, in terms both of the causes of the crises and of the difficulties in recovering from such crises. Their main conclusions are that stagnation after major financial crises becomes likely when the balance sheets of economic units are not quickly cleaned, when the nominal wage anchor breaks, and when there is no sizable and long-lasting stimulus by the state. Finally, Dodig and Herr draw tentative conclusions for the recent financial crisis and the Great Recession.

The remaining chapters of the book deal with the 2007–09 financial and economic crises by addressing the specific factors which have contributed to originating or transmitting the crises. In Chapter 5, Trevor Evans provides an overview of these factors. After briefly outlining the background to the 2007–08 international financial crisis, Evans then goes on to examine five of the main approaches that have been put forward to explain the crisis: the widespread presence of perverse incentives, the over-expansionary monetary policy of the US Federal Reserve, the impact of global imbalances and a so-called 'savings glut' in developing countries, the extensive deregulation of the financial system since the 1970s, and the attempt to generate an increasing return on the, in the recent decades vastly expanded, amount of financial capital and the associated pressure on wages. The chapter concludes with a brief note on the policy implications which follow from each of these explanations.

In Chapter 6, Jo Michell focuses on the relationship between changes in the distribution of income and the financial and economic crisis. According to Michell, the most widespread explanation for worsening inequality – technological change – is not convincing. He argues instead that the trends are better explained by the weakening of organized labour and the reduction of social protection that have taken place at the same time as the deregulation of trade and financial markets. The economic links between increasing inequality and rising household debt levels involve both household-level consumption behaviour and the macroeconomic effects of rising inequality. At the household level, Michell argues that rising debt levels were not the outcome of insurance against income volatility but were instead the result both of poor households being driven into debt by falling incomes and of imitative behaviour in which households attempted to emulate the 'conspicuous consumption' of households at the top of the distribution. At the macroeconomic level, inequality led to stagnationary tendencies, which were overcome by rising indebtedness and international imbalances.

Chapter 7 by Carlos A. Carrasco and Felipe Serrano surveys and analyses the economic literature on global and European imbalances and their connection with the global financial crisis. In the years preceding the crisis, there was increased attention paid to the existence of enormous current account imbalances among large economies worldwide. Research and policy papers can be divided into two positions regarding these imbalances. Some authors viewed global imbalances as part of a new equilibrium in the international financial system, while others urged policy intervention to reduce these imbalances. The Great Recession revived the debate over global imbalances and their influence on the gestation of the crisis. However, more recent work has clarified the relationship between the crisis and global imbalances, emphasizing the roots of the crisis in financial liberalization and the fragility of the international financial system. From this perspective, the authors highlight the need for deeper analysis of gross capital flows and the need to monitor credit levels as measures to prevent future financial crises.

Chapter 8 by Özgür Orhangazi deals with financial deregulation and its role in setting the conditions for the 2007–08 financial crisis. In the run-up to the crisis, deregulation created an environment in which mortgage lending expanded and speculation in other financial markets was heightened, even though riskiness was steadily increasing. Orhangazi first briefly reviews the history of regulation and deregulation in the USA and then discusses the channels through which financial deregulation contributed to the 2007–08 financial crisis. The author also reviews policy suggestions of those who see financial deregulation as the main contributor to the financial crisis and provides a critical assessment of these, while broadly situating financial deregulation within the context of the broader changes in capitalism since the early 1980s.

In Chapter 9, Giampaolo Gabbi, Alesia Kalbaska and Alessandro Vercelli explain the recent financial crisis and the subsequent Great Recession from the point of view of incentives that have changed as a consequence of securitization and contagion processes. The authors provide a critical analysis of the basic principles of the asymmetric information approach and its two branches that take different views on the evolution of banking and the role of securitization in it. The first focuses on the impact of securitization on the traditional model of commercial banking, whereas the latter sees the role of securitization in the emergence of a parallel banking system (shadow banking). This divergence between the two approaches leads to different policy implications that can be drawn from the analysis of the crisis, advocating, respectively, the elimination (or heavy mitigation) of securitization and shadow banking, or the strict regulation of shadow banking and all the credit transfer processes.

In Chapter 10, the final chapter, Sérgio Lagoa, Emanuel Leão and Ricardo Barradas discuss the role of risk management in the context of the subprime financial crisis. The reasons for the failure of financial institutions to manage risk appropriately are striking, since this is supposedly one of their main roles in the economy. The authors contrast the mainstream view, which argues that risk management will become more efficient with the expansion of finance and will ensure diversification and control of risk, with the financialization literature, which emphasizes that risk management by financial corporations will not be socially efficient in a context of deregulated markets and will ultimately lead to an increase of aggregate risk and crises. To assess the validity of such a claim, the authors review the literature on risk management during the subprime crisis, and identify failures that fall into three categories: technique and methodology, corporate governance and strategy, and regulation and external factors. Following the same categories they review potential remedies presented in the literature to the identified problems. The authors' conclusion is that the failures in risk management should be interpreted in light of the financialization perspective, which is therefore a valuable approach when addressing regulatory changes in the financial system.

1. The transition towards finance-dominated capitalism: French Regulation School, Social Structures of Accumulation and post-Keynesian approaches compared

Eckhard Hein, Nina Dodig and Natalia Budyldina

1.1 INTRODUCTION

This chapter provides a comparative overview of some important literature on financial, economic and social systems with an eye towards explaining the tendencies towards finance-dominated capitalism or 'financialization', broadly understood as 'the increasing role of financial motives, financial markets, financial actors and financial institutions in the operation of the domestic and international economies' (Epstein 2005a, p. 3). The chapter focuses on important strands of the literature, the French Regulation School, the Social Structures of Accumulation approach, mainly generated in the USA, and the contributions by several post-Keynesian authors, with a focus on the long-run views contained in Hyman Minsky's work, in particular. What these approaches have in common is the notion that capitalist development is embedded in social institutions and that there is a kind of interdependence between the set of institutions and economic development, each feeding back on the other. Therefore, in each of these approaches different stages of development, or different regimes, of modern capitalism can be distinguished, and some insights into the dynamics of these regimes can be obtained. These approaches are therefore particularly suited to provide the theoretical background for the examination of financialization tendencies, which have dominated modern capitalism to different degrees in different countries, roughly starting in the late 1970s or early 1980s in the USA and the UK and later in other developed capitalist economies, as well as in emerging market economies. Furthermore, these approaches provide some basic insights into the internal dynamics of financialization leading to the crisis of this stage of development of modern capitalism, which started in 2007 in the USA and rapidly spread all over the world. However, neither the precise analysis of the crisis from these different perspectives nor the long-run developments leading to the crisis are the focus of the present chapter. We will rather concentrate on the underlying and more fundamental analysis of the relationship and the interaction between the economic, financial and social systems in these approaches.

In order to take a comparative perspective, we have chosen the following four-step pattern for the outline of each of the approaches. First, we will sketch the basic structure of the approaches in order to single out how each of them views the interaction between social institutions and the economy and the related dynamics regarding the development of the institutional structure and the associated stages or regimes of economic development. Then we will tackle the question of how these approaches view the structural breaks or the regime shifts in the long-run development of modern capitalism, which have triggered or at least contributed to the emergence of a type of capitalism dominated by finance, or, in short, to the emergence of financialization. It should be noted already here that the terminology chosen in the different approaches is of course not homogeneous. But, as will be seen below, each of the approaches provides some ideas about the regime shift towards what is now widely called financialization. In the third step we will outline how these different approaches view the main characteristics and features of financialization, and in the fourth step we will deal with the respective views on the consequences of financialization for long-run economic and social development, including the crisis of this stage of development.

In section 1.2 we will apply this four-step method to the French Regulation School, and in section 1.3 we will address the Social Structures of Accumulation approach. As will be seen, these approaches are quite similar and show a high degree of overlapping, even in terms of contributing authors. In section 1.4 we will review some post-Keynesian contributions, and in section 1.5 we will focus on Minsky's work on different financial regimes in the long-run development of modern capitalism and his notion of 'money manager capitalism', which describes the most recent stage before the crisis. Although we consider Minsky to be part of post-Keynesian economics, we have decided to treat his approach separately, because he has provided a specific view about the dynamics and the succession of different financial regimes which merits separate and more extensive treatment. Section 1.6 will compare and conclude.

1.2   THE FRENCH REGULATION SCHOOL

1.2.1   Basic Structure of the Regulation Theory

Michel Aglietta, the founding father of the French Regulation School,[1] describes the main idea of his *A Theory of Capitalist Regulation* ([1976] 2000) as follows:

> The essential idea of *A Theory of Capitalist Regulation* is that the dynamism of capital represents an enormous productive potential but that it is also a blind force. It does not contain a self-limiting mechanism of its own, nor is it guided in a direction that would enable it to fulfil the capitalists' dream of perpetual accumulation. To put it another way, capitalism has the inherent ability to mobilize human energy and transform it into growth, but it does not have the capacity to convert the clash of individual interests into a coherent global system. (Aglietta 1998, p. 49)

The ultimately inevitable periods of crises in fact indicate breakdowns in the continuous reproduction of social relations and serve for the creation of new social relations. Robert Boyer (2000, 2005, 2010, 2013), another important proponent of the regulation theory, defines the aim of the regulation approach as explaining the rise and the subsequent crisis of modes of development. The mode of development is given by the combination of the 'accumulation regime' and the 'mode of regulation'.

The 'accumulation regime' refers to the organization of production and distribution of value and surplus value. The 'mode of regulation', on the other hand, refers to the institutions, norms and practices accompanying the 'accumulation regime' and providing the conditions for its long-run reproducibility. Jessop (1997, p. 291) describes the 'mode of regulation' as 'an emergent ensemble of rules, norms, conventions, patterns of conduct, social networks, organizational forms and institutions which can stabilize an accumulation regime'. The usual way to analyse and describe a mode of regulation is by examining five different dimensions (Jessop 1997; Guttmann 2012): the wage relation (organization of work, labour markets, wage bargaining, wages and employment); the enterprise form (organization, source of profits, form and degree of competition); the monetary regime (money, banking and credit system, monetary policy); the state (forms of intervention); and international regimes (regarding trade, direct investment, capital flows, international currency, exchange rate system, political arrangements). The specific combination of an accumulation regime and a mode of regulation, which sufficiently complement each other and are thus able to allow for relatively long-lasting capitalist expansion, is then called the 'mode of development'.

Over time, contradictions emerge in the mode of regulation, stemming from the conflicts between classes, firms, governments and political groups (Brenner and Glick 1991). This feeds back on the regime of accumulation and eventually results in a structural crisis. The transition from one mode of development to another is 'discontinuous, creatively destructive, and mediated through class conflict and institutional change' (Jessop 1997, p. 292). There is, in other words, no predictable outcome with respect to what the new mode of regulation, accumulation regime and thus mode of development will be. It will depend on the historical context, and 'out of these historically indeterminate processes of competitive economic war and socioeconomic and political struggle, one out of a range of alternative resolutions of the crisis is eventually hit upon' (Brenner and Glick 1991, p. 48).

In summary, the regulation theory rests on several important ideas, namely, that the society (and economic activities within it) is characterized by a network of social relations, which are inherently contradictory given the conflicting claims of various social groups. These contradictions make the ruptures in social relations, that is, crises, an expected state of affairs, whereas the non-crisis is more of a chance event. A prolonged stability in the reproduction of capital, that is, the accumulation regime, can be achieved when it is institutionalized in a set of practices, norms and conventions adopted by the society at the time, that is, in a mode of regulation (Lipietz 1987).

1.2.2 Structural Breaks or Regime Shifts towards Financialization and 'Finance-led' Growth

The regulation theory coined the term 'Fordist accumulation regime' to describe the prolonged period of stable growth following the Second World War in the United States (and France), based on an unprecedented compromise between capital and labour (Boyer 2010). Fordism can be broadly described as a mode of development based on an economic and institutional environment favourable to mass production and mass consumption. From the point of view of the social and economic functions of the state (government), the Fordist era was characterized by the 'Keynesian welfare state' (Jessop 1997). The principles of the Keynesian welfare state consisted in securing full employment under the conditions of relatively closed economies and influencing the distribution of income via collective bargaining regulation so that economic growth could be sustained by rising effective domestic demand. Collective mass consumption was thus a crucial feature of the Fordist mode of development.

In the early 1970s the Fordist accumulation regime and mode of development entered a structural crisis, manifesting itself as a crisis of productivity growth. A fall in the rate of profit from around the mid-1960s onwards was interpreted 'as a result of labour-productivity growth insufficient to raise the rate of surplus value to a degree that can counteract the rising organic composition of capital' (Brenner and Glick 1991, p. 97). This explanation of the crisis therefore rests on Marx's law of the tendency of the general rate of profit to fall due to technological change, as developed in *Capital*, Volume 3 (Marx 1894, Part III). This can be found in Aglietta's *A Theory of Capitalist Regulation* ([1976] 2000, p. 162) as well as in Boyer (1987).

Indeed Aglietta ([1976] 2000) gives two accounts of the crisis. Firstly, 'the watershed years of 1958–61 saw an acceleration in the fall in social wage costs proceeding from a sudden change in the forms of class struggle to the detriment of the wage earners' (Aglietta [1976] 2000, p. 99), which could be understood as a potential for a crisis of underconsumption. However, later on he argues that:

> the crisis of Fordism is first of all the crisis of a mode of labour organization. It is expressed above all in the intensification of class struggles at the point of production ... [T]hese struggles showed the limits to the increase in the rate of surplus-value that were inherent in the relations of production organized in this type of labour process ... The development of the department producing means of production encounters a constraint, since it no longer gives rise to technical mutations leading to a further mechanization of labour, capable of generating a sufficient saving in direct labour time to compensate for the increase in the organic composition of capital. (Aglietta [1976] 2000, p. 162)

Boyer (1987, pp. 30–31) also underlines the problems in generating sufficient productivity growth:

> Fordism is fairly efficient as regards labour and capital productivity when it replaces older systems, but it becomes harder and harder to get the same results when the issue is to deepen – and no more to extend – the same organizational methods. Hence a possible decline in productivity growth rates (in the US at the mid-Sixties) and/or in capital efficiency (in almost all OECD countries since the same period).

Boyer (2000) points out that, since the collapse of the Fordist mode of development, several different regimes have emerged. In particular, a 'finance-led growth regime' seems to have characterized the USA and the UK since the 1990s. Other regimes described in Boyer (2000) are, for instance, 'competition-led' (most of the OECD countries since the mid-1980s), 'service-led' (the USA during the 1980s), 'knowledge-based economy' (the USA during the 1990s), 'Toyotism' (Japan until the 1990s) and 'export-led growth' (East Asian emerging economics, until the 1997 crisis). He also argues that it is likely that, given the alternative regimes observed in various countries, a hybrid form based on their different characteristics will ultimately prevail, with each country emphasizing some features over others depending on its own political, social and economic legacy.

However, we will focus here on the literature surrounding the 'finance-led growth regime' which has been present primarily in the USA and, to some extent, the UK. The transition from Fordism to finance-led growth is considered to be a product of a longer structural transformation following a period of economic stagnation and crisis in the 1970s. Whereas Fordism was characterized by a compromise between managers and workers, the finance-led growth regime is dominated by alliances between investors/rentiers and managers. In particular, information technology and financial liberalization were driving and shaping the new growth regime (Aglietta and Breton 2001).

1.2.3   Characteristics of the Finance-led Growth Regime

In the USA, the changes brought about by the crisis of the Fordist regime were reflected in the increase in international trade and imports, financial liberalization and innovation, and labour market deregulation, all of which have contributed to eroding the bargaining power of trade unions, so that ultimately the managers began responding increasingly to the demands of financial markets relative to those of labour (Boyer 2010). A new 'social compromise' emerged from these developments: shareholders acknowledge the power of managers, and top managers take on the principles of shareholder value. The interests of workers are not represented in this new social compromise. 'This *new alliance* therefore brings *a shift in the hierarchy of institutional forms* and, at least potentially, makes possible a genuine accumulation regime' (Boyer 2010, p. 232, emphasis in the original). New financial players have thus gained the power to influence the decision-making of corporate managers.

The type of corporate governance determines (and can be seen from) the way in which profits are used and how the accumulation process is financed. Aglietta and Breton (2001) distinguish three types of corporate control through finance: 1) control through debt (exerted by banks, in bank-based financial systems); 2) control by the securities market, or direct control (the main players here are majority shareholders in market-based financial systems); and 3) control by shares or the stock market (minority shareholders and potential predators in market-based financial systems are most important players here). The latter type best describes the case of the USA in recent decades, and is the basis of shareholder value capitalism, according to Aglietta and Breton (2001).

The system of corporate governance based on control through debt promotes long-run company growth and is characterized by stable long-run relations among all parties involved in the process, because the creditors also tend to have relatively long-term relations with the firm (as with the traditional German or Japanese style of corporate governance). The other two types impose short-term profitability pressure on the management, and the impact on long-term growth becomes ambiguous (Aglietta and Breton 2001). Direct control through shares may be exercised by majority shareholders, which are usually institutional investors and also have relatively good information about the company. However, unlike banks, institutional investors do not provide long-term finance to the company and are thus less interested in its long-term prospects. Their targets are rather linked to the short-term financial performance of the company, and managers' pay is often linked with the company's financial performance, with other targets being subordinated. Finally, control by the stock market establishes a form of governance conducive to waves of corporate restructuring via mergers and acquisitions. Minority shareholders are very quick to sell or buy shares, and companies are encouraged indirectly – because of the fears of takeover or via incentive-based remuneration – to prioritize dividend distribution and adopt share price maximization over some other target. Dividend distribution, however, undermines accumulation, because the internal means of finance decrease.

In summary, the major characteristic of the finance-led growth regime is the central role played by finance and the shareholder–management alliances, as opposed to the capital–labour compromise, which was a dominant feature of the Fordist regime (Boyer 2000). In the finance-led growth regime, the wage relation is dominated by employment flexibility and wage moderation and an increasing relevance of profit sharing and pension funds for workers' households' income. Increasing financial liberalization intensifies the relationship between finance and the rest of the economy, making the overall economy more volatile and susceptible to financial instability, in turn. Stock market valuation is at the heart of the finance-led regime of accumulation (Boyer 2010), given that here it is the market that dictates the business strategies of companies. The more intense the market for corporate control is, the more the management will be focused on boosting the prices of shares because of fears of takeover (Aglietta and Breton 2001). Higher dividends are paid to maintain the minimum return on equity, and this shrinks the part of profits to be reinvested, ultimately undermining the growth of the firm itself.

1.2.4   Crisis of the Finance-led Growth Regime?

There has been no general agreement among regulation theorists on whether a finance-led accumulation regime is sustainable. Boyer (2000) develops a formal macroeconomic model, which incorporates the features of a finance-led accumulation regime in order to investigate the stability of the short-run equilibrium. Four configurations emerge, and, out of these, two show that an increase in the profitability norm imposed by shareholders on corporations and management can have a positive effect on demand (the so-called 'fully financialized system' and 'paradoxical wage system'). In other words, an accumulation regime is finance-led if an increase in the financial norm leads to higher growth. This happens when the financial markets 'lead to a generalization of investment behavior determined largely by profitability' (Boyer 2000, p. 127) and when wealth effects on consumption are well developed, generating sufficient aggregate demand and accelerating investment. However, further development of financial markets can take the economy towards the zone of structural instability: There is a threshold beyond which financialization is destabilizing for the macroeconomic equilibrium. Appropriate actions by the central bank, though, can stabilize the system by preventing financial bubbles.[2]

For the other two types of financialized systems ('financialized Fordist configuration' and 'hybrid financial system'), a rise in the profitability norm produces negative effects. This is usually a characteristic of the systems where the wage is the essential determinant of the mode of consumption ('an economy still dominated by wage-earning social relations', Boyer 2000, p. 127). The USA and, to some extent, the UK are the only two countries characterized by a finance-led accumulation regime, according to Boyer.

Although Boyer (2000) shows that it would be theoretically possible, mainly via the wealth effect on consumption, for a higher financial norm to have expansionary effects on the economy, the recent financial crisis originating in the USA may be seen as a structural crisis of this model of growth:

> The viability of a finance-led regime has long been a controversy among *regulationist* researchers: some perceived the process of financialization as irreversible (Aglietta 1998), whereas others considered that it was quite specific to the United States and the UK and ultimately bound to enter into a major crisis, as have any previous accumulation regimes (Boyer 2000). Nowadays history has delivered its assessment, and everybody agrees that with the successive bursting of the internet and real estate bubbles, this regime has shown its fragility. (Boyer 2010, p. 216, emphasis in the original)

In his more recent paper, Boyer (2013) writes about the 'transformation of finance' as the key to understanding the structural and systemic crisis that started in 2007. He identifies three processes of this transformation which acted as the originators of both the boom and the bust. Firstly, increased international competition in the 1960s and the demise of the capital–labour accord replaced the Fordist mass production/mass consumption regime with the finance-led growth regime. Yet this transition was accompanied by an increasing inequality of personal incomes, and in particular by the concentration of financial wealth at the very top of income distribution. Secondly, the dynamism of the new growth regime since the 1980s has rested upon financial innovation and the massive extension of credit to households. Given the moderate growth in real incomes of households, the lack of aggregate demand would have been an immediate obstacle to growth in the absence of debt-driven consumption. Increasing household debt, compensating for stagnating real incomes, exacerbated the fragility of the US economy. Finally, excess credit in the US economy and rising indebtedness of households were related to increasing imports from Asia, and huge capital inflows, from China in particular. This increased the likelihood of spillover effects of a financial crisis to other world regions and created structural imbalances in the world economy. Finance had, in fact, become 'dysfunctional with respect to recovery of accumulation, growth, and employment' (Boyer 2013, p. 22). The crisis was triggered by the occurrence of three deflationary processes that froze the US financial system: the bursting of the real estate bubble and the consequent fall in real estate prices which increased the real debt burden of households; the losses experienced by the financial system as a result of the loss in value of mortgage-backed securities; and, as a consequence, an increased risk-averseness of banks and other financial institutions, which stopped giving out credit. These three chain events invoked Irving Fisher's (1933) debt-deflation theory of depressions; only the immediate responses of governments and, in particular, central banks prevented a serious goods and labour markets deflation.

But is the finance-led growth regime disappearing? The process of cleaning the balance sheets will last for at least a decade, and the accumulation regime of the USA 'faces a structural block that can no longer be credit led', according to Boyer (2013, p. 15). Paradoxically, though, even in the aftermath of the financial crisis there appears to be a strong 'resilience of the power of finance' (Boyer 2013, p. 17). The major parts of the costs of the crisis have been shifted away from the financial sector and towards the taxpayer. Successful lobbying has prevented any significant attempt at regulation, and the alliance between managers and shareholders – the cornerstone of the mode of regulation in place since the 1980s – has not changed, according to Boyer (2013).

1.3 THE SOCIAL STRUCTURES OF ACCUMULATION (SSA) APPROACH

1.3.1 Basic Structure of the SSA Theory

Similar to the French Regulation School, the Social Structures of Accumulation (SSA) approach examines the interaction of potentially unstable capital accumulation and growth processes with social institutions or 'social structures' which 'tame' this instability and allow for longer periods of stable and rapid growth. The basic idea is that successful SSAs are finally undermined by endogenous processes within the SSA, which then give rise to systemic crises and – potentially – to a new SSA. The founding fathers of this approach were David Gordon, Michael Reich and Richard Edwards in the 1970s and early 1980s (McDonough et al. 2010).

The SSA stands for the set of institutions which favour investment (accumulation) in a certain period of time. These periods tend to last for several decades, and are thus best described as long waves or stages in the development of capitalism (Lippit 2010). The SSA theory aims to explain the stages of capitalism and describes and analyses the institutional arrangements that prevail in each of these stages. Institutions are to be considered broadly, and describe the specific economic (for instance, competition and organization of markets), political (the 'presence' of the government), ideological and cultural (education, religious beliefs, political ideologies) structures, which all reinforce each other during a particular SSA (McDonough et al. 2010). Given the importance of the various institutions in the formation (and the collapse) of any SSA, the construction of a new SSA, which will replace the old one, requires quite a lot of time. This is why periods of stagnation following the demise of an exhausted SSA can be so long-lasting.

Therefore, the relationship between long waves of growth followed by stagnation, observed in the history of capitalism, and changes in the institutional structures are at the core of the SSA approach. Both Marxian and Keynesian features can be found in the basic economic theory. However, unlike orthodox Marxian theory, the SSA approach focuses on the ability of capitalism 'to reinvent itself' after a period of prolonged stagnation and/or crisis.

So far in the literature on SSAs, four stages of capitalism in the United States have been described, as can be seen in Table 1.1. In this chapter we will focus on the last two SSAs, namely the post-war, or the regulated capitalist, SSA and the contemporary global neoliberal SSA.

Table 1.1   SSA theory on the history of capitalism in the United States

Period	Form	Characteristics
1) Mid- to late nineteenth century	Competitive SSA	Predominantly small and medium-sized firms, dominance of trade in international economic relations, laissez-faire government.
2) Late nineteenth century until the Great Depression	Monopoly SSA	Unions, oligopolistic market structure, US expansion in Latin America, creation of the Fed.
3) End of the Second World War until the 1970s 'Great Stagflation'	Regulated capitalist SSA	Capital–labour accord (strong unions), Keynesian welfare/warfare state, US international dominance, dollar as hegemonic currency.
4) Early 1980s to the present	Global neoliberal SSA	Dominance of capital over labour, separation of the financial from the non-financial sector, globalization, deregulation.

Source: Based on McDonough et al. (2010) and Kotz (2011).

1.3.2   Structural Breaks or Regime Shifts towards Financialization/Global Neoliberal SSA

According to Gordon et al. (1987), the prosperity of the post-war SSA in the USA was due to the following four factors that characterized that period: 1) a balanced capital–labour accord where, on the one hand, the workers were granted job security and rising real wages while, on the other hand, the unions were not strong enough to squeeze out profits; 2) the international hegemony of the USA ('Pax Americana'); 3) the government assured the traditional welfare state provisions, such as health care and social security; and 4) oligopolistic competition and relatively weak foreign economies.

Yet the prosperity came to an end in the 1970s, indicating the demise of the post-war SSA (see Table 1.2). In the SSA literature, the broad agreement appears to be that the cause of the crisis stemmed from the capital–labour relation or, more precisely, the decline in profitability (profit squeeze) due to the loss of power of capital relative to labour in the face of (close to) full employment (Gordon et al. [1994] 1998; Nilsson 1996, 1997; Kotz 2011).

In particular David Gordon, partly together with Samuel Bowles

Table 1.2   The rise and demise of the post-war SSA

Phase	Capital–labour accord	Pax Americana	Capital–citizen accord	Inter-capitalist rivalry
Boom: 1948–66	Cost of job loss rises; workers' resistance down.	US military dominance; terms of trade improve.	Government support for accumulation; profits main state priority.	Corporations insulated from domestic and foreign competition.
Erosion: 1966–73	Cost of job loss plunges; workers' resistance spreads.	Military power challenged; terms of trade hold steady.	Citizen movements take hold.	Foreign competition and domestic mergers begin to affect corporations.
Stalemate: 1973–79	Stagnant economy creates stalemate between capital and labour.	OPEC and declining dollar result in sharp deterioration in US terms of trade.	Citizen movements effect new fetters on business.	Pressure on foreign competition, and domestic rivalry intensifies.

Source: Gordon et al. (1987, p. 51).

and Thomas Weisskopf, focused his attention on the construction of macroeconom(etr)ic models which incorporate the insights of the post-Second World War SSA and its demise (Gordon 1981, 1995; Gordon et al. 1983, [1994] 1998). The basic feature of the models is the dependence of investment on expected profitability, with the latter being dependent on a constructed index of underlying capitalist power relative to (organized) labour. The main result is that the decline in the underlying capitalist power was the cause of the stagnation of investment during the 1970s and the 1980s, which eventually led to the collapse of the post-war accumulation regime and SSA.

The explanation of the crisis of the post-war SSA ('regulated capitalist SSA') as a crisis of profitability is also the one put forth by Kotz (2011). His idea is that different typologies of SSA will result in different forms of crises. In the case of the post-war SSA, we have a specific set of institutions, which are based on the capital–labour compromise and are ultimately supportive of the workers' position. Interventionist governments promote growth and high employment, labour unions are strong, competition among corporations is fairly restrained, and the financial sector is engaged mainly in the financing of productive activities of non-financial firms. In this framework of a 'mixed economy' (where the market, state and unions all play an important role), the problem that eventually arises is that of the *creation* of surplus value. There is thus not a problem of inadequate aggregate demand, but rather of decreasing profitability due to a 'loss of power on the part of capital' (Kotz 2011, p. 16). This type of crisis results not in an immediate crash but rather in a prolonged decline marked by a fall in the rate of capital accumulation and in the long-term growth rate, causing rising unemployment. Nilsson (1996) also focuses on the breakdown of the capital–labour accord as an explanation for the crisis of the regulated capitalist SSA. However, in his model the most significant factor causing the stagnation in profitability and investment was the loss of US hegemony.

The deep crisis of the post-war SSA finally gave rise to the 'global neoliberal SSA'. Tabb (2010) identifies four key developments in the regime shift from the post-war SSA to the global neoliberal SSA:

1. Leaps in innovation together with decreased transportation and communication costs led to a re-organization of production with ever expanding business opportunities. Complex production networks and commodity chains have spread internationally as a result of an increasing openness of markets.
2. Developments in information technology (IT) made the use of computerized data processing essential in various risk assessment calculations in the business environment.
3. The collapse of the system of fixed exchange rates (Bretton Woods) gave an impetus for speculation in exchange markets. Overall, financial innovation and derivatives allowed for greater speculation, higher leverage, and expansion of securitization.
4. The shareholder value orientation became the cornerstone of contemporary corporate governance; that is, a transition from manager-dominated capitalism to finance-dominated capitalism occurred.

The contemporary SSA, the 'global neoliberal SSA', began in the USA with the election of Ronald Reagan in 1980. The growth model of the global neoliberal SSA is based on, and dependent upon, finance and financial innovation, according to Tabb (2010, p. 149). In other words, the shift from the post-war SSA to the global neoliberal SSA has the embrace of financialization as its very central feature. It can actually be said that the keywords of the contemporary SSA are: financialization, globalization and neoliberalism.

Table 1.3   Key features of the post-war SSA and the neoliberal SSA

Regulated capitalist SSA (post-war SSA)	Neoliberal SSA
Capital–labour compromise	Capital dominates labour
Interventionist government	Retreat of government
Restrained competition among corporations	Unrestrained competition, price wars
Financial sector serving the non-financial sector	Separation of the financial from the non-financial sector, speculation in the former
'Mixed economy'	Unrestrained market (neoliberal ideology)

Source: Based on Kotz (2011).

1.3.3   Characteristics of the (Global) Neoliberal SSA

The neoliberal, or global neoliberal, SSA rests upon five key features, described by Kotz (2011). These features in fact appear to be the reverse of what characterized the previous, post-war SSA (Table 1.3). The capital–labour compromise ceased to exist, as such, and was replaced by the increasing dominance of capital over labour, resulting in an increasing gap between the growth of productivity and of real wages. Government activity was reduced, and waves of privatizations and deregulations in various sectors took place. With regard to the capital–capital relation, unrestrained competition, price wars and individualism were brought together under the umbrella of the free market and neoliberal ideology.

Most importantly, whereas in the regulated capitalist SSA the financial sector served the non-financial sector, the neoliberal SSA has seen an increasing separation of the financial from the non-financial sectors, with the former becoming progressively innovative and increasingly in pursuit of speculative profits. The neoliberal SSA has been characterized by increasing gearing ratios (that is, higher indebtedness of corporations), with more 'fictitious',[3] expectations-dependent capital (Tabb 2010). Crucially, there has been little provision for risk. Securitization and the extensive use of collateralized debt obligations (CDOs) induced large parts of the banking sector to reduce the standards of creditworthiness when granting credit. Finally, increasing debt levels and high leverage ratios undermined the financial stability of the system.

Other important features forming the global neoliberal SSA are globalization of trade and capital movements, as well as off-shoring. With the deregulation of labour markets and free capital movement, multinationals have succeeded in re-defining domestic labour contracts and, additionally, were successful in lobbying for lower taxation of profits. Both battles were fought under the flag of outsourcing (Boyer 2010). From the socio-political point of view, the major feature of the transition was that, following the shift of power towards multinational corporations, the power in both economic and political circles now shifted towards finance capital and financial markets. This is also apparent in that the elected officials or policymakers have not questioned the working of financial markets. Quite the contrary, it was the financial sector that – primarily via its monetary contributions to political candidates and elected officials – has been setting the issues on and/or off the political agenda (Tabb 2010). Over time, the financial industry became dominant over the non-financial sectors of the economy and thus over the production of goods and services.

This shift of power has had serious effects on income distribution. According to Boyer (2010), these developments were the prerequisites for the explosion of CEO remuneration. Managers did not have to respond any longer to workers' demands, but to those made by financial markets. Institutional investors who gained power via financial deregulation and high capital mobility have, since the mid-1980s, put the non-financial corporations increasingly under pressure by imposing their demands for higher rates of return on invested capital. Productive investment, in fact, has become more sensitive to profits than to expected demand, in particular in the USA and the UK, according to Boyer (2010).

The boom of CEO compensation in the period of financialization is seen as a reflection of the alliance of top managers with rentiers/shareholders under the flag of protection of the shareholder. It has not been justified by an unprecedented performance of the firms the CEOs were running. Rather, managers have occupied a unique position in the firm with regard to insider information and special knowledge about the firm. This caused an asymmetry of information between top managers and various boards,[4] resulting in an alliance between the two – a 'social compromise' (Boyer 2010, p. 231) – where the financiers acknowledge the power of managers, and managers take on the principles of shareholder value.

Tabb (2010) draws attention to the change in the ownership of corporate America: Since the 1980s the major shareholders have been institutional investors and pension funds, whose aim is the maximization of share prices in the short run. These types of shareholders enabled the transformation of *managerial capitalism*, 'understood as integrated unit dedicated to long-term growth' (Tabb 2010, p. 153), towards *finance capitalism*. Increasing dividend payments demanded by shareholders left less money to spend on productive investment or R&D, resulting in non-financial corporations engaging more in financial than in their core business activities.

One of the major consequences of this new social compromise and of the new practices in the banking sector was massive debt creation in the private household sector. Increasing household debt has been a result of stagnating real wages while the banking sector provided credit to finance consumption by relaxing credit constraints.

1.3.4 Crisis of the Neoliberal SSA – the Consequences of Financialization for Long-Run Development

Kotz and McDonough (2010) outline four factors which, in their view, have been contributing to the collapse of institutions of the global neoliberal SSA. These are:

1. increasing inequality in the distribution of functional income (between capital and labour) as well as personal income (among households);
2. a deregulated financial sector, which engaged massively in highly speculative and risky activities;
3. several asset bubbles preceding, and culminating in, the major housing bubble which burst with dramatic consequences in 2007; and
4. the degree of global economic and financial integration, which contained an increased risk of contagion after the outbreak of a crisis.

Along these lines, in his later work Kotz (2011) analyses the way in which the crisis of the neoliberal SSA manifested itself. He compares it with the demise of the post-war SSA (Table 1.4) and argues that, given the types of unsustainable trends produced by the neoliberal SSA, the crisis needed to be resolved in a sudden collapse, rather than in a long gradual decline, as in the case of the former SSA. The underlying cause of the crisis of the neoliberal SSA is not to be found in a profit squeeze and a falling rate of profit, as in the case of the regulated capitalist SSA, but rather in the weak growth of mass income-financed demand. From 1979 to 2007 the gap between real profits and real employee compensation widened, and 'in 2000–07 profits rose more than 8 times as fast as compensation' (Kotz

Table 1.4   The demise of the post-war and of the neoliberal SSA

Regulated capitalist SSA (post-war SSA)	Neoliberal SSA
Crisis of profitability	Crisis of 'over-investment'
Problem in the creation of surplus value	Problem in the realization of surplus value

Source: Based on Kotz (2011).

2011, p. 11). Inequality of household incomes grew, and was also made more pronounced by the reductions in social provisions.

However, the institutions of the neoliberal SSA were able to postpone the problem of realization of surplus value for several decades. Two features of the neoliberal SSA acted as 'delayers' of the collapse immanent in the neoliberal SSA: an increasingly speculative financial sector, and a series of large asset bubbles (Kotz 2011). A surplus of investable funds relative to productive investment opportunities – a consequence of rising inequality – fuelled a series of asset bubbles. These were accommodated by the deregulated, innovative and speculative financial sector. Owing to the wealth effect of increasing asset prices, a large part of the population was able to increase its consumption, notwithstanding slow or absent growth of household incomes.

However, several decades of consumption made possible by increasing indebtedness of households (the household debt to disposable income ratio had begun to increase steadily only since 1979, i.e. during the neoliberal SSA) became unsustainable so that the structural crisis of the neoliberal SSA occurred in 2008–09, after the collapse of the housing price bubble, beginning with a decline in consumer spending (Kotz 2011). The decline in business fixed investment followed afterwards. It appeared that, taking away the debt-financed consumption spending, productive capacities were much in excess of what was needed to satisfy effective demand. The crisis of the neoliberal SSA is thus interpreted as a crisis of over-investment caused by the difficulties in the realization of surplus value against the background of redistribution at the expense of wage incomes.

In other words, large asset bubbles and a deregulated financial system which allowed them to develop, the characteristics of the global neoliberal SSA, were necessary to temporarily 'resolve' the problem of weak demand caused by the redistribution of income immanent in this SSA. In practice, consumption was sustained by increasing debt levels. Unlike the crisis of the regulated (post-war) SSA, which was characterized by a longer and slower decline, this crisis occurred with a sudden economic collapse. The outcome was a financial crisis, a collapse in aggregate demand and presumably a long period of stagnation to follow (Kotz 2011).

1.4 POST-KEYNESIAN APPROACHES

1.4.1 Basic Structure

Post-Keynesian economics, that is, the school of thought based on the radical interpretation of John Maynard Keynes's work by Joan

Robinson, Richard Kahn, Nicholas Kaldor, Paul Davidson and others, as well as on Michal Kalecki's contributions, is built on several principles of a 'monetary theory of production', which distinguish this research programme from the mainstream 'real theories of exchange' as can be found in different modern versions of neoclassical economics (neoclassical synthesis, monetarism, new classical and new Keynesian economics). These post-Keynesian principles can be briefly summarized as follows.[5] In a monetary production economy, money, credit and monetary interest rates have real effects on distribution, employment and growth, and money and monetary policies are thus not neutral, neither in the short run nor in the long run. The levels of output and employment, as well as the rate of growth, are governed by the 'principle of effective demand', and the major real variables of the economic system are thus demand determined. The society consists of different social groups with different constraints (ownership of wealth and means of production, access to credit), different interests, and different behavioural commonalities within the groups (propensities to consume and to save). Monetary production economies are characterized by the conflict over the distribution of the social product and of national income and by power relationships affecting the outcome of this distribution conflict. Inconsistent distributional claims endowed with respective bargaining powers will generate conflict inflation. Economic and social processes take place in 'historical time', which means that '[t]oday is a break in time between an unknown future and an irrevocable past' (Robinson 1962, p. 26). Expectations under the conditions of 'fundamental uncertainty' regarding future events have therefore an important role to play when it comes to present economic behaviour, as do institutions, which emerge in order to cope with uncertainty. Post-Keynesian theories and models are thus historically and institutionally specific, and do not claim general and global validity. Model results ('equilibria' or, better, 'temporary states of rest') are not pre-determined by some general, ahistorical and exogenous structural factors, but are historically and institutionally specific, and they are 'path-dependent', being generated by the economy proceeding through 'historical time'. Furthermore, post-Keynesian models show that there are all sorts of fallacies of composition in monetary production economies. Individually purposeful, reasonable or 'rational' microeconomic behaviour may systematically generate unintended and counter-intuitive results at the level of the macroeconomy: the 'paradox of thrift' (Keynes [1936] 1973), the 'paradox of costs' (Rowthorn 1981), the 'paradox of debt' (Steindl [1952] 1976) and the 'paradox of tranquillity (stability)' (Minsky 1975) are the most prominent examples.[6] Finally, post-Keynesians hold that monetary production economies are struck with systemic instabilities and therefore require permanent stabilization policies in the short and in the long run.

From these basic principles it follows that, from a post-Keynesian perspective, institutions, 'the rules, laws, and customs that define acceptable social behaviour' (Cornwall and Cornwall 2001, p. 8), and power relationships are of utmost importance for the functioning of capitalist economies. Institutions are important in several respects (Pressman 2012). They are required to cope with fundamental uncertainty – money as a social construct and contracts as well as contract- and payment-enforcing institutions are important in this respect (Davidson 1988, 1994, Chapter 6).[7] Institutions are required to provide a stable monetary and financial system on both national and international levels. Institutions are important for containing and moderating the distribution conflict and preventing accelerating conflict inflation as an outcome of an unresolved distribution conflict, on the one hand, and macroeconomically dysfunctional redistributions, on the other hand. Therefore, appropriate labour market and wage bargaining institutions are particularly important for macroeconomic performance, but there are also other institutions affecting distributional struggle, for example central banks, as Palley (1996) and Setterfield (2007) have analysed for the USA and Hein (2002) for the Euro area.

Since monetary production economies are demand constrained in the short and in the long run, those institutions affecting private consumption and investment expenditure are of importance for short- and long-run economic performance, as are the institutions and regulations of government stabilization policies. Regarding the ability and the willingness to consume, institutions affecting income distribution and the degree of uncertainty of future income flows, as well as social norms affecting consumption expenditures, are important. Regarding investment, institutions affecting uncertainty with respect to future costs (wages, interest rates, exchange rate) and sales, and regulating access to the required means of finance seem to be most relevant. Finally, monetary and fiscal policies are important with respect to the determination of aggregate demand, output, employment and growth, both in the short and in the long run (Arestis and Sawyer 1998; Hein and Stockhammer 2010; Arestis 2013).

1.4.2 Structural Breaks and/or Regime Shifts towards Neoliberalism, Financialization or Finance-dominated Capitalism

Post-Keynesian explanations of regime shifts towards financialization/ finance-dominated capitalism or neoliberalism start with the analysis of the conditions for the 'Golden Age' period of the 1950s, 1960s and early 1970s, which provided high growth of output, investment and productivity, (close to) full employment and low inflation in the major capitalist economies. Cornwall and Cornwall (2001, Chapter 9) consider the 'social bargain' between capital, labour and the state as the very foundation of the 'Golden Age' in their evolutionary-Keynesian analysis. This was based on a long-run shift of political power towards social democratic and labour parties and of economic power towards trade unions, which had already started after the First World War, and was supported by the experience of the Great Depression and the following Second World War, as well as by the spread and broad acceptance of economic policy concepts based on Keynesian economics. Governments accepted full employment as a goal to be achieved by appropriate aggregate demand management and provided the institutional conditions for collective bargaining between employer associations and trade unions. The labour movement and the trade unions gave up the goal of overthrowing capitalism in exchange for full employment, social safety and increasing real wages. And capitalists accepted government intervention and labour's participation in productivity gains in exchange for keeping control over the firms and continuing exercising management functions. Cornwall and Cornwall (2001, p. 182) distinguish a 'social bargain group' of countries, consisting of Japan, Germany, France, Australia, Austria, Belgium, Denmark, Finland, the Netherlands, New Zealand, Norway, Sweden and Switzerland, from a 'market power group', containing the USA, the UK, Canada, Italy and Ireland. On average, over the period between 1960 and 1973, the two groups witnessed roughly equal rates of inflation, but the 'market power group' needed a much higher rate of unemployment in order to contain inflation than the 'social bargain' group.

Although, according to Cornwall and Cornwall (2001, pp. 169–170), the USA did not have a 'social bargain' at the national level, it acted as an international hegemon providing the international environment for high employment, high growth and low inflation in the 'social bargain' countries: the Bretton Woods system with fixed but adjustable exchange rates, the International Monetary Fund (IMF) and the World Bank, the General Agreement on Tariffs and Trade (GATT), and the European Recovery Program (Marshall Plan). In sum, these institutions established conditions such that the major constraints on employment and growth in many countries could be removed during the 'Golden Age' period:

- the demand constraint through active government demand management and real wages growing in line with productivity;
- the supply constraint through re-integration of demobilized soldiers, re-allocation of labour from agriculture to industry, increases in female labour participation, migration, and technology transfer

from the USA, which facilitated productivity in other countries to catch up;
- the inflation constraint through the 'social bargain' between labour, capital and the state, making target real wages grow in line with productivity, thus avoiding conflict inflation;
- the balance of payments constraint, in particular through capital transfers from the USA to Europe related to the European Recovery Program, the establishment of the European Payments Union dealing with intra-European imbalances, and later increased US military spending abroad; and
- the political constraint, because of the general acceptance of 'Big Government' and the absence of large government deficits and debt.

According to Cornwall and Cornwall (2001, Chapter 11) the 'Golden Age' crumbled because of the endogenous erosion of its most important institutional foundation, the 'social bargain' in several 'social bargain' countries:[8] 'Persistent low unemployment and rising living standards not only had increased labour's power, but had generated the belief that low unemployment and rising living standards were the norm. Anticipating continued growth and employment, people's aspirations rose, and their demands grew faster than the economy's ability to satisfy them' (Cornwall and Cornwall 2001, p. 227).

Wage aspirations not backed by productivity growth caused rising inflation rates, in both 'social bargain' and 'market power' countries, and made the inflation constraint binding again. Governments sacrificed full employment targets in favour of low inflation and international price competitiveness. The collapse of the Bretton Woods system in the early 1970s contributed to the end of the 'Golden Age', as did the deregulation of capital markets and the acceleration of economic and financial globalization in the 1970s and 1980s, which each contributed to reducing labour's bargaining power. A further contribution was the collapse of the Soviet Union in the late 1980s, which relieved business and governments of their fear of socialism. These developments led to the rise of neoliberalism starting in the mid-1970s replacing the 'Golden Age' institutions: 'Neoliberalism is a regime characterized by reduced government intervention, the deregulation of markets, cutbacks in the welfare state, and price stability as its overriding macroeconomic goal' (Cornwall and Cornwall 2001, p. 252).

In the neoliberal regime, the political constraint to full employment becomes binding again, enforced by institutional changes increasing the relative economic power of business. Central bank independence and constitutional amendments requiring balanced government budgets are the most prominent ones. However, the neoliberal regime suffers from severe problems and contradictions questioning the political and economic stability of the system, under the conditions of high unemployment, widespread poverty and increasing inequalities in the distribution of income.

Whereas Cornwall and Cornwall (2001) focus on the 'social bargain' and the transition from the 'Golden Age' constellation towards neoliberalism without explicitly mentioning the role of finance and financialization, Josef Steindl's ([1979] 1990, [1989] 1990) earlier long-run analysis takes a broader perspective regarding those factors explaining the rise and the fall of the 'Golden Age', on the one hand, and explicitly addresses those forces leading to the dominance of finance, on the other hand.[9] In Steindl ([1979] 1990) we find four reasons for high growth and low unemployment in the post-Second World War period:

1. Public spending increased tremendously after the Second World War, financed to a great extent by taxes on profits. This increased capacity utilization and fed back positively on firms' decisions to invest in capital stock.
2. Technological competition between East and West, the 'competition of the systems', had a strong impact on expenditures on R&D and education by governments, which spilled over to the private sector, boosting investment and productivity growth.
3. The post-war tensions triggered close cooperation between Western countries under the leadership of the USA. This included the world financial system of Bretton Woods, the Marshall Plan and American lending to Western European countries, which stabilized and provided the conditions for an increase in international trade. A higher level of international trade kept profit margins within limits and contributed to stabilizing wage shares.
4. European countries benefited from technological backwardness with respect to the USA and could make use of technological knowledge which had been generated and applied in the USA, thus making use of the 'catching-up' factor in economic growth.

Steindl ([1989] 1990) also mentions the low indebtedness of corporations right after the Second World War as a factor favourable to investment in capital stock and to GDP growth, as well as increasing the bargaining power of workers and trade unions associated with full employment which held mark-ups and profit shares in check and allowed for real wages to grow in step with productivity, thus providing the required demand growth.

Steindl ([1979] 1990) relates the causes of stagnation starting in the early or mid-1970s to the reduction of tensions between the superpowers, an increase in internal rivalries among the capitalist economies, a decay of US leadership and the collapse of the Bretton Woods international financial system, indicating the absence of the willingness and the ability for international cooperation. Further factors contributing to the re-emergence of stagnation were: the tendencies towards increasing capital productivity, reducing the required amounts of net investment to increase productive capacities; a trend towards an increasing marginal propensity to save from disposable income in prospering economies, weakening aggregate demand, capacity utilization, investment and growth; the fading out of the catching-up potential of Europe towards the USA associated with abnormally high rates of productivity growth in Europe over the post-war period; and increasing environmental and energy problems, with rising energy prices putting upward pressure on inflation rates and raising uncertainty with respect to future technological development.

However, the most important factor explaining the re-emergence of stagnation tendencies, according to Steindl ([1979] 1990), is 'stagnation policy' in the major capitalist economies. In this context, Steindl ([1979] 1990) refers to Kalecki's (1971, Chapter 12) 'Political Aspects of Full Employment', in which Kalecki argued that, although governments might know how to maintain full employment in a capitalist economy, they will not do so, because of capitalists' opposition. Whereas in Kalecki (1971, p. 144) the opposition of the capitalist class towards full employment policies will give rise to a 'political business cycle', Steindl ([1979] 1990, p. 9) argues that business opposition towards full employment policies gives rise to a 'political trend' causing or contributing to stagnation. In the course of the 1970s, governments, facing full employment and increasing rates of inflation, moved away from targeting full employment by means of active demand management towards targeting price stability and containing public deficits and debt, using higher rates of unemployment as an instrument.

In Bhaduri and Steindl (1985) these policies are associated with 'the rise of monetarism as a social doctrine', because monetarism is inherently linked with restrictive fiscal and monetary policies, which are supported by banks and the financial sector (or the rentiers). The application of monetarist policies thus indicates a shift of powers from industry to banks, or from the non-financial sector to the financial sector, which occurred in the course of national and international financial liberalization, as well as rapidly increasing financial activity in the 1970s and early 1980s (collapse of the Bretton Woods international financial system, rise of the eurodollar market, emergence of oil exporting countries to a class of 'international rentiers', emergence of international commercial banks). Starting in the

1980s, the tendencies towards stagnation and weak investment in capital stock have been amplified by an interest shift of corporations and their managers from production towards finance, and an increasing role of financial investment in comparison to real investment (Steindl [1989] 1990).

Smithin (1996) has explicitly analysed the rise and the fall of the 'Golden Age' in terms of the interests and power constellations of three social groups: business, labour and rentiers. The 'Golden Age' period is explained by a social compromise, in which aggregate demand, output and employment growth were sustained by economic policies inspired by Keynesian ideas, real wages grew in line with productivity growth, and real interest rates were kept at low levels by the monetary authorities, thus stimulating economic activity in production: 'This provided the space in which both "big business" and "big labour" could grow and prosper' (Smithin 1996, p. 5). What was important for this overall social compromise, according to Smithin (1996), was that real interest rates were kept low but remained positive, so that rentiers could at least maintain the 'real' value of their financial wealth.

This social compromise was shattered when, in the face of rising inflation rates due to an overheated US economy during the Vietnam War in the late 1960s and the oil price shocks of the early 1970s, central banks allowed real interest rates to turn negative during the 1970s. Although negative real interest rates are favourable for the actors in the real economy as borrowers, and thus for industrial capitalists and workers, they undermine the consent of the rentiers as lenders because their accumulated financial wealth is depreciated. This is what then caused a political revolution in the late 1970s, the 'Revenge of the Rentiers', 'the most important feature of which was the "capture" of central banks by rentier interests, and their conversion thereafter to exclusively "hard money", high interest, and anti-inflation policies' (Smithin 1996, p. 5).[10] Monetarism and an exclusive focus of economic policies on low inflation rates, balanced government budgets and stable exchange rates at the expense of aggregate demand management targeted towards full employment became the generally accepted doctrines, with the ultimate purpose of re-establishing positive real rates of return on financial capital. The major events were the appointment of Paul Volcker as chair of the US Fed in 1979 and the concomitant tight monetary policies in the USA, the election of Margaret Thatcher as British prime minister in 1979, which marked the start of draconian anti-inflation policies in Britain, and the establishment of the European Monetary System (EMS) with its exchange rate mechanism (ERM), which linked the central bank policies of member countries to the hard-line anti-inflation policy of the German Bundesbank.

This regime switch was successful in bringing down inflation, increasing real interest rates and initiating redistribution at the expense of labour. But it meant two policy-induced recessions in the early 1980s and the early 1990s, high unemployment and sluggish growth, in particular during the 1980s. According to Smithin (1996, p. 84) this points to a potential problem or contradiction in this regime, because 'policies designed to benefit the already-rich and the financial sector, when pushed to their logical conclusion, simply end up depressing the real economy on which everybody's livelihood ultimately depends'.

1.4.3 Characteristics of Finance-dominated Capitalism

Post-Keynesian contributions have focused on the 'macroeconomics of financialization', in particular. These contributions are based on detailed empirical case studies of the development of financialization, and include, for example, the contributions in Epstein (2005b), and by Krippner (2005) and Palley (2008, 2013, Chapter 2) for the USA, by van Treeck et al. (2007) and van Treeck (2009a) for Germany as compared to the USA, and by Stockhammer (2008) for Europe. Furthermore, the post-Keynesian macroeconomics of financialization can rely on some post-Keynesian and other 'microeconomic' contributions on the theory of the firm under the conditions of financialization, by Crotty (1990), Stockhammer (2005–06) and Dallery (2009), for example, and more recently on the effects of norms etc. (conspicuous consumption, 'keeping up with the Joneses') on household consumption behaviour by Cynamon and Fazzari (2008), Iacoviello (2008), Frank et al. (2014) and others.

As outlined in Hein and van Treeck (2010) and Hein (2012, Chapter 1) and explained in more detail by Hein and Dodig in Chapter 2 of this book, from a post-Keynesian macroeconomic perspective, finance-dominated capitalism can be characterized by the following elements:

1. With regard to distribution, financialization has been conducive to a rising gross profit share, including retained profits, dividends and interest payments, and thus a falling labour income share, on the one hand, and to increasing inequality of wages and top management salaries and thus of personal or household incomes, on the other hand. Hein (2013) has recently reviewed the evidence for a set of developed capitalist economies since the early 1980s and finds ample empirical support for falling labour income shares and increasing inequality in the personal/household distribution of market incomes with only a few exceptions, increasing inequality in the personal/household distribution of disposable income in most of the countries, and an increase

in the income share of the very top incomes, in particular in the USA and the UK, but also in several other countries for which data are available, with rising top management salaries as one of the major driving forces. Reviewing the empirical literature on the determinants of functional income distribution against the background of the Kaleckian theory of income distribution, it is argued that features of finance-dominated capitalism have contributed to the falling labour income share since the early 1980s through three main channels: falling bargaining power of trade unions, rising profit claims imposed in particular by increasingly powerful rentiers, and a change in the sectoral composition of the economy in favour of the financial corporate sector.

2. Regarding investment in capital stock, financialization has caused increasing shareholder power vis-à-vis firms and workers, a demand for an increasing rate of return on equity and bonds held by rentiers, and an alignment of management with shareholder interests through short-run performance-related pay schemes, such as bonuses, stock option programmes and so on. On the one hand, this has imposed short-termism on management and has caused decreasing management animal spirits with respect to real investment in capital stock and long-run growth of the firm and increasing preference for financial investment, generating high profits in the short run. On the other hand, it has drained internal means of finance available for real investment purposes from non-financial corporations, through increasing dividend payments and share buybacks in order to boost stock prices and thus shareholder value. These 'preference' and 'internal means of finance' channels should each have had partially negative effects on firms' real investment in capital stock. Econometric evidence for these two channels has been supplied by Stockhammer (2004), Orhangazi (2008), van Treeck (2008) and Onaran et al. (2011), confirming a depressing effect of increasing shareholder value orientation on investment in capital stock, in particular for the USA but also for other countries, such as the UK and France. In these studies either interest and dividend receipts or interest and dividend payments of non-financial firms are used as indicators for the degree of financialization.

3. Regarding consumption, financialization has generated an increasing potential for wealth-based and debt-financed consumption, thus creating the potential to compensate for the depressing demand effects of financialization, which were imposed on the economy via redistribution and the depressing impact of shareholder value orientation on real investment. Stock market and housing price booms have each increased notional wealth against which households were willing to

borrow. Changing financial norms, new financial instruments (credit card debt, home equity lending) and deterioration of creditworthiness standards, triggered by securitization of mortgage debt and the 'originate and distribute' strategies of commercial banks, made increasing credit available to low-income, low-wealth households, in particular. This allowed for consumption to rise faster than median income and thus to stabilize aggregate demand. But it also generated increasing debt–income ratios of private households. Several studies have shown that financial and housing wealth is a significant determinant of consumption, in particular in the USA, but also in countries like the UK, France, Italy, Japan and Canada (Ludvigson and Steindel 1999; Mehra 2001; Boone and Girouard 2002; Onaran et al. 2011). Furthermore, Cynamon and Fazzari (2008), Barba and Pivetti (2009), Guttmann and Plihon (2010) and van Treeck and Sturn (2012) have presented extensive case studies on wealth-based and debt-financed consumption, with a focus on the USA.

4. The liberalization of international capital markets and capital accounts has allowed for rising current account imbalances at the global but also at the regional levels, for example within the Euro area, as has been analysed by several authors, including Horn et al. (2009b), UNCTAD (2009), Hein (2012, Chapter 6), Hein and Mundt (2012) and van Treeck and Sturn (2012). Simultaneously, it created the problems of foreign indebtedness, speculative capital movements, exchange rate volatilities and related currency crises (Herr 2012).

1.4.4 Financialization and Long-Run Development

Based on the 'stylized facts' of financialization outlined in the previous section post-Keynesians have presented different models examining the long-run growth and stability effects of financialization, as reviewed in Hein and van Treeck (2010) and Hein (2012), and also by Hein and Dodig in Chapter 2 of this book.[11] Depending on the values of the model parameters, 'finance-led growth' regimes, as suggested by Boyer (2000), 'profits without investment' regimes, as found by Cordonnier (2006), or 'contractive' regimes may emerge. Only in the 'finance-led growth' regime is increasing shareholder power overall expansive with respect to the rates of capacity utilization, as an indicator for aggregate demand, profit and capital accumulation, as an indicator for growth, whereas in the 'profits without investment' regime the effects on the rates of capacity utilization and profit remain expansive but capital accumulation gets depressed, and in the 'contractive' regime there is a depressing effect on all three endogenous variables of the model. As shown in Hein (2012, Chapter 3), only the 'finance-led growth' regime yields long-run stability of the financial structure of the firm sector and of capital accumulation. This regime, however, requires a very special parameter constellation: only weakly negative effects of increasing shareholder power on management's animal spirits regarding real investment in capital stock, a low rentiers' propensity to save out of current income, a low profit share, a low elasticity of investment with respect to distributed profits and internal funds, and a high responsiveness with regard to capacity utilization (and to Tobin's q in some models). In particular, a long-run increase in the gross profit share associated with financialization may turn the stable financial structure into an unstable one. More realistic parameter constellations, giving rise to 'profits without investment' or 'contractive' regimes, turned out to yield cumulatively unstable long-run results regarding the financial structure of the firm sector and the rate of capital accumulation. In the face of rising shareholder power, a rising rentiers' rate of return, that is, increasing dividend rates and/or interest rates, and falling management animal spirits regarding investment in capital stock, these regimes are prone to systemic instability characterized by increasing outside finance–capital ratios, that is, rising debt plus rentiers' equity–capital ratios, and falling goods market equilibrium rates of capital accumulation. Falling labour income shares triggered by financialization increase the likelihood of these unstable regimes. Therefore, under the conditions of the 'contractive' and the 'profits without investment' regimes, there exists a considerable systemic long-run instability potential regarding the financial structure of the corporate sector of the economy and regarding capital accumulation.

'Profits without investment' regimes, as the regimes which empirically seem to have prevailed during the pre-2007 crisis financialization period (van Treeck et al. 2007; van Treeck 2009a, 2009b; Hein 2012, Chapter 6; Hein and Mundt 2012; van Treeck and Sturn 2012), can be driven by flourishing consumption demand, by rising export surpluses or by government deficits, each compensating for falling investment in capital stock. This is so because, from a macroeconomic perspective, the following equation, derived from national income accounting, has to hold, as pointed out by Kalecki (1971, p. 82):

Gross profits net of taxes = Gross investment + Capitalists' consumption + Government budget deficit + Export surplus − Workers' saving   (1.1)

Empirically, several countries, like the USA, the UK, Spain, Ireland and Greece, have relied on a 'debt-led consumption boom' type of development in the face of low investment in capital stock and redistribution at the expense of labour incomes, making use of the increasing potential for wealth-based and debt-financed consumption generated by financialization, as analysed by Hein (2012, Chapter 6), Hein and Mundt (2012) and van Treeck and Sturn (2012), for example. As has been shown in the models by Dutt (2005, 2006), Bhaduri et al. (2006), Bhaduri (2011a, 2011b) and Hein (2012, Chapter 5), reviewed by Hein and Dodig in Chapter 2 of this book, increasing credit to (workers') households may indeed be expansionary for consumption, aggregate demand (and hence profits) and growth in the short run, and the system will thus be debt-led. However, in the long run, a rising stock of debt and hence rising interest payments, and therefore redistribution of income, from debtor households with high propensities to consume to rentiers with low consumption propensities, have to be taken into account. Under certain conditions, these contractionary effects may over-compensate for the expansionary effect of higher credit, and the system may become debt-burdened in the long run. Furthermore, it has been shown that, as soon as households' debt–income ratios exceed some threshold values, this ratio itself will become unstable – as a macroeconomic effect of weakened standards of creditworthiness, for example.

Turning to the international dimension of financialization, 'profits without investment' regimes can also be driven by net exports and current account surpluses, as equation (1.1) shows. In the face of redistribution at the expense of (low) labour incomes, stagnating consumption demand and weak real investment, 'mercantilist export-led' strategies, relying on nominal wage moderation and suppressed domestic demand, are thus an alternative to generating aggregate demand. This type of development was found in countries like Austria, Belgium, Germany, the Netherlands, Sweden, Japan and China during the pre-2007 crisis financialization period (Hein 2012, Chapter 6; Hein and Mundt 2012; van Treeck and Sturn 2012). Since the 'debt-led consumption boom' economies were running increasing current account deficits, the 'mercantilist export-led' economies with increasing current account surpluses were the necessary counterpart at the global level. The financial crisis, which was triggered by over-indebtedness problems of private households in the leading 'debt-led consumption' economy, the USA, could thus quickly spread to the 'export-led mercantilist' economies through the foreign trade channel (collapse of exports) and the financial contagion channel (devaluation of financial assets), in particular.

Based on these analyses of the long-run effects of financialization on income distribution, capital accumulation, consumption and current account imbalances, post-Keynesian and other authors have argued that these developments, together with the liberalization and deregulation of national and international financial markets, should be considered to be the main causes of the global financial crisis and the Great Recession of 2007–09 (Fitoussi and Stiglitz 2009; Horn et al. 2009a, 2009b; UNCTAD 2009; Wade 2009; Palley 2010, 2012, 2013; Stockhammer 2010a, 2010b, 2012a, 2012b; Hein 2012). Focusing on developments in the financial sector, as in the following section dealing with Minsky's theory of money manager capitalism, is therefore necessary, but not sufficient, when it comes to providing a convincing explanation for the crisis of finance-dominated capitalism.

1.5 MINSKY'S MONEY MANAGER CAPITALISM

1.5.1 Basic Structure of Minsky's Approach: 'Stability Breeds Instability'

Following Keynes ([1936] 1973), Minsky (1975, [1986] 2008) rejected the neoclassical optimal market equilibrium hypothesis; instead, he argued that capitalist systems experience temporary states of relative tranquillity, in which, however, internally destabilizing forces operate and finally render the system unstable. These destabilizing forces derive from financial relations. Finance and financial relations are not by-products of economic development which may become important in certain stages or regimes, but are important and significant aspects of capitalism as such. Tranquillity in a capitalist economy, where firms operate with external finance, encourages increasing risk-taking and speculative behaviour, initially validated by the institutional structure, but finally generating deep crises and collapses: 'However, success breeds daring, and over time the memory of past disaster is eroded. Stability – even of an expansion – is destabilizing in that more adventuresome financing of investment pays off to the leaders, and others follow' (Minsky 1975, p. 127).

In Minsky's 'financial instability theory', investment is both the driving force and the most unstable component of aggregate demand. Investment decisions are made in a multiple period model. Previous investment and output decisions are validated by current investment based on expectations about future demand (and hence investment). This is so because Minsky, following Kalecki (1954) and – as a simplification – assuming that capitalists do not consume and workers do not save, holds that aggregate gross profits for the economy as a whole are determined by capitalist investment. Therefore, 'in a capitalist economy investment takes place now because it is expected that investment will take place in the future' (Minsky [1986] 2008, p. 146).

Since investment is partly externally financed by credit from banks or other financial intermediaries or by issuing bonds or selling equities, the volume of investment is affected by the assessment of lenders' and borrowers' risks (Minsky [1986] 2008, Chapter 8). Both of them are rising with the volume of investment and hence of external finance, and are thus restricting investment at a moment in time. However, if expectations regarding future yields associated with current output and investment decisions are fulfilled, lenders and borrowers, that is, rentiers and firms, are willing to reassess lenders' and borrowers' risks. They will reduce the margins of safety and will be willing to take more risk and thus to increase the level of external finance of investment projects and hence the indebtedness of the firm sector. This will increase the fragility of the financial system.

The fragility of the financial system is affected by the share of external finance in investment financing, by the liquidity in the system and by the relative proportions of 'hedge', 'speculative' and 'Ponzi' financing schemes in the system, as Minsky ([1986] 2008, Chapter 9) explains. Hedge financing is seen as the most stable scheme, because expected income allows both the interest and the principal to be paid back. Speculative finance means that investors expect to pay interest from future revenues but not the principal. They have to roll over debt and speculate for (further) rising asset prices. Ponzi finance means that investors do not expect revenues to be sufficient to pay interest, which means that they will have to rely on an increase in future debt in order to meet their payment commitments. If, during the period of tranquillity or stability (during an economic upswing), margins of safety are reduced, lenders' and borrowers' risks are scaled down, hedge units might turn into speculative units and speculative units might become Ponzi units, thus increasing the financial fragility of the whole system. External shocks in relatively small segments of the system are then sufficient to cause a general financial crisis and a collapse of the financial system, which requires the intervention of governments and central banks on a large scale in order to stop economic contraction and debt deflation processes.

Minsky's financial instability hypothesis can be seen as a theory not only of short-run cyclical fluctuations, but also of super-cyclical tendencies, which generate deep crises of the system.[12] Minsky (1995, p. 92) summarized this as follows:

> Over a timespan without a financial panic and a deep recession, the financial structure changes so that financial layering increases and the proportion of what I called speculative and Ponzi financial postures increase. The above can be called the first postulate of the Financial Instability hypothesis. The second postulate is that the increase in layering and the shift in the structure of payment commitments progressively increase the vulnerability of the financial system to a debt deflation process, which can usher in a deep depression business cycle.

However, the notion that 'stability generates instability' can be not only applied to explain deep financial crises, but also can be used as an approach towards the long-run succession of different financial regimes, as will be discussed next.

1.5.2   Structural Shifts towards 'Money Manager Capitalism'

According to Minsky, the economic system goes through 'stages' of capitalism, characterized by different institutional constellations and financial structures (Minsky 1996; Wray 2009a, 2009b; Tymoigne and Wray 2014, Chapter 2). After each recession, the system resurges with a new set of features, instruments and behavioural patterns which mark a change in a capitalist regime. Minsky ([1986] 2008) based his analysis on the US economic transitions; it is, however, also relevant for the global economy, as it has passed through similar transformations and in the course of globalization contributed to the tightening of international financial interrelations.

According to Minsky, the beginning of the twentieth century was marked by a shift from 'commercial capitalism' with its traditional commercial banking structure to 'early finance capitalism' during which investment banking started gaining momentum (Wray 2009a, 2009b). Debt financing was no longer obtained solely for trade, but to finance the purchase of expensive capital assets. The use of riskier practices resulted in the stock market collapse in 1929 and the ensuing years of the Great Depression. Major government and lender of last resort interventions, the New Deal reforms and massive military expenditures in the Second World War were needed to reboot the economy and steer it toward prosperity. This period is referred to as 'paternalistic capitalism' (Minsky and Whalen 1996; Wray 2009a, 2009b). The major features were: 'Big Government', that is, the increasing role of the public sector in economic activity, expansion of the social welfare system and counter-cyclical fiscal policies in order to stabilize the economy; government supervision and regulation of the financial system and guarantees of the monetary system (i.e. deposit insurance); 'Big Bank', that is the Federal Reserve system setting low short-term interest rates, stabilizing the financial system and acting as lender of last resort; buoyant consumer demand financed by increases in income; and post-depression reluctance to borrow, and hence a lesser role for the financial sector. In this period government deficits were increasing, in particular during the Second World War, but private sector balance sheets came out of the recession and the war with modest debt ratios, promising a sustainable future development (Minsky [1986] 2008, Chapter 4).

As this stable growth was believed to go ahead, uncertainty became a lesser concern, and following the pattern described in subsection 1.5.1 this encouraged financial innovation and risk-taking. The government continued to play a sizable role, but the same became true for large financial players such as investment and commercial banks and pension and mutual funds. The late 1960s and early 1970s marked a new stage in economic development – the transition towards 'money manager capitalism' with its increased riskiness, financial innovation, profit-seeking behaviour and growing leverage ratios:

> Capitalism in the United States is now in a new stage, *money manager* capitalism, in which the proximate owners of a vast proportion of financial instruments are mutual and pension funds. The total return on the portfolio is the only criteria used for judging the performance of the managers of these funds, which translates into an emphasis upon the bottom line in the management of business organizations. It makes the long view a luxury that only companies which are essentially owned by a single individual and which are not deeply dependent upon external financing can afford. (Minsky 1996, p. 1, emphasis in the original)

A widespread use of new position-making instruments, such as certificates of deposit (CDs), repurchase agreements, and borrowing in eurodollars enabled commercial banks to evade the Fed's reserve requirements, and hence adjust the volume of lending to their liking (Minsky [1986] 2008, Chapter 4). The institutional structure of commercial banking evolved as well; the emergence of fringe banking institutions, whose lenders of last resort were large banks, facilitated further detachment of the Fed from the de facto credit supply. This complex financial structure failed for the first time during the 1966 credit crunch; the lender of last resort stepped in, and prevented a recession, but validated risky practices (Minsky [1986] 2008, Chapter 4).

The 1970s decade was marked by a series of similar crises – the liquidity squeeze of 1970 and bank runs in 1974–75. The pattern was always more or less the same: higher leverage and riskiness, recession, the Fed's intervention to prevent asset prices from collapsing, and government running deficits to contain falling demand and business profits. Financial failures predictably influenced the real economy; growing unemployment, inflation and a permanent threat of debt deflation marked the end of the 'Golden Age' and became intrinsic features of the USA and global economy (Minsky [1986] 2008, Chapter 4).

The next step occurred in the 1980s with a decline in the importance of commercial banks and a simultaneous rise of financial markets. Commercial banks' profitability was squeezed after anti-inflationary policies implemented by Paul Volcker in 1979–80; furthermore, the tightly regulated banking system did not offer the perks of financial markets, where funds could be obtained at a lower cost. Together with financial globalization, these developments facilitated the widespread use of securitization techniques, which since then have become the bread and butter of financial institutions. As commercial banks have obtained the opportunity to resell their loans as an asset to investment banks, they no longer had to evaluate risks and stick to capital requirements; their primary aim became to give out as many loans as possible (Wray 2009a).

The elimination of the Glass–Steagall Act in 1999 put an end to functional separation of different types of banking, making it even easier for financial institutions to earn profits. The development of futures markets was responsible for the financialization of new sectors; in particular, severe social and economic implications were caused by commodities price hikes, which had little to do with real terms. Low interest rates and increased competition on financial markets resulted in rising credit availability and leverage, profit-seeking and financial innovation (Wray 2009a).

1.5.3 Characteristics of Money Manager Capitalism

As Wray (2009a, p. 55) argued, money manager capitalism is dominated by 'highly leveraged funds seeking maximum returns in an environment that systematically under-prices risk'. The definition highlights the main features of the system: the increased role of credit, concentration of financial and market power, and the moral hazard effect of short-term-oriented activities (Minsky 1996).

Financialization has provided generous opportunities for profit making by means of 'speculative finance'. The rise of financial markets starting in the 1980s opened access to cheaper financing for firms, and the US low interest rate policies in the 2000s combined with competition among banks made it even more affordable (Wray 2009a). In speculative and Ponzi dominant regimes, new borrowing is necessary to repay previous debt or even to pay interest (Minsky [1986] 2008, Chapter 3). The shareholder value model generated high and a constantly rising trend of share and asset prices, which in turn induced further lending. Securitization and globalization of financial markets created a dense and highly interrelated network of financial institutions, funds and enterprises with common interests, while the age of financial innovation when capital assets can be easily financed and traded allowed for speculative growth of asset prices (Wray 2009b). This 'snowball effect' tends to erase the real foundations of economic growth, pushing the system towards fragility and susceptibility to price bubbles.

Reduced supervision is predictably disastrous for a financial system ruled by myopic profit-oriented agents and creates fertile ground for unscrupulous behaviour. With rising revenues from investment trading, fraud has become a widespread practice. Share price manipulations, betting against debts of large enterprises and whole governments, speculative raids detached from any real macroeconomic indicators – all of this has contributed to the series of economic crises starting from the 1970s (Wray 2009b).

The rise of finance and concentration of market power in the hands of 'too big to fail' institutions have resulted in a paradoxical economic constellation of a self-regulated financial system and anti-laissez-faire state policies. In a money manager capitalist state, the regulatory role of 'Big Government' has become passive and downsized. However, in the case of an economic downswing, the government inevitably has to step in and become the ultimate stabilizer of aggregate demand (Wray 2009b).

Similar tendencies can be observed with respect to the lender of last resort functions of the 'Big Bank'. With the replacement of the Fed's traditional discount window by open-market operations, commercial banks were freed from senior influence and could therefore engage in more risk-taking (Minsky [1986] 2008, Chapter 3). In a money manager capitalist regime, commercial banks are no different from any other profit-seeking corporations; they function on high leverage ratios, speculate and adjust lending to their liking. The Fed is detached from the endogenous money-creating processes in an economy, but it has to provide guarantees for and liquidity of otherwise unmarketable assets, turning into the 'ultimate fallback source of financing' for other banking institutions (Minsky [1986] 2008, p. 48). Decades of market failures and state interventions validating risky schemes have resulted in the concentration of financial power in the hands of money managers while worsening inequality in the economy and society. Therefore, consumption increasingly has to be supported by borrowing. However, this again increases financial fragility as a result of the increasing debt–income ratios of households.

1.5.4 Consequences of Money Manager Capitalism for Long-Run Development

The expansion of the financial sector since the 1960s has gone hand in hand with more uncertainty, financial structure fragility, and the need for frequent government stabilization of demand and economic activity, as well as lender of last resort interventions of the central bank. An economy, where a 'long view (is) a luxury' (Minsky 1996, p. 1) and short-term external financing dominates, becomes vulnerable to sudden disruptions, such as interest rate increases or cash flow shortfalls. This is especially true for periods of economic expansion, when firms reduce their safety margins to a minimum in response to favourable expectations and, hence, to further forthcoming credit. A temporary shift from a hedge to speculative financial profiles can be handled by entities themselves; in a money manager capitalist economy, however, the whole financial sector tends to engage in speculative or Ponzi financing. The increasing relevance of financial markets and large corporations increasingly assuming the characteristics of financial institutions makes growth in money manager capitalism increasingly unstable and requires more frequent and more extensive government and central bank stabilization.

Wray (2011) establishes a direct connection between money manager capitalism and the global financial crisis. He singles out four important aspects of money manager capitalism which finally led to the crisis: 1) the rise of 'managed money' (pension funds, sovereign wealth funds, insurance funds, etc.) and the shift towards focusing on total returns (yields plus appreciation); 2) Wall Street firms going public by issuing traded shares and thus enjoying the advantage of issuing shares in a boom; 3) deregulation and de-supervision, which allowed financial institutions to engage in ever riskier activities, that is, holding riskier assets, taking more illiquid positions and increasing leverage; and 4) the rise of fraud as normal business procedure. These changes indicate the institutional and behavioural dimension of Minsky's credo that 'stability is destabilizing', and Wray (2011, p. 16) concludes: 'The current financial crisis is a natural outcome of these processes – an unsustainable explosion of real estate prices, mortgage debt, and leveraged positions in collateralized securities and derivatives in conjunction with a similarly unsustainable explosion of commodities prices and equities. The crash was inevitable.'

1.6   COMPARISON AND CONCLUSIONS

In this chapter we have surveyed some of the important literature on financial, economic and social systems with an eye towards explaining the tendencies towards financialization. We have focused on the French Regulation School, the US-based Social Structures of Accumulation approach, several contributions of post-Keynesian authors and, finally, in particular, the long-run views based on Hyman Minsky's work. These approaches have in common the notion that capitalist development is embedded in social institutions and that institutions and economic development are mutually interdependent. In each of these approaches, different stages of development, or different regimes, of modern capitalism could be distinguished, the latest being the 'finance-led growth regime' (Regulation School), or the '(global) neoliberal social structure of accumulation' (SSA approach), or 'finance-dominated capitalism' (post-Keynesians) or 'money manager capitalism' (Minsky), each describing the period of financialization, which started in the USA and the UK in about the late 1970s and early 1980s and somewhat later in other capitalist economies. The analysis has followed a four-step pattern for each of the approaches in order to facilitate comparison. First, we have sketched the basic structure of each of the approaches in order to single out how these approaches view the interaction between social institutions and the economy and the related dynamics regarding the development of the institutional structure and associated stages or regimes of economic development. We have then dealt with the question of how these approaches view the structural breaks or the regime shifts in the long-run development of modern capitalism that triggered, or at least contributed to, the emergence of financialization. In the third step we have outlined how these different approaches view the main characteristics and features of financialization, and in the fourth step we have dealt with the respective views on the consequences of financialization for long-run economic and social development, including the crisis of this stage of development. Therefore, we can now summarize and compare the four approaches in the four steps just mentioned:

1. Regarding the basic structures, all approaches consider 'capitalist' (Regulation School, SSA), 'monetary production' (post-Keynesians) or 'financial' (Minsky) economies to be inherently unstable and argue that these economies require stabilizing social institutions. Whereas the Regulation School and the SSA approach, based on the Marxian approach, view this instability as rooted in class conflict between capital and labour in the spheres of production and distribution, post-Keynesians present several requirements for institutions, which are rooted in their views of the nature of a 'monetary production economy', among them the need to cope with fundamental uncertainty, to provide stable monetary and financial relations, to constrain distribution conflict, and to stabilize aggregate demand in the short and in the long run. Minsky's view on institutions is based on the nature of financial economies, which is prone to the 'stability breeds instability' principle obviously rooted in human behaviour. Interestingly, the Regulation School and in particular the SSA approach, as well as Minsky provide an endogenous mechanism of institutional change, basically arguing that existing regimes are undermined by their success, which sets in motion certain processes that make the regime finally collapse. In the post-Keynesian approaches, institutional changes seem to be contingent on exogenous shocks, changing power relations and economic policy failures, without following definite 'laws of motion'.

2. According to the Regulation School and the SSA approach, the transition towards a 'finance-led growth regime' (Regulation School) or a 'global neoliberal SSA' (SSA approach) was based on the collapse of profitability in the previous regime, 'Fordism' or the 'regulated capitalist SSA'. Whereas the Regulation School draws on Marx's law of the tendency of the rate of profit to fall and argues that the crisis of profitability was caused by technological change, the SSA approach follows the Marxian profit squeeze theory and argues that, under the conditions of full employment, workers were able to squeeze the rate of surplus value and hence the profit share. This crisis of profitability had a negative impact on investment and growth and made the manager–worker compromise (Regulation School) or the capital–labour accord (SSA), and thus the most important pillar of the previous regime, collapse. Post-Keynesian authors have also drawn attention to the collapse of a 'social bargain' or a 'social compromise' as the cause for the erosion of the 'Golden Age' period of the 1950s until the early 1970s, which they relate to increasing inflation rates in the 1970s and the following economic policy responses. Cornwall and Cornwall (2001) argue that workers' and trade unions' excessive wage demands as compared to productivity under the conditions of full employment caused rising inflation rates and the 'social bargain' of the 'Golden Age' to collapse. Smithin (1996), however, considers the rising inflation rates of the 1970s to be the result of exogenous shocks and, in his view, it was monetary policies accepting negative real interest rates which made rentiers quit the social compromise of the 'Golden Age' period. Steindl ([1979] 1990) holds a similar view, arguing that the capitalist class as a whole became dominated by rentiers' interests, which then caused the implementation of anti-Keynesian 'stagnation policies'. Minsky's approach differs from those previously outlined in that he views the transition towards money manager capitalism rather as a gradual process, driven by the stability of 'paternalistic capitalism', and based on his credo 'stability breeds instability' by increasing appetite for risk etc.

3. When it comes to the main characteristics of the financialization period, we see some convergence among the different approaches, and no fundamental differences but some complementarities. In particular the Regulation School, the SSA approaches and the post-Keynesian contributions seem to agree that the financialization period is characterized by the deregulation and liberalization of national and international financial markets, goods markets and labour markets, by the reduction of government intervention in the market economy, by a rentier/shareholder–manager coalition dominating labour, by a

pronounced shareholder value and short-term profitability orientation of firms at the expense of long-run profitable investments in
capital stock, by redistribution of income from wages to broad profits,
and among wages from direct labour to managers, and by increasing
opportunities of creating household debt for consumption purposes,
as well as structural changes in the banking sector through securitization, in particular. Minsky's contribution is more narrowly focused on
the characteristics of the financial sector in 'money manager capitalism', highlighting the role of leveraging, the shift towards speculative
and Ponzi financing, the role of frauds, and the increasing instability
generated hereby. Whereas these observations are complementary to
the other approaches, highlighting the instability properties acknowl-
edged by the other approaches too, the Minskyan view on the role
of governments seems to be slightly different from the rest. Whereas
the other approaches seem to argue that financialization is characterized by downsizing governments, the Minskyan approach highlights
the changed role of governments and central banks as rescuer of last
resort in the case of crisis, without necessarily claiming that government has been downsized in money manager capitalism.

4. Finally, regarding the effects of financialization on long-run development, Regulation School and SSA approaches seem to have given
up their Marxian supply-side explanations of deep crises, that is, the
falling rate of profit due to technological development argument and
the profit squeeze approach, and seem to acknowledge that monetary
production economies, at least nowadays, are demand constrained.
Therefore, they now seem to accept the post-Keynesian argument that,
in particular, redistribution at the expense of (lower) wages during the
financialization period has caused a major problem for aggregate
demand, which only temporarily could be overcome by increasing
household debt, which then triggered the crisis. Therefore, there seems
to be a common understanding now among the members of these
schools regarding the importance of wage stagnation driving household debt, at least in some countries, and regarding the fragility of
this process, underpinned by financial deregulation and innovations,
as Setterfield (2011) has also pointed out. However, post-Keynesian
contributions have clearly spelled out the macroeconomic conditions and constraints and have also highlighted that there are different types of development under financialization, with the 'debt-led
consumption boom' type and the 'export-led mercantilist' type at
the extremes, which immediately links the issues of inequality and of
global current account imbalances as causes for the worldwide Great
Recession. Again, the Minskyan contribution is much narrower and

more focused on the developments within the financial sector, highlighting the increasing instability potentials, which finally triggered the crisis. Following Palley (2010), we would therefore argue that the Minskyan contributions are important and complementary to the other approaches, but that they are not sufficient to explain the worldwide Great Recession – and the following developments. For this, redistribution as the fundamental feature of financialization, increases in household debt in several countries, and rising global current account imbalances have to be considered as well.

NOTES

1. 'Regulation, or regulationist, theory' and 'regulation approach' are used interchangeably in the literature. The term *régulation* ought to mean social regularization (Jessop 1997), rather than legal or state regulation. In the regulation theory the state is considered as (only) one among the institutions which are involved in regulation.
2. Juego (2011) and Tickell (2000) criticize Boyer (2000) for suggesting that financial innovations could provide the stability of this accumulation regime while disregarding the significant potential for political instability. Some other criticisms that have surrounded this work relate to the absence of the public sector in the model and the focus of analysis on a national economy (Tickell 2000; van Treeck 2009a), because it is quite impossible to theorize about a finance-led growth regime without more explicit reference to the political economy of international finance. Furthermore, the Boyer model lacks any systematic analysis of firms' and households' financial decisions as well as any stock–flow interactions of household deficits and debt. The non-consideration of these factors may have contributed to the underestimation of potentials for instability in finance-led growth economies.
3. Tabb (2010, p. 156) compares the financial innovation characteristic of the present SSA to Marx's notion of 'fictitious capital', that is, 'paper claims to ownership of capital that does not (or does not yet) exist in material form'.
4. There is also an asymmetry of information between the managers (insiders) and the capital markets. This enabled the firms to – quite often – misrepresent the performance of the firm to the capital markets. In the USA, the Generally Accepted Accounting Principles (GAAP) gave substantial freedom for interpretation (Boyer 2010, pp. 226–227), which resulted in a years-long overestimation of the publicly quoted corporations' and thus the stock market's performance. Additionally, during the second half of the 1990s the stock options granted to managers were not considered as a cost to corporations, making the corporate profits appear higher and consequently obtaining higher valuation of the shares.
5. See Lavoie (2006, Chapter 1, 2011) for an overview of 'presuppositions and key characteristics' of post-Keynesian economics and other heterodox schools of thought.
6. Lavoie (2011) also adds the 'paradox of liquidity' (Nesvetailova 2007) and the 'paradox of risk' (Wojnilower 1980).
7. Therefore, monetary production economies are contract economies, based on money as a unit of account, which then require institutions, hence a legal system, of contract and payments enforcement. Chartalists even argue that the very existence of money is based on the existence of the state and that 'money (broadly speaking) is a unit of account, designated by a public authority for the codification of social debt obligations' (Tcherneva 2006, p. 69). On modern money theory as the most recent incarnation of chartalism, see Wray (2012) and for an assessment see Lavoie (2013).

8. 'The exceptions were Austria, Japan, Norway, Sweden and Switzerland, where social bargains and full employment persisted until the early 1990s' (Cornwall and Cornwall 2001, p. 223).
9. A major purpose of Steindl's ([1979] 1990, [1989] 1990) contribution was, of course, to explain why the stagnation tendencies in mature capitalism he had detected in his earlier book, that is in Steindl ([1952] 1976), did not materialize in the post-Second World War period.
10. See also Epstein (1992), who has presented a three-class model of industrial capitalists, financial capitalists and workers, in which central bank policies are determined by capital–labour relations, industry–finance relations, the degree of central bank independence and the position of the economy in the world economy.
11. See for example Godley and Lavoie (2007, Chapter 11), Lavoie (2008), Skott and Ryoo (2008a, 2008b) and van Treeck (2008).
12. See for examples Palley's (2013, Chapter 8) notion of a 'Minsky super cycle'.

REFERENCES

Aglietta, M. (1976), *Régulation et crises du capitalisme: L'expériences des Etats-Unis*, Paris: Calmann-Lévy. English translation, *A Theory of Capitalist Regulation: The US Experience*, London: Verso, 2000.
Aglietta, M. (1998), 'Capitalism at the turn of the century: regulation theory and the challenge of social change', *New Left Review*, **232**, 41–90.
Aglietta, M. and R. Breton (2001), 'Financial systems, corporate control and capital accumulation', *Economy and Society*, **30**, 433–466.
Arestis, P. (2013), 'Economic theory and policy: a coherent post-Keynesian approach', *European Journal of Economics and Economic Policies: Intervention*, **10**, 243–255.
Arestis, P. and M. Sawyer (1998), 'Keynesian economic policies for the new millennium', *Economic Journal*, **108**, 181–195.
Barba, A. and M. Pivetti (2009), 'Rising household debt: its causes and macroeconomic implications – a long-period analysis', *Cambridge Journal of Economics*, **33**, 113–137.
Bhaduri, A. (2011a), 'Financialisation in the light of Keynesian theory', *PSL Quarterly Review*, **64**, 7–21.
Bhaduri, A. (2011b), 'A contribution to the theory of financial fragility and crisis', *Cambridge Journal of Economics*, **35**, 995–1014.
Bhaduri, A. and J. Steindl (1985), 'Monetarism as a social doctrine', in P. Arestis and T. Skouras (eds), *Post-Keynesian Economic Theory*, Brighton: Wheatsheaf.
Bhaduri, A., Laski, K. and M. Riese (2006), 'A model of interaction between the virtual and the real economy', *Metroeconomica*, **57**, 412–427.
Boone, L. and N. Girouard (2002), 'The stock market, the housing market and consumer behaviour', *OECD Economic Studies*, **35**, 175–200.
Boyer, R. (1987), 'Technical change and the theory of regulation', CEPREMAP Working Paper No. 8707, March, Paris.
Boyer, R. (2000), 'Is a finance-led growth regime a viable alternative to Fordism? A preliminary analysis', *Economy and Society*, **29**, 111–145.
Boyer, R. (2005), 'How and why capitalisms differ', MPIfG Discussion Paper No. 05(4), Max Planck Institute for the Study of Societies.
Boyer, R. (2010), 'The rise of CEO pay and the contemporary social structure of

accumulation in the United States', in T. McDonough, M. Reich and D.M. Kotz (eds), *Contemporary Capitalism and Its Crises: Social Structure of Accumulation Theory for the 21st Century*, Cambridge, UK: Cambridge University Press.

Boyer, R. (2013), 'The present crisis: a trump for a renewed political economy', *Review of Political Economy*, **25**, 1–38.

Brenner, R. and M. Glick (1991), 'The regulation approach: theory and history', *New Left Review*, **188**, 45–119.

Cordonnier, L. (2006), 'Le profit sans l'accumulation: la recette du capitalisme dominé par la finance', *Innovations, Cahiers d'Economie de l'Innovation*, **23**, 51–72.

Cornwall, J. and W. Cornwall (2001), *Capitalist Development in the Twentieth Century: An Evolutionary-Keynesian Analysis*, Cambridge, UK: Cambridge University Press.

Crotty, J. (1990), 'Owner–management conflict and financial theories of investment instability: a critical assessment of Keynes, Tobin, and Minsky', *Journal of Post Keynesian Economics*, **12**, 519–542.

Cynamon, B. and S. Fazzari (2008), 'Household debt in the consumer age: source of growth – risk of collapse', *Capitalism and Society*, **3** (2), 1–30.

Dallery, T. (2009), 'Post-Keynesian theories of the firm under financialization', *Review of Radical Political Economics*, **41**, 492–515.

Davidson, P. (1988), 'A technical definition of uncertainty and the long-run non-neutrality of money', *Cambridge Journal of Economics*, **12**, 329–337.

Davidson, P. (1994), *Post Keynesian Macroeconomic Theory*, Aldershot, UK and Brookfield, VT, USA: Edward Elgar Publishing.

Dutt, A.K. (2005), 'Conspicuous consumption, consumer debt and economic growth', in M. Setterfield (ed.), *Interactions in Analytical Political Economy: Theory, Policy and Applications*, Armonk, NY: M.E. Sharpe.

Dutt, A.K. (2006), 'Maturity, stagnation and consumer debt: a Steindlian approach', *Metroeconomica*, **57**, 339–364.

Epstein, G.A. (1992), 'Political economy and comparative central banking', *Review of Radical Political Economics*, **24**, 1–30.

Epstein, G.A. (2005a), 'Introduction: financialization and the world economy', in G.A. Epstein (ed.), *Financialization and the World Economy*, Cheltenham, UK and Northampton, MA, USA: Edward Elgar Publishing.

Epstein, G.A. (ed.) (2005b), *Financialization and the World Economy*, Cheltenham, UK and Northampton, MA, USA: Edward Elgar Publishing.

Fisher, I. (1933), 'The debt-deflation theory of great depressions', *Econometrica*, **1**, 337–357.

Fitoussi, J.-P. and J. Stiglitz (2009), 'The ways out of the crisis and the building of a more cohesive world', OFCE Document de Travail 2009-17, OFCE.

Frank, R.H., A.S. Levine and O. Dijk (2014), 'Expenditure cascades', *Review of Behavioral Economics*, **1**, 55–73.

Godley, W. and M. Lavoie (2007), *Monetary Economics: An Integrated Approach to Credit, Money, Income, Production and Wealth*, Basingstoke: Palgrave Macmillan.

Gordon, D. (1981), 'Capital–labor conflict and the productivity slowdown', *American Economic Review, Papers and Proceedings*, **71** (2), 30–35.

Gordon, D. (1995), 'Growth, distribution, and the rules of the game: social structuralist macro foundations for a democratic economic policy', in G.A. Epstein and H.M. Gintis (eds), *Macroeconomic Policy after the Conservative Era*, Cambridge, UK: Cambridge University Press.

Gordon, D., T.E. Weisskopf and S. Bowles (1983), 'Long swings and the nonre-productive cycle', *American Economic Review, Papers and Proceedings*, **73** (2), 152–157.

Gordon, D., T.E. Weisskopf and S. Bowles (1987), 'Power, accumulation and crisis: the rise and demise of the postwar social structure of accumulation', in R. Cherry (ed.), *The Imperiled Economy*, Book I, New York: Union for Radical Political Economics (URPE).

Gordon, D.M., S. Bowles and T.E. Weisskopf (1994), 'Power, profits, and investment: an institutional explanation of the stagnation of U.S. net investment after the mid-1960s', Working Paper No. 12, New School for Social Research. Reprinted in S. Bowles and T.E. Weisskopf (eds) (1998), *Economics and Social Justice: Essays on Power, Labor and Institutional Change*, Cheltenham, UK and Lyme, NH, USA: Edward Elgar Publishing.

Guttmann, R. (2012), 'The heterodox notion of structural crisis', available at: http://www.assoeconomiepolitique.org/political-economy-outlook-for-capitalism/wp-content/uploads/2012/06/Guttmann-Heterodox_Notion_of_Structural_Crisis.pdf.

Guttmann, R. and D. Plihon (2010), 'Consumer debt and financial fragility', *International Review of Applied Economics*, **24**, 269–283.

Hein, E. (2002), 'Monetary policy and wage bargaining in the EMU: restrictive ECB policies, high unemployment, nominal wage restraint and inflation above the target', *Banca Nazionale del Lavoro Quarterly Review*, **55**, 299–337.

Hein, E. (2012), *The Macroeconomics of Finance-dominated Capitalism – and its Crisis*, Cheltenham, UK and Northampton, MA, USA: Edward Elgar Publishing.

Hein, E. (2013), 'Finance-dominated capitalism and re-distribution of income – a Kaleckian perspective', *Cambridge Journal of Economics*, advance access, 2013, doi:10.1093/cje/bet038.

Hein, E. and M. Mundt (2012), 'Financialisation and the requirements and potentials for wage-led recovery: a review focusing on the G20', Conditions of Work and Employment Series No. 37, International Labour Organization.

Hein, E. and E. Stockhammer (2010), 'Macroeconomic policy mix, employment and inflation in a post-Keynesian alternative to the New Consensus model', *Review of Political Economy*, **22**, 317–354.

Hein, E. and T. van Treeck (2010), '"Financialisation" in post-Keynesian models of distribution and growth – a systematic review', in M. Setterfield (ed.), *Handbook of Alternative Theories of Economic Growth*, Cheltenham, UK and Northampton, MA, USA: Edward Elgar Publishing.

Herr, H. (2012), 'International monetary and financial architecture', in E. Hein and E. Stockhammer (eds), *A Modern Guide to Keynesian Macroeconomics and Economic Policies*, Cheltenham, UK and Northampton, MA, USA: Edward Elgar Publishing.

Horn, G., K. Dröge, S. Sturn, T. van Treeck and R. Zwiener (2009a), 'From the financial crisis to the world economic crisis: the role of inequality', IMK Policy Brief, October, Macroeconomic Policy Institute (IMK) at the Hans Böckler Foundation, Düsseldorf.

Horn, G., H. Joebges and R. Zwiener (2009b), 'From the financial crisis to the world economic crisis (II). Global imbalances: Cause of the crisis and solution strategies for Germany', IMK Policy Brief, December, Macroeconomic Policy Institute (IMK) at the Hans Böckler Foundation, Düsseldorf.

Iacoviello, M. (2008), 'Household debt and income inequality, 1963–2003', *Journal of Money, Credit and Banking*, **40**, 929–965.

Jessop, B. (1997), 'Survey article: the regulation approach', *Journal of Political Philosophy*, **5**, 287–326.

Juego, B. (2011), 'Whither regulationism: reflections on the regulation approach', *Interdisciplinary Journal of International Studies*, **7** (1), 55–66.

Kalecki, M. (1954), *Theory of Economic Dynamics*, London: George Allen & Unwin.

Kalecki, M. (1971), *Selected Essays on the Dynamics of the Capitalist Economy, 1933–70*, Cambridge, UK: Cambridge University Press.

Keynes, J.M. (1936), *The General Theory of Employment, Interest, and Money*. Reprinted in *The Collected Writings of J.M. Keynes*, Vol. VII, London: Macmillan, 1973.

Kotz, D.M. (2011), 'Social structures of accumulation, the rate of profit, and economic crises', paper written for a Festschrift in honour of Thomas E. Weisskopf, University of Massachusetts, 1 October, available at: http://www.peri.umass.edu/fileadmin/pdf/conference_papers/weisskopf/D._Kotz_paper.doc.

Kotz, D.M. and T. McDonough (2010), 'Global neoliberalism and the contemporary social structure of accumulation', in T. McDonough, M. Reich and D.M. Kotz (eds), *Contemporary Capitalism and Its Crises: Social Structure of Accumulation Theory for the 21st Century*, Cambridge, UK: Cambridge University Press.

Krippner, G.R. (2005), 'The financialization of the American economy', *Socio-Economic Review*, **3**, 173–208.

Lavoie, M. (2006), *Introduction to Post-Keynesian Economics*, Basingstoke: Palgrave Macmillan.

Lavoie, M. (2008), 'Financialisation issues in a post-Keynesian stock-flow consistent model', *European Journal of Economics and Economic Policies: Intervention*, **5**, 331–356.

Lavoie, M. (2011), 'History and methods of post-Keynesian economics', in E. Hein and E. Stockhammer (eds), *A Modern Guide to Keynesian Macroeconomics and Economic Policies*, Cheltenham, UK and Northampton, MA, USA: Edward Elgar Publishing.

Lavoie, M. (2013), 'The monetary and fiscal nexus of neo-chartalism: a friendly critique', *Journal of Economic Issues*, **47**, 1–31.

Lipietz, A. (1987), 'Rebel sons: the regulation school, an interview by Jane Jenson', *French Politics and Society*, **5** (4), 17–26.

Lippit, V.D. (2010), 'Social structure of accumulation theory', in T. McDonough, M. Reich and D.M. Kotz (eds), *Contemporary Capitalism and Its Crises: Social Structure of Accumulation Theory for the 21st Century*, Cambridge, UK: Cambridge University Press.

Ludvigson, S. and C. Steindel (1999), 'How important is the stock market effect on consumption?', *Federal Reserve Bank of New York Economic Policy Review*, July, 29–51.

Marx, K. (1894), *Das Kapital: Kritik der politischen Ökonomie*, Dritter Band: *Der Gesamtprozeß der kapitalistischen Produktion*, edited by F. Engels. Reprinted in *Marx-Engels-Werke*, Vol. 25, Berlin: Dietz Verlag, 1964. English translation, *Capital: A Critique of Political Economy*, Vol. 3: *The Process of Capitalist Production as a Whole*, New York: International Publisher, 1967.

McDonough, T., M. Reich and D.M. Kotz (2010), 'Introduction: social structure of accumulation theory for the 21st century', in T. McDonough, M. Reich and D.M. Kotz (eds), *Contemporary Capitalism and Its Crises: Social Structure of Accumulation Theory for the 21st Century*, Cambridge, UK: Cambridge University Press.

Mehra, Y.P. (2001), 'The wealth effect in empirical life-cycle aggregate consumption equations', *Federal Reserve Bank of Richmond Economic Quarterly*, **87** (2), 45–68.

Minsky, H. (1975), *John Maynard Keynes*, London: Macmillan.

Minsky, H. (1986), *Stabilizing an Unstable Economy*. Reprinted by McGraw-Hill, New York, 2008.

Minsky, H. (1995), 'Longer waves in financial relations: financial factors in the more severe depressions II', *Journal of Economic Issues*, **29**, 83–96.

Minsky, H. (1996), 'Uncertainty and the institutional structure of capitalist economies', Working Paper No. 155, April, Jerome Levy Economics Institute, Annandale-on-Hudson, New York.

Minsky, H. and C.J. Whalen (1996), 'Economic insecurity and the institutional prerequisites for successful capitalism', Working Paper No. 165, May, Jerome Levy Economics Institute, Annandale-on-Hudson, New York.

Nesvetailova, A. (2007), *Fragile Finance: Debt, Speculation and Crisis in the Age of Global Credit*, Basingstoke: Palgrave Macmillan.

Nilsson, E.A. (1996), 'The breakdown of the U.S. postwar system of labor relations: an econometric study', *Review of Radical Political Economics*, **28** (1), 20–50.

Nilsson, E.A. (1997), 'The growth of union decertification: a test of two nonnested theories', *Industrial Relations*, **36**, 324–348.

Onaran, Ö., E. Stockhammer and L. Grafl (2011), 'Financialisation, income distribution and aggregate demand in the USA', *Cambridge Journal of Economics*, **35**, 637–661.

Orhangazi, Ö. (2008), 'Financialisation and capital accumulation in the non-financial corporate sector: a theoretical and empirical investigation on the US economy: 1973–2003', *Cambridge Journal of Economics*, **32**, 863–886.

Palley, T. (1996), 'Restoring prosperity: why the US model is not the answer for the United States or Europe', *Journal of Post Keynesian Economics*, **20**, 337–351.

Palley, T. (2008), 'Financialisation: what it is and why it matters', in E. Hein, T. Niechoj, P. Spahn and A. Truger (eds), *Finance-led Capitalism? Macroeconomic Effects of Changes in the Financial Sector*, Marburg: Metropolis.

Palley, T. (2010), 'The limits of Minsky's financial instability hypothesis as an explanation of the crisis', *Monthly Review*, **61** (11), 28–43.

Palley, T. (2012), *From Crisis to Stagnation: The Destruction of Shared Prosperity and the Role of Economics*, Cambridge, UK: Cambridge University Press.

Palley, T. (2013), *Financialization: The Economics of Finance Capital Domination*, Basingstoke: Palgrave Macmillan.

Pressman, S. (2012), 'Institutionalism', in J.E. King (ed.), *The Elgar Companion to Post Keynesian Economics*, 2nd edn, Cheltenham, UK and Northampton, MA, USA: Edward Elgar Publishing.

Robinson, J. (1962), *Essays in the Theory of Economic Growth*, London: Macmillan.

Rowthorn, R. (1981), 'Demand, real wages and economic growth', Thames Papers in Political Economy, Autumn, London.

Setterfield, M. (2007), 'The rise, decline and rise of incomes policies in the US during the post-war era: an institutional-analytical explanation of inflation and the functional distribution of income', *Journal of Institutional Economics*, **3** (2), 127–146.

Setterfield, M. (2011), 'Anticipations of the crisis: on the similarities between post-Keynesian economics and regulation theory', *Revue de la Régulation*, **10**, available at: http://regulation.revues.org/9366.

Skott, P. and S. Ryoo (2008a), 'Macroeconomic implications of financialization', *Cambridge Journal of Economics*, **32**, 827–862.

Skott, P. and S. Ryoo (2008b), 'Financialization in Kaleckian economics with and without labor constraints', *European Journal of Economics and Economic Policies: Intervention*, **5**, 357–386.

Smithin, J. (1996), *Macroeconomic Policy and the Future of Capitalism: The Revenge of the Rentiers and the Threat to Prosperity*, Cheltenham, UK and Brookfield, VT, USA: Edward Elgar Publishing.

Steindl, J. (1952), *Maturity and Stagnation in American Capitalism*, 2nd edn, New York: Monthly Review Press, 1976 .

Steindl, J. (1979), 'Stagnation theory and stagnation policy', *Cambridge Journal of Economics*, **3**, 1–14. Reprinted in J. Steindl, *Economic Papers, 1941–88*, Basingstoke: Macmillan, 1990.

Steindl, J. (1989), 'From stagnation in the 30s to slow growth in the 70s', in M. Berg (ed.), *Political Economy in the Twentieth Century*, Oxford: Philip Allan. Reprinted in J. Steindl, *Economic Papers, 1941–88*, Basingstoke: Macmillan, 1990.

Stockhammer, E. (2004), 'Financialisation and the slowdown of accumulation', *Cambridge Journal of Economics*, **28**, 719–741.

Stockhammer, E. (2005–06), 'Shareholder value orientation and the investment–profit puzzle', *Journal of Post Keynesian Economics*, **28**, 193–215.

Stockhammer, E. (2008), 'Some stylized facts on the finance-dominated accumulation regime', *Competition and Change*, **12**, 189–207.

Stockhammer, E. (2010a), 'Income distribution, the finance-dominated accumulation regime, and the present crisis', in S. Dullien, E. Hein, A. Truger and T. van Treeck (eds), *The World Economy in Crisis – The Return of Keynesianism?*, Marburg: Metropolis.

Stockhammer, E. (2010b), 'Neoliberalism, income distribution and the causes of the crisis', Research on Money and Finance Discussion Paper No. 19, Department of Economics, SOAS, London.

Stockhammer, E. (2012a), 'Financialization, income distribution and the crisis', *Investigación Económica*, **71** (279), 39–70.

Stockhammer, E. (2012b), 'Rising inequality as a root cause of the present crisis', Working Paper Series No. 282, Political Economy Research Institute (PERI), University of Massachusetts Amherst.

Tabb, W.K. (2010), 'Financialization in the contemporary social structure of accumulation', in T. McDonough, M. Reich and D.M. Kotz (eds), *Contemporary Capitalism and Its Crises: Social Structure of Accumulation Theory for the 21st Century*, Cambridge, UK: Cambridge University Press.

Tcherneva, P. (2006), 'Chartalism and the tax-driven approach to money', in P. Arestis and M. Sawyer (eds), *A Handbook of Alternative Monetary Economics*, Cheltenham, UK and Northampton, MA, USA: Edward Elgar Publishing.

Tickell, A. (2000), 'Finance-led growth after Fordism: observation on Boyer, R. (2000) Is a finance-led growth regime a viable alternative to Fordism?', comments presented at ESRC/International Centre for Labour Studies Workshop,

November 1999, Manchester University, available at: http://www2.cddc.vt.edu/ digitalfordism/fordism_materials/Tickell.pdf.

Tymoigne, E. and L.R. Wray (2014), *The Rise and Fall of Money Manager Capitalism: Minsky's Half Century from World War Two to the Great Recession,* London: Routledge.

UNCTAD (2009), *The Global Economic Crisis: Systemic Failures and Multilateral Remedies,* New York: UNCTAD.

van Treeck, T. (2008), 'Reconsidering the investment–profit nexus in finance-led economies: an ARDL-based approach', *Metroeconomica,* **59,** 371–404.

van Treeck, T. (2009a), 'The political economy debate on "financialisation" – a macroeconomic perspective', *Review of International Political Economy,* **16,** 907–944.

van Treeck, T. (2009b), 'A synthetic stock-flow consistent macroeconomic model of "financialisation"', *Cambridge Journal of Economics,* **33,** 467–493.

van Treeck, T. and S. Sturn (2012), 'Income inequality as a cause of the Great Recession? A survey of current debates', Conditions of Work and Employment Series No. 39, International Labour Organization.

van Treeck, T., E. Hein and P. Dünhaupt (2007), 'Finanzsystem und wirtschaftliche Entwicklung: neuere Tendenzen in den USA und in Deutschland', IMK Studies 5/2007, Macroeconomic Policy Institute (IMK) at the Hans Böckler Foundation, Düsseldorf.

Wade, R. (2009), 'From global imbalances to global reorganisations', *Cambridge Journal of Economics,* **33,** 539–562.

Wojnilower, A.M. (1980), 'The central role of credit crunches in recent financial history', *Brookings Papers on Economic Activity,* **2,** 277–326.

Wray, L.R. (2009a), 'Money manager capitalism and the global financial crisis', *Real-World Economics Review,* **51,** 55–69.

Wray, L.R. (2009b), 'The rise and fall of money manager capitalism: a Minskian approach', *Cambridge Journal of Economics,* **33,** 807–828.

Wray, L.R. (2011), 'Minsky's money manager capitalism and the global financial crisis', *International Journal of Political Economy,* **40** (2), 5–20.

Wray, L.R. (2012), *Modern Money Theory: A Primer on Macroeconomics for Sovereign Monetary Systems,* Basingstoke: Palgrave Macmillan.

2. Finance-dominated capitalism, distribution, growth and crisis – long-run tendencies

Eckhard Hein and Nina Dodig

2.1 INTRODUCTION

In this chapter we provide a macroeconomic perspective on 'financialization' or 'finance-dominated capitalism', as a long-run trend which has dominated modern capitalism, to different degrees in different countries, starting in about the late 1970s or early 1980s in the USA and the UK and later in other developed capitalist economies and also in emerging market economies. We will also link this trend with the recent financial and economic crises. From a macroeconomic point of view, financialization has four important features (Hein 2012):

1. With regard to distribution, financialization has been conducive to a rising gross profit share, including retained profits, dividends and interest payments, and thus a falling labour income share, on the one hand, and to increasing inequality of wages and top management salaries, on the other hand. The major reasons for this have been falling bargaining power of trade unions, rising profit claims imposed in particular by increasingly powerful rentiers, and a change in the sectoral composition of the economy in favour of the financial corporate sector.
2. Regarding investment in the capital stock, financialization has been characterized by increasing shareholder power vis-à-vis management and workers, an increasing rate of return on equity and bonds held by rentiers, and an alignment of management with shareholder interests through short-run performance-related pay schemes, such as bonuses, stock option programmes, and so on. On the one hand, this has imposed short-termism on management and has served to decrease management's animal spirits with respect to real investment in the capital stock and the long-run growth of the firm and to increase the preference for financial investment which generates high

profits in the short run. On the other hand, it has drained internal means of finance for real investment purposes from corporations, through increasing dividend payments and share buybacks, in order to boost stock prices and thus shareholder value. These 'preference' and 'internal means of finance' channels have each had partially negative effects on firms' real investment in the capital stock, and hence also on the long-run growth potential of the economy to the extent that productivity growth is capital embodied.

3. Regarding consumption, financialization has generated increasing potential for wealth-based and debt-financed consumption, thus creating the potential to compensate for the demand-depressing effects of financialization, which were imposed on the economy via redistribution and the impact on real investment. Stock market and housing price booms have each increased notional wealth against which households were willing to borrow. Changing consumption norms (conspicuous consumption, 'keeping up with the Joneses'), new financial instruments (credit card debt, home equity lending) and deterioration of creditworthiness standards, triggered by debt securitization and the 'originate and distribute' strategies of banks, made credit increasingly available to low-income, low-wealth households, in particular. This allowed for consumption to rise faster than the median income in several countries and thus to stabilize aggregate demand. But it also generated increasing debt–income ratios of private households and thus increasing financial fragility.

4. The deregulation and liberalization of international capital markets and capital accounts have created the potential to run and finance persistent current account deficits for one set of countries, and for mercantilist strategies with current account surpluses for another set of countries. Simultaneously, they have created the problems of foreign indebtedness, speculative capital flows, exchange rate volatilities and related currency crises.

These characteristics of financialization led to the dominance of 'profits without investment' regimes in several countries during the pre-2007 crisis financialization period, in which a long-run tendency of rising levels of profits (not only profit shares) but relatively weak investment in the capital stock could be observed (van Treeck et al. 2007; van Treeck 2009b; Hein 2012, Chapter 6; Hein and Mundt 2012; van Treeck and Sturn 2012). This is shown in Figure 2.1 for the USA and in Figure 2.2 for Germany, as outstanding examples. In both countries, investment and profits had increased broadly in line until the late 1970s or early 1980s. In the USA the divergence of profits from investment started in the 1980s and was only

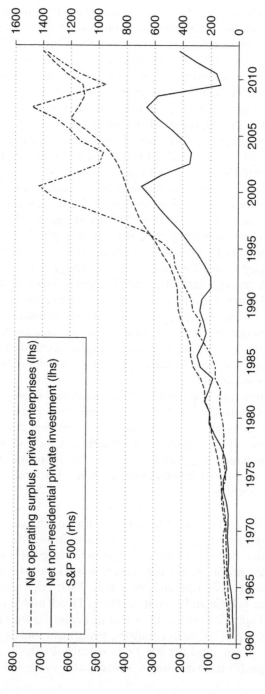

Source: Bureau of Economic Analysis (2013); Federal Reserve Bank of St. Louis (2013); authors' calculations.

Figure 2.1 Investment, profits (index 1980=100) and share prices, USA, 1960–2012

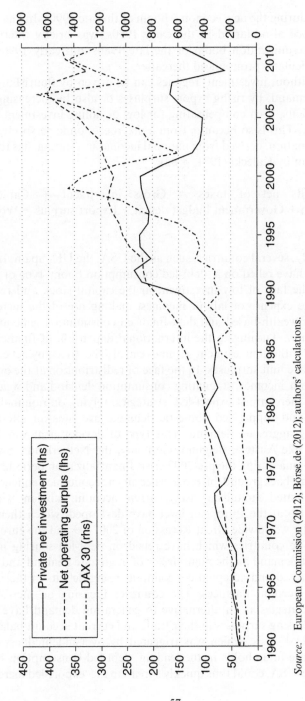

Source: European Commission (2012); Börse.de (2012); authors' calculations.

Figure 2.2 Investment, profits and share prices (index 1980=100), Germany, 1960–2012

interrupted during the new economy boom of the late 1990s. In Germany, the divergence also started in the early 1980s, was briefly interrupted during the re-unification boom of the late 1980s and early 1990s, and became particularly pronounced thereafter.

'Profits without investment' regimes can be driven by flourishing consumption demand, by rising export surpluses or also by increasing government deficits, each compensating for low or falling investment in the capital stock. This is so because, from a macroeconomic perspective, the following equation, derived from national income accounting, has to hold, as pointed out by Kalecki (1971, p. 82):

Gross profits net of taxes = Gross investment + Capitalists' consumption + Government budget deficit + Export surplus − Workers' saving

Empirically, several countries, such as the USA, the UK, Spain, Ireland and Greece, have relied on a 'debt-led consumption boom' type of development in the face of low investment in the capital stock and redistribution at the expense of labour incomes, making use of the increasing potential for wealth-based and debt-financed consumption generated by financialization. Turning to the international dimension of financialization, 'profits without investment' regimes can also be driven by net exports and current account surpluses. In the face of redistribution at the expense of (low) labour incomes, stagnating consumption demand and weak real investment, 'mercantilist export-led' strategies, relying on nominal wage moderation and suppressed domestic demand, are thus an alternative to generating aggregate demand. This type of development was found in countries like Austria, Belgium, Germany, the Netherlands, Sweden, Japan and China during the pre-2007 crisis financialization period.[1]

Against the background of these basic macroeconomic tendencies of finance-dominated capitalism, rising current account imbalances at the global but also at the European level have developed, which then contributed to the worldwide Great Recession of 2007–09 and the euro crisis thereafter. The countries which have relied on debt-led soaring private consumption demand as the main driver of aggregate demand and GDP growth generated and accepted concomitant rising deficits in their trade and current account balances. The countries focusing on mercantilist export-led strategies as an alternative to generating demand have accumulated increasing surpluses in their trade and current account balances.

The financial crisis, which was triggered by over-indebtedness problems of private households in the leading 'debt-led consumption boom' economy, the USA, could thus quickly spread to the 'export-led mercantilist' economies through the foreign trade channel (collapse of exports) and the financial contagion channel (devaluation of financial assets) and thus cause the worldwide Great Recession.

Based on stylized facts and econometric results obtained from a literature review supporting the relevance of the macroeconomic features of financialization mentioned above, we will provide an overview of theoretical models which have included these features in distribution and growth models. Basically, two types of models have been used so far: 1) demand-driven small analytical models;[2] and 2) large scale, so-called stock–flow consistent (SFC) models.[3] Whereas the first type of models allows for general analytical results regarding the distribution and growth effects of changes in parameters related to financialization, in the second type the effects can be obtained only through numerical simulations. However, the advantage of the second type of models is that it can take into account the features of the financial and economic sectors of the economy in a more detailed way. Of course, both types are complementary, and the results obtained should, in principle, not contradict each other. Small analytical models should be stock–flow consistent, too, and SFC models can be simplified, so that analytical solutions can be computed. Each of these model types allows for the generation of different types of regimes, depending on the model parameters and coefficients in the behavioural equations: 'finance-led growth' regimes, 'profits without investment' regimes and 'restrictive' regimes in the face of increasing dominance of finance and shareholders. They also allow for the treatment of the sustainability of certain regimes.

In this chapter we will proceed as follows. In section 2.2 we will review and interpret the effects of financialization on income distribution. In section 2.3 we will integrate the distribution effects with the effects on investment in the capital stock and on consumption and will discuss the outcomes in a closed economy framework. Section 2.4 will then introduce the open economy dimension, and section 2.5 will summarize and conclude.

2.2 FINANCIALIZATION AND REDISTRIBUTION OF INCOME SINCE THE EARLY 1980s[4]

2.2.1 Empirical Evidence

The period of finance-dominated capitalism has been associated with a massive redistribution of income. First, functional income distribution has changed at the expense of labour and in favour of broad capital income. The labour income share, as a measure taken from the national accounts and corrected for the changes in the composition of employment regarding

Table 2.1 *Labour income share as percentage of GDP at current factor costs, average values over the trade cycle, early 1980s to 2008*

	1. Early 1980s to early 1990s	2. Early 1990s to early 2000s	3. Early 2000s to 2008	Change (3 − 1), percentage points
Austria	75.66	70.74	65.20	−10.46
Belgium	70.63	70.74	69.16	−1.47
France	71.44	66.88	65.91	−5.53
Germany	67.11	66.04	63.34	−3.77
Greece[1]	67.26	62.00	60.60	−6.66
Ireland	70.34	60.90	55.72	−14.61
Italy	68.31	63.25	62.37	−5.95
Netherlands	68.74	67.21	65.57	−3.17
Portugal	65.73	70.60	71.10	5.37
Spain	68.32	66.13	62.41	−5.91
Sweden	71.65	67.04	69.16	−2.48
UK	72.79	71.99	70.67	−2.12
USA	68.20	67.12	65.79	−2.41
Japan[1]	72.38	70.47	65.75	−6.64

Notes:
The labour income share is given by the compensation per employee divided by GDP at factor costs per person employed. The beginning of a trade cycle is given by a local minimum of annual real GDP growth in the respective country.
1   Adjusted to fit in a three-cycle pattern.

Data Source: European Commission (2010); author's calculations.
Source: Hein (2012, p. 13).

employees and the self-employed, shows a falling trend in the developed capitalist economies considered here from the early 1980s until the Great Recession. This is shown in Table 2.1, which presents cyclical averages in order to eliminate cyclical fluctuations due to the well-known counter-cyclical properties of the labour income share.

Second, personal income distribution became more unequal in most countries from the mid-1980s until the late 2000s. Taking the Gini coefficient as an indicator, this is true for the distribution of market income, with the Netherlands being the only exception in the data set (Table 2.2). If redistribution via taxes and social policies by the state is included and the distribution of disposable income is considered, Belgium, France, Greece, Ireland and Spain have not seen an increase in their Gini coefficients. The other countries, however, have also experienced increasing inequality in the distribution of disposable income during the period of finance-dominated capitalism.

Table 2.2   Gini coefficients for households' income

Gini coefficient for households' market income

Country	Mid-1980s	Around 1990	Mid-1990s	Around 2000	Mid-2000s	Late 2000s	Change from mid-1980s, around 1990 or mid-1990s until late 2000s
Austria	–	–	–	–	0.433	0.472	–
Belgium	0.449	–	0.472	0.464	0.494	0.469	0.020
Finland	0.387	–	0.479	0.478	0.483	0.465	0.078
France	–	–	0.473	0.490	0.485	0.483	0.010
Germany	0.439	0.429	0.459	0.471	0.499	0.504	0.065
Greece	0.426	–	0.446	0.466	0.454	0.436	0.010
Ireland	–	–	–	–	–	–	–
Italy	0.420	0.437	0.508	0.516	0.557	0.534	0.114
Netherlands	0.473	0.474	0.484	0.424	0.426	0.426	−0.047
Portugal	–	0.436	0.490	0.479	0.542	0.521	0.085
Spain	–	–	–	–	–	0.461	–
Sweden	0.404	0.408	0.438	0.446	0.432	0.426	0.022
UK	0.419	0.439	0.453	0.512	0.500	0.506	0.087
USA	0.436	0.450	0.477	0.476	0.486	0.486	0.050
Japan	0.345	–	0.403	0.432	0.443	0.462	0.117

Gini coefficient for households' disposable income

Country	Mid-1980s	Around 1990	Mid-1990s	Around 2000	Mid-2000s	Late 2000s	Change mid-1980s or around 1990 until late 2000s
Austria	0.236	–	0.238	0.252	0.265	0.261	0.025
Belgium	0.274	–	0.287	0.289	0.271	0.259	−0.015
Finland	0.209	–	0.218	0.247	0.254	0.259	0.050
France	0.300	0.290	0.277	0.287	0.288	0.293	−0.007
Germany	0.251	0.256	0.266	0.264	0.285	0.295	0.044
Greece	0.336	–	0.336	0.345	0.321	0.307	−0.029
Ireland	0.331	–	0.324	0.304	0.314	0.293	−0.038
Italy	0.309	0.297	0.348	0.343	0.352	0.337	0.028
Netherlands	0.272	0.292	0.297	0.292	0.284	0.294	0.022
Portugal	–	0.329	0.359	0.356	0.385	0.353	0.024
Spain	0.371	0.337	0.343	0.342	0.319	0.317	−0.054
Sweden	0.198	0.209	0.211	0.243	0.234	0.259	0.061
UK	0.309	0.354	0.336	0.352	0.331	0.342	0.033
USA	0.337	0.348	0.361	0.357	0.38	0.378	0.041
Japan	0.304	–	0.323	0.337	0.321	0.329	0.025

Note: Gini coefficient is based on equivalized household income.

Data Source: OECD (2012); authors' calculations.
Source: Hein (2013, p. 7).

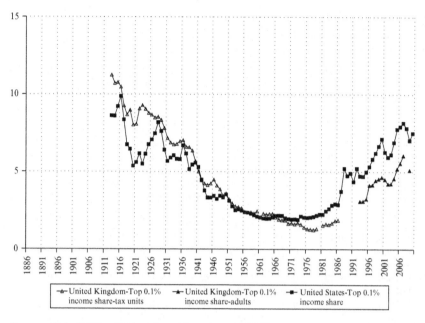

Source: Hein (2013, p. 9); data from Alvaredo et al. (2012).

Figure 2.3   Top 0.1 per cent share in national income in the UK and the USA, in percentages

Third, as data based on tax reports provided by Alvaredo et al. (2012) have shown, there has been an explosion of the shares of the very top incomes since the early 1980s in the USA and the UK, which, prior to the present crisis, reached the levels of the mid-1920s in the USA and the mid-1930s in the UK (Figure 2.3). In France, Germany, the Netherlands, Spain, Portugal, Italy, Ireland, Japan and Sweden (Figures 2.4–2.7), however, the shares of the top 0.1 per cent have not returned to the high levels of the period prior to the Second World War. But, with the exception of Germany, Ireland and the Netherlands, a slightly upward trend can be observed in these countries since the early 1980s, too. Although Germany has not yet seen a marked increase, it should be noted that the share of the top 0.1 per cent has been substantially higher in this country for longer periods of time and that it was only surpassed by the USA and the UK in the mid-1980s and the mid-1990s, respectively (Figure 2.4).[5]

Taking a look at the composition of top incomes, the increase in the income share of the top 0.1 per cent in the US has mainly been driven by an increase in top salaries (wages and salaries, bonuses, exercised stock

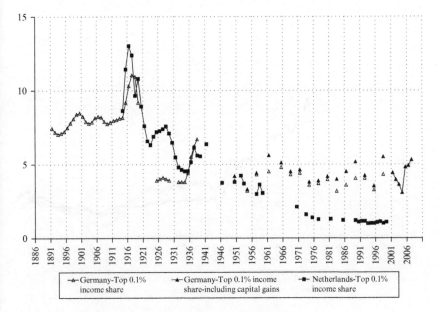

Source: Hein (2013, p.9); data from Alvaredo et al. (2012).

Figure 2.4   *Top 0.1 per cent share in national income in Germany and the Netherlands, in percentages*

options and pensions) since the 1970s, and since the mid-1980s also in entrepreneurial income (Figure 2.8). Remuneration of top management ('working rich') has therefore contributed significantly, but not exclusively, to rising inequality in the US from the early 1980s until 2006. The decomposition of top incomes is provided for only a few countries in the data set by Alvaredo et al. (2012). Out of these, the 'working rich' phenomenon can also be found in Spain, where the share of top management salaries in the top 0.1 per cent of incomes has seen a rising trend from the early 1980s until the early 2000s, and in the Netherlands, where such an increase could be observed in the course of the 1990s. In Italy we find only a slight increasing tendency since the early 1980s, and in France there has not been such an increase at all.[6] Whereas top management salaries have contributed up to more than 50 per cent to the income of the top 0.1 per cent income share in the USA, top management salaries in Germany have played a minor role. However, their share increased from 15 per cent in 1992 to 22.4 per cent in 2003 (Bach et al. 2009). Therefore, the 'working rich' phenomenon seems to arise in Germany as well.

Since top management salaries are part of the compensation of

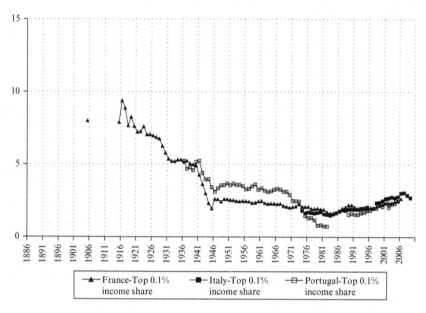

Source: Hein (2013, p. 10); data from Alvaredo et al. (2012).

Figure 2.5 *Top 0.1 per cent share in national income in France, Italy and Portugal, in percentages*

employees in the national accounts and are thus included in the labour income share considered above, the increase in top management salaries has dampened the fall in the measured labour income share since the early 1980s. Excluding top management salaries from the labour income share would therefore give an even more pronounced fall in the share of 'direct labour', as has been shown by Buchele and Christiansen (2007) and Glyn (2009) for the USA and by Dünhaupt (2011) for Germany and the USA.

2.2.2 A Kaleckian Interpretation of the Effects of Financialization on Income Shares

According to Atkinson (2009), the trends and determinants of functional income distribution provide the key to the explanation of the other dimensions of redistribution. The analysis of factor shares provides the link between incomes at the macroeconomic or the national accounting level and incomes at the level of a household, thus helping in understanding the development of inequality in personal distribution, and providing an indicator of the relative powers of different groups. For example, an

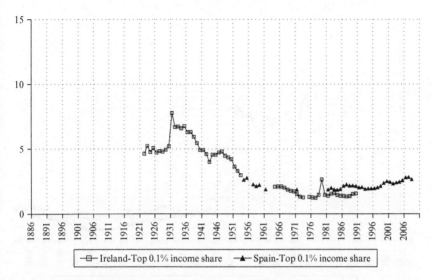

Source: Hein (2013, p. 10); data from Alvaredo et al. (2012).

Figure 2.6   Top 0.1 per cent share in national income in Ireland and Spain, in percentages

increase in the profit share and a decrease in the wage share will also increase the inequality of income distribution across households if financial and economic wealth generating profits is distributed unequally. Hein (2013) has therefore reviewed the recent empirical literature on the determinants of income shares against the background of the Kaleckian theory of distribution, in order to identify the channels through which financialization and neoliberalism have affected functional income distribution (Table 2.3).[7]

According to the Kaleckian approach (Kalecki 1954, Part I), the gross profit share in national income, which includes retained earnings, dividends, and interest and rent payments, as well as overhead costs (and thus top management salaries), has three major determinants.

First, the profit share is affected by firms' pricing in incompletely competitive goods markets, that is, by the mark-up on unit variable costs. The mark-up itself is determined by three different factors:

a. by the degree of industrial concentration and by the relevance of price competition relative to other instruments of competition (marketing, product differentiation) in the respective industries or sectors, that is, by the degree of price competition in the goods market;

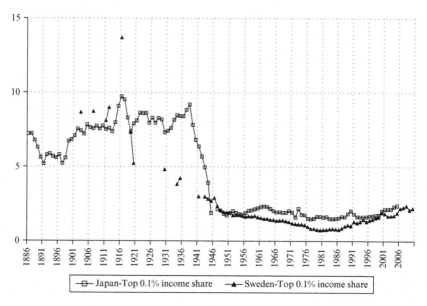

Source: Hein (2013, p. 11); data from Alvaredo et al. (2012).

*Figure 2.7   Top 0.1 per cent share in national income in Japan and
Sweden, in percentages*

b.   by the bargaining power of trade unions, because, in a heterogeneous
     environment with differences in unit wage cost growth between
     firms, industries or sectors, the firm's or the industry's ability to shift
     changes in nominal wage costs to prices is constrained by competi-
     tion with other firms or industries which do not have to face the same
     increase in unit wage costs; and
c.   by overhead costs and gross profit targets, because the mark-up has to
     cover overhead costs and distributed profits.

   Second, with mark-up pricing on unit variable costs, that is, material
plus wage costs, the profit share in national income is affected by unit
imported material costs relative to unit wage costs. With a constant mark-
up, an increase in unit material costs will thus increase the profit share in
national income.
   And, third, the aggregate profit share of the economy as a whole is a
weighted average of the industry or sector profit shares. Since profit shares
differ among industries and sectors, the aggregate profit share is affected
by the industry or sector composition of the economy.

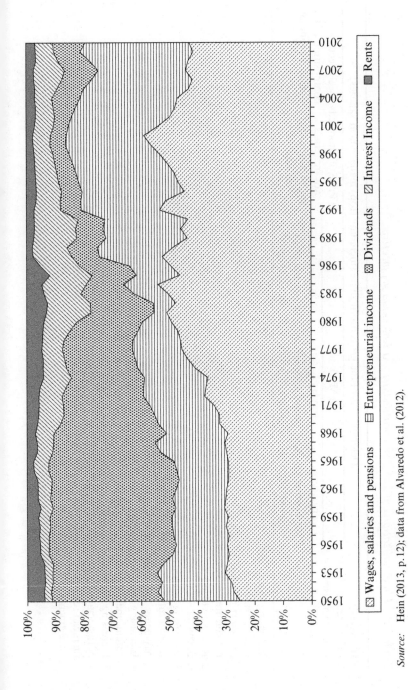

Source: Hein (2013, p.12); data from Alvaredo et al. (2012).

Figure 2.8 Composition of top 0.1 per cent income, USA, 1950–2010

Table 2.3 Financialization and the gross profit share – a Kaleckian perspective

Stylized facts of financialization (1–7) and neoliberalism (8–9)	Determinants of the gross profit share (including (top) management salaries)				
	1) Mark-up			2) Price of imported raw materials and semi-finished products	3) Sectoral composition of the domestic economy
	1.a) Degree of price competition in the goods market	1.b) Bargaining power and activity of trade unions	1.c) Overhead costs and gross profit targets		
1. Increasing shareholder value orientation and short-termism of management	…	+	+	…	…
2. Rising dividend payments	…	…	+	…	…
3. Increasing interest rates or interest payments	…	…	+	…	…
4. Increasing top management salaries	…	…	+	…	…
5. Increasing relevance of financial to non-financial sector (investment)	…	+	…	…	+

6. Mergers and acquisitions	+	...	+	+
7. Liberalization and globalization of international finance and trade	−	+/−	+/−	+
8. Deregulation of the labour market	...	...	...	...
9. Downsizing of government	...	...	...	+

Note: + positive effect on the gross profit share; − negative effect on the gross profit share; ... no direct effect on the gross profit share.

Source: Based on Hein (2013, p. 15).

Integrating some stylized facts of financialization and neoliberalism into this approach and reviewing the respective empirical literature, it can be argued that there is some convincing empirical evidence that financialization and neoliberalism have contributed to the rising gross profit share and hence to the falling labour income share since the early 1980s through three main channels (Hein 2013).

First, the shift in the sectoral composition of the economy from the public sector and the non-financial business sector with higher labour income shares towards the financial business sector with a lower labour income share has contributed to the fall in the labour income share for the economy as a whole.

Second, the increase in management salaries as a part of overhead costs together with rising profit claims of rentiers, that is, rising interest and dividend payments of the corporate sector, has in sum been associated with a falling labour income share, although management salaries are part of the compensation of employees in the national accounts, and thus of the labour income share.

Third, financialization and neoliberalism have weakened trade union bargaining power through several channels: an increasing shareholder value and short-term profitability orientation of management; sectoral shifts away from the public sector and the non-financial business sector with stronger trade unions in many countries to the financial sector with weaker unions; abandonment of government demand management and full employment policies; deregulation of the labour market; and liberalization and globalization of international trade and finance.

These developments not only have triggered falling labour income shares, but also should have been conducive to the observed increases in inequality of personal/household incomes.

2.3 FINANCIALIZATION, DISTRIBUTION, INVESTMENT AND CONSUMPTION – MACROECONOMIC EFFECTS

2.3.1 Financialization, Shareholder Value Orientation, and Investment – Macroeconomic Effects

2.3.1.1 Empirical results
Econometric evidence in favour of the hypothesis that financialization has caused a slowdown in capital accumulation through a 'preference' channel and an 'internal means of finance' channel has been presented by Stockhammer (2004), van Treeck (2008), Onaran et al. (2011) and

Orhangazi (2008). Stockhammer (2004) takes the share of interest and dividends in the profits of non-financial business as an indicator for the dominance of short-term profits in firms' or management's preferences. Short-term financial investment is hence preferred over long-term real investment in the capital stock, and the share of dividends and interest in profits should therefore be negatively associated with real investment. Using annual data for the business sector and applying time series estimations for France (1978–97), Germany (1963–90), the UK (1970–96) and the USA (1963–97), Stockhammer finds evidence in favour of his hypothesis for France, the US and maybe also the UK, but not for Germany. Van Treeck (2008) introduces interest and dividend payments, each in relation to the capital stock, into the estimation of the determinants of the rate of capital accumulation in the non-financial corporate sector of the USA (1965–2004), using annual data for his time series estimations. He finds that dividend and interest payments each have a statistically significant negative effect on capital accumulation, indicating the finance constraint given by internal means of finance. The value of the negative coefficient on dividend payments also exceeds that on interest payments, which is interpreted as evidence for the 'shareholder value orientation' of management: dividend payments thus negatively affect investment not only via internal means of finance but also via firms' (or management's) preferences. Onaran et al. (2011) in their time series study for the USA (1962–2007) find a positive effect of the non-rentier profit share on real gross private domestic investment, but a negative effect of the rentier profit share (net dividends and net interest payments of domestic industry as a share of nominal GDP), which severely dampens the positive impact of unit gross profits on investment through the 'internal means of finance' channel. Orhangazi (2008) has used firm-level data on non-financial firms in the USA (1972–2003) with a focus on the manufacturing sector in a dynamic panel-estimation approach. He finds that financial profits have a negative impact on real investment for large firms, indicating a shift in favour of short-term financial profits and at the expense of long-term profits from investment in the capital stock. For small firms, however, the effect of financial profits (the sum of interest and equity income in net earnings) on real investment is positive, because financial profits seem to ease the financing constraint for these firms. The effect of financial payments (interest expenses, cash dividends, purchase of firms' own stocks) on investment is negative for the whole panel.

2.3.1.2 Macroeconomic models deriving different regimes

Based on these effects of financialization on investment in the capital stock, including the effects on functional income distribution outlined in section 2.2, post-Keynesians have presented different models examining the long-run growth and stability effects of financialization, as reviewed in Hein and van Treeck (2010) and Hein (2012, Chapter 3), without open economy issues yet.[8] Depending on the values of the model parameters, 'finance-led growth' regimes, as suggested by Boyer (2000), 'profits without investment' regimes, as found by Cordonnier (2006), or 'contractive' regimes may emerge.

Only in the 'finance-led growth' regime is increasing shareholder power overall expansive with respect to the rates of capacity utilization, as an indicator for aggregate demand, profit and capital accumulation, whereas in the 'profits without investment' regime the effects on the rates of capacity utilization and profit remain expansive but capital accumulation gets depressed, and in the 'contractive' regime there is a depressing effect on all three endogenous variables of the model. As will be shown below, only the 'finance-led growth' regime yields long-run stability of the financial structure of the firm sector and of capital accumulation. This regime, however, requires a very special parameter constellation: only weakly negative effects of increasing shareholder power on management's animal spirits regarding real investment in the capital stock; a low rentiers' propensity to save out of current income (based on strong wealth effects on consumption); a low profit share; a low elasticity of investment with respect to distributed profits and internal funds; and a high responsiveness with regard to capacity utilization (and to Tobin's q in some models). In particular, a long-run increase in the gross profit share associated with financialization may turn the stable financial structure unstable. More realistic parameter constellations giving rise to 'profits without investment' or 'contractive' regimes have turned out to yield cumulatively unstable long-run results regarding the financial structure of the firm sector and the rate of capital accumulation. In the face of rising shareholder power, a rising rentiers' rate of return, that is, increasing dividend rates and/or interest rates, and falling management animal spirits regarding investment in the capital stock, these regimes are susceptible to systemic instability, characterized by increasing outside finance–capital ratios, that is, rising debt plus rentiers' equity–capital ratios, and falling goods market equilibrium rates of capital accumulation. Falling labour income shares triggered by financialization increase the likelihood of these unstable regimes. Therefore, under the conditions of the 'contractive' and the 'profits without investment' regimes, there exists a considerable systemic long-run instability potential regarding the financial structure of the corporate sector of the economy and regarding capital accumulation. These results can be demonstrated using a simple model with fixed prices in the goods and financial markets, as suggested by Hein (2012, Chapter 3).

2.3.1.3 A simple model of financialization, shareholder dominance, distribution and growth[9]

The basic model Let us assume a closed economy without economic activity of the state, which produces just one type of commodity, which can be used for consumption and investment purposes, with a fixed-coefficients production technology. The basic model can be described by the following equations.

Pricing and distribution:

$$p = [1 + m(\rho)]wa, \qquad m > 0, \frac{\partial m}{\partial \rho} \geq 0, \tag{2.1}$$

$$h = \frac{\Pi}{pY} = 1 - \frac{1}{1 + m(\rho)}, \qquad \frac{\partial h}{\partial \rho} \geq 0, \tag{2.2}$$

$$r = \frac{\Pi}{pK} = \frac{\Pi}{pY} \frac{Y}{Y^p} \frac{Y^p}{K} = hu\frac{1}{v} \tag{2.3}$$

Financing of capital stock and rentiers' income:

$$pK = B + E_R + E_F, \tag{2.4}$$

$$\gamma = \frac{B + E_R}{pK}, \tag{2.5}$$

$$\varphi = \frac{E_F}{pK}, \tag{2.6}$$

$$\Pi = \Pi_F + R, \tag{2.7}$$

$$R = \rho(E_R + B). \tag{2.8}$$

Saving, investment and goods market equilibrium:

$$\sigma = \frac{S}{pK} = \frac{\Pi - R + s_R R}{pK} = r - (1 - s_R)\rho\gamma, \qquad 0 < s_R \leq 1, \tag{2.9}$$

$$g = \frac{pI}{pK} = \alpha + \beta u + \tau h - \theta\rho\gamma \qquad \beta, \tau, \theta \geq 0, \tag{2.10}$$

$$g = \sigma, \tag{2.11}$$

$$\frac{\partial\sigma}{\partial u} - \frac{\partial g}{\partial u} > 0 \qquad \Rightarrow \qquad \frac{h}{v} - \beta > 0. \tag{2.12}$$

Variables:

p: price; m: mark-up; ρ: rentiers' rate of return on equity and bonds; w: nominal wage rate; a: labour–output ratio; h: gross profit share; Π: gross profits; Y: real income; r: rate of profit; K: real capital stock; Y^p: full capacity output determined by the capital stock; u: rate of capacity utilization; v: capital–full capacity output ratio; B: bonds held by rentiers; E_R: equity held by rentiers; E_F: equity held by firms/owner-managers; γ: outside finance–capital ratio; φ: inside finance–capital ratio; Π_F: retained profits by firms; R: rentiers' income; σ: saving–capital rate; S: saving; s_R: propensity to save out of rentiers' income; g: rate of capital accumulation; I: investment; α, β, τ, θ: coefficients in the investment function.

Firms set prices (p) according to a mark-up (m) on constant unit labour costs (wa) up to full capacity output. The mark-up is determined by the degree of price competition in the goods market, by the bargaining power of labour in the labour market, and by overhead costs and gross profit targets (equation 2.1; Table 2.3). The profit share (h), that is, the proportion of profits (Π) in nominal output (pY), is therefore determined by the mark-up (equation 2.2). The mark-up and the profit share may become elastic with respect to the rentiers' rate of return on equity and bonds (ρ) in the long run. The profit rate (r) relates the annual flow of profits to the nominal capital stock and can be decomposed into the rate of capacity utilization (u), the profit share (h), and the inverse of the capital–full capacity output ratio (v) (equation 2.3).

Long-term finance of the capital stock consists of firms' accumulated retained earnings (E_F), long-term credit granted by rentiers' households (B), and equity issued by the firms and held by rentiers' households (E_R) (equation 2.4). The rentiers' share in the capital stock, the outside finance–capital ratio, is given by γ (equation 2.5), whereas φ denotes the accumulated retained earnings–capital ratio or the inside finance–capital ratio (equation 2.6). It is assumed that these ratios are constant in the short run, but become variable, and hence are to be endogenously determined in the long run of the model.

Total profits (Π) split into firms' retained profits (Π_F), on the one hand, and dividends plus interest paid to rentiers' households (R), on the other hand (equation 2.7). Interest payments to rentiers' households are given by the rate of interest and the stock of debt, with the rate of interest as a distribution parameter being an exogenous variable for income generation and capital accumulation, mainly determined by monetary policies and risk and liquidity assessments of banks and rentiers, following the post-Keynesian 'horizontalist' view of endogenous money and credit.[10] Dividend payments, given by the dividend rate and the stock of equity held by rentiers' households, are also determined by the power struggle between rentiers (shareholders) and firms (management), with rentiers being interested in high dividends for income purposes and management being in favour of retained earnings for firms' real investment and growth purposes. In order to further simplify the analysis, dividend and interest payments to rentiers are synthesized and just one rentiers' rate of return on bonds and equity (ρ) is considered, which, together with the stock of equity and bonds held by rentiers, determines rentiers' income (equation 2.8).

Changes in the rentiers' rate of return may cause a change in the mark-up in firms' pricing in incompletely competitive goods markets (equation 2.1). If these changes occur, distribution between gross profits, as the sum of retained profits, and interest and dividends received by rentiers' households, on the one hand, and wages, on the other hand, will be affected (equation 2.2). In the face of increasing shareholder power, we consider the mark-up to be dividend-inelastic in the short run. Therefore, in the short run, only the distribution of income between firms and rentiers is affected by rising shareholder power. But in the long run the mark-up, and hence the profit share, are likely to become dividend-elastic, for the reasons outlined in section 2.2.

In order to simplify the analysis, workers are assumed not to save. The portion of profits retained is completely saved by definition. The portion of profits distributed to rentiers' households, the interest and dividend payments, is used by those households according to their propensity to save (s_R). Therefore, we get the saving–capital rate (σ) in equation (2.9), which relates total saving to the nominal capital stock. The accumulation rate (g) relates net investment (I) to the capital stock, and equation (2.10) provides an extended post-Kaleckian investment function.[11] Investment decisions are assumed to be positively affected by 'animal spirits' (α), expected sales and unit profits (or the profit share), because the latter two both increase the (expected) profit rate. Expected sales are determined by the rate of capacity utilization. Unit profits are given by the profit share and are thus determined by the mark-up in firms' pricing in the goods market. Distributed profits, the dividends and interest payments to rentiers, have a negative impact on investment, because they reduce retained earnings and firms' own means of finance, which are required for investment following Kalecki's (1937) 'principle of increasing risk'.

Short-run equilibrium and the effects of financialization and increasing shareholder power   The goods market equilibrium is determined by the equality of saving and investment decisions (equation 2.11). The goods market stability condition requires that the saving–capital rate responds more elastically to changes in capacity utilization than the capital accumulation rate does (condition 2.12). The model generates the following goods market equilibrium values:

$$u^* = \frac{\alpha + \tau h + \rho\gamma(1 - s_R - \theta)}{\frac{h}{v} - \beta},$$ (2.13)

$$r^* = \frac{\frac{h}{v}[\alpha + \tau h + \rho\gamma(1 - s_R - \theta)]}{\frac{h}{v} - \beta},$$ (2.14)

$$g^* = \frac{\frac{h}{v}(\alpha + \tau h) + \rho\gamma\left[\beta(1 - s_R) - \theta\frac{h}{v}\right]}{\frac{h}{v} - \beta}.$$ (2.15)

For the short-run analysis, firms' outside finance–capital ratio is assumed to be constant (or only slowly changing), and the mark-up, and therefore the profit share, are considered to be dividend-inelastic, because the determinants of the mark-up change rather slowly. An increase in shareholder power will thus affect the goods market equilibrium, firstly through the effects on management's preferences regarding real investment in the capital stock (as compared to more profitable financial investments in the short run), and hence through the animal spirit variable in the accumulation function, and secondly through the effects of an increasing rentiers' rate of return (higher dividend payments) on firms' internal means of finance in the accumulation function. An increase in the shareholder value orientation of management, and hence a decrease in animal spirits, as indicated by α in the investment function, has uniquely negative effects on the endogenous variables, as can easily be seen from equations (2.13)–(2.15): $\frac{\partial u^*}{\partial \alpha} > 0$, $\frac{\partial r^*}{\partial \alpha} > 0$ and $\frac{\partial g^*}{\partial \alpha} > 0$. An increase in the rentiers' rate of return, however, has ambiguous effects. It affects firms' investment through the availability of internal funds and the access to external financing, but it also has an influence on the income of rentiers' households, and hence on consumption:

$$\frac{\partial u^*}{\partial \rho} = \frac{(1 - s_R - \theta)\gamma}{\frac{h}{v} - \beta},$$ (2.13a)

$$\frac{\partial r^*}{\partial \rho} = \frac{\frac{h}{v}(1 - s_R - \theta)\gamma}{\frac{h}{v} - \beta},$$ (2.14a)

$$\frac{\partial g^*}{\partial \rho} = \frac{\gamma\left[\beta(1 - s_R) - \theta\frac{h}{v}\right]}{\frac{h}{v} - \beta}.$$ (2.15a)

Table 2.4   Short-run cases for a change in the rentiers' rate of return

	'Normal' case $1 - s_R < \theta$	'Intermediate' case $\theta < 1 - s_R < \frac{\theta h}{v\beta}$	'Puzzling' case $\frac{\theta h}{v\beta} < 1 - s_R$
$\frac{\partial u^*}{\partial p}$	−	+	+
$\frac{\partial r^*}{\partial p}$	−	+	+
$\frac{\partial g^*}{\partial p}$	−	−	+

Source: Hein (2012, p. 52).

Table 2.5   Short-run accumulation regimes under the conditions of financialization and rising shareholder power

	'Contractive' regime	'Profits without investment' regime	'Finance-led growth' regime
Effect via management's animal spirits	Weak/strong	Weak	Weak
Effect via rentiers' rate of return	'Normal' case	'Intermediate' case	'Puzzling' case

Source: Hein (2012, p. 53).

Assuming that the stability condition (2.12) for the goods market equilibrium holds, 'normal', 'intermediate' and 'puzzling' cases are obtained for the effects of increasing shareholder power through the 'internal means of finance' channel, as shown in Table 2.4. Adding the effects of increasing shareholder power through the 'preference' channel, the regimes shown in Table 2.5 may emerge.

The 'normal' case of a negative impact of an increase in the rentiers' rate of return on the equilibrium values of capacity utilization, the profit rate and the rate of capital accumulation will be given if: $1 - s_R < \theta$. Therefore, this case is the more likely the higher the rentiers' propensity to save and the higher the responsiveness of firms' real investment with respect to distributed profits, and hence to internal funds, is. With this parameter constellation, the increase in consumption demand associated with a redistribution of income from firms to rentiers' households is insufficient to compensate for the negative effects on firms' investment. In the 'normal' case, the effect of an increasing rentiers' rate of return on the equilibrium rates of capacity utilization, profit and capital accumulation amplifies the negative effects of rising shareholder power via management's animal spirits on these variables, and we obtain the overall 'contractive' regime.

In the 'puzzling' case, we have an opposite parameter constellation: $1 - s_R > \theta\frac{h}{v\beta}$. A low propensity to save out of rentiers' income, a low responsiveness of investment with respect to distributed profits and internal funds, and a high elasticity with respect to capacity utilization allow for a positive effect of an increasing rentiers' rate of return on the equilibrium rates of capacity utilization, profit and capital accumulation. In the 'puzzling' case, the effects of an increasing rentiers' rate of return on the equilibrium rates of capacity utilization, profit and capital accumulation may over-compensate for the negative effects of rising shareholder power via management's animal spirits. If this condition holds, we will obtain a 'finance-led' accumulation regime, and hence an overall positive effect of increasing shareholder power on the rates of capacity utilization, profit and capital accumulation.

Finally, an 'intermediate' case may arise if: $\theta < 1 - s_R < \theta\frac{h}{v\beta}$. In this case, an increase in the rentiers' rate of return is accompanied by rising rates of capacity utilization and profit, but by a falling equilibrium rate of capital accumulation. What is required for the 'intermediate' case, on the one hand, is a low rentiers' propensity to save, which boosts consumption demand in the face of redistribution in favour of rentiers, and a low responsiveness of firms' investment with respect to distributed profits, and hence internal funds, which limits the negative effects of redistribution on firms' investment. On the other hand, however, in the 'intermediate' case we also have a low responsiveness of investment with respect to capacity utilization, which, in sum, is not able to over-compensate for the negative effects of a rise in the rentiers' rate of return through internal funds. Under the conditions of the 'intermediate' case, the negative effects of increasing shareholder power via management's preferences (animal spirits) may be over-compensated by the effects of a rising rentiers' rate of return with respect to capacity utilization and the profit rate, but the negative effect on capital accumulation is not. For the former, it is again required that increasing shareholder power is associated with a strong effect of the increase in the rentiers' rate of return, but with a low effect via management's animal spirits. If these conditions hold, we will obtain a 'profits without investment' regime.

Long-run (in)stability　In the long run of the model, the financial structure of the economy and hence the inside and outside finance–capital ratios are no longer exogenous, but have to be determined endogenously. Since $\gamma + \phi = 1$, it is sufficient to analyse the dynamics of γ in the face of changing shareholder power and rentiers' rates of return. The accumulation of bonds and equity held by rentiers is given by rentiers' income and the propensity to save out of this income:

$$\Delta(E_R + B) = s_R\rho(E_R + B) \tag{2.16}$$

For the growth rate of debt plus equity held by rentiers we get:

$$\frac{\Delta(E_R + B)}{(E_R + B)} = s_R\rho. \tag{2.17}$$

If we assume that prices remain constant, which means that mark-ups and distribution may change, but not the price level, the growth rate of the outside finance–capital ratio depends on the growth rate of outside finance and on the growth rate of the real capital stock. From equation (2.6) we get:

$$\hat{\gamma} = \frac{\Delta(E_R + B)}{(E_R + B)} - \hat{K} = s_R\rho - g. \tag{2.18}$$

In the long-run equilibrium, the endogenously determined value of γ has to be constant; hence $\hat{\gamma} = 0$ has to hold. Introducing this condition into equation (2.18) and making use of equation (2.15) yields the following long-run equilibrium value for the outside finance–capital ratio:

$$\gamma^* = \frac{s_R\rho\left(\frac{h}{v} - \beta\right) - \frac{h}{v}(\alpha + \tau h)}{\rho\left[\beta(1 - s_R) - \theta\frac{h}{v}\right]}. \tag{2.19}$$

This long-run equilibrium will be stable if $\frac{\partial\hat{\gamma}}{\partial\gamma} < 0$. Starting from equation (2.18) and making use of equation (2.15) yield:

$$\frac{\partial\hat{\gamma}}{\partial\gamma} = \frac{-\rho\left[\beta(1 - s_R) - \theta\frac{h}{v}\right]}{\frac{h}{v} - \beta}. \tag{2.20}$$

Taking into account that we assume the goods market equilibrium to be stable, it follows for the long-run stability condition of the outside finance–capital ratio:

$$\frac{\partial\hat{\gamma}}{\partial\gamma} < 0 \text{ if:} \qquad \beta(1 - s_R) - \theta\frac{h}{v} > 0 \Leftrightarrow 1 - s_R > \frac{\theta h}{v\beta} \tag{2.20'}$$

As can easily be checked with Tables 2.4 and 2.5, this is the condition which gives the 'puzzling case' and the 'finance-led growth' regime. Only in this regime will the financial structure hence be stable in the long run, whereas the financial structure in the 'contractive' and the 'profits without investment' regimes will be unstable. In these regimes, slight deviations of the actual outside finance–capital ratio from its equilibrium value will make it further diverge from this value. As is discussed more extensively in Hein (2012, Chapter 3), these disequilibrium processes may then show a macroeconomic 'paradox of outside finance': a rise (fall) in the outside finance–capital ratio will induce firms to reduce (raise) capital accumulation in order to reduce (raise) their individual outside finance–capital ratio; however, the macroeconomic outcome will be such that the outside finance–capital ratio will continue to rise (fall). Furthermore, it should be noted that a rise in the mark-up and the profit share in the long run may turn a stable 'finance-led growth' regime into an unstable 'profits without investment' regime.[12] These are the major results of this simple model: even if the goods markets are stable, 'contractive' regimes and 'profits without investment' regimes, the latter having prevailed during the pre-2007 crisis financialization period in several economies (van Treeck et al. 2007; van Treeck 2009a, 2009b; Hein 2012, Chapter 6; Hein and Mundt 2012; van Treeck and Sturn 2012), are prone to a considerable systemic long-run instability potential regarding the financial structure of the corporate sector of the economy and regarding capital accumulation. Of course, there may be other forces in the economy which either dampen or exacerbate instability in more complex models.[13]

So far, 'profits without investment' regimes in this section have been based on low propensities to save out of distributed profits, without yet considering wealth effects on consumption and household debt. This will be the focus of section 2.3.2.

2.3.2 Financialization, Household Debt and Consumption – Macroeconomic Effects

2.3.2.1 Empirical evidence

Econometric studies have shown that (financial and housing) wealth is a statistically significant determinant of consumption – not only in the USA. For the USA, Ludvigson and Steindel (1999) and Mehra (2001) have estimated marginal propensities to consume out of wealth between 3 and 7 per cent, applying time series econometrics to different periods. Onaran et al. (2011), carefully distinguishing between propensities to consume out of wages, non-rentier profits, rentier profits, financial wealth and housing wealth, find smaller values for the USA (1962–2007): the propensity to consume out of net financial wealth is estimated to be 0.7 per cent, whereas the estimate for the propensity to consume out of gross housing wealth is 2 per cent. Boone and Girouard (2002) find marginal propensities to consume out of wealth between 2 and 4 per cent for the USA, the UK, France, Italy and Japan (1980–99), with a higher value only for Canada. Applying dynamic panel regression for 14 OECD countries

(1979–99), Dreger and Slacalek (2007) obtain that the marginal propensity to consume out of financial and housing wealth in capital-market-based countries was 3.7 per cent, whereas in bank-based countries it was just 0.7 per cent.

Furthermore, Cynamon and Fazzari (2008, 2013), Zezza (2008), Barba and Pivetti (2009), Guttmann and Plihon (2010), Palley (2012, Chapter 3) and van Treeck and Sturn (2012) have presented extensive case studies on the importance of wealth-based and debt-financed consumption focusing on the USA.[14] Some of them highlight imitation and conspicuous consumption effects in the face of increasing inequality of household incomes ('keeping up with the Joneses'), building on the relative income hypothesis (Duesenberry 1949); others focus on the role of financial innovations, in particular securitization of credit card and mortgage debt. With respect to consumption demand, increases in household debt, based on (notional) financial or housing wealth and/or conspicuous consumption may thus become a substitute for higher wages:

> Household debt thus appears to be capable of providing the solution to the fundamental contradiction between the necessity of high and rising levels of consumption, for the growth of the system's actual output, and a framework of antagonistic conditions of distribution, which keeps within limits the real income of the vast majority of the society. (Barba and Pivetti 2009, p. 127)

However, in a recent empirical study, Kim (2013) has found that, although new credit to households will boost aggregate demand and output, the effect of household debt variables on output in the USA was negative for the 1982–2009 period, whereas for the 1951–81 period no effect could be detected.

2.3.2.2 Debt-financed consumption in macroeconomic models
Bhaduri et al. (2006) have explicitly focused on the wealth effect on consumption in their model, implying that increases in financial wealth stimulate households' willingness to consume. However, stock market wealth (and also housing wealth) is purely 'virtual wealth', and increasing consumption is hence associated with increasing gross indebtedness of private households. Therefore, a wealth-based credit boom may be maintained over a considerable period of time. Finally, however, the expansive effects of consumer borrowing may be overwhelmed in the long run by rising interest obligations, which reduce households' creditworthiness and eventually require higher saving. A debt-led consumption boom will then turn into a debt-burdened recession. Although the authors consider the debt–income ratio of households as a major determinant of creditworthiness and hence of access to new borrowing, the dynamics of this ratio are not

traced in the long run of their model. Potential 'paradoxes of debt' are not at issue, and distributional and investment effects of 'finance-dominated capitalism' on household indebtedness and growth are also missing in the long-run dynamics. The same is true for Bhaduri's (2011a, 2011b) extensions of this approach, which attempt to show how a debt-financed consumption boom supported by rising asset prices ultimately leads to a credit crunch and debt deflation.

Kapeller and Schütz (2012) have integrated the Veblenian concept of conspicuous consumption into a post-Keynesian distribution and growth model in the tradition of Bhaduri and Marglin (1990). They argue that relative consumption and imitation concerns matter primarily within a social group, here within the working class. It is assumed that an increase in the profit share is distributed unevenly among workers. Efforts to 'keep up with the Joneses' may then increase consumption and generate a 'consumption-driven profit-led' regime. However, this regime is based on increasing debt of those workers who have suffered from income losses, and thus may not be sustainable. But the debt dynamics and the sustainability conditions are not examined explicitly.

The contradictory macroeconomic effects of household indebtedness for consumption purposes have already been included by Palley (1994) in a multiplier–accelerator business cycle model: an increase in household debt initially stimulates aggregate demand, transferring purchasing power from lending high-income households with a low marginal propensity to consume to borrowing low-income households with a high propensity to consume. But interest payments on debt subsequently become a burden on aggregate demand, because purchasing power is redistributed in the opposite direction. This model is then extended to include Minskyan 'tranquillity' effects and to examine interactions of financial fragility and tranquillity. However, this business cycle model in level variables does not treat the development of stock–flow (debt–income) or stock–stock (debt–capital) ratios; neither are changes in income distribution or in the propensities to invest in real capital stock examined.

Kim et al. (2014), applying the relative income hypothesis to a stationary economy with zero net investment, have slightly modified Palley's basic result, arguing that the dampening effects of the stock of household debt on consumption only shows up if debtor households do not or cannot use their saving as a buffer in order to service debt and to maintain the level of consumption simultaneously. The obvious limitation of this argument is that we have increasing debt (and hence debt services) but constant income in the model, so that such a kind of behaviour will be able only to postpone but not to eliminate the depressing effect of the stock of debt on consumption. As soon as net debt servicing obligations exceed saving out of current income, consumption has to contract – or debtor households have to default – and the economy will have to face a 'sudden stop' and/or a financial crisis. The assumption of a stationary economy is an obvious limitation to this model – the dynamics and effects of household debt should better be analysed within the framework of a growing economy.

Dutt (2005, 2006) has analysed the effects of conspicuous consumption and easier access to consumer credit associated with deregulation of the financial sector within a Steindlian model of growth and income distribution, making use of a mechanism similar to that of Palley (1994). Credit-based consumption of workers, facilitated by the deregulation of the financial system allowing home equity lending, adjustable consumer loans and securitization, stimulates effective demand and growth in the short run. However, in the long run, contractive effects arise because interest payments imply redistribution of income from workers to capitalists, who have a lower propensity to consume. These effects may overwhelm the expansive effects so that higher workers' debt has long-run contractive effects on capital accumulation and growth under certain conditions. However, with a low rate of interest, high levels of autonomous investment and a low profit share, the long-run effects of workers' debt may remain expansive, according to Dutt. The model sketched below is similar to Dutt's models. However, Dutt's models include a built-in stabilizer, because he assumes that the desired lending of capitalists (or rentiers) to workers' households, or the desired debt of workers' households from the perspective of the capitalists (or rentiers), is determined and thus restricted by workers' income net of interest payments. He thus excludes the cumulative increases, and hence instability, of workers' debt–income or debt–capital ratios. The model below will not make such a restrictive assumption and rather will assume that creditors, because of the institutional changes in the age of financialization mentioned above, do not care much about workers' net income or wealth when granting credit. This allows to focus on the issue of the long-run stability of workers' debt–capital ratios, and to treat the major effects of finance-dominated capitalism in a direct and explicit way.

2.3.2.3   A simple model of financialization, redistribution, household debt and growth[15]

The basic model and short-run equilibrium   The assumptions regarding production, pricing and distribution in the model are as outlined in section 2.3.1.3: We assume a closed one-good economy without a government, operating with a fixed-coefficient technology in which functional income distribution is determined by mark-up pricing of firms in the incompletely competitive goods market. The share of profits in national income ($h = \Pi/pY$) is therefore a function of those variables determining the mark-up (m), in particular the degree of competition in the goods market, the bargaining power of trade unions in the labour market, and overhead costs and gross profit targets:

$$h = h(m). \tag{2.21}$$

There are two types of households, rentiers and workers, and a firm sector in the model. It is assumed that the capital stock of the firm sector (pK) is completely financed by equity issued by the firms and held by the rentiers' households (E_R). Rentiers receive all the profits made by the firms (Π) as dividend payments (Π_R), and there are no retained earnings of the firm sector in this model:

$$\Pi = \Pi_R = hpY. \tag{2.22}$$

From this it also follows that the dividend rate ($d = \Pi_R/E_R$) is equal to the rate of profit on capital stock ($r = \Pi/pK$), which can be decomposed into the profit share (h), the rate of utilization of productive capacities given by the capital stock (u), and the capital–potential output ratio (v):

$$d = \frac{\Pi_R}{E_R} = \frac{\Pi}{pK} = \frac{\Pi}{pY}\frac{Y}{Y^p}\frac{Y^p}{K} = hu\frac{1}{v} = r. \tag{2.23}$$

Workers' consumption (pC_W) is determined by their wage income ($W = (1-h)Y$), on the one hand, and by credit received from rentiers (ΔB_W) net of interest payments on their stock of debt (iB_W) to rentiers, on the other hand:

$$pC_W = W + \Delta B_W - iB_W = (1 - h)pY + \Delta B_W - iB_W. \tag{2.24}$$

Loans from rentiers to workers thus have a twofold effect. On the one hand, they increase available financial resources and boost consumption. On the other hand, they increase workers' households' stock of debt, and thus interest payments, which reduce workers' consumption. The net effect may be positive or negative. The rate of interest is again given by monetary policies of the central bank, setting the base rate of interest in the money market, and by rentiers' liquidity and risk assessments as well as the degree of competition in the credit and financial markets, determining the mark-up on the base rate, and thus the rate(s) of interest in these markets. The rate of interest is an exogenous variable in the model.

Rentiers' consumption (pC_R) is determined by their total income, consisting of distributed profits of firms ($hpY = \Pi_R$) plus the interest payments from workers' households (iB_W), and their propensity to consume (c_R):

$$pC_R = c_R(hpY + iB_W), \qquad 0 < c_R < 1. \qquad (2.25)$$

There are only two types of assets available for rentiers' saving: equity issued by the firm sector and debt of workers' households. It is assumed that rentiers' saving (S_R), determined by their propensity to save ($s_R = 1 - c_R$) out of their total income, is split into fixed proportions between additional lending to workers and buying additional equity issued by the firms:

$$\Delta B_W = \delta S_R = \delta s_R(hpY + iB_W), \qquad (2.26)$$

$$\Delta E_R = (1 - \delta)S_R = (1 - \delta)s_R(hpY + iB_W). \qquad (2.27)$$

Different from Dutt (2005, 2006), because of the institutional changes in the age of financialization, rentiers tend not to care much about workers' net income or indebtedness when granting credit. Therefore, as a first approximation, rentiers' loans to workers are considered to be a fixed proportion (δ) of rentiers' saving. This proportion is determined by several factors: workers' households' willingness to go into debt, rentiers' households' willingness to supply credit to workers, hence workers' households' creditworthiness as perceived by rentiers and affected potentially, but not necessarily, by workers' debt–capital or debt–income ratios, the regulation of the credit market, and thus the standards for creditworthiness, and other factors influencing creditworthiness.

Normalizing equations (2.24)–(2.26) by the capital stock yields:

$$\frac{pC_W}{pK} = (1 - h)\frac{u}{v} + \hat{B}_W\lambda_W - i\lambda_W, \qquad (2.28)$$

$$\frac{pC_R}{pK} = c_R\left(h\frac{u}{v} + i\lambda_W\right), \qquad (2.29)$$

$$\frac{\Delta B_W}{pK} = \hat{B}_W\lambda_W = \delta s_R\left(h\frac{u}{v} + i\lambda_W\right). \qquad (2.30)$$

The workers' debt–capital ratio ($\lambda_W = B_W / pK$) is treated as a constant in the short-run analysis but will be endogenously determined in the long run of the model. Finally, $\hat{B}_W = \Delta B_W/B_W$ is the rate of change of workers' debt. Including the creditor–debtor relationship between rentiers' households and workers' households in the three basic equations of the Kaleckian model and the stability condition for the goods market equilibrium yields:

$$g = \frac{pI}{pK} = \alpha + \beta u, \qquad 0 < \beta, \qquad (2.31)$$

$$\sigma = \frac{S}{pK} = s_R\left(h\frac{u}{V} + i\lambda_W\right), \qquad 0 < s_R < 1, \qquad (2.32)$$

$$g = (1 - \delta)\sigma, \qquad (2.33)$$

$$(1 - \delta)s_R\frac{h}{V} - \beta > 0. \qquad (2.34)$$

The rate of investment (I) in capital stock (g) is determined by (expected) sales, and hence by the rate of capacity utilization and by animal spirits of the firm sector (α), so that a basic neo-Kaleckian function for capital accumulation in equation (2.31) is obtained. Equation (2.32) defines the saving rate (α), that is, saving in relation to the capital stock, which is determined by rentiers' income normalized by the capital stock and their propensity to save. Equation (2.33) is the goods market equilibrium, and condition (2.34) presents the usual Kaleckian/Keynesian goods market equilibrium stability condition.

For the short-run equilibrium the workers' debt–capital ratio is taken as given and constant. From equations (2.31)–(2.33), the short-run equilibrium rates of capacity utilization (u^*) and capital accumulation (g^*) are obtained:

$$u^* = \frac{\alpha - (1 - \delta)s_R i\lambda_W}{(1 - \delta)s_R\dfrac{h}{V} - \beta}, \qquad (2.35)$$

$$g^* = \frac{(1 - \delta)s_R\left(\alpha\dfrac{h}{V} - \beta i\lambda_W\right)}{(1 - \delta)s_R\dfrac{h}{V} - \beta}. \qquad (2.36)$$

Long-run equilibrium and stability In the long run, the workers' debt–capital ratio is considered to be variable and has to be determined endogenously. Long-run equilibrium requires the endogenously determined value of this ratio to be constant. If we assume again goods market prices to be constant – mark-ups may change but the price level remains the same, which means that unit labour costs will have to vary inversely with the mark-up – the rate of change in the workers' debt–capital ratio is given as:

$$\hat{\lambda}_W = \hat{B}_W - \hat{K} = \hat{B}_W - g. \qquad (2.37)$$

In long-run equilibrium $\hat{\lambda}_W = 0$ is required, and therefore:

$$\hat{B}_W = g. \tag{2.38}$$

From equations (2.30) and (2.35) it is obtained:

$$\hat{B}_W = \frac{\delta s_R\left(\alpha\dfrac{u}{v} - \beta i\lambda_W\right)}{\lambda_W\left[(1 - \delta)s_R\dfrac{h}{v} - \beta\right]}. \tag{2.39}$$

Inserting equation (2.36) and equation (2.39) into equation (2.38) yields two long-run equilibrium values for the workers' debt–capital ratio:

$$\lambda_{W1}^{**} = \frac{\delta}{1 - \delta} \tag{2.40}$$

and

$$\lambda_{W2}^{**} = \frac{\alpha h}{\beta i v}. \tag{2.41}$$

Stability of the long-run equilibrium workers' debt–capital ratio requires:

$$\frac{\partial\hat{\lambda}_W}{\partial\lambda_W} < 0. \tag{2.42}$$

Starting from equation (2.37), inserting equations (2.36) and (2.39) yields:

$$\hat{\lambda}_W = \frac{s_R\left[\alpha\delta\dfrac{h}{v}\lambda_W^{-1} + \beta(1 - \delta)i\lambda_W - \alpha(1 - \delta)\dfrac{h}{v} - \beta\delta i\right]}{(1 - \delta)s_R\dfrac{h}{v} - \beta}. \tag{2.43}$$

From this it is obtained:

$$\frac{\partial\hat{\lambda}_W}{\partial\lambda_W} = \frac{s_R\left[\beta(1 - \delta)i - \alpha\delta\dfrac{h}{v}\lambda_W^{-2}\right]}{(1 - \delta)s_R\dfrac{h}{v} - \beta}. \tag{2.43a}$$

Since the denominator will be positive, if only stable short-run goods market equilibria are considered, stability of long-run equilibrium is given if the numerator in equation (2.43a) is negative. Therefore, stability is obtained under the following condition:

$$\frac{\partial \hat{\lambda}_w}{\partial \lambda_w} < 0 \quad \text{if}: \lambda_w < \sqrt{\frac{\delta}{(1-\delta)} \frac{\alpha h}{\beta i v}} \Rightarrow \lambda_w < \sqrt{\lambda_{w1}^{**} \lambda_{w2}^{**}}. \quad (2.43a')$$

Instability will hence prevail under the following condition:

$$\frac{\partial \hat{\lambda}_w}{\partial \lambda_w} < 0 \quad \text{if}: \lambda_w > \sqrt{\frac{\delta}{(1-\delta)} \frac{\alpha h}{\beta i v}} \Rightarrow \lambda_w > \sqrt{\lambda_{w1}^{**} \lambda_{w2}^{**}}. \quad (2.43a'')$$

Since two equilibrium values for the workers' debt–capital ratio are obtained and the benchmark for stability is given by the root of the product of these two values, only the lower value is stable, whereas the upper value is unstable. This is shown in Figure 2.9, where it is assumed that $\lambda_{w1}^{**} = \delta/(1-\delta)$ and $\lambda_{w2}^{**} = (\alpha h)/(\beta i v)$. In this case, λ_{w1}^{**} is stable, whereas λ_{w2}^{**} is unstable. As shown below this is the only constellation which is consistent with economically meaningful stable goods market equilibrium values for capacity utilization and capital accumulation.

The long-run equilibrium values for capacity utilization and capital accumulation associated with the first long-run equilibrium value for the workers' debt–capital ratio in equation (2.40) are:

$$u_1^{**} = \frac{\alpha - \delta s_R i}{(1-\delta)s_R \dfrac{h}{v} - \beta}, \quad (2.44)$$

$$g_1^{**} = \frac{s_R \left[\alpha(1-\delta)\dfrac{h}{v} - \beta \delta i \right]}{(1-\delta)s_R \dfrac{h}{v} - \beta}. \quad (2.45)$$

For a positive long-run equilibrium rate of capacity utilization, with short-run goods market stability assumed to hold, we need: $\alpha > \delta s_R i$, and for a positive equilibrium rate of capital accumulation it is required that: $\alpha > [\delta/(1-\delta)][(\beta i v)/h]$. Note that the latter implies that:

$$\lambda_{w1}^{**} = \frac{\delta}{1-\delta} < \lambda_{w2}^{**} = \frac{\alpha h}{\beta i v}. \quad (2.46)$$

For the second (unstable) long-run equilibrium value for the workers' debt–capital ratio given in equation (2.41) the related long-run equilibrium rates of capacity utilization and capital accumulation are:

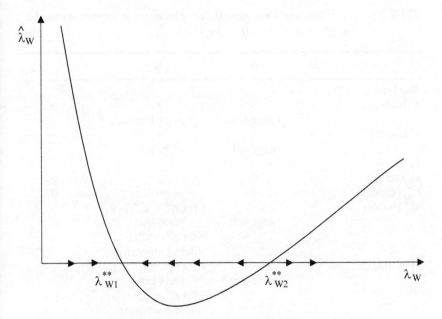

Figure 2.9   *Long-run equilibrium values for workers' debt–capital ratio and their stability*

$$u_2^{**} = \frac{\alpha\left[1 - (1 - \delta)\dfrac{s_R h}{\beta v}\right]}{(1 - \delta)s_R \dfrac{h}{v} - \beta},$$ (2.47)

$$g_2^{**} = 0.$$ (2.48)

Short- and long-run effects of financialization   Table 2.6 summarizes the short- and long-run effects of financialization on capacity utilization, capital accumulation and the workers' debt–capital ratio. In the short run, taking the workers' debt–capital ratio as given, falling animal spirits of the firm sector with respect to investment in real capital stock and redistribution at the expense of workers have negative effects on both capacity utilization and capital accumulation. However, these contractive effects of financialization may be compensated by increasing lending of rentiers to workers for consumption purposes. Also, a lower rentiers' propensity to save and a lower rate of interest on workers' debt help to stabilize private consumption and thus contribute to compensating for the depressing

Table 2.6 *Short-run and long-run effects of changes in exogenous model variables, assuming* $\alpha > \delta s_R i$

	α	h	δ	i	s_R	λ_W
Short run						
u^* (stable)	+	− (wage-led)	+ (debt-led)	−	−	−
g^* (stable)	+	− (wage-led)	+ (debt-led)	−	−	−
Long run						
λ_{W1}^{**} (stable)	0	0	+	0	0	...
λ_{W2}^{**} (unstable)	+	+	0	−	0	...
u_1^{**} (stable)	+	− (wage-led)	+ for $r_1^{**} = d_1^{**} > i$ (debt-led) − for $r_1^{**} = d_1^{**} < i$ (debt-burdened)	−	−	...
g_1^{**} (stable)	+	− (wage-led)	+ for $r_1^{**} = d_1^{**} > i$ (debt-led) − for $r_1^{**} = d_1^{**} < i$ (debt-burdened)	−	−	...

Note: ... denotes not applicable.

Source: Hein (2012, p. 105).

effects of low animal spirits and redistribution of income at the expense of workers.

In the long run, the endogeneity of the workers' debt–capital ratio has to be taken into account. The model yields two potential long-run equilibrium values for this ratio. For economically meaningful results for stable equilibrium capacity utilization, the lower equilibrium value for the workers' debt–capital ratio is stable, whereas the upper value is unstable. Therefore, within the limits given by the unstable upper equilibrium value, the workers' debt–capital (and debt–income) ratio will converge towards a definite value. Only if it exceeds the upper equilibrium will it become unstable and explode.

Lower animal spirits of the firm sector with respect to real investment, and a higher rate of interest each have a negative effect on the upper equilibrium value for the workers' debt–capital ratio and thus compress the corridor of stability, whereas a higher profit share extends it. A higher proportion of rentiers' saving lent to workers increases the stable equilibrium value of the workers' debt–capital ratio, but this compresses the corridor of upwards stability.

The long-run effects of lower animal spirits, a higher profit share and also a higher rate of interest or a higher rentiers' propensity to save on equilibrium capacity utilization and capital accumulation are each negative. However, increasing lending of rentiers to workers can be expansive also in the long run, taking the negative feedback effects of increasing debt and higher interest payments on workers' consumption into account, provided that the exogenous rate of interest is lower than the endogenously determined rate of profit. But, if the rate of interest is higher than the rate of profit, the negative feedback effect of increasing debt and higher interest payments over-compensates for the short-run expansive effect of increasing lending to workers and turns it contractive in the long run.

Depending on the rate of interest relative to the rate of profit, we may therefore have two stable long-run constellations in the face of higher lending of rentiers to workers. With a relatively low rate of interest, a higher proportion of rentiers' saving being lent to workers (causing a higher workers' debt–capital ratio) will be accompanied by higher rates of capacity utilization and capital accumulation. Aggregate demand and growth will hence be debt-led. With a relatively high rate of interest, however, a higher proportion of rentiers' saving lent to workers (causing a higher workers' debt–capital ratio) will be accompanied by lower rates of capacity utilization and capital accumulation. In this case, aggregate demand and growth will be debt-burdened. Both constellations are locally stable. However, the upwards corridor of stability will shrink owing to the increase in the equilibrium workers' debt–capital ratio in each constellation.

Since the model economy in the short run is always debt-led, a higher proportion of rentiers' saving lent to workers will always be accompanied by higher rates of capacity utilization and capital accumulation. Moving from the short to the long run, the stock–flow dynamics may turn the short-run debt-led into a long-run debt-burdened constellation if the rate of interest is too high relative to the rate of profit. With a low rate of interest, relative to the rate of profit, however, this will not happen and the economy remains debt-led in the long run, too.

In the long run, a shift from debt-led aggregate demand and growth to a debt-burdened constellation will take place only if there is a change in parameters which affect the long-run equilibrium rate of profit relative to the rate of interest. A fall in animal spirits, a rise in the profit share, an increase in the rentiers' propensity to save, or a rise in the exogenous rate of interest will each lower the long-run equilibrium rate of profit and may make it fall below the rate of interest.

It should be noted that the considerations so far apply only if $\alpha > \delta s_R$

i, because this condition ensures that there is a stable and economically meaningful goods market equilibrium associated with a stable long-run workers' debt–capital ratio. If this condition is violated in the course of finance-dominated capitalism, by the decrease in animal spirits, by the increase in the proportion of rentiers' saving lent to workers, by an increasing rate of interest or by an increasing rentiers' propensity to save, economically meaningful goods market equilibria would have to be unstable (or the stable goods market equilibrium rate of capacity utilization would be negative), and the system would turn unstable in the short and in the long run.

In summary, what this little model shows is that increasing (workers') household debt for consumption purposes may indeed have expansionary effects, both in the short and in the long run, over-compensating for the contractive effects of financialization on aggregate demand and growth via redistribution and via repressed capital accumulation.[16] However, the conditions for such expansionary and stable effects are highly restrictive. And, even if they exist, they tend to be undermined by financialization itself, through redistribution at the expense of the labour income share, which has a depressing effect on income growth in a wage-led economy and may turn a debt-led economy debt-burdened, through lending too much to deficit households and through depressing animal spirits, which may each turn a stable workers' debt–capital ratio unstable.

2.4 FINANCIALIZATION, OPEN ECONOMY EFFECTS AND CURRENT ACCOUNT IMBALANCES

2.4.1 Empirical Evidence

The interconnectedness of rising income inequality, widening global current account imbalances, and crises has come to the fore during recent developments in the world economy. Wage moderation[17] and the polarization of income distribution led to deficiencies in effective demand in most countries. To cope with this, countries adopted different strategies based on institutional, macroeconomic and other factors which will be discussed below. Broadly speaking, two types of 'capitalism under financialization' developed: the 'debt-led consumption boom' type and the 'export-led mercantilist' type.[18] These two types mutually reinforced each other and, in the context of financial liberalization, contributed to rising global current account imbalances. The 'debt-led consumption boom' type generated a 'profits without investment' regime relying on debt-financed consumption demand for the realization of profits, as we have outlined in section 2.3.2. Since this strategy was associated with higher unit labour cost growth, higher inflation and more dynamic domestic demand than in the 'export-led mercantilist' economies, it meant large current account deficits as a consequence. The 'export-led mercantilist' type, which may also give rise to a 'profits without investment' regime, relies instead on export and current account surpluses as an alternative for generating demand and realizing profits.

These two types of development were complementary. The dynamic 'debt-led consumption boom' type of development in the USA and the other countries following this model relied on the willingness and the ability of private households to go into debt, and on ever rising notional wealth, in particular rising residential property prices, (seemingly) providing collateral for credit, and on the willingness of the rest of the world – notably the 'export-led mercantilist' countries – to run current account surpluses and thus to supply credit in order to finance the related current account deficits in the 'debt-led consumption boom' economies. The slowly growing or stagnating 'export-led mercantilist' economies, on the other hand, relied on the willingness and the ability of the rest of the world – notably the 'debt-led consumption boom' economies – to go into debt, because their moderate or weak growth rates were dependent on dynamic growth of world demand and their export markets.

Figure 2.10 illustrates the development of the global current account imbalances since 1980. In the course of the recovery from the bursting of the new economy boom of the late 1990s, the global current account imbalances exploded from the early 2000s until the outbreak of the global financial crisis in 2007–08. Particularly large were USA current account deficits towards Asian countries, primarily towards China and Japan. As Fitoussi and Stiglitz (2009) pointed out, in the USA growth was maintained through increasing private and public indebtedness. This was financed partly by East Asia, where the People's Bank of China kept the currency artificially undervalued, leading to current account surpluses and, by definition, higher savings, and partly by Europe. The current account of the Euro area as a whole was relatively balanced but, below the surface, massive intra-Euro area imbalances had built up, with Germany in particular accumulating surpluses, and the countries of Southern Europe experiencing rising current account deficits (Stockhammer 2010a, 2010b; Hein et al. 2012).

In Hein (2012, Chapter 6), cyclical average data for the trade cycle of the early 2000s were analysed with the aim of distinguishing the two regimes mentioned above – the 'debt-led consumption boom' type and the 'export-led mercantilist' type – and identifying the countries which

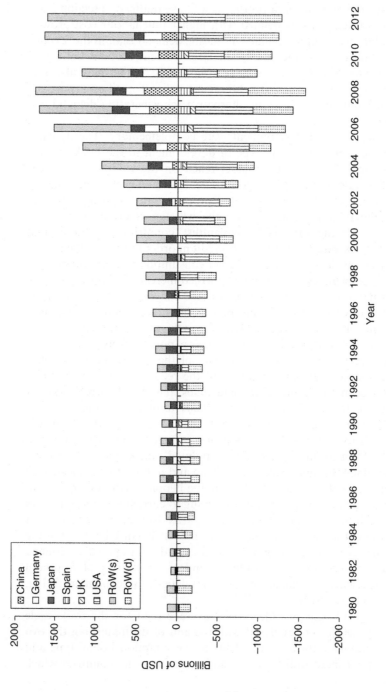

Note: RoW(s): rest of the world, current account surplus countries; RoW(d): rest of the world, current account deficit countries.

Source: IMF (2013); authors' calculations.

Figure 2.10 Current account balances, 1980–2012

followed each of these patterns. The USA, the UK, Greece, Ireland and Spain were found to have followed the 'debt-led consumption boom' type of aggregate demand and growth. It is notable that all these economies saw considerable increases in residential property prices and/or in wealth–income ratios in the cycle of the early 2000s. This was conducive to soaring consumption demand, and hence to considerable growth contributions of private consumption and domestic demand. Strong domestic demand growth in the 'debt-led consumption boom' countries was accompanied by negative growth contributions of the balance of goods and services in all of these countries.[19] The 'debt-led consumption boom' economies were thus the world demand engines of the cycle from the early 2000s to 2008. As a counterpart to these economies, an 'export-led mercantilist' group was identified, containing the economies of, notably, China and Germany, but also of Austria, Belgium, the Netherlands, Sweden and Japan. These economies were characterized by surpluses in the balances of goods and services and in the current accounts. The financial balances of the private sectors were strongly positive in each of these countries.

Empirically, the link between rising inequality and current account imbalances was tested recently. In the face of rising inequality and falling labour income shares, financial globalization – so the argument goes – provided the conditions for 'debt-led consumption boom' economies running into persistent current account deficits, and 'export-led mercantilist' economies with persistent current account surpluses, thus fuelling global current account imbalances. In the former group of countries, increasing inequality of personal incomes triggered a spike in economic activity, owing to imitation effects where lower-income groups went into debt to 'keep up with the Joneses', but also higher inflation rates, which contributed to a rise of current account deficits. In the latter group, stagnating domestic demand and lower inflation contributed to increasing current account surpluses. In a cross-sectional econometric study for 18 OECD countries (1968–2006) Kumhof et al. (2012) confirm that an increase in top income shares and financial liberalization are associated with larger current account deficits. A one percentage point increase in the top 5 per cent income share is associated with a current account–GDP deterioration of 0.8 percentage points. Similarly, Behringer and van Treeck (2013) find a strong negative link between top-end income inequality and the current account balance in a panel regression of 20 countries (1972–2007). In addition, they show that an increase in the corporate financial balance associated with a falling wage share leads to an improvement of the current account. Therefore, according to their view, it makes a difference whether redistribution at the expense of labour leads to an improvement in the share of retained profits or to a rise in distributed profits and thus in top household incomes.

2.4.2   Inequality and Current Account Imbalances in Macroeconomic Models

In an open economy dynamic stochastic general equilibrium (DSGE) model, Kumhof and Ranciere (2010) analyse the links between increasing inequality, current account imbalances and crisis. In the model, the top 5 per cent group (investors), whose income and wealth increase relative to the bottom 95 per cent group (workers), finances the bottom group, as well as foreigners. In a country with less developed financial markets or institutional impediments to private household debt, financing of foreigners is predominant, and the country's growth model turns export-driven (as, for example, in China). Otherwise (as, for example, in the USA), the bottom group will be able to sustain its consumption despite decreasing real wages, increasing the bottom households' debt–income ratios over time. Higher leverage in turn increases financial fragility, leading eventually to a financial crisis: In a run-up to the crisis, both inequality and leverage increase simultaneously, as was the case prior to the Great Depression as well as the Great Recession.

Open economy SFC models, as in Godley and Lavoie (2007, Chapters 6, 12), provide another framework for the study of the interactions between two countries or regions, and for the emanating current account imbalances. For example, the build-up of the USA current account deficits vis-à-vis Chinese surpluses can be well examined in this framework, as was done by Barbosa de Carvalho (2012). The models have since been enlarged to include three countries, which appears particularly suitable for the analysis of world current account imbalances between the three major players: the USA, China and the Euro area. Among these models, Belabed et al. (2013) take into explicit account the effects that rising income inequality can have on the build-up of current account imbalances. Here the developments in both personal and functional income distribution are analysed and used to explain various patterns of consumption in different countries. The authors employ an extended version of Duesenberry's (1949) relative income hypothesis, where the household's consumption depends not only on disposable income, but also on consumption of the household's social reference group.[20] With upward-looking comparisons, the model gives rise to expenditure cascades, as proposed by Frank et al. (2014), whose appearance and scope depend crucially on where in the (personal) income distribution ladder inequality begins to rise. In order to analyse the effects of rising inequality on current account (im)balances, Belabed et al. (2013) essentially examine two hypotheses. The first one states that an increase in personal inequality (in particular in top income shares) leads, ceteris paribus, to a decrease in households' saving and an increase in household debt, which has a negative effect on the current account balance. The USA economy fits very well with this proposition. The second hypothesis states that a shift in functional income distribution at the expense of wages leads, ceteris paribus, to an improvement of the current account as a result of the lack of consumption and a concomitant increase of private sector saving, since firms and rich households save more than poor households. This is broadly the description of developments in the surplus economies of Germany and China. For China in particular, the authors argue that personal inequality has increased as well, but given the under-development of financial markets, where the lower and middle classes are not able to borrow in order to finance consumption, expenditure cascades cannot develop as in the case of the USA. The other effect – changing functional income distribution – thus dominates, leading to an export-oriented growth model in the face of weak domestic demand. Their model simulations confirm both ypotheses.

2.4.3   A Simple Model of Financialization, Redistribution, Current Account Imbalances and Growth

Here we sketch a simple open economy distribution and growth model without economic activity by the government, in which a 'profits without investment' regime under the conditions of increasing financialization is driven by net exports or current account surpluses. The model is based on the works by Blecker (1989), Bhaduri and Marglin (1990) and Hein and Vogel (2008).[21] We assume a fixed-coefficient production technology, no technological progress, and functional income to be mainly determined by mark-up pricing of firms in incompletely competitive goods markets. Financialization is assumed to have the following effects: first, a redistribution of income at the expense of the wage share in favour of the gross profit share, as outlined in section 2.2; second, decreasing animal spirits of firms with respect to investment in the capital stock ('preference' channel), as outlined in section 2.3.1 – for the sake of simplicity we do not explicitly consider the effect of increasing dividend payments and share buybacks ('internal means of finance' channel) here; and, third, rising demand in the foreign economy, which is assumed to follow a 'debt-led consumption boom' type of development, that is, rising consumption demand based on increasing (workers') household debt, as discussed in section 2.3.2. We will analyse the effects on domestic capacity utilization and capital stock growth, derive the conditions for a 'profits without investment' regime of the domestic economy driven by net exports and current account surpluses and, finally, briefly reflect on the sustainability of such a regime.

Let us start with the well-known goods market equilibrium condition for an open economy without economic activity of the state: planned saving (S) has to be equal to net investment (pI) plus net exports (NX), the difference between exports (X) and imports (M) of goods and services:

$$S = pI + X - M = pI + NX. \tag{2.49}$$

Normalizing equation (2.49) by the nominal capital stock (pK) yields the following goods market equilibrium relationship between the saving rate ($\sigma = S/pK$), the accumulation rate ($g = I/K$) and the net export rate ($b = NX/pK$):

$$\sigma = g + b. \tag{2.50}$$

For the sake of simplicity we assume that saving consists only of saving out of profits (S_Π) – workers are assumed not to save. Since the rate of capacity utilization is the relation of output to potential output ($u = Y/Y^p$) and the capital–potential output ratio relates the capital stock to potential output ($v = K/Y^p$), we obtain for the saving rate:

$$\sigma = \frac{S_\Pi}{pK} = \frac{s_\Pi \Pi}{pK} = s_\Pi h \frac{u}{v}, \quad 0 < s_\Pi \leq 1. \tag{2.51}$$

Investment is modelled following the Rowthorn (1981) and Dutt (1984, 1987) version of the Kaleckian model, the neo-Kaleckian version, making investment decisions of firms dependent on 'animal spirits' (α) and on aggregate demand relative to productive capacities and hence on the rate of capacity utilization:

$$g = \alpha + \beta u, \quad \alpha, \beta > 0. \tag{2.52}$$

As will be shown below, this investment function makes sure that the effect of a change in functional income distribution on domestic demand and accumulation – leaving the effects on net exports aside – is wage-led; an increase in the profit share causes lower rates of capacity utilization, profit and capital accumulation. This is the result found for most examined countries in many empirical studies applying a more extensive post-Kaleckian investment function including the profit share or unit profits as a positive determinant, following Bhaduri and Marglin (1990)

(Naastepad and Storm 2007; Hein and Vogel 2008; Stockhammer et al. 2009, 2011; Onaran et al. 2011; Onaran and Galanis 2012; Hein 2014, Chapter 7).

The net export rate is positively affected by international price competitiveness, provided that the Marshall–Lerner condition can be assumed to hold and the sum of the absolute values of the price elasticities of exports and imports exceeds unity. Under this condition, the real exchange rate will have a positive effect on net exports. The real exchange rate itself is assumed to be positively related with the profit share.[22] But net exports also depend on the developments of foreign and domestic demand. An increase in domestic demand, and hence in the domestic rate of capacity utilization, has a negative impact on net exports, ceteris paribus, and an increase in foreign demand and hence in the foreign rate of capacity utilization (u_f) has a positive effect, with the coefficients being affected by the income elasticities of the demand for exports and imports, respectively:

$$b = \psi e_r(h) - \phi u + \varepsilon u_f, \quad \psi, \phi, \varepsilon > 0. \tag{2.53}$$

Stability of the goods market equilibrium requires that saving responds more elastically to a change in the endogenous variable, the rate of capacity utilization, than investment and net exports do together:

$$\frac{\partial \sigma}{\partial u} - \frac{\partial g}{\partial u} - \frac{\partial b}{\partial u} > 0 \quad \Rightarrow \quad s_\Pi \frac{h}{v} - \beta + \phi > 0. \tag{2.54}$$

The equilibrium rates of capacity utilization, capital accumulation and net exports are given by:

$$u^* = \frac{\alpha + \psi e_r(h) + \varepsilon u_f}{s_\Pi \dfrac{h}{v} - \beta + \phi}, \tag{2.55}$$

$$g^* = \frac{\alpha \left(s_\Pi \dfrac{h}{v} + \phi \right) + \beta[\psi e_r(h) + \varepsilon u_f]}{s_\Pi \dfrac{h}{v} - \beta + \phi}, \tag{2.56}$$

$$b^* = \frac{\left(s_\Pi \dfrac{h}{v} - \beta \right)[\psi e_r(h) + \varepsilon u_f] - \phi \alpha}{s_\Pi \dfrac{h}{v} - \beta + \phi}. \tag{2.57}$$

Whereas equilibrium capacity utilization indicates equilibrium activity with given productive capacities, equilibrium capital accumulation determines the development of productive capacities or potential output. The effects of a change in the profit share on the equilibrium rates of capacity utilization, capital accumulation and net exports are as follows:

$$\frac{\partial u^*}{\partial h} = \frac{\psi \frac{\partial e_r}{\partial h} - s_\Pi \frac{u}{v}}{s_\Pi \frac{h}{v} - \beta + \phi}, \tag{2.55a}$$

$$\frac{\partial g^*}{\partial h} = \frac{\beta \left(\psi \frac{\partial e_r}{\partial h} - s_\Pi \frac{u}{v} \right)}{s_\Pi \frac{h}{v} - \beta + \phi}, \tag{2.56a}$$

$$\frac{\partial b^*}{\partial h} = \frac{\left(s_\Pi \frac{h}{v} - \beta \right) \psi \frac{\partial e_r}{\partial h} + \phi s_\Pi \frac{u}{v}}{s_\Pi \frac{h}{v} - \beta + \phi}. \tag{2.57a}$$

As equations (2.55a) and (2.56a) show, the negative effect of a change in the profit share on the rates of capacity utilization and capital accumulation via domestic demand may be over-compensated by the positive effect on net exports via improved price competitiveness, so that the total demand and growth regime may turn profit-led. In this case equation (2.57a) will have to be positive, too.

As pointed out above, we would like to include the following effects of financialization (Ω) in our little model:

1. declining animal spirits of firms with respect to investment in the capital stock: $\frac{\partial \alpha}{\partial \Omega} < 0$;
2. redistribution at the expense of the wage share: $\frac{\partial h}{\partial \Omega} > 0$;
3. acceleration of foreign demand due to a 'debt-led consumption boom' type of development in the foreign economy: $\frac{\partial u_f}{\partial \Omega} > 0$.

Through these channels, increasing financialization has the following effects on the equilibrium values of the domestic economy:

$$\frac{\partial u^*}{\partial \Omega} = \frac{\frac{\partial \alpha}{\partial \Omega} + \frac{\partial h}{\partial \Omega} \left(\psi \frac{\partial e_r}{\partial h} - s_\Pi \frac{u}{v} \right) + \frac{\partial u_f}{\partial \Omega} \varepsilon}{s_\Pi \frac{h}{v} - \beta + \phi}, \tag{2.55b}$$

$$\frac{\partial g^*}{\partial \Omega} = \frac{\frac{\partial \alpha}{\partial \Omega}\left(s_\Pi \frac{h}{v} + \phi\right) + \beta\left[\frac{\partial h}{\partial \Omega}\left(\psi \frac{\partial e_r}{\partial h} - s_\Pi \frac{u}{v}\right) + \frac{\partial u_f}{\partial \Omega}\varepsilon\right]}{s_\Pi \frac{h}{v} - \beta + \phi}, \quad (2.56b)$$

$$\frac{\partial b^*}{\partial \Omega} = \frac{-\frac{\partial \alpha}{\partial \Omega}\phi + \frac{\partial h}{\partial \Omega}\left[\left(s_\Pi \frac{h}{v} - \beta\right)\psi \frac{\partial e_r}{\partial h} + s_\Pi \frac{u}{v}\phi\right] + \frac{\partial u_f}{\partial \Omega}\varepsilon\left(s_\Pi \frac{h}{v} - \beta\right)}{s_\Pi \frac{h}{v} - \beta + \phi}.$$

$$(2.57b)$$

A 'profits without investment' regime driven by net exports/current account surpluses requires: $\frac{\partial u^*}{\partial \Omega} > 0, \frac{\partial g^*}{\partial \Omega} < 0, \frac{\partial b^*}{\partial \Omega} > 0$. Assuming the stability condition for the goods market equilibrium to hold, we therefore have:

$$\frac{\partial u^*}{\partial \Omega} > 0, \text{if: } \frac{\partial \alpha}{\partial \Omega} + \frac{\partial h}{\partial \Omega}\left(\psi \frac{\partial e_r}{\partial h} - s_\Pi \frac{u}{v}\right) + \frac{\partial u_f}{\partial \Omega}\varepsilon > 0, \quad (2.55b')$$

$$\frac{\partial g^*}{\partial \Omega} < 0, \text{if: } \frac{\partial \alpha}{\partial \Omega} + \left(s_\Pi \frac{h}{v} + \phi\right) + \beta\left[\frac{\partial h}{\partial \Omega}\left(\psi \frac{\partial e_r}{\partial h} - s_\Pi \frac{u}{v}\right) + \frac{\partial u_f}{\partial \Omega}\varepsilon\right] < 0,$$

$$(2.56b')$$

$$\frac{\partial b^*}{\partial \Omega} > 0, \text{if: } -\frac{\partial \alpha}{\partial \Omega}\phi + \frac{\partial h}{\partial \Omega}\left[\left(s_\Pi \frac{h}{v} - \beta\right)\psi \frac{\partial e_r}{\partial h} + s_\Pi \frac{u}{v}\phi\right] + \frac{\partial u_f}{\partial \Omega}\varepsilon\left(s_\Pi \frac{h}{v} - \beta\right) > 0.$$

$$(2.57b')$$

A positive effect of increasing financialization on equilibrium capacity utilization requires that the negative effect via the 'animal spirits' channel is over-compensated by the increase of aggregate demand through the foreign demand channel and the redistribution channel, as is shown in condition (2.55b'). The former depends on the increase of foreign demand (through debt-led consumption) and on the income elasticity of the demand for exports of the domestic economy. The latter requires that aggregate demand is profit-led and that the dampening effects of redistribution on domestic demand are over-compensated by an increase in net exports via higher price competitiveness, which has to rely on high price elasticities of demand for exports, in particular. However, it should be noticed that, even if overall demand were wage-led, increasing financialization could nonetheless have expansionary effects on capacity utilization, if the negative effects via animal spirits and redistribution in favour of profits are small, and the foreign demand effects are extremely strong. If none of these constellations are given, an increase in financialization will depress domestic capacity utilization and the economy will rather be in a contractive regime.

If the effects of increasing financialization on domestic capacity utilization are expansionary through the foreign demand and the redistribution channels, the effect on domestic equilibrium capital accumulation may be negative nonetheless. As shown in condition (2.56b'), this will occur in particular if the accelerator term in the investment function is weak and thus the increase in domestic capacity utilization has only small effects on capital accumulation which are then insufficient to compensate for the negative direct effects through weakened 'animal spirits'. With a strong accelerator effect, however, capital accumulation may be stimulated overall and the economy would then be in a 'finance-led growth' regime driven by net exports.

Condition (2.57b') shows the effects of increasing financialization on the equilibrium net export rate. The effect via the 'animal spirits' channel will be positive, whereas the effects via the distribution and foreign demand channels will be definitely positive only if: $s_\Pi \frac{h}{v} - \beta > 0$. But with a strong accelerator effect as in the 'finance-led growth' regime, which we have ruled out for the 'profits without investment' regime, the foreign demand channel may have negative effects on net exports, without, however, making the total effect of financialization on net exports necessarily negative.[23]

Having so far spelled out the conditions for 'profits without investment' regimes driven by net exports, we finally take a look at the associated dynamics of foreign assets and liabilities. For the sake of simplicity, we do not explicitly treat cross-border flows of primary incomes, in particular interest and dividend payments associated with foreign assets and liabilities, and therefore treat net exports of goods and services as equivalent to the current account balance. Positive net exports, and hence current account surpluses, for the domestic economy mean that its stock of net foreign assets (A) improves: $NX = \Delta A_d$, whereas the reverse is true for the foreign economy. In a two-country model, net foreign assets of the domestic economy (A_d), which we continue to assume to be in a 'profits without investment' regime driven by net exports and current account surpluses, and hence to follow an 'export-led mercantilist' type of development, are equal to net foreign liabilities of the foreign economy (L_f), which we assume to be in a 'profits without investment' regime driven by debt-financed household consumption, thus following a 'debt-led consumption boom' type of development accepting concomitant negative net exports and current account balances:

$$A_d = L_f. \tag{2.58}$$

Positive (negative) net exports and current accounts mean a change in net foreign assets (liabilities) and hence:

$$\Delta A_d = \Delta L_f. \tag{2.59}$$

Dividing equation (2.59) by equation (2.58), it follows that the growth rate of net foreign assets of the domestic economy has to be equal to the growth rate of net foreign liabilities of the foreign economy:

$$\hat{A}_d = \frac{\Delta A_d}{A_d} = \hat{L}_f = \frac{\Delta L_f}{L_f}. \tag{2.60}$$

A constant net foreign assets–GDP ratio, or a constant net foreign liabilities–GDP ratio, requires that net foreign assets, or net foreign liabilities, and nominal GDP ($pY = Y^n$) of the respective economy grow at the same rate:

$$\frac{A_d}{Y_d^n} \text{ constant, if: } \hat{A}_d = \hat{Y}_d^n, \tag{2.61}$$

$$\frac{L_f}{Y_f^n} \text{ constant, if: } \hat{L}_f = \hat{Y}_f^n. \tag{2.62}$$

Taking into account equation (2.60) this means that the constancy of both the net foreign assets–GDP ratio of the domestic economy and the net foreign liabilities–GDP ratio of the foreign economy requires that the two economies have to grow at the same rate:

$$\frac{A_d}{Y_d^n} \text{ and } \frac{L_f}{Y_f^n} \text{ constant, if } \hat{A}_d = \hat{Y}_d^n = \hat{L}_f = \hat{Y}_f^n. \tag{2.63}$$

From equations (2.60)–(2.62) we also obtain that the long-run net foreign assets–GDP ratio for the domestic country and the net foreign liabilities–GDP ratio of the foreign economy are given as:

$$\hat{A}_d = \frac{\Delta A_d}{A_d} = \frac{\dfrac{\Delta A_d}{Y_d^n}}{\dfrac{A_d}{Y_d^n}} \Rightarrow \frac{A_d}{Y_d^n} = \frac{\dfrac{\Delta A_d}{Y_d^n}}{\hat{Y}_d^n}, \tag{2.64}$$

$$\hat{L}_f = \frac{\Delta L_f}{L_f} = \frac{\dfrac{\Delta L_f}{Y_f^n}}{\dfrac{L_f}{Y_f^n}} \Rightarrow \frac{L_f}{Y_f^n} = \frac{\dfrac{\Delta L_f}{Y_f^n}}{\hat{Y}_f^n}. \tag{2.65}$$

With constant current account surplus–GDP ratios, or current account deficit–GDP ratios, and constant nominal GDP growth rates, the net foreign assets–GDP ratio, or the net foreign liabilities–GDP ratio, will converge towards a definite value. As should be clear from the arguments put forward above, this can only hold for both economies simultaneously if their GDP growth rates are the same.

By definition, in a two-country model net foreign assets have to grow at the same rate as net foreign liabilities. However, nominal GDP growth rates of the domestic economy and the foreign economy will not necessarily be equal. If this is the case, only one country can see a constant net foreign liabilities–/net foreign assets–GDP ratio, whereas the other will witness continuously falling or rising net foreign liabilities–/net foreign assets–GDP ratios. Let us distinguish two constellations:

1. In the first constellation, the current account deficit country, the foreign economy following the 'debt-led consumption boom' type of development grows at a higher rate than the current account surplus country, the domestic economy following the 'export-led mercantilist' strategy: $\hat{Y}_d^n < \hat{Y}_f^n$. In this case, either a constant foreign assets–GDP ratio of the domestic economy will be accompanied by a falling foreign liabilities–GDP ratio of the foreign economy, or a rising foreign assets–GDP ratio of the domestic economy will be accompanied by a constant foreign liabilities–GDP ratio of the foreign economy. Or one may obtain both, rising foreign assets–GDP ratios of the domestic economy and falling foreign liabilities–GDP ratios of the foreign economy.
2. In the opposite constellation, the current account deficit 'debt-led consumption boom' economy grows at a lower speed than the current account surplus 'export-led mercantilist' economy: $\hat{Y}_d^n > \hat{Y}_f^n$. In this case, either a constant foreign assets–GDP ratio of the domestic economy will be accompanied by a rising foreign liabilities–GDP ratio of the foreign economy, or a falling foreign assets–GDP ratio of the domestic economy will be accompanied by a constant foreign liabilities–GDP ratio of the foreign economy. Or we obtain both, falling foreign assets–GDP ratios of the domestic economy and rising foreign liabilities–GDP ratios of the foreign economy.

In the first constellation, in which the current account deficit country grows at a higher rate than the current account surplus country, there is no immanent movement towards ever rising foreign liabilities–GDP ratios, and hence towards foreign over-indebtedness. Of course, this constellation may run into problems associated with increasing household debt being the driver of growth in the current account deficit country – as analysed in section 2.3.2. Long-run growth problems may also arise owing to weak investment and capital stock growth in this country. However, this might not affect the growth differential with respect to the current account surplus countries, because both countries will suffer from the long-run growth problems embedded within a 'profits without investment' regime. But in the first constellation there are no inherent or systemic problems of foreign indebtedness as such. This is completely different in the second constellation, in which the current account surplus country grows at a higher rate than the current account deficit country. It is this constellation which generates a tendency towards cumulatively rising foreign liabilities– GDP ratios of the current account deficit country, which might finally trigger problems of over-indebtedness with the rest of the world.

2.5 SUMMARY AND CONCLUSIONS

In this chapter we have reviewed the empirical and theoretical literature on the effects of changes in the relationship between the financial sector and the non-financial sector of the economy – that is financialization – on distribution, growth, instability and crisis. We have taken a macroeconomic perspective and have examined four macroeconomically relevant features of financialization: first, the effect on income distribution; second, the effects on investment in the capital stock; third, the effects on household debt and consumption; and, fourth, the effects on net exports and current account balances. For each of these features we have briefly reviewed some empirical and econometric literature, and some theoretical and modelling literature examining the macroeconomic effects of these features, and finally we have presented small models generating the most important macroeconomic outcomes. We have chosen as a starting point for all these considerations the empirical observation that several countries in the pre-Great Recession financialization period were characterized by redistribution in favour of profits and by 'profits without investment' regimes – which require explanation from a macroeconomic perspective.

We started with the examination of the redistribution tendencies of financialization in different respects – functional distribution, personal/ household distribution and top incomes shares in national income – and we have shown that the financialization period was characterized by increasing inequalities in all these dimensions. Then we applied a Kaleckian approach towards the explanation of the falling labour income shares in the financialization period, taking into account broad empirical research in this area. We argued that this redistribution was mainly due to a shift in the sectoral composition of the economy, at least in some countries, from the public sector and the non-financial business sector with higher labour income shares towards the financial business sector with a lower labour income share, to rising profit claims of the rentiers, that is, rising interest payments (in the 1980s) and higher dividend payments of the corporate sector, and to the weakening of trade union bargaining power through several channels.

Regarding investment in the capital stock, we have reviewed supportive econometric evidence for the 'preference' channel and the 'internal means of finance' channel. According to the first channel, financialization and shareholder value orientation have caused decreasing management's animal spirits with respect to real investment in the capital stock and long-run growth of the firm and increasing preference for financial investment generating high profits in the short run. And, according to the second channel, financialization and shareholder value orientation have drained internal means of finance for real investment purposes from the corporations, through increasing dividend payments and share buybacks in order to boost stock prices and thus shareholder value. Implementing these channels in macroeconomic distribution and growth models yields different regimes, depending on the values of the model parameters: 'finance-led growth' regimes, 'profits without investment' regimes or 'contractive' regimes. Only the 'finance-led growth' regime yields long-run stability of the financial structure of the firm sector and of capital accumulation, whereas the empirically more realistic 'profits without investment' and 'contractive' regimes yield cumulatively unstable long-run results regarding the financial structure of the firm sector and the rate of capital accumulation, that is, rising debt plus rentiers' equity–capital ratios, and falling rates of capital accumulation. Falling labour income shares triggered by financialization increase the likelihood of these unstable regimes. Therefore, under the conditions of the 'contractive' and the 'profits without investment' regimes there exists a considerable systemic long-run instability potential regarding the financial structure of the corporate sector of the economy and regarding capital accumulation.

Considering the effects of financialization on consumption and household debt, we have argued that there is increasing evidence for (notional) wealth effects on household consumption as well as for the relative income hypothesis regarding households' decisions to consume, each of them associated with increasing indebtedness in order to finance consumption expenditure exceeding current income. We have shown that increasing (workers') household debt for consumption purposes may indeed have expansionary effects, over-compensating the contractive effects of financialization on aggregate demand and growth via redistribution and via repressed capital accumulation, both in the short and in the long run.

However, the conditions for such expansionary and stable effects are highly restrictive. And, even if they exist, they tend to be undermined by financialization itself, first, through redistribution at the expense of the labour income share, which has depressing effects on income growth in a wage-led economy and which may turn a debt-led economy debt-burdened, second, through lending too much to deficit households and, third, through depressing animal spirits, which may each turn a stable workers' debt–capital ratio unstable.

The alternative to a 'profits without investment' regime, driven by a 'debt-led consumption boom' type of development, is an 'export-led mercantilist' strategy. In section 2.4 we therefore dealt with this international dimension of financialization, which led to increasing current account imbalances at the global level in the pre-crisis financialization period. We specified the conditions for such a strategy and found that, in particular, strong growth in current account deficit countries, driven by debt-led consumption booms, high income elasticities of the demand for exports of the current account surplus country and also high price elasticities are supportive, as are only weakly negative effects on investment in the capital stock. Examining the dynamics of foreign assets and liabilities associated with 'export-led mercantilist' strategies, we have found that there is no immanent or systemic dynamics towards ever rising foreign liabilities–GDP ratios, and hence towards foreign over-indebtedness, if the current account deficit countries grow at a higher rate than the current account surplus countries. However, as soon as this constellation turns into its opposite, a tendency towards cumulatively rising foreign liabilities–GDP ratios of the current account deficit country will arise. This might finally trigger problems of over-indebtedness with the rest of the world if the current account deficit country is not the country issuing the world key currency, which is accepted irrespective of the dynamics of the ratio of debt held by foreigners to GDP of this country.

Summing up, we have shown that, against the background of redistribution of income at the expense of the labour income share and depressed investment in the capital stock, each a major feature of financialization, short- to long-run dynamic 'profits without investment' regimes may emerge. However, each type of these regimes, the 'debt-led consumption boom' type and the 'export-led mercantilist' type, contains internal contradictions, with respect to household debt in the first regime and with respect to foreign debt of the counterpart current account deficit countries in the second regime, which finally undermine the sustainability of these regimes and lead to financial and economic crises, as in 2007–09. This crisis was triggered by problems associated with the over-indebtedness of private households in the leading 'debt-led consumption boom' economy, the USA. The crisis then quickly infected the 'export-led mercantilist' economies through the collapse of their export markets (foreign trade channel) and through the devaluation of their capital exports into risky and now collapsing financial markets in the 'debt-led consumption boom' economies (financial contagion channel).

NOTES

For helpful comments we would like to thank Daniel Detzer, Trevor Evans, Hansjörg Herr, Natalia Budyldina, and the participants in the FESSUD Annual Conference 2013 in Amsterdam. Remaining errors are, of course, ours. For a more extensive version, see also Hein (2014, Chapter 10).

1. For the analysis of 'debt-led consumption boom' and 'export-led mercantilist' economies see, for example, Stockhammer (2010a, 2010b, 2012a, 2012b), Hein (2012, Chapter 6), Hein and Mundt (2012) and van Treeck and Sturn (2012), with slightly different terminologies.
2. See, for example Dutt (1995, 2005, 2006), Lavoie (1995, 2009), Boyer (2000), Cordonnier (2006), Hein (2012) and Isaac and Kim (2013).
3. SFC models treating financialization issues have been presented by Lavoie (2008), Skott and Ryoo (2008a, 2008b), Zezza (2008), van Treeck (2009a) and Dallery and van Treeck (2011), among others.
4. This section draws on Hein (2012, Chapter 2, 2013).
5. See Hein (2013) for results on further countries.
6. See Hein (2013) for results and figures for these countries.
7. Neoliberalism is a broader concept than financialization, aiming at the deregulation of labour, financial and goods markets, a reduction of government intervention in the market economy and of government demand management, and a redistribution of income from wages to profits.
8. See for example Lavoie (2008), Skott and Ryoo (2008a, 2008b) and van Treeck (2008).
9. This section draws on Hein (2012, Chapter 3).
10. The post-Keynesian 'horizontalist' view of endogenous money was pioneered by Kaldor (1970, 1982, 1985), Lavoie (1984, 1992, pp.149–216, 1996) and Moore (1988, 1989). For a survey of the post-Keynesian endogenous money approach and its implementation in post-Keynesian models of distribution and growth see Hein (2008).
11. For an introduction to Kaleckian distribution and growth theory and the distinction between neo- and post-Kaleckian models, see Hein (2014).
12. For further effects of a long-run increase in the profit share see Hein (2012, Chapter 3).
13. See, for example, Meirelles and Lima (2006), Lima and Meirelles (2007), Charles (2008a, 2008b), Fujita and Sasaki (2011) and Ryoo (2013), who have added the Minskyan distinction between 'hedge', 'speculative' and 'Ponzi' finance to similar models and derived more differentiated results for the (in)stability issues.
14. See also Rajan (2010) and Stiglitz (2012).
15. This section draws on Hein (2012, Chapter 5).
16. For the treatment of household debt in more complex models, simultaneously with corporate debt, see Isaac and Kim (2013) and also the earlier work, using simulations in stock–flow consistent models, by Godley and Lavoie (2007, Chapter 11), Lavoie (2008) and van Treeck (2009a).
17. Wage moderation means that real wages do not increase in line with increases in productivity, or that nominal wages do not increase in line with productivity plus inflation.
18. For similar analyses see van Treeck et al. (2007), Bibow (2008), Fitoussi and Stiglitz (2009), Horn et al. (2009), Sapir (2009), UNCTAD (2009), van Treeck (2009b), Wade (2009), Hein and Truger (2010, 2011, 2012/13) and Stockhammer (2010a, 2010b).
19. The exception here is Ireland, where the growth contribution of external demand was

positive. Its current account deficit (and the positive financial balance of the external sector) was not due to a deficit in external trade but rather a deficit in the cross-border flows of primary incomes.

20. More technically, it depends on a parameter capturing consumption emulation, which itself depends again on the institutional context, for example corporate and government veils, labour market, etc.

21. For more elaborated open economy models of a similar type see Blecker (1998, 2011).

22. As shown in Hein and Vogel (2008), an increase in the real exchange rate, and hence in price competitiveness, may be associated with a fall in the profit share if it is based on a fall in the mark-up. However, the econometric estimations by Stockhammer et al. (2009, 2011) do not find such an effect; their results suggest that improved price competitiveness is usually obtained by means of nominal wage moderation or nominal devaluation of the currency, which are both associated with an increase in the profit share.

23. A strong accelerator effect in the investment function has to be compensated for by a strong (negative) domestic income effect in the net export function, that is, a high income elasticity of the demand for imports, in order not to violate the goods market equilibrium condition.

REFERENCES

Alvaredo, F., A.B. Atkinson, T. Piketty and E. Saez (2012), The World Top Incomes Database, available at: http://g-mond.parisschoolofeconomics.eu/topincomes.

Atkinson, A.B. (2009), 'Factor shares: the principal problem of political economy?', *Oxford Review of Economic Policy*, **25** (1), 3–16.

Bach, S., G. Corneo and V. Steiner (2009), 'From bottom to top: the entire distribution of market income in Germany, 1992–2003', *Review of Income and Wealth*, **55**, 303–330.

Barba, A. and M. Pivetti (2009), 'Rising household debt: its causes and macroeconomic implications – a long-period analysis', *Cambridge Journal of Economics*, **33**, 113–137.

Barbosa de Carvalho, L. (2012), 'Current account imbalances and economic growth: a two-country model with real–financial linkages', manuscript.

Behringer, J. and T. van Treeck (2013), 'Income distribution, aggregate demand and current account: a sectoral perspective', IMK Working Paper No. 125, Macroeconomic Policy Institute (IMK) at the Hans Böckler Foundation, Düsseldorf.

Belabed, C.A., T. Theobald and T. van Treeck (2013), 'Inequality and current account imbalances – a stock–flow consistent approach', IMK Working Paper No. 126, Macroeconomic Policy Institute (IMK) at the Hans Böckler Foundation, Düsseldorf.

Bhaduri, A. (2011a), 'Financialisation in the light of Keynesian theory', *PSL Quarterly Review*, **64** (256), 7–21.

Bhaduri, A. (2011b), 'A contribution to the theory of financial fragility and crisis', *Cambridge Journal of Economics*, **35**, 995–1014.

Bhaduri, A. and S. Marglin (1990), 'Unemployment and the real wage: the economic basis for contesting political ideologies', *Cambridge Journal of Economics*, **14**, 375–393.

Bhaduri, A., K. Laski and M. Riese (2006), 'A model of interaction between the virtual and the real economy', *Metroeconomica*, **57**, 412–427.

Bibow, J. (2008), 'The international monetary (non-)order and the "global capital flows paradox"', in E. Hein, T. Niechoj, P. Spahn and A. Truger (eds), *Finance-led Capitalism? Macroeconomic Effects of Changes in the Financial Sector*, Marburg: Metropolis.

Blecker, R.A. (1989), 'International competition, income distribution and economic growth', *Cambridge Journal of Economics*, **13**, 395–412.

Blecker, R.A. (1998), 'International competitiveness, relative wages, and the balance-of-payments constraint', *Journal of Post Keynesian Economics*, **20**, 495–526.

Blecker, R.A. (2011), 'Open economy models of distribution and growth', in E. Hein and E. Stockhammer (eds), *A Modern Guide to Keynesian Macroeconomics and Economic Policies*, Cheltenham, UK and Northampton, MA, USA: Edward Elgar Publishing.

Boone, L. and N. Girouard (2002), 'The stock market, the housing market and consumer behaviour', *OECD Economic Studies*, **35**, 175–200.

Börse.de (2012), 'DAX-Historie', available at: http://www.boerse.de/historische-kurse/DAX/DE0008469008.

Boyer, R. (2000), 'Is a finance-led growth regime a viable alternative to Fordism? A preliminary analysis', *Economy and Society*, **29**, 111–145.

Buchele, R. and J. Christiansen (2007), 'Globalization and the declining share of labor income in the United States', paper prepared for the 28th International Working Party on Labor Market Segmentation, Aix-en-Provence, France, 5–7 July, available at: http://gesd.free.fr/paper419.pdf.

Bureau of Economic Analysis (2013), NIPA tables, available at: http://www.bea.gov/index.htm.

Charles, S. (2008a), 'Corporate debt, variable retention rate and the appearance of financial fragility', *Cambridge Journal of Economics*, **32**, 781–795.

Charles, S. (2008b), 'A post-Keynesian model of accumulation with a Minskyan financial structure', *Review of Political Economy*, **20**, 319–331.

Cordonnier, L. (2006), 'Le profit sans l'accumulation: la recette du capitalisme dominé par la finance', *Innovations, Cahiers d'Economie de l'Innovation*, **23**, 51–72.

Cynamon, B. and S. Fazzari (2008), 'Household debt in the consumer age: source of growth – risk of collapse', *Capitalism and Society*, **3** (2), 1–30.

Cynamon, B. and S. Fazzari (2013), 'Inequality and household finance during the consumer age', Working Paper No. 752, Levy Economics Institute of Bard College.

Dallery, T. and T. van Treeck (2011), 'Conflicting claims and equilibrium adjustment processes in a stock–flow consistent macro model', *Review of Political Economy*, **23**, 189–211.

Dreger, C. and J. Slacalek (2007), 'Finanzmarktentwicklung, Immobilienpreise und Konsum', *DIW Wochenbericht*, **74**, 533–536.

Duesenberry, J.S. (1949), *Income, Saving and the Theory of Consumer Behaviors*, Cambridge, MA: Harvard University Press.

Dünhaupt, P. (2011), 'Financialization, corporate governance and income distribution in the USA and Germany: introducing an adjusted wage share indicator', in T. Niechoj, Ö. Onaran, E. Stockhammer, A. Truger and T. van Treeck (eds), *Stabilising an Unequal Economy? Public Debt, Financial Regulation, and Income Distribution*, Marburg: Metropolis.

Dutt, A.K. (1984), 'Stagnation, income distribution and monopoly power', *Cambridge Journal of Economics*, **8**, 25–40.

Dutt, A.K. (1987), 'Alternative closures again: a comment on "Growth, distribution and inflation"', *Cambridge Journal of Economics*, **11**, 75–82.

Dutt, A.K. (1995), 'Internal finance and monopoly power in capitalist economies: a reformulation of Steindl's growth model', *Metroeconomica*, **46**, 16–34.

Dutt, A.K. (2005), 'Conspicuous consumption, consumer debt and economic growth', in M. Setterfield (ed.), *Interactions in Analytical Political Economy: Theory, Policy and Applications*, Armonk, NY: M.E. Sharpe.

Dutt, A.K. (2006), 'Maturity, stagnation and consumer debt: a Steindlian approach', *Metroeconomica*, **57**, 339–364.

European Commission (2010), AMECO Database, Spring, available at: http://ec.europa.eu/economy_finance/db_indicators/ameco/index_en.htm.

European Commission (2012), AMECO Database, Spring, available at: http://ec.europa.eu/economy_finance/db_indicators/ameco/index_en.htm.

Federal Reserve Bank of St. Louis (2013), FRED database, available at: http://research.stlouisfed.org/fred2/series/SP500/downloaddata.

Fitoussi, J.-P. and J. Stiglitz (2009), 'The ways out of the crisis and the building of a more cohesive world', OFCE Document de Travail No. 2009-17, OFCE.

Frank, R.H., A.S. Levine and O. Dijk (2014), 'Expenditure cascades', *Review of Behavioral Economics*, **1**, 55–73.

Fujita, S. and H. Sasaki (2011), 'Financialization and its long-run macroeconomic effects in a Kalecki–Minsky model', Discussion Paper No. E-11-001, Research Project Center, Graduate School of Economics, Kyoto University.

Glyn, A. (2009), 'Functional distribution and inequality', in W. Salverda, B. Nolan and T.M. Smeeding (eds), *The Oxford Handbook of Economy Inequality*, Oxford: Oxford University Press.

Godley, W. and M. Lavoie (2007), *Monetary Economics: An Integrated Approach to Credit, Money, Income, Production and Wealth*, Basingstoke: Palgrave Macmillan.

Guttmann, R. and D. Plihon (2010), 'Consumer debt and financial fragility', *International Review of Applied Economics*, **24**, 269–283.

Hein, E. (2008), *Money, Distribution Conflict and Capital Accumulation: Contributions to 'Monetary Analysis'*, Basingstoke: Palgrave Macmillan.

Hein, E. (2012), *The Macroeconomics of Finance-dominated Capitalism – and Its Crisis*, Cheltenham, UK and Northampton, MA, USA: Edward Elgar Publishing.

Hein, E. (2013), 'Finance-dominated capitalism and re-distribution of income – a Kaleckian perspective', *Cambridge Journal of Economics*, advance access, doi:10.1093/cje/bet038.

Hein, E. (2014), *Distribution and Growth after Keynes: A Post-Keynesian Guide*, Cheltenham, UK and Northampton, MA, USA: Edward Elgar Publishing.

Hein, E. and M. Mundt (2012), 'Financialisation and the requirements and potentials for wage-led recovery: a review focusing on the G20', Conditions of Work and Employment Series No. 37, International Labour Organization.

Hein, E. and A. Truger (2010), 'Financial crisis, global recession and macroeconomic policy reactions – the case of Germany', in S. Dullien, E. Hein, A. Truger and T. van Treeck (eds), *The World Economy in Crisis – The Return of Keynesianism?*, Marburg: Metropolis.

Hein, E. and A. Truger (2011), 'Finance-dominated capitalism in crisis – the case for a Keynesian New Deal at the European and the global level', in P. Arestis and M. Sawyer (eds), *New Economics as Mainstream Economics, International Papers in Political Economy*, Basingstoke: Palgrave Macmillan.

Hein, E. and A. Truger (2012/13), 'Finance-dominated capitalism in crisis – the case for a global Keynesian New Deal', *Journal of Post Keynesian Economics*, **35**, 183–210.

Hein, E. and T. van Treeck (2010), '"Financialisation" in post-Keynesian models of distribution and growth – a systematic review', in M. Setterfield (ed.), *Handbook of Alternative Theories of Economic Growth*, Cheltenham, UK and Northampton, MA, USA: Edward Elgar Publishing.

Hein, E. and L. Vogel (2008), 'Distribution and growth reconsidered – empirical results for six OECD countries', *Cambridge Journal of Economics*, **32**, 479–511.

Hein, E., A. Truger and T. van Treeck (2012), 'The European financial and economic crisis: alternative solutions from a (post-)Keynesian perspective', in P. Arestis and M. Sawyer (eds), *The Euro Crisis, International Papers in Political Economy*, Basingstoke: Palgrave Macmillan.

Horn, G., K. Dröge, S. Sturn, T. van Treeck and R. Zwiener (2009), 'From the financial crisis to the world economic crisis: the role of inequality', IMK Policy Brief, October, Macroeconomic Policy Institute (IMK) at the Hans Böckler Foundation, Düsseldorf.

IMF (2013), World Economic Outlook Database, available at: http://www.imf.org/external/pubs/ft/weo/2013/01/weodata/index.aspx.

Isaac, A.G. and Y.K. Kim (2013), 'Consumer and corporate debt: a neo-Kaleckian synthesis', *Metroeconomica*, **64**, 244–271.

Kaldor, N. (1970), 'The new monetarism', *Lloyds Bank Review*, **97**, 1–17.

Kaldor, N. (1982), *The Scourge of Monetarism*, Oxford: Oxford University Press.

Kaldor, N. (1985), 'How monetarism failed', *Challenge: The Magazine of Economic Affairs*, **28** (2), 4–13.

Kalecki, M. (1937), 'The principle of increasing risk', *Economica*, **4**, 440–447.

Kalecki, M. (1954), *Theory of Economic Dynamics*, London: George Allen & Unwin.

Kalecki, M. (1971), *Selected Essays on the Dynamics of the Capitalist Economy, 1933–70*, Cambridge, UK: Cambridge University Press.

Kapeller, J. and B. Schütz (2012), 'Conspicuous consumption, inequality and debt: the nature of consumption-driven profit-led regimes', Working Paper No. 1213, Department of Economics, Johannes Kepler University of Linz.

Kim, Y.K. (2013), 'Household debt, financialization, and macroeconomic performance in the United States, 1951–2009', *Journal of Post Keynesian Economics*, **35** (4), 675–694.

Kim, Y.K., M. Setterfield and Y. Mei (2014), 'A theory of aggregate consumption', *European Journal of Economics and Economic Policies: Intervention*, **11** (1), 31–49.

Kumhof, M. and R. Ranciere (2010), 'Inequality, leverage and crises', IMF Working Papers 268, International Monetary Fund.

Kumhof, M., C. Lebarz, R. Ranciere, A.W. Richter and N.A. Throckmorton (2012), 'Income inequality and current account imbalances', IMF Working Papers 12/08, International Monetary Fund.

Lavoie, M. (1984), 'The endogenous flow of credit and the post-Keynesian theory of money', *Journal of Economic Issues*, **18**, 771–797.

Lavoie, M. (1992), *Foundations of Post-Keynesian Economic Analysis*, Aldershot, UK and Brookfield, VT, USA: Edward Elgar Publishing.

Lavoie, M. (1995), 'Interest rates in post-Keynesian models of growth and distribution', *Metroeconomica*, **46**, 146–177.

Lavoie, M. (1996), 'Horizontalism, structuralism, liquidity preference and the principle of increasing risk', *Scottish Journal of Political Economy*, **43**, 275–300.

Lavoie, M. (2008), 'Financialisation issues in a post-Keynesian stock–flow consistent model', *European Journal of Economics and Economic Policies: Intervention*, **5**, 331–356.

Lavoie, M. (2009), 'Cadrisme within a post-Keynesian model of growth and distribution', *Review of Political Economy*, **21**, 369–391.

Lima, G.T. and A.J.A. Meirelles (2007), 'Macrodynamics of debt regimes, financial instability and growth', *Cambridge Journal of Economics*, **31**, 563–580.

Ludvigson, S. and C. Steindel (1999), 'How important is the stock market effect on consumption?', *Federal Reserve Bank of New York Economic Policy Review*, July, 29–51.

Mehra, Y.P. (2001), 'The wealth effect in empirical life-cycle aggregate consumption equations', *Federal Reserve Bank of Richmond Economic Quarterly*, **87** (2), 45–68.

Meirelles, A.J.A. and G.T. Lima (2006), 'Debt, financial fragility, and economic growth: a Post Keynesian macromodel', *Journal of Post Keynesian Economics*, **29**, 93–115.

Moore, B.J. (1988), *Horizontalists and Verticalists: The Macroeconomics of Credit Money*, Cambridge, UK: Cambridge University Press.

Moore, B.J. (1989), 'The endogeneity of credit money', *Review of Political Economy*, **1**, 65–93.

Naastepad, C.W.M. and S. Storm (2007), 'OECD demand regimes (1960–2000)', *Journal of Post Keynesian Economics*, **29**, 211–246.

OECD (2012), OECD.StatExtracts, available at: http://stats.oecd.org/Index.aspx.

Onaran, Ö. and G. Galanis (2012), 'Is demand wage- or profit-led? National and global effects', Conditions of Work and Employment Series No. 40, International Labour Organization.

Onaran, Ö., E. Stockhammer and L. Grafl (2011), 'Financialisation, income distribution and aggregate demand in the USA', *Cambridge Journal of Economics*, **35**, 637–661.

Orhangazi, Ö. (2008), 'Financialisation and capital accumulation in the non-financial corporate sector: a theoretical and empirical investigation on the US economy: 1973–2003', *Cambridge Journal of Economics*, **32**, 863–886.

Palley, T. (1994), 'Debt, aggregate demand, and the business cycle: an analysis in the spirit of Kaldor and Minsky', *Journal of Post Keynesian Economics*, **16**, 371–390.

Palley, T. (2012), *From Crisis to Stagnation: The Destruction of Shared Prosperity and the Role of Economics*, Cambridge, UK: Cambridge University Press.

Rajan, R. (2010), *Fault Lines: How Hidden Fractures Still Threaten the World Economy*, Princeton, NJ: Princeton University Press.

Rowthorn, R.E. (1981), 'Demand, real wages and economic growth', Thames Papers in Political Economy, Autumn, London.

Ryoo, S. (2013), 'The paradox of debt and Minsky's financial instability hypothesis', *Metroeconomica*, **64**, 1–24.

Sapir, J. (2009), 'From financial crisis to turning point: how the USA "subprime crisis" turned into a world-wide one and will change the global economy', *Internationale Politik und Gesellschaft*, **1/2009**, 27–44.

Skott, P. and S. Ryoo (2008a), 'Macroeconomic implications of financialization', *Cambridge Journal of Economics*, **32**, 827–862.

Skott, P. and S. Ryoo (2008b), 'Financialization in Kaleckian economics with and without labor constraints', *European Journal of Economics and Economic Policies: Intervention*, **5**, 357–386.

Stiglitz, J. (2012), *The Price of Inequality: How Today's Divided Society Endangers Our Future*, New York: W.W. Norton.

Stockhammer, E. (2004), 'Financialisation and the slowdown of accumulation', *Cambridge Journal of Economics*, **28**, 719–741.

Stockhammer, E. (2010a), 'Income distribution, the finance-dominated accumulation regime, and the present crisis', in S. Dullien, E. Hein, A. Truger and T. van Treeck (eds), *The World Economy in Crisis – The Return of Keynesianism?*, Marburg: Metropolis.

Stockhammer, E. (2010b), 'Neoliberalism, income distribution and the causes of the crisis', Research on Money and Finance, Discussion Paper No. 19, Department of Economics, SOAS.

Stockhammer, E. (2012a), 'Financialization, income distribution and the crisis', *Investigación Económica*, **71** (279), 39–70.

Stockhammer, E. (2012b), 'Rising inequality as a root cause of the present crisis', Working Paper Series No. 282, Political Economy Research Institute (PERI), University of Massachusetts Amherst.

Stockhammer, E., Ö. Onaran and S. Ederer (2009), 'Functional income distribution and aggregate demand in the Euro area', *Cambridge Journal of Economics*, **33**, 139–159.

Stockhammer, E., E. Hein and L. Grafl (2011), 'Globalization and the effects of changes in functional income distribution on aggregate demand in Germany', *International Review of Applied Economics*, **25**, 1–23.

UNCTAD (2009), *The Global Economic Crisis: Systemic Failures and Multilateral Remedies*, New York: UNCTAD.

van Treeck, T. (2008), 'Reconsidering the investment–profit nexus in finance-led economies: an ARDL-based approach', *Metroeconomica*, **59**, 371–404.

van Treeck, T. (2009a), 'A synthetic stock–flow consistent macroeconomic model of financialisation', *Cambridge Journal of Economics*, **33**, 467–493.

van Treeck, T. (2009b), 'The political economy debate on "financialisation" – a macroeconomic perspective', *Review of International Political Economy*, **16** (5), 907–944.

van Treeck, T. and S. Sturn (2012), 'Income inequality as a cause of the Great Recession? A survey of current debates', Conditions of Work and Employment Series No. 39, International Labour Organization.

van Treeck, T., E. Hein and P. Dünhaupt (2007), 'Finanzsystem und wirtschaftliche Entwicklung: neuere Tendenzen in den USA und in Deutschland', IMK Studies 5/2007, Macroeconomic Policy Institute (IMK) at the Hans Böckler Foundation, Düsseldorf.

Wade, R. (2009), 'From global imbalances to global reorganisations', *Cambridge Journal of Economics*, **33**, 539–562.

Zezza, G. (2008), 'US growth, the housing market and the distribution of income', *Journal of Post Keynesian Economics*, **30**, 375–402.

3. Theories of financial crises as cumulative processes – an overview

Daniel Detzer and Hansjörg Herr

3.1 INTRODUCTION

Financial crises are no new phenomena. Even before market mechanisms dominated the whole economy, financial crises were possible. One of the most widely cited examples, the 'Tulip Mania', was a speculative bubble in 1637 in the Netherlands marked by extreme price increases of newly introduced tulip bulbs. When the bulb prices suddenly collapsed in a panic, many speculators became over-indebted and fell into bankruptcy. From the late eighteenth century on, when modern capitalism in England unfolded, financial crises were regular companions of capitalist development, however with different intensity in different historical periods. By the nineteenth century, economists had already started to develop models to try to understand financial crises. Karl Marx and John Stuart Mill, among others, famously analysed financial crises. The aim of this chapter is not to present a history of economic thought, and will thus not discuss early theories in great detail. However, as will be shown, many of the theories developed by economists of that time have been incorporated into later approaches to understanding financial crises. The present analysis is restricted to dynamic unsustainable processes which lead to financial crises in a medium-term horizon. By way of further clarification, this chapter will not focus on different capitalist regimes that may be more or less prone to financial crises. We also do not look at international financial crises. However, many of the approaches discussed can be easily transferred to the international level.

Knut Wicksell's ([1898] 1936) analysis of the interaction of two rates of return seems to us a suitable framework for discussing financial crises. Wicksell belongs to the Swedish school of neoclassical economists, which differed in many ways from the 'traditional' neoclassical school that later came to dominate mainstream economic thought. John Maynard Keynes and Hyman Minsky also followed the Wicksellian approach with fundamental alterations. In the Wicksellian approach, dynamic economic

115

processes are explained by the interaction of two rates of return, which typically diverge or at least do not tend to equilibrium. Both neoclassical and Keynesian economists agree that the money interest rate is important, but disagree on the second rate of return with which to compare it. In the neoclassical paradigm it is the natural rate of return which is determined in the real sphere. In the Keynesian paradigm it is the expected rate of return for investment in the business sector.

In section 3.2 we discuss financial crises in the neoclassical paradigm. These models stress the point that the monetary sphere, in one way or another, can for a certain period of time develop independently of the real sphere. As, according to the neoclassical dichotomy, the real sphere in the end dominates economic development, the monetary sphere sooner or later has to adjust. The general idea is that the monetary sphere in the short and medium term can become a disturbing factor for the real sphere. Irving Fisher and Milton Friedman, the icons of monetarist thinking in the twentieth century, made this point very strongly. In extreme cases developments in the monetary sphere can lead to financial crises with far-reaching repercussions for the real sphere. Knut Wicksell, Friedrich von Hayek, the Keynes of *A Treatise on Money* and Irving Fisher will be discussed in this section. We add Schumpeter to this list, in spite of the fact that he cannot be clearly subordinated under a specific paradigm.

Later, in his General Theory, John Maynard Keynes criticized the neoclassical dichotomy between a real and a monetary sphere. Instead, he proposed a model of a monetary production economy. In such an approach, money plays a key role and penetrates all spheres of the economy. Instabilities and financial crises all develop within the framework of a monetary production economy. Keynes and Minsky are presented in section 3.3.

There are also approaches which concentrate their analyses on the explanation of cumulative processes without presenting an overall economic model. Behavioural finance has particularly contributed to these types of models, which will be discussed in section 3.4. More specifically, Robert Shiller is taken as a representative of this school of thinking. In section 3.5, the different approaches to explaining financial crises will be compared. In section 3.6 we develop our own theory of financial crises on the basis of the Keynesian paradigm. Section 3.7 draws conclusions.

3.2 FINANCIAL CRISES AS DISTURBING FACTORS OF A STABLE REAL SPHERE

In this section neoclassical approaches, predominantly drawn from older neoclassical economists, to financial crises will be discussed. The reason for this is that modern versions of neoclassical thinking, which base their models on the assumption of efficient financial markets and rational expectations, are not suitable for explaining financial crises. In these approaches, an average economic agent acts on the basis of fundamentals and is perfectly informed about those fundamentals, and all endogenous variables reflect fundamentals. Changes in fundamentals immediately lead to a new equilibrium without any possibility of speculation. In this framework, systemic crises simply have no place. The same is the case in general equilibrium models in the tradition of Léon Walras, which cannot even introduce money in any meaningful way.

We start the analysis with *Knut Wicksell* ([1898] 1936, [1906] 1935), who explained the dynamics of capitalist economies by the interaction of two rates of return, the so-called natural rate of interest and the money interest rate.[1] The natural rate of interest is the interest rate of the neoclassical real sphere in an equilibrium constellation. It is the interest rate which, in the neoclassical capital market without money, equalizes savings and investment.

> There is a certain rate of interest on loans which is neutral in respect to commodity prices, and tends neither to raise nor to lower them. This is necessarily the same as the rate of interest which would be determined by supply and demand if no use were made of money and all lending were effected in the form of real capital goods. It comes to much the same thing to describe it as the current value of the natural rate of interest on capital. (Wicksell [1898] 1936, p. 102)

The money interest rate is determined in the monetary sphere mainly by the central bank and the banking system. As soon as the money interest rate is lower than the natural interest rate, a cumulative investment process is triggered. 'The number of people becoming entrepreneurs will be abnormally increased' (Wicksell [1898] 1936, p. 106). The resulting expansion leads to an inflationary process. Financing does not restrict expansionary processes, as the monetary system is 'elastic' (Wicksell [1898] 1936, p. 110). If the money interest rate is above the natural interest rate, a deflationary contraction process is triggered.

It is important to point out that, as soon as the two interest rates are not the same, a cumulative process develops which has no endogenous tendency towards equilibrium. For example, if the money rate is below the natural rate, the economy will come into a situation of overheating which has no tendency to be corrected. The economy is not understood as a pendulum, which after a disturbance finds its way back to equilibrium. The correct picture is rather a cylinder in motion on an inclined plane. As long as the money interest rate is not equal to the natural interest rate, 'the cylinder continues to move in one direction. Indeed it will, after some time, start "rolling": the motion is an acceleration one' (Wicksell [1898] 1936, p. 101). Only the central bank can stop the inflationary expansion by increasing the interest rate. Money supply becomes endogenous, whereas the central bank has to use the interest rate as the main policy tool. According to Wicksell, the natural rate of interest is not stable. Many changes in the real sphere can change the natural rate, for example changes in technology or changes of households' preference which lead to a new saving behaviour. This implies that the central bank, with its interest rate policy, has to follow the natural interest rate in a discretionary way.

Wicksell's approach serves as a suitable framework to explain financial crises. It stresses the character of capitalist development as a sequence of cumulative expansions and contractions which affect the whole economy. Methodologically, Wicksell starts in a constellation with full employment and price-level stability. A cumulative expansion period is triggered exogenously and leads to increasing instability and fragility. A fall of the money interest rate, for example, increases asset prices (prices of factories, houses, etc.) and aggregate demand at the same time, sparking an inflationary process and a change in relative prices. The production of goods with increasing relative prices is stimulated and, given full employment, the production of goods with falling relative prices is reduced.[2] Wicksell ([1898] 1936, p. 96) expects that increasing prices 'will in some measure "create its own drought". When prices have been rising steadily for some time, entrepreneurs will begin to reckon on the basis not merely of the prices already attained, but of a further rise of prices.' Given the arguments so far and assuming a certain difference between the natural rate of interest and the money interest rate, price-level changes will stabilize at a certain level. However, in a typical inflationary process, purely speculative activities based on expectations of further increasing asset prices stimulate an accelerating inflationary expansion. Such speculation destroys any anchor of the inflation rate, and the latter increases faster and faster. Any cumulative expansion must come to its end, giving way to a cumulative contraction phase which, if sharp enough, leads to systemic problems in the financial system.

Wicksell's model of cumulative expansions and contractions was taken over by a large number of economists in the early twentieth century. Hayek, in his business cycle model, and Keynes, in his *Treatise on Money*, were especially important.[3] For Hayek ([1929] 2012, [1931] 2012), the modern organization of credit faces an eminently difficult dilemma. Say's law postulates that aggregate supply exactly creates the aggregate demand to sell all products. For a barter economy this is obvious, because to offer a good also means to demand a good. A mismatch between demand and supply in a single market is possible, but there can never be a mismatch between aggregate supply and aggregate demand. Say's law crucially depends on the non-existence of money hoarding. As soon as money hoarding becomes possible, a situation can develop where nobody wants to buy and everybody wants to sell. Dishoarding can lead to excess demand. For Hayek, the interaction between savings and (net) investment is especially important. In the usual neoclassical capital market, savings imply the supply of additional credit in a certain period, and net investment means an additional demand for credit in the same period. The interest rate – determined in the real sphere, with the marginal productivity of capital on the one side and time preference of households on the other side – equalizes savings and investment in such a way that Say's law also holds in an economy with credit.

One of the key arguments of Hayek is that the modern credit system does not fit the vision of the neoclassical capital market. The influence 'of money should be sought in the fact that when the volume of money is elastic, there may exist a lack of rigidity in the relationship between saving and the creation of real capital' (Hayek [1929] 2012, p. 101). Funds for investment, according to the argument, come from savings and money creation. Hayek was very much impressed by the German economist Albert Hahn (1920), who had pointed out that in modern credit systems with commercial banks a credit creates a deposit, and not the other way round. The central bank has no direct instrument to stop a credit and deposit expansion when banks want to give credits. But now a problem is created for Hayek, who basically agreed with Hahn's theory. In modern credit organizations, the volume of credit becomes independent of savings. The volume of credit given by banks does not necessarily reflect the volume of savings. If credit demand increases for investment, for whatever reason, the interest rate does not act as a 'brake' for investment as it would if the neoclassical capital market worked as assumed according to the neoclassical model.

For Hayek, many factors can lead to an increase in investment without a corresponding increase in ex-ante savings, according to fundamentals in the real sphere. The credit system will respond with credit expansion without bankers knowing that credit demand is not driven by long-term fundamentals. Processes in the banking sector even support an endogenous credit expansion. A bank which does not follow the general trend of credit expansion is flooded with liquidity in the form of deposits and has the incentive to give more credit as well. During such a process, the monetary sphere becomes, in a sense, independent of the real sphere. However, in the long run the real sphere will dominate the nominal sphere. During an expansion real investment materializes which in the medium term is not profitable. An expansion not financed by savings leads to an 'artificial' increase in investment which is not able to earn the required long-term rate of return which is given by marginal productivity in equilibrium. Sooner or later a credit expansion must come to an end. During the following contraction the artificially increased capital stock will be destroyed. A crisis with the potential of a systemic financial crisis is the outcome.

John Maynard Keynes (1930) follows Wicksell and Hayek. However, he adds one important argument which later became one of the cornerstones of the Keynesian paradigm. From national accounting, Keynes deduces his so-called fundamental equations of the value of money. In a closed economy the net domestic product or national income (Y) equals wages (W) plus profits. The latter are divided into normal profit (Q_N) and extra or windfall profits (Q_E). Windfall profits are identical with undistributed profits of the enterprise sector. With P as the price level and Y_r as real income ($Y = Y_rP$) it follows $Y = Y_rP = W + Q_N + Q_E$. Isolating the price level, the equation of the value of money becomes $P = (W/Y_r) + (Q_N/Y_r) + (Q_E/Y_r)$. The term ($W/Y_r$) expresses unit-labour costs, the term (Q_N/Y_r) normal profits per unit of output or unit-profit costs.[4] Normal profits represent interest costs but also 'normal' dividends and other non-labour income flowing to households. It is assumed that in equilibrium all profits are distributed to households. Keynes, implicitly assuming monopolistic competition, argues that increases in unit-labour costs and profit costs are rolled over by firms and increase the price level.[5] Falling costs, of course, lead to a falling price level. Cost and price-level changes are independent of the demand constellation. A direct price–price effect is assumed as soon as macroeconomic cost levels change. This means that, in the framework of a closed economy and a comparative-static equilibrium analysis, firms are able to roll over costs without excess demand. If all firms in an industry, for example, need oil as an input and are confronted with higher oil prices, they will increase their output prices. If nominal unit-labour costs in the industry increase, firms will react in the same way.[6] This is an important difference to neoclassical models of price-level changes which use only excess demand or excess supply in the goods market as drivers for inflation and deflation.

Thus, in the model presented above, costs depend on (W/Y_r) and (Q_N/Y_r). Normal profits per output unit can change, but not in the same dynamic way as nominal unit-labour costs. Unit-labour costs depend on wage per hour and labour productivity. This can be shown when numerator and denominator in (W/Y_r) are divided by labour input. Productivity changes, at least in developed countries, are not very high and relatively stable. This implies that the most important factor that determines changes in costs and the price level is changes in nominal wages.[7] With this argument, Keynes presented a key additional factor for cumulative expansion and contraction processes.

Let us come to (Q_E/Y_r). From national accounting it follows that wind-fall profits are identical with investment minus household savings. Thus we get $Q_E = I - S_H$, with I as net investment and S_H as household savings.[8] Net investment higher than household saving implies excess demand in the goods market and an increase of the price level. In the opposite con-stellation a lack of demand leads to a goods market deflation. The more investment exceeds household savings, the higher the increase in the price level and the higher undistributed profits. Windfall profits used for invest-ment and consumption of capitalists or wealth owners lead to further demand and even higher profits; they become a 'widow's cruse' which remains undepleted whatever is spent. On the other hand, the more firms cut investment expenditure in a situation of a loss, the more losses they realize. Firms suffer from a 'Danaid jar' which can never be filled (Keynes 1930, p. 125).[9] With the widow's cruse and the Danaid jar, Keynes intro-duced an additional dynamic element into his model which leads to cumu-lative processes. In the General Theory, Keynes implicitly argues that in a situation of unused capacities higher demand leads to higher output. Higher demand in a situation of full capacity utilization increases the price level. This is the assumption made in the *Treatise*. Of course, there is an area of price–quantity effects when, during an expansion period, bottle-necks are reached in some industries and not in others.

In the *Treatise on Money*, explicitly referring to Wicksell, the interest rate which balances net investment and household savings and makes undistributed profits zero was called by Keynes the natural rate of inter-est. 'Every departure of the market rate from the natural rate tends . . . to set up a disturbance of the price level' (Keynes 1930, p. 139). As in all Wicksellian frameworks, money must be considered to be endogenous.

In the tradition of the *Treatise on Money* several constellations between cost inflation/cost deflation and demand inflation/demand deflation can be distinguished, which all are important for dynamic processes:

a. A combination of demand inflation and cost inflation leads to a cumulative expansion. A boom phase which, according to Keynes, can be caused by many factors typically leads sooner or later to such a constellation. As soon as bottlenecks are reached, economic expansions trigger demand inflations. Resulting higher profits in the enterprise sector typically stimulate further investment and luxury consumption of profit receivers. Both will lead to further undistributed profits. The expansion will lead to higher employment and in the end higher nominal wages. Furthermore, workers may defend their real wages and demand higher wages when a demand inflation starts. Both inflationary forces now reinforce each other and lead to a cumulative expansion.

b. A second cumulative constellation results from a combination of demand deflation and cost deflation. Shrinking demand decreases output and prices and increases unemployment. Higher unemployment can lead to nominal wage cuts and a further stimulation of the deflationary process. As soon as the wage anchor breaks, a cumulative deflationary wage price spiral together with a lack of demand and high losses of the enterprise sector develops. A systemic financial crisis in a system with high stocks of debt is then all but impossible to avoid.

c. The combination of cost inflation and demand deflation characterizes a constellation where, owing to a lack of demand, firms are not able to roll over all cost increases but the price level still rises. Such a stagflation leads to a profit squeeze. A stagflation is typical at the end of an expansion, for example when central banks start to fight inflation. Of course, other explanations of a stagflation are possible, such as a collapse of investment due to a negative expectation shock or price increase of natural resources in an overall stagnating economy.

Theoretically, the combination of cost deflation and demand inflation is also possible. Such a constellation fits, for example, a demand stimulating policy in a country suffering from a deflationary wage decrease.[10]

According to Keynes, nominal wages should not be flexible and nominal wages should never decrease – this is what Keynes repeatedly recommended. Nominal wage development should become a nominal anchor for price-level development (Riese 1986; Herr 2009). Actually, the nominal wage level should increase according to medium-term productivity development plus the target rate of inflation, thus becoming a nominal anchor for the desired inflation rate because, in this case, nominal unit-labour costs increase in line with the desired inflation rate. Keynes did not discuss financial crises explicitly, but for him it was clear that falling nominal wages are a disaster. 'Thus it is fortunate that the workers, though unconsciously, are instinctively more reasonable economists than the classical school, inasmuch as they resist reduction of money-wages' (Keynes 1936, p. 14). This leads us directly to Irving Fisher, who discussed the disastrous effects of goods market deflations.

Irving Fisher (1911) is the founder of the modern version of the quantity theory of money which was set out by David Hume and taken over by David Ricardo and almost all classical economists. Fisher argues, following the classical and neoclassical paradigm, that in the long run money is neutral and changes of money supply in the end affect only the price level. But what is important here is that changes in the money supply can have deep and destabilizing effects on the economy in the short and medium term. Periods of 'transition' from one equilibrium to another after an increase in the supply of money lead to 'action and reaction' and 'a cycle of "prosperity" and "depression"' (Fisher 1911, p. 72). Asset price bubbles and financial crises are extreme versions of such destructive disturbances created in the monetary sphere. Milton Friedman (1968) later argued in exactly the same way. Also, for him, money can become a fundamentally disturbing factor for the real economy. His recommendation to follow strict monetary targeting as an economic policy rule had the purpose of enforcing the neutrality of money also in the short run.

Under the impact of the Great Depression in the United States, Fisher (1933) wrote a paper which remains one of the cornerstones for understanding the destructive power of deflationary processes. For Fisher, a business cycle with its ups and downs is difficult to avoid and poses no fundamental threat. A problem is, however, that under certain conditions a 'normal' business cycle can get out of control, triggering a development which leads to a cumulative breakdown of the economy. In an almost Keynesian manner, Fisher argues that over-optimistic expectations lead to periods of expansion, including asset price bubbles. Herding and speculative behaviour trigger asset price inflations, which are usually combined with a large credit expansion. These are also phases of high GDP growth and high employment. When asset price inflations come to an end, asset price deflations are the ultimate result. The bigger the bubble is, the bigger will be the following asset price deflation. The end of an expansion period – like the beginning – depends on many factors and can only be clarified in a historical analysis. Asset price deflations lead to the destruction of wealth as well as to problems for speculators and other economic units in paying back their debt. Non-performing loans start to grow. Assets are sold under distress to be able to service debt, and panic leads to sharply falling asset prices.

Asset price inflations and following asset price deflations and non-performing loan problems are normal during capitalist development and over the business cycle. However, as mentioned, an economic downturn can spiral out of control, and developments like the Great Depression in the 1930s can result. The difference between a normal crisis and a disaster leading to a systemic financial crisis with deep repercussions for production and employment is a goods market deflation. A constellation of high debt and goods market deflation leads to an increase of the real debt burden by all debtors in the domestic currency.

> Then, *the very effort of individuals to lessen their burden of debts increases it, because of the mass effect of the stampede to liquidate in swelling each dollar owed.* Then we have the great paradox which, I submit, is the chief secret of most, if not all, great depressions: *The more the debtors pay, the more they owe.* (Fisher 1933, p. 344, emphasis in the original)

The non-performing loan problem explodes, credit chains break, credit supply freezes, and the coherence of financial markets erodes. The economic boat capsizes, as Fisher (1933) calls it. He also shows empirically that the deflation during the Great Depression increased the real debt burden in the USA in spite of the fact that nominal debt had been paid back.

For Fisher, the key channel between an asset market deflation and a goods market deflation is the lack of demand for goods and services and, at the same time, an increase of supply because firms with non-performing loans try to sell everything in an attempt to survive. The lack of demand is also caused by collapsing investment and decreasing consumption demand. Both shrink because of deflationary expectations, lower income and rising unemployment. Fisher remains a theorist of the quantity theory of money, as the only channel of goods market deflation is a lack of demand in relation to supply. The role of the nominal wage level as a nominal anchor against deflation does not exist in Fisher's thinking.

Nevertheless with his real debt effect of deflation, Fisher stressed one of the most destructive and important effects which creates a financial crisis and leads to a cumulative breakdown of the financial system. What can be learned from Fisher is that a goods market deflation in a situation of high domestic debt is one of the worst possible developments in a capitalist economy. And a capitalist economy without substantial debt is not imaginable. Minsky (1982, p. 393) correctly wrote: 'when Fisher . . . identified the characteristics of a debt deflation process . . . [he] identified essential forces which make for the observed instability of capitalist economies'.[11]

Joseph Schumpeter ([1911] 1934, [1961] 2008) developed a model of a boom–bust cycle which also includes the possibility of financial crises. Starting from an equilibrium situation, some entrepreneurs implement a new innovation (a new technology, a new product, a different organization of production, etc.). A stock of new inventions is always available. It is the entrepreneur who selects some of them and triggers economic development.[12] Entrepreneurship, which is very close to the Keynesian category of 'animal spirits' (Keynes 1936, p. 161), plays the key role during an expansion process. For Schumpeter, a precondition for a new wave of innovations is that the occurred instabilities due to previous innovation waves are settled and the economy is in an overall stable constellation. Capitalist development cannot take place without credit. Credit is created ad hoc (out of nothing) (Schumpeter [1911] 1934, p. 107) by the banking system. 'The essential function of credit in our sense consists in enabling the entrepreneur to withdraw the producers' goods which he needs from their previous employment, by exercising a demand for them, and thereby to force the economic system into new channels' (Schumpeter [1911] 1934, p. 106). New credit leads to demand inflation and forced household savings, as entrepreneurs enter the goods market as additional demanders to get the means to realize their investments.

Schumpeter assumes a kind of herding behaviour of firms following the innovative entrepreneurs. The 'followers' imitate the innovation to capture some of the extra profits which can be earned in the new markets. They are also forced to do so by competition. If they do not follow they will sooner or later be eliminated by the market. Driven by high investment and credit expansion, a boom phase develops. The expansion phase is accompanied by a further, often bigger and more visible, phenomenon (Schumpeter [1961] 2008, Chapter 4). The positive economic development stimulates companies without innovating to expand or enter the new markets. Speculation, in the narrow sense, can occur and lead to asset price inflations. Last but not least, private households may take consumption loans and further stimulate credit expansion and demand. Schumpeter divides credit into productive and unproductive credit, where the former leads to new innovations or increases productivity, while the latter does not.

For Schumpeter the end of an expansion period depends, like the beginning, on history and cannot be explained mechanically. However, herding of entrepreneurs and followers leads to fast increases of capacities accompanied with credit expansion. For Schumpeter, it is clear that such a development is unsustainable and must sooner or later come to an end. What is important is that, during the crisis phase when investment, demand in general and output shrink, not all firms will survive. Firms which were not innovative enough will go bankrupt. In particular, unproductive loans to firms with low innovative power and to consumers lead to problems. Economic crises and, to a certain extent, financial crises as well are part of the normal process of capitalist development and its capacity to increase productivity and innovate. Schumpeter ([1942] 1976) speaks about a process of creative destruction which is very close to Karl Marx's ([1867] 2008) idea of relative surplus value creation, which is stimulated by the chance of extra profits innovative firms can earn. In Schumpeter's theoretical model, the economy falls back into an equilibrium constellation, however with a higher level of productivity and new products. A new expansion can start when entrepreneurial spirits are high again and finance is available.

However, Schumpeter ([1961] 2008, p. 158f.) also argued that crises can spin out of control. In such a case, not only are less innovative firms eliminated, but good firms also break down. Such a development is dysfunctional and harmful for economic development. He makes a difference here between a recession, as the normal process that follows the expansion, and a depression, which describes this dysfunctional development. The depression is characterized by an undershooting of the new equilibrium, where cumulative processes (for example Fisher's debt deflation) drive the economy further away from the equilibrium constellation. Whether the recession turns into a depression depends, according to Schumpeter, on external circumstances and is not predictable. However, some factors make it more likely to happen, including, for example: the general mentality and mood in the business community and the general public; the extent of credit expansion (in particular unproductive credit) during the phase of prosperity; and the extent of occurred maladjustment of capacities and of deceptive business practices.

3.3 THE KEYNESIAN APPROACH WITH NO DICHOTOMY BETWEEN A REAL AND A MONETARY SPHERE

3.3.1 Keynes's Fundamental Modification of the Wicksellian Approach

In the General Theory, Keynes criticized the Wicksellian approach, especially based on two points. Firstly, Keynes gave up the idea of a natural rate of interest:

> In my *Treatise on Money* I defined what purported to be a unique rate of interest, which I called the *natural rate* of interest – namely the rate of interest which . . . preserved equality between the rate of saving . . . and the rate of investment . . . I had, however, overlooked the fact that in any given society there is, on this definition, a *different* natural rate of interest for each hypothetical level of employment. (Keynes 1936, p. 242, emphasis in the original)

With this insight the natural sphere as a reference point of the money interest rates no longer exists. Secondly, Keynes criticized the idea of all Wicksellians that credit supply is the sum of savings plus money creation by the banking system, whereby the latter becomes a disturbing factor and creates all types of complications. This idea 'has led to the worst muddles of all' (Keynes 1936, p. 183). Wicksellians conclude that, 'if the quantity of money could only be kept *constant* in all circumstances, none of these complications would arise, since the evils supposed to result from the supposed excess of investment over savings proper would cease to be possible. But at this point we are in deep water.'[13] Keynes came to the conclusion that in a capitalist economy a market between savings and investment, which is equalized by an interest rate, simply does not exist. In such a case, the credit market is composed of credit supply and credit demand (as stocks), but savings (as flows) are of no importance. With this insight, Say's law also breaks down and the law of effective demand becomes the key to determining output and employment.

Instead of the concept of an interaction between a real sphere and a monetary sphere, which can lead to instability and financial crises, Keynes developed a model of a *monetary production economy* (Keynes [1933] 1973). He supported the view of Karl Marx ([1867] 2008) that the nucleus of a capitalist economy can be expressed by $M - C - (M + \Delta M)$, with M as money, C as commodities and ΔM as profit. Money is invested in productive processes to earn more money. C also stands for the production process, which is an income creating process as well. Both Keynes and Marx ([1894] 2010) distinguished between management, which is investing in productive capital, and economic agents, which finance firms. Marx ([1894] 2010) imagined a production process, which is embedded in credit relationships, with the formula $(M_{Fin} - M) - C - (M + \Delta M) - (M_{Fin} + \Delta M_{Int})$ with $(M_{Fin} - M)$ showing that management gets funds from financial institutions and private wealth owners (M_{Fin}) to invest in productive capital. From the money flowing back to firms, loans have to be paid back to creditors including interest. This is shown by $(M + \Delta M) - (M_{Fin} + \Delta M_{Int})$. The important point is that credit given to firms and investment in productive capital must be considered as a potentially unstable process. For example, not enough or too much capital might be invested to serve consumption demand. The whole system of money advances may also break down on a large scale and end in a situation where credit cannot be paid back.

For Keynes, uncertainty plays a central role in a monetary production economy. It is not only the uncertainty which exists in all societies, for example, about the harvest in the coming years; what is important is uncertainty created by the market mechanism itself. Uncertainty means that all future events are unknown and probability models are insufficient to overcome uncertainty. Economic agents know that there are known unknowns and even unknown unknowns. The construct of a real sphere, including a capital market with savings as supply and net investment as demand, in Keynesian thinking, does not exist. A real sphere also cannot serve as an anchor for expectations. It follows that expectations must be considered unstable under certain conditions. Economic agents can also have different expectations and expectations can be wrong. Former decisions, which may have seemed rational at the time they were taken, may be judged irrational with hindsight (Herr 2011b). In the Keynesian paradigm for equilibrium models, expectations have to be considered as exogenous. They depend on historical developments not only in the economic sphere but also on social and political developments and institutions. A large part of economic development then depends on exogenously given expectations. From this perspective, economic development can be modelled as a sequence of time periods all shaped from historical specific expectations. Long-term economic trends as a result of a development of a real sphere do not exist. Empirically, measured trends are the result of the string of shorter sequences all shaped by expectations (F. Hahn 1981).[14]

Uncertainty leads to certain techniques or behaviour by economic agents to cope with uncertainty. Keynes gives three examples of such behaviour:

> Agents assume that the present is a much more serviceable guide to the future than a candid examination of past experiences would show . . . We assume that the *existing* state of opinion as expressed in prices and the character of existing output is based on a correct summing up of future prospects . . . Knowing that our own individual judgment is worthless, we endeavour to fall back on the judgement of the rest of the world . . . The psychology of a society of individuals each of whom is endeavouring to copy the others leads to what we may strictly term a *conventional* judgment. (Keynes 1937c, p. 214)

Many different techniques are possible to simplify decisions in a world of uncertainty, and Keynes analysed only some of them. The tendency towards a conventional judgement or 'state of confidence' (as Keynes 1936, Chapter 12, called it) especially leads to herding behaviour. Herding is one of the most powerful feedback mechanisms leading to unsustainable expansions and financial crises. Keynes is very close here to some ideas later developed within behavioural economics and especially behavioural finance.[15] This allows the integration of research results from behavioural economics into Keynesian thinking (see for example King 2013).

Keynes (1936, 1937c) followed Wicksell in modelling the economic system as the interaction of two rates of return. One of the two rates is the money interest rate. It is not simply fixed by the central bank; it is given by the intersection between the money supply function and the money demand function. Money supply is given exogenously by the central bank. Money demand depends on the demand for money for transaction purposes and hoarding. The latter fulfils the function to protect individual agents in an uncertain world from the imponderability of a capitalist economy and earns a liquidity premium. The marginal liquidity premium decreases with increases of money holdings for hoarding purposes. A household will hoard money as long as the marginal liquidity premium is higher than the money interest rates. This makes the demand for hoarding a function of the interest rate under the condition of a given level of uncertainty. The equilibrium interest rate is given at the intersection of money demand and money supply. An increase in the level of uncertainty leads to a higher level of the liquidity premium, a desire to hold more liquidity. Given the demand for transaction purposes and money supply, the market outcome is an increase of the interest rate. From a modern post-Keynesian perspective, this model is a step backwards compared to the *Treatise on Money*, where money supply was implicitly endogenous. However, it allows Keynes to give credit supply, and thus the creditor, an active function in economic development (see Herr 2014).[16]

The second rate of return is the marginal efficiency of capital, a rate of return of investment expressed as an interest rate and calculated by management carrying out investment in productive capital. Keynes (1936, p. 135) defines it as follows: 'I define the marginal efficiency of capital as being equal to that rate of discount which would make the present value of the series of annuities given by the returns expected from the capital-asset during its life just equal to its supply price.' The marginal efficiency of capital has nothing to do with a marginal productivity of capital. It is determined mainly by the expected future yields an investment project creates, but also by the sum of money which has to be spent today to invest. The marginal efficiency of capital in the end depends on animal spirits or, as Schumpeter called it, entrepreneurship.

Keynes models economic dynamics via the interaction between the interest rate and the marginal efficiency of capital. As long as the latter is higher than the former, investment will be carried out and an investment–income creation process starts. As soon as the marginal efficiency of capital falls below the interest rate, investment will collapse. The consequence is a fall in income and employment. As in Wicksell, there is no market mechanism which could adjust the two rates of return automatically or quickly. The opposite is the case: when, owing to a negative expectation shock, the marginal efficiency of capital collapses as future yields are calculated more cautiously, the money interest rate increases as demand for money for hoarding increases. In periods of optimism, the marginal efficiency of capital increases and the interest rate simultaneously decreases (see Keynes 1936, Chapter 22, 1937c). The interaction between the two rates leads to periods of high investment and high income creation and periods of low or no investment and shrinking income creation. Also possible in the Keynesian framework is a period of long-term stagnation, based on depressed animal spirits and a conventional judgement which does not change. There is no anchor for the marginal efficiency of capital in any kind of fundamentals as in a neoclassical tradition. In Keynes's approach the economy is part of society and there are many linkages between economic development and development in the society as a whole. Expectations are one of these linkages. Especially in an economy without stabilizing institutions, expectations may change quickly and substantially. This 'openness' of the Keynesians system makes the economic system potentially very unstable, and can result in financial crises.

Keynes distinguished between expectations of managers and expectations of agents in the stock market. Managers, like all economic agents, can become more or less optimistic. However, their expectations are based on the situation and a relatively good knowledge about the industry. Agents in the stock market are less informed about the situation in an industry, or even do not care about it. One consequence is that expectations in stock markets typically change more violently than expectations of managers, and stock markets can thus be used as casinos for speculation. In the stock market, even 'professional investment may be linked to those newspaper competitions in which the competitors have to pick out the six prettiest faces from a hundred photographs, the prize being awarded to the competitor whose choice most nearly corresponds to the average preferences of the competitors as a whole' (Keynes 1936, p. 156). This kind of speculation can lead to self-reflexive developments in asset markets and to extreme asset price inflations and ensuing asset price deflations. Such developments are not restricted to stock markets. These same principles can be extended to all kinds of asset markets, like real estate, gold or currencies.

Let us come back to the topic of an endogenous money supply. Keynes (1936, 1937c) gave creditors an active role in economic development. The disadvantage of Keynes's approach is that money supply is given exogenously, and the banking system is absolutely passive. The key role in determining credit supply and the interest rate is taken over by wealth owners who increase or decrease their credit supply (desire for hoarding). The finance motive of Keynes (1937a, 1937b) delivers elements of an endogenous money supply, but Keynes's approach remains insufficient (see also Lucarelli 2013). Post-Keynesian models have long since followed the idea of an endogenous supply of money. The central bank sets the interest rate, whereas the commercial banking system decides how much credit it takes. Credit expansion by commercial banks depends on credit demand by the enterprise sector or other borrowers. For macroeconomic credit supply, wealth owners usually play a subordinate role, as the commercial banking system, together with the central bank, dominates the credit market (for an overview of the broad literature about endogenous money supply see Lavoie 2011).[17]

In modern Keynesian thinking, there are two channels to give banks an active role. Banks take credits in order to give credits. Usually they take short-term deposits or other forms of short-term debt and grant long-term credits. The interest spread between taking a credit and lending covers not only the costs of banking and bank profit, but also what can be called an 'uncertainty premium'. According to the level of uncertainty, the uncertainty premium will be high or low. The existence of an uncertainty premium implies that the central bank cannot dictate long-term interest rates, which are important for investment in productive capital. The power of the central bank is asymmetric. It can always push up the long-term interest rate by increasing the refinancing rate. But it cannot reduce the long-term interest rate to very low levels even if the refinancing rate is zero when banks have a high uncertainty premium.

Credit rationing by the banking system also plays an important role in determining the availability of credit. In a world of uncertainty not all credit demanders will be satisfied. It is one of the big shortcomings in the standard model of asset markets to assume that credit demand and credit supply functions intersect and all credit demanders get credit at the market interest rate.[18] Banks check whether a debtor has adequate collateral, offers a viable investment project, has high expected income, and so on. Credit demanders who do not fulfil certain standards do usually not get credit. Even a very high interest rate cannot convince a creditor to give credit when she or he expects that the credit cannot be paid back. In a situation of asymmetric information banks and other credit suppliers also will not increase the interest rate to the level the market would allow. They know that a high interest rate leads to adverse selection, as the serious credit demanders leave the market and the risk-loving and desperate debtors, with a high likelihood of default, are left. The intensity of credit rationing depends on the level of uncertainty. In a boom, when positive expectations prevail, banks are relatively lax about giving out credit. When confidence breaks down in a crisis, banks will follow a policy of strict credit rationing. Credit rationing by commercial banks significantly reduces the power of central banks to stimulate the economy. In a situation of high uncertainty, even very low interest rates do not help to overcome strict credit rationing. From a New Keynesian point of view, credit rationing, based on asymmetric information, has been demonstrated by Stiglitz and Weiss (1981) and Stiglitz and Greenwald (2003). Wolfson (1996) shows from a post-Keynesian perspective that, under uncertainty, credit rationing can occur simply by asymmetric expectations, that is, the same information is evaluated differently by borrower and lender.

Keynes also highlighted the importance of borrower's and lender's risk:

> Two types of risks affect the volume of investment which have not commonly been distinguished ... The first is the entrepreneur's or borrower's risk and arises out of doubts in his own mind as to the probability of his actually earning the prospective yields for which he hopes ... [A] second type of risk is relevant which we may call the lender's risk. This may be due either to moral hazard ... or ... involuntary default due to the disappointment of expectations. (Keynes 1936, p. 144)

However, he never explicitly developed a model of credit and financial crises. All elements for such a model exist within Keynes's writings, but were never formally put together. It was Hyman Minsky who developed a Keynesian model with the explicit analysis of credit relationships and financial crises.

3.3.2 Minsky's Financial Instability Hypothesis

Hyman Minsky (see especially 1975, 1982, [1986] 2008) had already developed his financial instability hypothesis by the 1960s. He describes his contribution to economics as an interpretation of the essence of Keynes's publication of *The General Theory of Employment, Interest and Money* in 1936. His theory was also influenced by Schumpeter's credit view of money. Minsky's theory is based on two key theorems: firstly, an economy has financing regimes under which it is stable and financing regimes under which it is unstable; and, secondly, during periods of prosperity the economy can move from stable to unstable regimes. Minsky, therefore, does not interpret financial instability as caused by exogenous shocks, but rather sees the occurrence of financial instability and financial crisis as inherent features of capitalist economies (Minsky 1992). This section will outline Minsky's main theoretical concepts.

An economic unit has payment commitments out of its debt liabilities. Those commitments are fixed in nominal terms and have to be paid at predefined dates. At the same time, it expects incoming cash flows to serve those commitments. Cash flows, in turn, are uncertain and depend on conditions in product markets, and so on. Minsky defines cash flow–debt relations for three types of economic units: hedge, speculative and ultra-speculative/Ponzi units. A hedge unit has sufficient expected cash flows to serve all future payment commitments (interest and principal) when they occur. A hedge unit often exhibits a high share of equity in relation to debt. A speculative unit expects cash receipts that are sufficient to cover interest payments, but not to pay back the principal. Only in the long run are expected cash flows sufficient to reimburse the lenders in full. Until then, a speculative unit needs to roll over its debt. Incoming cash flows of a Ponzi unit are not even expected to be sufficient to cover the interest payments in any period. Only during the final periods are large cash flows expected, thus allowing for repayment. Until then, a Ponzi unit needs to capitalize interest payments. Hence, it needs to roll over the principal and find new financing for the accruing interest. A financial system can be described as robust if small changes in cash flows, capitalization rates or commitments currently served will not inhibit the ability of most units to meet their financial commitments. The opposite is true for fragile systems. Here, small changes in the above-mentioned variables will have detrimental effects so that many units fail to meet their financial commitments. Therefore, the economy becomes more fragile when the relative weight of hedge units to speculative and Ponzi units declines (Minsky 1982, pp. 66–68, 105–108).

Minsky modelled the investment decision as the interrelation between current output prices and asset prices. Current output prices of investment goods can be seen as the supply price for new investment. It depends on money wages, labour productivity, the short-run interest rate and a profit mark-up. This price is regarded as stable in the short run when capacity utilization is at normal levels. Prices in asset markets are the valuation of already existing investment goods and determine the demand price for new investment.[19] Asset prices are equal to the present value of expected net cash flows from investment goods and depend mainly on the state of uncertainty and the capitalization rate. The capitalization rate is given by the interest rate. For investment to take place, it is necessary that the demand price is above the supply price. If this condition is fulfilled and there are no financing constraints, firms will invest until the demand price of investment projects is equal to their supply prices. Even if the demand price does not change, supply prices will start to increase as soon as the economy approaches full capacity utilization. Investment demand, however, is usually restricted by finance before this point is reached. A firm will only be able to invest without changing its current debt and liquidity position as long as the investment is financed by free cash flows. Higher investment requires external finance. If external debt finance is used, the borrower will incur fixed future payment commitments, while profits from the investment project remain uncertain. This increases the risk of insolvency. The borrower will discount a 'margin of safety' from the demand price, accounting for the borrower's risk he or she perceives. Higher indebtedness also increases the lender's risk, because the equity buffer, as protection for the lender, in relation to debt decreases and the debtor moves towards a more fragile situation. As compensation for this perceived lender's risk the lender will ask for higher interest payments, higher collateral and so on to secure the lending. Therefore, perceived borrower's risk decreases the demand price and lender's risk increases the supply price. Thus, when firms keep increasing their borrowing, demand prices will progressively decrease and, at the same time, supply prices will continuously increase. As soon as both prices become equal, investment stops. Investment determined in this way will usually be much smaller than without the existence of borrower's and lender's risks. The discount taken from the demand price and the surcharge on the supply price are the so-called 'margins of safety'. The higher the perceived risks are, the higher the discount and surcharge.

Based on those theoretical foundations, Minsky was then able to model how an economic system can create a boom and how it moves during the boom from financial stability to financial fragility, which then turns into a bust. Minsky developed a model of an endogenous beginning of an expansion phase. It is assumed that the economy has just gone through a crisis, whereby most speculative units have been wiped out. Borrowers and lenders are very conservative regarding finance after their recent crisis experience. Low indebtedness leads to a phase of stability – investment and profits are low but stable. In this phase, expectations are fulfilled. Minsky now assumes that a phase of stability leads to higher confidence. Borrowers become more optimistic in their profit expectations and are gradually willing to take more credit. At the same time a phase of stable profits and low indebtedness allows lenders to register low default rates. Thus, they will reduce their margins of safety; that is, they are willing to provide more finance at lower cost. A higher level of debt-financed investment is now possible.

There are further feedback mechanisms. Higher investment leads to higher profits as a result of increasing output at given prices. Higher profits in turn have three feedback effects. Firstly, they allow borrowers to fulfil their past debt commitments. This, as mentioned, encourages lenders and borrowers to reduce their margins of safety and, therefore, increases the share of debt-financed investment. Secondly, if the positive developments of current profits are regarded as permanent, it will increase expected funds for internally financed investment. Here, Minsky follows the Kaleckian relation between profits and investment expenditures. Thirdly, it increases the expectations about future cash flows from new investment. These three mechanisms lead to a further increase in internally and externally financed investment. The feedback loop can start again.

Minsky held an endogenous money view, which implies that money is created by banks' credit expansions during a period of high investment.

The higher stock of money will (with given portfolio preferences) in turn lead to an increase in the demand for assets. Resulting higher asset prices will further stimulate investment and increase the value of collateral. Additionally, following Keynes's (1936, 1937c) argument, the desire to hoard money depends on the level of uncertainty. The overall increased confidence, as a result of higher profits and the validation of expectations, will lower the desire to hold money. Therefore, the public will be willing to hold more illiquid assets instead. This again increases asset prices and stimulates investment even further (De Antoni 2006).

During a boom phase the indebtedness of all economic units in the economy swells and leverage ratios increase. The margins of safety are reduced and expected cash flows exceed payment commitments only slightly and not throughout all future periods. More short-term lending will also take place. The relative weight of Ponzi and speculative units increases during the boom. As a result, only small deviations from expectations can lead to defaults of borrowers. The system moves from a financial structure that is stable to one that is more and more fragile (Minsky 1975, 1986).

There is an often criticized inconsistency in Minsky's theory. If investment leads to profits and profits to investment, the debt–equity ratio will not necessarily increase. The criticism holds if one assumes a closed economy in which there is only one firm, workers consume all their income, and profits are not distributed. However, as soon as many heterogeneous firms exist, investment of one firm will not necessarily correspond to the profits of that particular firm. Therefore, while the debt–equity ratio of the sector as a whole may not deteriorate, in parts of the enterprise sectors this ratio may increase. The distribution of profits and workers' savings are also important. In this case firms are forced to borrow to finance investment. If a firm wants to increase its debt-to-equity ratio (for example to increase its return on equity) it can always do so by increasing its pay-outs or by share buybacks. See for the debate Toporowski (2007), as well as Lavoie and Seccareccia (2001).

In Minsky's theory, the boom comes to an end when investment collapses. Typically it is the central bank which curbs investment. Inflationary pressure due to the boom will persuade the central bank to increase its interest rate. Bottlenecks in the financial system, for example due to liquidity or capital constraints, will also lead to an increase in the interest rate on loans. According to Minsky (1982) financial innovations can stimulate and extend a boom phase, but in the end an increase in interest rates will stop a boom.

The increase in the interest rate leads to the negative net worth of some Ponzi units. The net worth of speculative and hedge units also decreases.

Credit ratings of borrowers are lowered. This, together with the increase in the interest rate, leads to further declining investment. Moreover, speculative and Ponzi-financed firms get into trouble refinancing their debt and, therefore, cannot fulfil their obligations to banks. Actual cash flows of banks fall below expected cash flows, so that these also need to raise new finance or sell assets. Furthermore, other units in the system will try to fulfil their commitments by selling assets. Therefore, asset values fall and an asset price deflation is triggered. Distress in the financial system and the shortage of liquidity further reduce investment. Because of this, profits decline, and this further depresses prices for assets. Additionally, cash flows of firms are lower than expected. As a result, some hedge units become speculative units. Increasing defaults decrease the confidence of lenders and borrowers, who will realize their margins of safety were too low. Borrowers' and lenders' risk increases further. Thus, cash flows by firms will not be used for new investment projects but rather to reduce their debt ratio or to buy financial assets. Financial institutions also try to deleverage by reducing credits. In this circumstance, firms', financial institutions' and even private wealth owners' main objectives are to repair their balance sheets. Negative wealth effects dampen consumption demand. All these developments lead to a process of shrinking aggregate demand intensified by negative multiplier effects in the goods market (Minsky 1975, 1986).

Whether this process turns into a deep depression or just a mild recession can be influenced by the action taken by the central bank and the government. Minsky argued that the main task of the central bank is to stabilize asset prices. This can be done either by direct interventions in the asset market or by providing liquidity to units that have trouble refinancing their positions. The government should increase its deficit during a downturn to stabilize the cash flows of firms.

Minsky's work delivers, without a doubt, the most distinct explanation for the causes of financial instabilities and crisis in an economy. The basis of his theoretical approach is the Keynesian paradigm whereby he introduced the dimension of debt and debt quotas into the analysis, something Keynes neglected. Minsky constructed a whole set of feedback mechanisms which lead to cumulative processes, in the tradition of Wicksell. Many of them were later discussed in more detail in behavioural finance.

Charles Kindleberger explicitly built his historical analysis of financial crises on Minsky's approach (see Kindleberger and Aliber 2011).[20] His historical analysis added to the understanding of financial crises. Firstly, several factors that could lead to herding behaviour were distinguished, for example the belief that others are better informed, the psychology of group thinking, a slow adjustment of individuals to a conventional judgement, hysteria in the light of increasing asset prices, and investors' beliefs in the wrong model. Secondly, in the last phase of a bubble, greed and fraud are common phenomena. Thirdly, the role of the central bank as lender of last resort is stressed. Finally, the historical analysis required that international crises and the contagion mechanism should explicitly be taken into account.

3.4 BEHAVIOURAL FINANCE

3.4.1 Basics of Behavioural Finance

Behavioural finance tries to explain people's economic decisions by combining findings of behavioural and cognitive research with traditional economics and finance. It was, in particular, driven by the failure of conventional theory (utility maximization of rational investors in efficient markets) to explain many empirical developments. Behavioural economics started developing in the 1960s and 1970s, when psychologists began to examine economic decision-making processes. Among the most famous of those psychologists are Kahneman and Tversky (1974), who detailed the heuristics and biases of humans who make decisions under uncertainty. Their later developed prospect theory was awarded a Nobel Prize. At the same time, increasing empirical findings that raised doubts about the validity of some key ideas in finance – the efficient market hypothesis and the capital asset pricing model – were collected. It was found that in many instances the behaviour and decisions of market participants did not fit the assumptions of standard theories. There is a vast and growing amount of literature in this field. Baker and Nofsinger (2010) identified four prevalent key themes: heuristics, framing, emotions and market impact.

Heuristics are means of reducing the cognitive resources necessary to find solutions to certain problems. They can be described as mental shortcuts and are often referred to as rules of thumb. They help individuals to make decisions under uncertainty with a limited ability to quantify the likelihood of outcomes. Researchers have identified a vast and still growing number of heuristics that have an effect on financial decision-making processes. Among them are affect, representativeness, availability, anchoring, adjustment, familiarity, overconfidence, the status quo, loss and regret aversion, ambiguity aversion, conservatism, and mental accounting.

Framing means that the decisions taken by people who have different options are strongly influenced by how their choices are framed.

Essentially, people confronted with exactly the same problem may choose different alternatives, depending on how the problem is presented to them.

Emotions and associated human unconscious needs, fantasies and fears also drive decisions. The underlying idea is that emotions and feelings influence psychic reality in manifold ways and areas. They may explain sudden changes in expectations and abrupt breakdowns of markets. Some of the research in this category investigates relations between investors' moods, which depend on factors like sunshine, weather or sporting events, and their investment decisions. Others found that most investors assume they are cleverer than the average investor and are convinced they can beat the market. It also was found that investors believe that an increase in asset prices will go on for ever – in spite of historical precedent.

The last key theme in this field of research focuses on *market impact.* This investigates whether and how cognitive errors and biases of individuals or groups affect market outcomes and prices and prevent financial markets from being efficient. In efficient markets agents use all information about the value of an asset available to them. In stock markets, so to speak, all agents calculate the future cash flows of all companies and calculate their present value, all investors having the same knowledge and believing in the same model to explain the world. If some investors make mistakes in their expectations, the mistakes have a normal distribution and cancel each other out. If this is not the case, arbitrage trades by the majority of informed investors correct any errors in the market. Under such assumptions asset prices will be ruled by fundamentals (Black 1986). Shleifer (2000, p. 24) stated that 'market efficiency only emerges as an extreme special case unlikely to hold under plausible circumstances'. He names two key conditions in the theory that explain the deviations from efficient market outcomes – limits to arbitrage and investors' sentiment. Limited arbitrage prevents the informed investors from trading away price deviations caused by irrational investors. Investors' sentiment is responsible for disturbance of efficient prices in the first place. Research, for example, has shown that, if noise traders'[21] sentiments are unpredictable and correlated, arbitrage may not take place. If arbitrageurs have limited horizons and their risk-bearing capacity is limited, they have to worry about having to liquidate the asset in mispriced markets even if they believe, in the end, the fundamentals work out. Therefore, the aggressiveness of arbitrageurs may be limited, and large divergences between fundamental and market prices can occur (Shleifer 2000).

It is often argued that well-informed arbitrageurs are professional investment fund managers who use outside investors' money. However, it has been discovered that investment fund managers follow the market and enforce herding. If investment fund managers tried to gain through an arbitrage strategy and the prices in the short and medium term deviated still further from their fundamental value, funds would make a temporary loss. Owing to the short-sightedness of outside investors, this would lead to a withdrawal of funds away from arbitrageurs, so that they might be forced to close their positions and realize losses. This contributes additionally to the 'irrational trend'. Managers who, in the short term, are not as successful as others will probably lose their jobs. When a bubble later comes to an end, all managers realize losses and then the market is made responsible for the development. As investment managers know these mechanisms, they do not follow arbitrage strategies but follow the herd, even if they have superior knowledge.

Studies have found that some investors base their investment decisions on extrapolative expectations and trend chasing. Additionally, there are some technical features in financial markets that lead to positive feedback mechanisms like stop-loss orders, or liquidations after unfulfilled margin calls. As opposed to conventional theory, better-informed arbitrageurs will not trade prices back to fundamental levels but will jump on the bandwagon and try to increase gains by anticipating the trading strategy of uninformed investors. Therefore, they will rationally amplify the bubble in the hope of selling assets before the bubble comes to its end. This case is very close to Keynes's example of the beauty contest explained in section 3.3.1 (Shleifer 2000).

While there is a large catalogue of empirical findings of human behaviour and a growing volume of literature that tries to integrate these behavioural findings in models of financial markets, behavioural finance does not provide a unified framework or even an alternative paradigm to standard mainstream theory. Currently, there is a range of models which all focus on different specific points. They all show that financial markets do not work in the way the neoclassical model, including the theory of efficient financial markets, assumes. In section 3.4.2, this chapter presents the views of Robert Shiller, who combines many findings from behavioural economics and psychology to explain the occurrence of bubbles.

3.4.2 Robert Shiller's Explanation of Asset Price Bubbles

As a student, Shiller was influenced by Charles Kindleberger and, thus, similarities between his views and Kindleberger's perceptions of bubbles and financial crises are not surprising. Shiller (2005, 2012) analysed the new economy stock market bubble in the 1990s and the real estate bubble in the 2000s which led to the Great Recession in 2009. From this, he developed a more general theory of bubbles, which he defines as:

a situation in which news of price increases spur investors' enthusiasm, which spreads by psychological contagion from person to person, in the process amplifying stories that might justify the price increases and bringing in a larger and larger class of investors, who despite doubts about the real value of an investment, are drawn to it partly through envy of others' successes and partly through a gambler's excitement. (Shiller 2012, p. 245)

A bubble develops as follows:

1. There are some initial price increases (precipitating factors).
2. These are supported by certain feedback loops, which lead to further price increases.
3. News media draw attention towards some stories. New era stories are of special relevance.
4. Those stories justify the price increases.
5. This draws more people into the market to buy, which in turn increases prices even more.

The precipitating factors are exogenous and reflect unique historical developments, which lead to an initial upward movement in prices. To explain how the initial price increases reproduce themselves, feedback loops are introduced. Here, Shiller mentions direct price–price feedbacks, where further price increases are triggered via investors' enthusiasm and expectations based on initially increasing prices. Additional feedback mechanisms are propagated through the real economy. Increasing asset prices lead, through a wealth effect, to higher economic activity. Consumption demand is stimulated as well as credit expansion via higher values of collateral. At the same time, company profits increase. All this leads to further increases in asset prices and demand for assets.

News media play a particularly essential role. They shape public opinion and categories of thought, and actively direct the attention of the audience to certain stories. By doing this, news media can strengthen feedback mechanisms. Also, they can be responsible for attention cascades, where the attention of the audience is directed to a certain fact that, then, leads attention to a range of other factors leading to changes in public perception. New era stories also play an essential part in the creation of a boom. The stories[22] justify the enormous price increases. However, the stories do not normally cause the boom, but rather emerge as a subsequent interpretation of an asset market boom that has already advanced for a while. A new era story implies the general perception that the future is brighter and less uncertain than the past. In each loop the new era stories spread further and bring new demand to the market, which leads to further asset price increases. There is no endogenous turnaround that leads to the end of a bubble. There are countervailing forces from those who know what is going on and are willing to bet against the bubble. However, those activities are limited, since in certain constellations it is hard to determine with precision whether there is a bubble or not and it is even harder to determine its turning points.

Shiller (2005, 2012) tries to advance from popular theories of bubbles, which talk about euphoric or panic-stricken behaviour where investors blindly follow the herd. He uses findings from social psychology to explain the behaviour of investors. There is a range of what he calls 'brain bugs' active, which influence people's decision making. Speculative bubbles are the result of those brain bugs affecting the entire financial system. In the following the most relevant of those psychological factors will be outlined.

There are patterns of human behaviour that suggest price anchors in asset markets that would not persist if markets were entirely rational. Quantitative anchors indicate the appropriate level of prices, and people use them to determine whether the market is over- or under-priced. Consequently, those anchors give them an indication for their buying and selling decisions. The argument is drawn from a psychological phenomenon. If people have to answer a quantitative question about a number and the situation is ambiguous, they take whatever number is at hand as an orientation. Shiller assumes this can also be applied to markets; if people are supposed to make judgements about, for example, the level of stock prices, the most likely anchor is the most recently remembered price. This would explain certain continuity in prices. The anchor can also be the rate of change. This means that, when prices have gone up by a certain degree in the recent past, people, not sure about future changes, will simply extrapolate past growth rates (Shiller 2005, pp. 148–149).

Moral anchors are psychological factors that influence the decision of people about holding their investment or selling it and consuming the proceeds. When asset prices increase, people holding the asset become wealthier. When prices become high enough, a discrepancy between the consumption and the wealth level of people will occur. People will be induced to sell part of their assets to increase their consumption to a higher level. This will moderate the asset price increases. Therefore, for the stock prices to stay on a high level or even to climb further, from a certain point on people need to have strong reasons not to sell their assets. Those moral anchors are not quantitative but take the form of storytelling and justification. One example of such a story is the narrative spread in the 1990s that most people do not become millionaires by earning exceptional incomes but rather by being frugal savers. This was partly the moral anchor needed for sustaining the bull market in the USA in the 2000s (Shiller 2005, pp. 149–152).

Shiller (2005, pp. 152–155) further describes psychological findings about human nature that he also saw related to the behaviour of asset markets. According to those findings, people are *overconfident*, indicating that people assume their judgement or reasoning is right with a high probability. This overconfidence strengthens psychological anchors, because people tend to believe strongly in stories or reasons once they have adopted them initially. Another related finding is *magical thinking*. People believe that, if they take certain actions, they will be lucky, even though they should know by rational thinking that their action will not affect the probabilities of the outcome. This can translate, at least at some intuitive level, to thinking of the form 'If I buy this stock, it will go up', and therefore contribute to overconfidence and speculative bubbles. Investors also seem to judge the future from observed past outcomes (*representative heuristics*). This strengthens quantitative anchors. Overall, market participants seem, according to questionnaires by Shiller, to make decisions by intuition and, because of their overconfidence, put great trust in this intuition and the stability of anchors.

However, anchors are fragile, which can be explained by *non-consequentialist reasoning*. According to this finding, humans cannot make certain decisions in advance, since there are emotional elements that one cannot appreciate before the event occurs. Therefore, only when the event occurs can one discover how one 'feels' about it and then make the decision based on this newly discovered information. Therefore, it is hard to predict the breaking of a psychological anchor (Shiller 2005, pp. 155–156). An example of this is an investor believing that, in the long term, shares are the best investments. Therefore, he follows a long-term investment strategy and plans also to stay invested even during downturns. However, when the downturn actually occurs and prices start falling, even though he rationally had concluded to stay in the market, he may experience certain emotions, for example fear, that will change his decision.

While these anchors work on an individual level, it is hard to suggest that all people have the same anchor and act at the same time. Therefore, Shiller (2005) uses further findings from psychology that could explain the synchronizing of thought and behaviour among investors. One important argument is that people are ready to believe majority opinions or the opinions of an authority even if those plainly contradict matter-of-fact judgements. Therefore, if a critical mass is achieved in a market, believing in a certain story, it is likely that more people will convert to this story and act accordingly. Herd behaviour can also be caused by information cascades. It is assumed that economic agents have only certain information about a situation. Decisions are taken in sequence so that the second decision taker can observe the decision of the first one, the third decision taker can observe the decision of the first and the second one, and so on. However, they do not know the reasons for those decisions. Now, while they all have the same fundamental information, the second decision maker has the additional information about the decision of the first decision maker. If the fundamental information is ambiguous, it may be rational for the second decision maker to assume that the first decision maker had some additional information, which led to the first decision maker's choice. Therefore, the second decision maker might make the same decision. Accordingly, when the information that investors possess is not revealed, herd behaviour can become rational. Shiller (2005, p. 160) provides a telling example. Take the decision of choosing between two restaurants, where the only information provided is the appearance of the restaurant from the outside. The first visitor has only this information on which to make a decision, while a second visitor can see the first decision maker from the outside and may assume that the first decision maker knows that the chosen restaurant is good. Thus, the second visitor will follow the first one. The third decision maker now sees two people in the restaurant and, taking this as a quality signal, follows the first visitor as well. Therefore, a situation can occur where all restaurant visitors eat in the same restaurant, while the other restaurant is empty, without there being any objective difference between them.

There are additional reasons for exuberance and herd-like behaviour in the way humans communicate. A first point is that humans are more likely to communicate stories about interesting things. For example, if it is about stock markets it is rather the story about a hot stock than the plain conversation about price–earnings ratios. Therefore, usually an exchange of stories, rather than of fundamental information, takes place. Another interesting finding is that humans can have conflicting ideas coexisting in their minds. While they can think markets are not predictable, they may at the same time think they can make correct market forecasts. One explanation for this phenomenon is that very often ideas were received from some expert and were believed. Humans assume, despite the fact that two opinions contradict each other at a first glance, that both ideas are correct and experts have on a professional level solved the perceived contradiction. Depending on the outside circumstances one or the other view may become dominant, which may explain sudden fluctuations and swings in markets. Social-based selectivity of attention is another human characteristic. Normally, humans can pay attention to only a certain small number of things at the same time. Additionally, they tend to focus their attention on things that others focus their attention on. This can lead to shifts of focus on certain events or information, and to the disregard of other information, collectively, and so lead to herd behaviour in markets (Shiller 2005, pp. 160–170).

Behavioural finance shows that investors do not act rationally, as is assumed in the theoretical approaches of rational expectations and the efficient market hypothesis. It tries to give a more accurate picture of human behaviour in financial markets. Additionally, it shows that, even though there might be rational, well-informed investors in the market, their ability to correct prices is limited. Behavioural finance shows that cumulative processes are part of market processes in financial markets, and bubbles in financial markets have to be expected. Shiller tried to combine different findings from the field of behavioural finance to create a theory of asset price bubbles. He emphasized the importance of external factors to start the bubble, which then are amplified by feedback loops. Stories are important to sustain a boom. He underpinned his theory with findings from other sciences such as psychology and sociology, which explain herd-like behaviours. These observations made the theory particularly valuable. Even though Shiller's model and behavioural finance in general concentrate on asset markets and have many loose ends and undrawn conclusions, they can fill in unexplained gaps in other theories of financial crises presented here. Without doubt, behavioural finance allows a deeper understanding of Keynes's (1936, 1937c) argument of conventional judgement or the state of confidence and sudden changes of expectations.

A usual consequence of behavioural finance is that asset prices do not reflect fundamentals and only by chance reach fundamentals. A large bundle of psychological effects and models exist to support this. Andrei Shleifer makes this clear. Each explanation drawn from behavioural finance and behavioural economics in general:

> has some intuitive appeal, and, each may account for some piece of the puzzle. Each, moreover, has some support from the lab or from other market data. Yet we still do not know which one of them is driving U.S. stock prices today, or which will drive them in the future. In fact, we do not even know that we have the right theory on the list. (Shleifer 2000, pp. 185–186)

However, the role of fundamentals in behavioural finance remains ambiguous. It is argued that economic agents do not act according to neoclassical assumptions, and even if economic agents could act according to neoclassical assumptions they could not determine prices, as arbitrage processes are limited. This leads to the question: what role do fundamentals play when they are unimportant for markets? One could argue that clever economists can calculate fundamentals. But there is no guarantee that clever economists do not follow one of the behaviours described by behavioural finance. And different clever economists may come to different outcomes, even having the same information. It seems to be theoretically much clearer to assume that there are no fundamentals which determine asset prices. Also, in the long term, trend development of asset prices does not follow trend development of fundamentals. In a world of uncertainty, future cash flows simply cannot be objectively calculated. In such a Keynesian world, asset prices have no anchor in fundamentals whatsoever.

3.5   COMPARISON OF FINANCIAL CRISIS THEORIES

In this section the different financial crisis theories are compared. In spite of deep differences between various paradigms, there are several important points that all financial crisis theories share.

Firstly, in all models financial crises are the result of an unsustainable boom phase. It is assumed that market processes do not tend to an equilibrium and potentially follow cumulative processes. The boom phase in asset markets can create asset price inflations, or it can, in the sphere of production, create overcapacities in relation to consumption demand via too high investment and inflationary developments. Both spheres can be affected by unsustainable boom phases. For example, Wicksell and Hayek stress more booms in the sphere of production, whereas behavioural finance concentrates on processes in asset markets, and Fisher, Keynes and Minsky integrate both spheres in their models.

Secondly, in all financial crisis models, feedback mechanisms play the key role during expansion phases, as well as during contraction phases. There are objective and subjective feedback mechanisms. Objective feedback mechanisms are, for example, developments in asset prices and product market prices, wealth effects, changes in income, real interest rate effects, effects on cash flows and profits, and so on which improve or worsen the economic situation of an economic unit and lead to certain reactions. Subjective feedback mechanisms are, for example, changes in perceptions which lead to more positive or more negative expectations and, in this way, change the behaviour of economic units. Here, mass psychological phenomena are discussed which can, among many other things, lead to exuberance and panic. Different financial crisis models stress different feedback mechanisms. In neoclassical financial crisis models, subjective feedback mechanisms are in the background, whereas subjective feedback mechanisms are stressed by behavioural finance. Financial crisis models in the Keynesian tradition stress both feedback mechanisms.

Thirdly, in all models of financial crises, exogenous factors trigger an expansion or a boom. It can be a new innovation, a deregulation of a certain area in the economy, the end of a war, the election of a political party or a period of unjustified low interest rates, to name only a few. Only Minsky tries to model an endogenous trigger of a boom. In Wicksell and Hayek, as well as in the Keynes of the *Treatise on Money*, as soon as the money interest rate is below the natural interest rate, a cumulative expansion is triggered. However, these economists argued it would be wrong to hold central banks responsible for boom and bust phases. According to them, many factors can change the natural interest rate. The money interest rate has to follow the natural interest rate in a discretionary way. As monetary authorities cannot observe the natural interest rate, this can become very demanding for monetary policy makers and requires a high level of theoretical and historical understanding.[23] In Keynes's (1936) book *The General Theory of Employment, Interest and Money* and in Minsky's theory, a dynamic interplay between two rates of return also exists. However, they substituted the natural interest rate for the expected rate of return for investment. During the boom phase, and before the crisis, a cumulative development towards more and more fragility takes place in all models. In the end, it is a question of taste to assume an endogenous or exogenous end of a boom. It must come to an end! However, which factor will stop the boom, and when, is open to history. The dynamic crisis models analysed in this chapter are substantially different from real business cycle models in the tradition of Robert Lucas (1977). In the latter, shocks in the real sphere lead to changes in real GDP growth and employment, whereas the economy is always in equilibrium. In the crisis models, expansion and crisis phases are largely triggered by exogenous factors, but the dynamic processes which follow and systemic financial crisis are endogenous to a market economy. Both Kindleberger and Shiller have furthered the knowledge about the triggers of boom phases and of bust phases in the framework of their historical analyses (see also Dodig and Herr, Chapter 4 in this volume).

Fourthly, all approaches assume, implicitly or explicitly, an elastic financial system which is able to create sufficient endogenous credit to feed expansions. In Wicksell's, Hayek's or Schumpeter's approach, credit expansion and money creation are endogenous. Minsky and many economists in the post-Keynesian camp followed this argument. All these economists assume that monetary policy is interest rate policy and central banks are not able to successfully control a monetary aggregate.

In his book *The General Theory of Employment, Money and Interest*, Keynes (1936) used hoarding and dishoarding to give the economic model elasticity for cumulative expansions and contractions. Keynes's approach is, at this point, unsatisfactory, because changes in hoarding are hardly able to create the dynamic of capitalism we find. It is not convincing that hoarding and dishoarding can substitute for an endogenous approach of money creation. In later papers, Keynes introduced the finance motive, which allowed him to introduce some elements of endogenous money supply in his model. Later, as mentioned, post-Keynesian economists stressed the endogeneity of money much earlier than the mainstream, which continues to believe in the quantity theory of money.

In spite of the common points mentioned above, there are fundamental differences between the different approaches. Firstly, from a Keynesian perspective the interaction between a natural rate of interest and the money interest rate is misleading. There is no natural rate of interest which depends in equilibrium on the marginal productivity of physical capital and the time preference of households. To cut the economy into a real sphere, where money does not play a role, and a monetary sphere, is a theoretical construct which is not useful in understanding a capitalist economy. A market where investment and savings meet and are balanced by an interest rate is a mirage. In the neoclassical approach, the natural rate of interest will change according to developments in the real sphere. Such changes can lead to disturbances in the economy and to financial crises. However, it must be assumed that disturbances in the Keynesian approach of the General Theory are potentially much deeper, including the possibility of long-term stagnation. The marginal efficiency of capital, as Keynes called the expected rate of return of investment, has no anchor in the real sphere. It is driven by expectations based on a state of confidence or conventional judgement and can change in a quick and violent way, triggering expansions and contractions. The state of confidence and conventional judgement reflect the institutional, social and political constellation in a country and connect the economy with developments in society.

Secondly, behavioural finance does not present a comprehensive macroeconomic approach. It focuses on asset market developments and sharpens the understanding of herding and other phenomena in asset markets. This is not a critique, but it gives behaviour finance a specific status. It can be used to show that the neoclassical approaches of the efficient financial market hypothesis and rational expectations are far from any reality and, most importantly, are incorrect abstractions of the behaviour of economic agents. Different behaviours lead to different market equilibriums, and it is not possible to predict which behaviour will dominate at what time and whether a new behaviour can dominate markets at any time. Behavioural finance does not belong to a certain economic paradigm. It can be incorporated in different paradigms. Adding conclusions from behavioural finance in neoclassical models allows one to show a large bundle of 'exceptions' from the neoclassical equilibrium. Most work in the field of behavioural finance seems to be in such a tradition, and it does not try to become part of a new alternative paradigm, fundamentally criticizing neoclassical thinking. But behavioural finance can also be used to deepen the understanding of the economic system in the Keynesian paradigm. Keynes developed ideas which were very close to those that were later developed in behavioural finance. This allows the integration of research results from behavioural economics into Keynesian thinking.

Thirdly, Schumpeter has made clear that the dynamism of a capitalist economy is unthinkable without the key role played by the financial system in economic development. In neoclassical thinking it is the efficiency of the financial system that improves optimal allocations and, in this way, growth. Schumpeter goes much beyond this. Entrepreneurs need new credits to realize their innovation. Also, in Keynesian thinking, a credit system delivering sufficient and cheap credit is a precondition for satisfactory investment and full employment. Both Minsky and Schumpeter stress that the start of a boom phase typically needs a period of economic and political stability.

Fourthly, from a Keynesian perspective, Minsky delivered the most comprehensive model of financial crises. Keynes integrated asset market bubbles in general boom–bust cycles of the economy. However, he did not explicitly analyse indebtedness of economic agents and financial crises. Minsky, who based his framework on Keynes, explicitly added indebtedness of economic units and analysed the fragility which indebtedness can create. His approach can become the basis for further developing models of financial crises.

3.6   A MODEL OF FINANCIAL CRISES

In this section a comprehensive model of financial crises in the Keynesian tradition is presented. Several streams of economic thinking can be combined. Of key importance are: Knut Wicksell's cumulative process; John Maynard Keynes's analysis to determine output and inflation and of uncertainty, expectations and herding; Hyman Minsky's analysis of debt quotas and changing leverages; and Irving Fisher's analysis of goods market deflation and his debt-deflation theory. Approaches in the tradition of behavioural finance can substantially add to the understanding of cumulative processes during periods of expansion and contraction.

Not all contraction processes lead to a financial crisis, but there is always the danger that a contraction process will get out of control and develop into a deep financial crisis. The higher credit expansion and asset price inflation are, and the higher debt quotas of economic units become during an expansion, the greater the probability that a financial crisis will follow and the greater the probability that the financial crisis will be severe. Financial crises can develop even without asset price bubbles, for example when huge overcapacity is built up during the expansion and/or households become highly indebted. Financial crises can be triggered by asset price bubbles without an overheating in the sphere of production. For example, stock market or real estate bubbles driven by credit can throw a whole economy into a crisis. It is obvious that the danger of a deep financial crisis is especially high when a strong economic expansion, which creates high overcapacity and increased debt quotas, is combined with a strong asset price bubble that is driven by credit expansion.

Financial crises typically develop after medium-term boom–bust cycles, which are usually not longer than a single decade. However, also possible are long-term developments over several decades, which create fragile economic constellations. This occurs, for example, when the debt–income quotas of economic units increase over a longer period of time (see Hein and Dodig, Chapter 2 in this volume). Given a constellation where debt quotas are already high, a medium-term boom–bust cycle with a systemic financial crisis at its end, then, must be considered as especially deep. Financial crises can lead to long-term stagnation, as new booms do not necessarily or automatically follow after a financial crisis. Japan after the bubble in the second half of the 1980s is an example of this. A financial crisis can also bring a long-term regime to an end. The subprime crisis and the Great Recession are probably a historical example of such a 'break' in a long-term development.

In what follows, a stylized model of financial crises based on the Keynesian paradigm, including Minsky, is presented. The main drivers of systemic financial crises are, as mentioned, objective and subjective feedback mechanisms, which work during the creation of a boom or a bubble and during a contraction, leading to a financial crisis. A graphical exposition of a stylized expansion–contraction cycle with a systemic financial crisis is shown in Figure 3.1. The beginning of an expansion is triggered by exogenous factors. This does not exclude the possibility that a period of stable economic development will improve the state of confidence and expectations in such a way that an unsustainable expansion phase is triggered. However, a period of stagnation can reproduce itself permanently and can lead, over a long time, to a very slow or not growing economy without an endogenous mechanism that could lead to an expansion. Of course, following Minsky, if there is no financial crisis for a long time and the memory of a previous crisis begins to fade from society's collective consciousness, the conditions for a new expansion improve as long as balance sheets are cleaned and debt quotas of all economic agents are low.

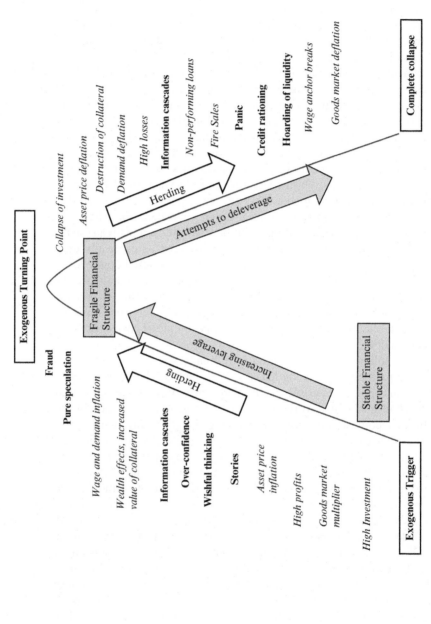

Exogenous Turning Point

Fraud

Pure speculation

Collapse of investment

Asset price deflation

Destruction of collateral

Demand deflation

High losses

Information cascades

Non-performing loans

Fire Sales

Panic

Credit rationing

Hoarding of liquidity

Wage anchor breaks

Goods market deflation

Complete collapse

Herding

Attempts to deleverage

Fragile Financial Structure

Increasing leverage

Herding

Wage and demand inflation

Wealth effects, increased value of collateral

Information cascades

Over-confidence

Wishful thinking

Stories

Asset price inflation

High profits

Goods market multiplier

High Investment

Stable Financial Structure

Exogenous Trigger

150

Notes: Italics = objective factors, bold = subjective factors.

Source: Own illustration.

The start of an expansion is characterized by a low interest rate, sufficient finance, and a high expected rate of return for investment in the enterprise sector (which may be the result of the exogenous trigger). History decides which factors start an expansion and which will later lead to a bubble and a systemic financial crisis. From the financing side, a typical supportive factor for an expansion is a period of very low real (especially when interest rates were high before) or even negative real interest rates. Looking at the investment side, a wide range of factors can trigger an expansion, for example an innovation, a real shortage in production capacities or in housing, the end of a war, or political developments.

Objective feedback mechanisms are the goods market multiplier, which stimulates consumption demand when investment increases. High investment via the goods market multiplier leads to high capacity utilization and, through the accelerator effect, encourages further investment. Part of normal profits usually is not distributed to households and allows self-financing, which can further stimulate investment. High demand in a situation of bottlenecks leads to demand inflation and even higher undistributed profits. High self-financing of investment, added to by investment financed by credit, leads to waves of investment with higher debt quotas in the firm sector, in spite of self-financing.

During an expansion, banks reduce credit rationing and advance a higher volume of credit. The uncertainty premium of banks is low. Private wealth owners reduce their liquidity hoarding and also start to expand credit to the enterprise sector and/or buy shares or other assets. Typically the expansion in the real economy driven by high investment and increasing consumption demand is accompanied by a development of increasing asset prices. This triggers very strong feedback mechanisms in the financial sector. As the value of collateral increases, banks are willing to give more credit. Higher collateral also stimulates credit demand. Firms with increasing collateral and more confidence about their cash flows feel it is safe to take on more credit. Lender's and borrower's risk is perceived as low, which further stimulates investment.

Additionally, because of higher income, on the basis of a real expansion with higher income creation and lower unemployment, and positive wealth effects on the basis of higher asset prices, households are able and willing to take more credit to increase their consumption, or to buy more assets, or to start speculating in asset markets.

During an expansion, a whole set of subjective feedback mechanisms exist. Animal spirits or the state of confidence improves during the expansion. Optimism turns into over-optimism and wishful thinking. Information cascades and stories, which justify the development, lead to herding, which further increases asset prices. Different groups of economic actors can have different expectations. Positive expectations of managers, expressed in a high expected rate of return for investment, lead to high investment. Such investment processes take time and lead to excess demand, which can make management even more optimistic. Wealth owners, including financial institutions without the knowledge of firms' managers, may even have more positive expectations. Asset prices start to increase sharply. As, for example, stock prices have no objective anchor, they can increase to very high levels driven by high current profits of firms and fantasies of future profits. A clear sign of euphoria is increasing asset prices to levels not imaginable before, but justified now by new era stories.

Pure speculation is triggered. Agents who do not have a long-term horizon enter asset markets. They buy assets even if they believe prices will fall in the long run. They are convinced they are clever enough to sell before the mass of investors and speculators do so. Risk-loving investors speculating with credit also enter the market. Fraud and greed can become widespread. High asset prices further stimulate investment in the firm sector as high share prices allow companies to get cheap finance by issuing new shares. High real estate prices make it profitable for real estate developers to build houses and sell them in the market. Consumption demand is also further stimulated by high asset prices.

During the expansion, several instabilities build up. The most important point is that all sectors in the economy increase their gross debt. High profits and the widow's cruse may slow down the increasing indebtedness of firms. Nevertheless, other firms may build up high indebtedness. At the same time financial institutions become more indebted and increase credits given in relation to equity. Some private households also become highly indebted. An overall extension of balance sheets of many economic units takes place.

Typically, asset price inflations are often accompanied by a strong economic expansion with high real GDP growth and falling unemployment. Such a development will sooner or later lead to goods market inflation. The latter is driven by excess demand in the goods market and typically by a developing wage–price spiral. For unions it is very difficult to prevent inflationary nominal wage increase as a demand inflation reduces real wages and increases profits, firms' development looks good and unemployment rates are decreasing. As long as the central bank does not increase interest rates, inflation can further stimulate the expansion.

What is important here is that the economy moves into a more and more fragile constellation. Indebtedness of all sectors in the economy increases, and the levels of margins of safety for debtors and borrowers are low. Asset prices increase to very high levels. However, speculators betting on even higher prices push asset prices further up. High investment in production capacities (including real estate markets) makes it less and less likely that all capacities in the future will be able to be utilized. In the last phase of a bubble, when speculation seems to become very rewarding, adventurers of all types are attracted. And, at the same time, some projects are already less profitable than expected and fraud can become common.

It is clear that the expansion must eventually come to an end. Many factors can trigger the end of the expansion. For example, monetary policy may increase interest rates, and companies in some economic sectors may realize less profits than expected and have difficulties fulfilling their debt service, increasing lender's risk and borrower's risk, and may halt a credit expansion. Asset prices may stop increasing further, and this may lead to problems for some speculators, or expectations may change without any narrow economic explanation.

During a contraction period, the problem of non-performing loans becomes the centre of attention. When speculative activities in stock or real estate or other asset markets, financed by credit, do not materialize, when firms' investment projects do not earn the cash flows expected, or when private households cannot pay back their consumption or mort-gage debt – either because asset prices do not increase further or because income increases are below expectations – financial difficulties spread. Objective and subjective feedback mechanisms stimulate a cumulative contraction process.

An important objective feedback mechanism is the interaction between the fall in asset prices, financial problems of speculators, firms and finan-cial institutions, and fire sales of economic units with liquidity and sol-vency problems. Fire sales can lead to an extremely quick and substantial collapse of asset prices and cause escalating problems of speculative units. The more firms, financial institutions and households sell assets to be able to fulfil financial obligations, the faster asset prices will decline. Falling asset prices trigger further objective feedback mechanisms. They lead to a fall in the value of collateral and a destruction of equity. Financial institu-tions intensify credit rationing partly enforced by a destruction of equity in their own balance sheets and partly because of a decrease in the value of the collateral of debtors.

An important subjective feedback mechanism is the erosion of the state of confidence, reflecting the increase of the level of uncertainty. Because of a more cautious judgement of lender's risk, financial institutions follow a more restrictive attitude towards granting loans. Credit rationing becomes more intensive. In extreme cases even the credit market between financial institutions for short-term credit can break down. Investment by firms collapses as animal spirits erode. Advances of firms in productive activi-ties are reduced. Part of a more pessimistic judgement by investors is a higher borrower's risk. Higher levels of uncertainty stimulate hoarding of liquidity by private wealth holders, firms and financial institutions. In such a situation, liquidity in the market dries up. Economic agents thirst for money like a poor soul for relief.[24] Euphoria during the last phase of the boom gives way to over-pessimism and panic. It is worth stressing that panic becomes a frequent ingredient of a cumulative downturn. For example, negative information cascades are much faster than positive ones. The market in general, and especially asset markets, follows the logic of a game of 'Musical Chairs', where everybody tries to secure a chair before the music stops. Such behaviour creates strong cumulative processes, expressed in fire sales, liquidity hoarding and extreme credit rationing.[25]

Losses in the enterprise sector, caused by decreasing demand, further weaken investment. At this point, the goods market multiplier and falling consumption caused by negative income, wealth effects and expectations intensify the reduction in output and employment. Reduced aggregate demand leads to increasing financial problems in firms and to bankruptcies. Unemployment and shrinking household income lead to increasing non-performing loans for consumption and real estate credits.

In the centre of negative feedback factors are the permanent erosion of wealth and confidence and the increasing problem of economic units to fulfil debt service. These developments in asset markets have severe repercussions for the development of output and employment. Shrinking output and higher unemployment further weaken aggregate demand in the goods market and aggravate financial stress in asset markets. A systemic financial crisis, accompanied by a steep drop in output and employment, is the outcome.

There is one very powerful feedback mechanism left which, if it starts to become effective, leads to deep systemic financial crises. A lack of goods market demand and a shrinking of production and employment can lead to deflationary tendencies. As far as a demand deflation is concerned, such deflationary processes, typically shown in a reduction of the inflation rate, are normal for phases after the end of a boom. But, as soon as unemployment becomes very high or labour market institutions are weak, the probability that nominal wages will fall increases. As soon as unit-labour costs start to decrease, a cost-driven deflationary process is triggered. A sharp deflation under the condition of high debt is the most brutal objective feedback mechanism, which tears an economy into a widespread systemic financial crisis. This is so because a deflation increases the debt burden of all debtors in the domestic currency. In addition to this, deflationary expectations lead to a collapse of investment by firms, which do not want to compete with other firms that later buy productive capital for a lower price. Households also reduce their consumption demand for durables if deflationary expectations spread. Production and employment fall further, and additional nominal wage cuts can follow as unemployment deepens.

Without the central bank taking on the role of lender of last resort, many even moderate downturns end up in deep systemic financial crises. Before Walter Bagehot ([1873] 1999) wrote his *Lombard Street* and before central banks understood their function as lender of last resort, this is what happened. Almost all financial crises in the first half of the nineteenth century led to the collapse of large parts of the financial system. However, in spite of the power of a central bank to fight against liquidity problems, during a period of deflation it becomes not much more than an observer, since monetary policy cannot cut nominal interest rates below zero and, even if the central bank offers high liquidity, banks do not increase credit expansion when they follow credit rationing.[26]

3.7   CONCLUSIONS

Above, we have analysed financial crises as the outcome of dynamic unsustainable processes from a theoretical point of view. The Wicksellian cumulative process, with the interaction of two rates of return, seems to us the best framework for analysing such unsustainable processes. Neoclassical as well as Keynesian economists use Wicksell's approach. Neoclassical authors stress the interaction between a rate of return of a real sphere in relation to the interest rate, which comes from the monetary sphere. Keynesians overcome the neoclassical dichotomy and focus on the interaction of two rates of return in a monetary production economy. Behavioural finance supports the Keynesian approaches and adds to the understanding of cumulative processes.

Economic boom phases combined with credit expansions and higher indebtedness of economic units are the key explanation of a later systemic financial crisis. To prevent financial crises, unsustainable credit expansions have to be prevented. Microeconomic prudential regulations are important, but not sufficient to prevent an unsustainable expansion. The individual banker, the individual firm and the individual buyer of real estate may all believe that they act in a responsible and rational way, in spite of an unsustainable credit expansion. Short-term speculation in asset markets, which are often linked with credit expansion and fraud, has no positive social function. Measures should be taken to prevent credit-financed speculation of this type.

Without credit, economic dynamics in a capitalist economy cannot take place. Credit is needed to channel resources into investment and innovative production, which lead to economic development. Rather than a system which simply does not allow credit for expansion, what is most desirable is a system which supports credit expansion in productive areas and prevents unsustainable increases in debt quotas.

Goods market deflation creates one of the strongest destructive feedback mechanisms in financial crises. As soon as the nominal wage anchor breaks, deflation can snowball uncontrollably. To prevent a deflation-driven financial crisis, labour market institutions must be strong enough to hinder nominal unit-labour costs from falling, even when high unemployment prevails. In addition, demand management is needed to prevent a demand-driven deflationary process.

NOTES

For helpful comments we would like to thank Nina Dodig, Dirk Ehnts, Trevor Evans, Eckhard Hein, Rainer Stachuletz, Natalia Budyldina, Barbara Schmitz and the participants in the FESSUD Annual Conference 2013 in Amsterdam. Remaining errors are, of course, ours.

1. In the classical paradigm the 'natural' price was the long-run equilibrium price, in contrast to the market price, which fluctuates around the natural price. In a similar way the natural interest rate has the meaning of an equilibrium interest rate determined by fundamentals.
2. In Wicksell's framework, during an expansion employment does not increase, but changes its structure. Of course, on a more concrete level of analysis, changes in the volume of employment were also considered. However, Wicksell did not know the law of aggregate demand and had no theoretical tools to analyse a quantitative expansion process.
3. Important also were Ludwig von Mises ([1912] 1953) and Dennis Robertson (1940), who will, however, not be discussed here.
4. Normal profits are, as mentioned, considered as costs. In the General Theory, Keynes argued that a liquidity premium determines the interest rate and the interest rate the profit rate (Keynes 1930, Chapter 17). Profit as a cost can be presented in a much more differentiated way (see for example Herr and Kazandziska 2011 or Hein 2012). But this is not the topic of this chapter.
5. Of course, in oligopolistic and monopolistic markets firms also have power to change prices.
6. One consequence of this argument is that in a situation of unemployment higher nominal wages do not lead to additional real demand and not to an increase of output and employment up to full capacity utilization.
7. Nominal exchange rate movements can also influence the domestic price level.
8. For simplification we only look at the household and enterprise sector. Under this condition in national accounting $Y = I + C$ with C as consumption demand. It also holds $Y = C + S_H + Q_E$, whereas Q_E are undistributed profits. Total saving obviously is $S = S_H + Q_E$. From the two definitions of Y it follows: $Q_E = I - S_H$.
9. The relationship between investment demand (including consumption out of profits) and profits was stressed by many economists (see especially Kalecki 1954).
10. China after the Asian crisis in 1997 or Japan's fiscal policy in the 1990s and 2000s fits this constellation.
11. See also Vercelli (2011). The neoclassical model including the model with aggregate demand and aggregate supply argues that a deflation has stabilizing effects, as net monetary wealth in real terms will increase. This positive wealth effect then increases

aggregate demand. Independent of the question as to whether net monetary wealth in a model with endogenous money exists, such an effect must be considered as unimportant compared to the Fisher effect (see Tobin 1980).

12. According to Schumpeter, technological development is not determined by 'objective' factors. Which technologies are used and developed depends on entrepreneurs.

13. Keynes then quotes *The Wild Duck* by Henrik Ibsen, where the duck dives down to the bottom of the lake, as deep as possible, and is trapped in the weed and tangle and all the rubbish that is down there.

14. The school of rational expectations explains expectations endogenously. This is possible as it is assumed that expectations of at least the average economic agent are identical with the equilibrium outcome of the model. It is obvious that under such an assumption expectations cannot have a systematic effect on economic outcomes.

15. This led Davidson (2010, p. 254) to call Keynes the 'first behavioural economist'.

16. In modern post-Keynesian approaches an active role of credit supply is modelled in another way (see below).

17. For a model of endogenous money supply including the commercial banking system and deposit holding of the public see Heine and Herr (2013).

18. The difficulty in understanding the functioning of credit markets is also created by the fact that in many cases the asset market is modelled as demand and supply of money. In this type of model the credit market is hidden behind the money market.

19. Minsky does not distinguish between stockholders' and managers' evaluation and interests as clearly as Keynes. Here, he rather seems to follow Tobin's q, where stockholders' and managers' expectations and interests are identical.

20. The first edition of the book was published in 1978 with Kindleberger as the only author.

21. Noise traders are traders who react to irrelevant information (noise) or do not act rationally according to the normative economic model (Shleifer 2000). Conversely, information traders trade on the basis of all relevant information about the value of an asset (Black 1986).

22. Stories associated with the recent bubble were for example the myth that house prices in the USA needed to increase in the face of population and economic growth with limited land resources. Different varieties of this story were circulating, based on land scarcity, increasing construction costs, etc. (Shiller 2008). During the boom preceding the stock market crash of 1929, price increases in the stock market were justified by productivity increases due to prohibition (Galbraith [1954] 1992).

23. After the Second World War, for neoclassical economists the central bank itself became the most important disturbing factor as soon as it followed discretionary monetary policy. On the one hand, the central bank might not be able to understand economic development (for example the time lag between an interest rate change and its effect on the economy); on the other hand politicians might force central banks to short-sighted policies to achieve short-term positive economic effects (for example before an election). Monetary targeting and independent central banks therefore became the policy recommendations for these types of monetarists (see as a representative Friedman 1969).

24. 'O God, you are my God; early will I seek you: my soul thirsts for you, my flesh longs for you in a dry and thirsty land, where no water is' (Psalms 63:1).

25. Humans in panic show the same behaviour as some animals, for example mice or ants. In panic, for example, behaviour is copied, individuals attempt to move faster than normal, interactions between individuals become physical, and better options are overlooked. For example, in a room with two doors most individuals run in panic to one door (Hamilton 1971).

26. Boom–bust cycles on an international level are very similar to boom–bust cycles on a national level (Williamson 2005). They typically develop in the following sequence (Herr 2008, 2011a). International capital flows become deregulated and/or there is a change in expectations about the future economic development of a country. Stories

and new era ideas also play an important role in international boom–bust cycles. When a country is considered to be a good investment location, domestic and foreign entrepreneurs, financial institutions and wealth owners typically share the same positive expectations. Capital starts to flow into the country. A domestic credit expansion is usually further stimulated or even driven by foreign credits. The key point is that foreign gross indebtedness increases. Most countries in the world suffer from the so-called 'original sin' (Eichengreen et al. 2003), indicating they only get foreign credit in foreign currency. Foreign debt denominated in foreign currency is extremely dangerous, because a real depreciation of the domestic currency leads to an increase of the real debt burden in domestic currency. When a boom, in combination with foreign indebtedness, comes to an end, foreign capital inflows stop and capital flight becomes widespread. The collapse of the exchange rate and twin crises, a crisis of the domestic financial system and a balance-of-payments crisis, become unavoidable (Kaminsky and Reinhart 1999).

REFERENCES

Bagehot, W. (1873), *Lombard Street: A Description of the Money Market*. Reprinted Wiley, Hoboken, NJ, 1999.

Baker, H.K. and J.R. Nofsinger (2010), 'Behavioral finance: an overview', in H.K. Baker and J.R. Nofsinger (eds), *Behavioral Finance*, Hoboken, NJ: Wiley.

Black, F. (1986), 'Noise', *Journal of Finance*, **41** (3), 529–543.

Davidson, P. (2010), 'Behavioral economists should make a turn and learn from Keynes and Post Keynesian economics', *Journal of Post Keynesian Economics*, **33** (2), 251–254.

De Antoni, E. (2006), 'Minsky on financial instability', in P. Arestis and M. Sawyer (eds), *A Handbook of Alternative Monetary Economics*, Cheltenham, UK and Northampton, MA, USA: Edward Elgar Publishing.

Eichengreen, B., R. Hausmann and U. Panizza (2003), 'Currency mismatches, debt intolerance and original sin: why they are not the same and why it matters', NBER Working Paper 10036, National Bureau of Economic Research.

Fisher, I. (1911), *The Purchasing Power of Money: Its Determination and Relation to Credit, Interest and Crises*, New York: Macmillan.

Fisher, I. (1933), 'The debt deflation theory of great depressions', *Econometrica*, **1**, 337–357.

Friedman, M. (1968), 'The role of monetary policy', *American Economic Review*, **58** (1), 1–17.

Friedman, M. (1969), *The Optimum Quantity of Money and Other Essays*, London: Macmillan.

Galbraith, J.K. (1954), *The Great Crash*. Reprinted Penguin, London, 1992.

Hahn, A. (1920), *Volkswirtschaftliche Theorie des Bankkredits*, 3rd edn, Tübingen: Mohr.

Hahn, F. (1981), 'General equilibrium theory', in D. Bell and I. Kristol (eds), *The Crisis in Economic Theory*, New York: Basic Books.

Hamilton, W.D. (1971), 'Geometry for the selfish herd', *Journal of Theoretical Biology*, **31** (2), 295–311.

Hayek, F.A. von (1929), *Monetary Theory and the Trade Cycle*. Reprinted in *Collected Works of F.A. Hayek*, Vol. 7, Chicago: University of Chicago Press, 2012.

Hayek, F.A. von (1931), *Prices and Production*. Reprinted in *Collected Works of F.A. Hayek*, Vol. 7, Chicago: University of Chicago Press, 2012.

Hein, E. (2012), *Macroeconomics of Finance-dominated Capitalism – And Its Crisis*, Cheltenham, UK and Northampton, MA, USA: Edward Elgar Publishing.

Heine, M. and H. Herr (2013), *Volkswirtschaftslehre: Paradigmenorientierte Einführung in die Mikro- und Makroökonomie*, München: Oldenburg.

Herr, H. (2008), 'Financial systems in developing countries and economic development', in E. Hein, T. Niechoj, P. Spahn and A. Truger (eds), *Finance-Led Capitalism? Macroeconomic Effects of Changes in the Financial Sector*, Marburg: Metropolis.

Herr, H. (2009), 'The labour market in a Keynesian economic regime: theoretical debate and empirical findings', *Cambridge Journal of Economics*, 33, 949–965.

Herr, H. (2011a), 'International monetary and financial architecture', in E. Hein and E. Stockhammer (eds), *A Modern Guide to Keynesian Macroeconomics and Economic Policies*, Cheltenham, UK and Northampton, MA, USA: Edward Elgar Publishing.

Herr, H. (2011b), 'Money, expectations, physics and financial markets: paradigmatic alternatives in economic thinking', in H. Ganssmann (ed.), *New Approaches to Monetary Theory: Interdisciplinary Perspectives*, London: Routledge.

Herr, H. (2014), 'An analytical framework for the post-Keynesian macroeconomic paradigm', *Izmir Review of Social Sciences*, 1 (2), 73–116.

Herr, H. and M. Kazandziska (2011), *Macroeconomic Policy Regimes in Western Industrial Countries*, London: Routledge.

Kahneman, D. and A. Tversky (1974), 'Judgment under uncertainty: heuristics and biases', *Science*, New Series, 185 (4157), 1124–1131.

Kalecki, M. (1954), *Theory of Economic Dynamics*, London: George Allen & Unwin.

Kaminsky, G.L. and C. Reinhart (1999), 'The twin crises: the causes of banking and balance-of-payments problems', *American Economic Review*, 89, 473–512.

Keynes, J.M. (1930), *A Treatise on Money*, Vol. I: *The Pure Theory of Money*, Cambridge, UK: Cambridge University Press.

Keynes, J.M. (1933), *A Monetary Theory of Production*. Reprinted in *Collected Writings*, Vol. XIII, London: Macmillan, 1973.

Keynes, J.M. (1936), *The General Theory of Employment, Interest and Money*, Cambridge, UK: Cambridge University Press.

Keynes, J.M. (1937a), 'Alternative theories of the rate of interest', *Economic Journal*, 47, 241–252.

Keynes, J.M. (1937b), 'The "ex-ante" theory of interest', *Economic Journal*, 47, 693–699.

Keynes, J.M. (1937c), 'The general theory of employment', *Quarterly Journal of Economics*, 51, 209–223.

Kindleberger, C.P. (1978), *Manias, Panics and Crashes: A History of Financial Crises*, New York: Basic Books.

Kindleberger, C.P. and R.Z. Aliber (2011), *Manias, Panics, and Crashes: A History of Financial Crises*, 6th edn, Houndmills, Basingstoke: Palgrave Macmillan.

King, J.E. (2013), 'Should post-Keynesians make a behavioural turn?', *European Journal of Economics and Economic Policies: Intervention*, 10 (2), 231–242.

Lavoie, M. (2011), 'Money credit and central banks in post-Keynesian economics', in E. Hein and E. Stockhammer (eds), *A Modern Guide to Keynesian*

Macroeconomics and Economic Policies, Cheltenham, UK and Northampton, MA, USA: Edward Elgar Publishing.

Lavoie, M. and M. Seccareccia (2001), 'Minsky's financial instability hypothesis: a missing macroeconomic link?', in R. Bellofiore and P. Ferri (eds), *Financial Fragility and Investment in the Capitalist Economy: The Economic Legacy of Hyman Minsky*, Vol. II, Cheltenham, UK and Northampton, MA, USA: Edward Elgar Publishing.

Lucarelli, B. (2013), 'Endogenous money: a note on some post-Keynesian controversies', *Review of Political Economy*, **25**, 348–359.

Lucas, R.E., Jr (1977), 'Understanding business cycles', *Carnegie–Rochester Conference Series on Public Policy*, **5**, 7–29.

Marx, K. (1867), *Das Kapital: Kritik der politischen Ökonomie*, Erstere Band: *Der Produktionsprozeß des Kapitals*. Reprinted Rosa-Luxemburg-Stiftung (ed.), Karl Dietz Verlag, Berlin, 2008.

Marx, K. (1894), *Das Kapital: Kritik der politischen Ökonomie*, Dritter Band: *Der Gesamtprozeß der kapitalistischen Produktion*. Reprinted Rosa-Luxemburg-Stiftung (ed.), Karl Dietz Verlag, Berlin, 2010.

Minsky, H.P. (1975), *John Maynard Keynes*, New York: Columbia University Press.

Minsky, H.P. (1982), *Can 'It' Happen Again? Essays on Instability and Finance*, New York: M.E. Sharpe.

Minsky, H.P. (1986), *Stabilizing an Unstable Economy*. Reprinted McGraw-Hill, New York, 2008.

Minsky, H.P. (1992), 'The financial instability hypothesis', Working Paper No. 74, Levy Economics Institute.

Mises, L. von (1912), *The Theory of Money and Credit*. Reprinted Yale University Press, New Haven, CT, 1953.

Riese, H. (1986), *Theorie der Inflation*, Tübingen: Mohr.

Robertson, D.H. (1940), *Essays in Monetary Theory*, London: Staples Press.

Schumpeter, J. (1911), *The Theory of Economic Development*. Reprinted Harvard University Press, Cambridge, MA, 1934.

Schumpeter, J. (1942), *Capitalism, Socialism and Democracy*, New York: Harper & Brothers. Reprinted George Allen & Unwin, London, 5th edn, 1976.

Schumpeter, J. (1961), *Konjunkturzyklen: Eine theoretische, historische und statistische Analyse des kapitalistischen Prozesses*. Reprinted Vandenhoeck & Ruprecht, Göttingen, 2008.

Shiller, R. (2005), *Irrational Exuberance*, Princeton, NJ: Princeton University Press.

Shiller, R. (2008), *The Subprime Solution*, Princeton, NJ: Princeton University Press.

Shiller, R. (2012), *Finance and the Good Society*, Princeton, NJ: Princeton University Press.

Shleifer, A. (2000), *Inefficient Markets: An Introduction to Behavioral Finance*, Oxford: Oxford University Press.

Stiglitz, J.E. and B. Greenwald (2003), *Towards a New Paradigm in Monetary Economics*, Cambridge, UK: Cambridge University Press.

Stiglitz, J.E. and A. Weiss (1981), 'Credit rationing in markets with imperfect information', *American Economic Review*, **71** (3), 333–421.

Tobin, J. (1980), *Asset Accumulation and Economic Activity: Reflections on Contemporary Macroeconomic Theory*, Chicago: University of Chicago Press.

Toporowski, J. (2007), 'Minsky's "induced investment and business cycles"', *Cambridge Journal of Economics*, **32** (5), 725–737.
Vercelli, A. (2011), 'A perspective on Minsky moments: revisiting the core of the financial instability hypothesis', *Review of Political Economy*, **23** (1), 49–67.
Wicksell, K. (1898), *Interest and Prices*. Reprinted Sentry Press, New York, 1936.
Wicksell, K. ([1906] 1935), *Lectures on Political Economy*, Vol. 2, London: Routledge.
Williamson, J. (2005), *Curbing the Boom–Bust Cycle: Stabilizing Capital Flows to Emerging Markets*, Washington, DC: Peterson Institute for International Economics.
Wolfson, M.H. (1996), 'A post-Keynesian theory of credit rationing', *Journal of Post-Keynesian Economics*, **18** (3), 443–470.

4. Financial crises leading to stagnation – selected historical case studies

Nina Dodig and Hansjörg Herr

4.1 INTRODUCTION

Capitalist development is not characterized by smooth economic development measured as a stable GDP growth rate or stable development of other economic indicators like employment, the inflation rate or credit expansion. Rather, historically capitalism is characterized by a cyclical development pattern that produces a positive GDP growth rate in most countries in the long run. The ups and downs do not follow the regular swings of the sinusoidal curve. Periods of high growth can be more or less pronounced. Crises can be more or less deep and long. This chapter focuses on deeper economic downturns. Usually, cyclical downturns fade out within a short period of time and make room for a new expansion period. However, one can observe throughout history that periods of economic crises can spiral out of control and that the market mechanism cannot save the economy from a cumulative shrinking. History has also demonstrated that economic crises can lead to a lasting period of stagnation. Typically, these two negative scenarios, cumulative shrinking and long-term stagnation, follow after a deep financial crisis.

The Great Recession that occurred in 2009 after the outbreak of the subprime financial crisis and affected the whole developed world is a prime example of a sharp financial crisis. In comparison to the Great Depression in the early 1930s, the cumulative collapse of many economies could be avoided. But the unresolved question is whether GDP growth will be low for a long period in the crisis countries and what negative repercussions for employment, living conditions and political developments in societies can be expected. This chapter tries to answer this question by analysing severe financial crises observed throughout the history of capitalism which led to a long period of stagnation. There are several key questions that must be answered in understanding historical financial crises:

a. What triggers deep financial crises? This question focuses on explaining what causes the economic boom or the asset price bubble before the financial crisis.
b. Which factors intensify the financial crises further?
c. Most importantly, which factors prevent the return to prosperity for an extended period of time? Which factors cause low growth or even stagnation for a long period?

This leads us to the question of which financial crises should be selected. This question is not easy to answer, because capitalist history is full of financial crises. Capitalism, defined as a comprehensive system dominating production and employment, was established in some European countries at the end of the nineteenth century. In earlier centuries, financial crises existed, for example the Dutch tulip crisis in 1637, but they were of a different character, because the capitalist system was not yet well developed. During the first half of the nineteenth century, though, when the capitalist mode of production became dominant, the industrialized world began to experience a sequence of financial crises. Monetary policy at that time did not understand how to stabilize economies, and financial market regulations did not exist – for example, private banks could issue their own banknotes. Owing to certain regulatory attempts later on, such as the Bank Act in England of 1844, economic stability could be improved. However, in the second half of the nineteenth century, severe and prolonged crises hit what was then considered the developed world. The 'Long Depression' of 1873–96 inaugurated a period of recurring financial crises and low GDP growth. The following decades up until the First World War (1914–18) were marked by a relative stability and high growth rates under the regime of the classical Gold Standard – with the exception of the short 1907 banking panic in the United States (USA). This system came to an end with the First World War. After the First World War the re-establishment of the classical Gold Standard failed. Long-term prosperity could not be achieved.

This chapter will concentrate its analysis on crises during the twentieth and twenty-first centuries. Three crises, in our view, are of particular importance, because all three led to a long-term period of low GDP growth:

1. the Great Depression in the early 1930s, which could only be overcome with the beginning of the Second World War or during the preparation for it;
2. the crisis in Latin America in the 1980s, which reached well into the 1990s;

3. the Japanese stagnation after the bubble in the 1980s. This crisis is
    of special interest to us because Japan has not been able to overcome
    stagnation and low GDP growth to this day. Furthermore, it has
    been debated whether the USA or Europe might follow in Japan's
    footsteps.

Whereas the Great Depression and the Japanese crisis were mainly triggered by financial problems inside the countries,[1] the crisis in Latin
America was triggered by foreign indebtedness denominated in foreign
currency.

In what follows we analyse the logic of the three crises, approaching
them in chronological order. Subsequently we compare the crises and
draw conclusions.

4.2   THE GREAT DEPRESSION

4.2.1   The Background

The 'Roaring Twenties' were usually considered a period of high economic
prosperity in the USA. Rapid growth began after a deflationary recession
in 1920–21. The first half of the 1920s saw an unprecedented expansion of
industrial production and trade (Figure 4.1a). Non-agricultural employment[2] increased by 40 per cent between 1921 and 1929 (Figure 4.1b). This
reflects the tendency towards Fordist mass production, made available by
new technologies and production methods and sufficient demand. Cars,
telephones, electrical kitchen appliances, radio and film were brought to
the middle class on a large scale. In the aftermath of the First World War,
the USA became the richest country in the world measured in GDP per
capita, with a booming industry and a society adapting to consumerism.

However, despite the initial boom, the volume of production and trade
did not increase much from 1923 to 1929. The early end of the boom has to
do with the fact that the prosperity was not combined with equal income
distribution. Income inequality was increasing throughout the 1920s and
dampened demand based on household income. Despite the potential for
mass production after the First World War, Fordism was not fully realized
until after the Second World War when sustainable, income-based mass
consumption was enabled by a more equitable income distribution.

What we observe for the 1920s, however, is an increase in household consumption, in particular of durable goods and real estate, largely financed
with credit. Instalment buying accounted for much of households' credit
in the 1920s (Olney 1999). Figure 4.2 shows how non-mortgage debt as a

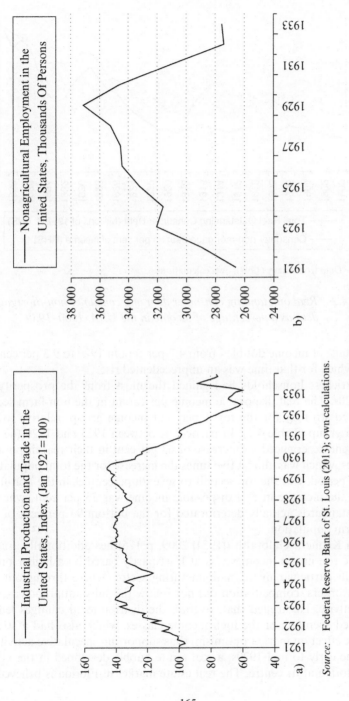

Source: Federal Reserve Bank of St. Louis (2013); own calculations.

Figure 4.1 (a) Production and (b) employment in the USA, 1921–33

The demise of finance-dominated capitalism

Source: Data from Olney (1999); own calculations.

Figure 4.2   Real outstanding consumer debt and consumer non-mortgage debt as a percentage of income in the USA, 1900–1939

percentage of income doubled from 4.7 per cent in 1920 to 9.3 per cent in 1929, which for that time was an unprecedented rise.

The richest households had gained the most from the prosperity of the 1920s. The real disposable income per capita in the non-farm sector increased strongly for the top 1 per cent income group, relative to the bottom group (Table 4.1). In particular, between 1923 and 1929 the top 1 per cent experienced an increase of 63 per cent in their real disposable incomes, which was almost five times the increase for the total population in that period. For the top second to seventh percentiles in the non-farm sector, the increase in real disposable income was 23 per cent, whereas living standards actually deteriorated for the bottom 93 per cent of the non-farm population.

John Kenneth Galbraith ([1954] 2009, p.175) has additionally argued that the rise in top incomes was at least partly based on a higher profit share, in particular in the manufacturing sector, where throughout the 1920s workers' compensation did not follow the substantial increases in productivity. He argued that, overall, the distributional changes led to increased spending of the high income classes, which also had a strong positive effect on market optimism, thus supporting speculative activities.

In the early to mid-1920s, a real estate bubble developed in the USA, with Florida at its centre. The real estate market in Florida is believed to

Table 4.1 Disposable income per capita for the USA, 1920–29

| | Per capita income in constant 1929 dollars | | | | | | | | | | % change |
	1920	1921	1922	1923	1924	1925	1926	1927	1928	1929	1923–29
Total population	543	477	548	613	613	633	640	649	675	693	13
Non-farm population											
Entire non-farm population	659	599	683	754	745	761	769	775	807	825	9
Top 1%	7962	8379	9817	9641	10512	12719	12606	13563	15666	15721	63
2nd–7th %	1698	1837	2034	2197	2268	2498	2490	2522	2674	2700	23
Lowest 93%	513	435	497	566	542	521	531	525	527	544	–4
Farm population	269	183	213	244	256	280	270	278	280	295	21

Source: Holt (1977, Table 3).

Notes: Data on residential wealth comprise the market value of structures and estimated value of land (in current dollars); for computing details, see Grebler et al. (1956, pp. 359–376, Appendix D).

Source: Data from Grebler et al. (1956, Appendix L, Table L-6); own calculations.

Figure 4.3   Non-farm residential mortgage debt as a percentage of non-farm residential wealth

have had the strongest boom and then crash in the 1920s, but unfortunately no data on house prices are available. Nicholas and Scherbina (2011) constructed a real estate price index for Manhattan for the same period, showing that, between the fourth quarter of 1922 and the second quarter of 1926, house prices increased by 54 per cent. Over the next two years, that is, until the second quarter of 1928, real estate prices fell 28 per cent. While the bubble was developing, households were more than encouraged to speculate in the real estate market. Figure 4.3 shows the huge mounting up of mortgage debt relative to residential wealth in the USA.

The collapse of the real estate bubble, as mentioned, came in 1926, and thousands of households were left homeless. The rate of foreclosures was increased dramatically (see Figure 4.4), and the situation only worsened after the end of the stock market bubble in 1929. Between 1928 and 1933, the index of housing prices fell by 25 per cent. Foreclosures, which had been an issue since the burst of the real estate bubble in 1926, remained a problem throughout the entire 1930s and well into the 1940s.

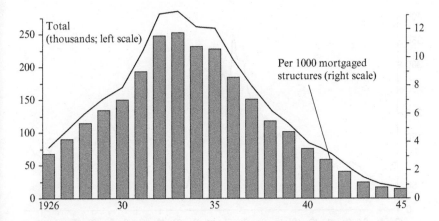

Notes: Left-hand side: number of foreclosed mortgaged properties, in thousands; right-hand side: foreclosure rates (foreclosures per 1000 mortgaged properties).

Source: IMF (2012, p. 104).

Figure 4.4 Foreclosures during the Great Depression in the USA

After the end of the real estate bubble a new bubble was under way, this time in the stock market. In 1928, speculation began feeding the stock market bubble. Although stock prices on the New York Stock Exchange had already begun to climb in 1924, the sharpest rise came during 1928 and 1929 (see Figure 4.5). Although there are no precise data, speculative activity of the rich in real estate and stock markets was high, and became an increasing source of income for the small group of wealthy individuals in the 1920s.[3] It is unclear to what extent, but speculation was also driven by credit. Galbraith ([1954] 2009, p. 177) mentions that 'the proportion of personal income received in the form of interest, dividends, and rent – the income, broadly speaking, of the well-to-do – was about twice as great as in the years following the Second World War'.

4.2.2 The Crisis

In 1929 the stock market had been on the rise for nine consecutive years, leading Irving Fisher, one of the most well-known economists of his time, to proclaim that the 'stock prices have reached what looks like a permanently high plateau' (Fisher 1929) on 17 October, just days before the collapse. In spring 1929 the Federal Reserve tried to contain the bubble by announcing it would increase interest rates. At that time, the collapse was avoided only because the head of the National City Bank offered

Source: Federal Reserve Bank of St. Louis (2013); own illustration.

Figure 4.5   Dow Jones Industrial Stock Price Index for the USA (dollars per share), 1920–42

to lend enough money to the public to offset the 'turmoil' caused by the Fed (Galbraith [1990] 1994). In August 1929, however, there was a drop in industrial production, raising negative sentiment towards the stock market. After a weak performance of the stock market, on 21 October a mass panic occurred, accompanied by heavy selling of shares. On 29 October the stock market declined by 23 per cent (Desai 2011, p. 193). The so-called 'Black Tuesday' has since been remembered as one of the most disturbing days in the history of the New York Stock Exchange.

The stock market crash triggered a deep recession in the USA. Nominal national income more than halved from 1929 until 1932 in the USA (Kuznets 1937). Owing to deflation, the contraction in real terms was somewhat lessened, but at 41 per cent it was significant nonetheless (see Figure 4.6). The decline in real per capita national income registered a dramatic fall of 43 per cent from 1929 to 1932.

In 1933 industrial production was half of its 1929 value and, along with the decline in production and output, unemployment rose to dramatic levels. By 1933 a quarter of the working population – approximately 13 million people – were unemployed (Galbraith [1954] 2009) (see Table 4.2). Household debt-to-income ratios exploded, as shown in Figure 4.7, rising from over 60 per cent at the peak of the bubble to well over 80 per cent in 1932.

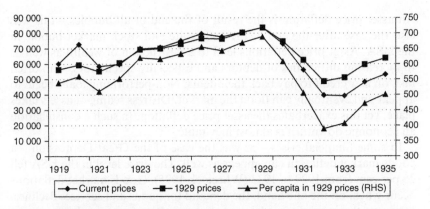

Notes: Left-hand scale: national income in current prices and in 1929 prices; right-hand scale: national per capita income in 1929 prices.

Source: Data from Kuznets (1937, Table 1); own calculations.

Figure 4.6 Nominal national income, total (in millions of US dollars) and per capita, 1919–35

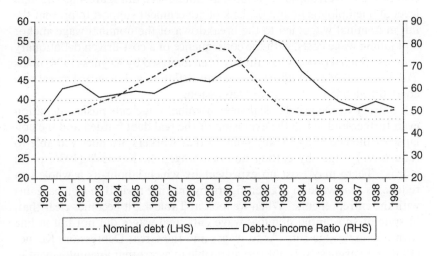

Source: IMF (2012, p. 104).

Figure 4.7 Household debt (in billions of US dollars) during the Great Depression in the USA, and debt-to-income ratio (as percentage)

An asset price deflation is the result of the end of all bubbles – this was also the case after the end of the real estate and stock market bubble in the USA. Asset price deflations lead to a destruction of wealth as well as to increasing difficulties of debtors and especially speculators, who often take on new credit to pay back their debts. Non-performing loans begin to appear and eventually can flood the market. Distress selling of assets takes place, yet this exacerbates the asset price deflation. In such a constellation an economic downturn is almost inevitable.

In some financial crises – as was the case of the Great Depression – a goods market deflation can appear as well. The price level in the USA fell 25 per cent from 1929 to 1933 (Wheelock 1995). Goods market deflations occur when, on the one hand, the demand for goods and services declines, owing to the breakdown of investment, resulting in unemployment and depressed consumption demand. But, on the other hand, supply can increase, despite the declining demand, when firms with liquidity and solvency problems still desperately try to sell everything in their fight for survival. The huge drop in the price level during the Great Depression cannot be explained by disequilibrium between goods market demand and supply alone. The most important factor to explain the deflation was the fall in unit labour costs. Nominal (hourly) wages declined by more than 20 per cent in the USA from 1929 to 1933, as can be seen in Figure 4.8. The high level of unemployment and the lack of government support to prevent the fall in nominal wages led to the breakdown of the nominal wage anchor and falling wage costs, with the consequence of a cost-driven deflationary process.[4] Such a process has already been analysed by Keynes (1930) in his *Treatise on Money*. With goods market deflation a downward spiral was created which led to the Great Depression.

Contrary to the neoclassical view, nominal wage cuts pushed deflation even further and led to the explosion of the real debt burden and the collapse of the economy. A key point is that workers are not even able to reduce real wages by cutting nominal wages. In Keynes's (1936, p. 13) words: 'There may exist no expedient by which labour as a whole can reduce its *real* wage to a given figure by making revised *money* bargains with the entrepreneurs.' When we look at Table 4.2 it becomes clear that, in spite of substantial nominal wage cuts, real wages did not fall in line with nominal wage cuts. As to wages and the Great Depression, Keynes (1936, p. 9) argues: 'It is not very plausible to assert that unemployment in the United States in 1932 was due either to labour obstinately refusing to accept a reduction of money-wages or to its obstinately demanding a real wage beyond what the productivity of the economic machine was capable of furnishing.'

Deflation is one of the biggest feedback mechanisms leading to a

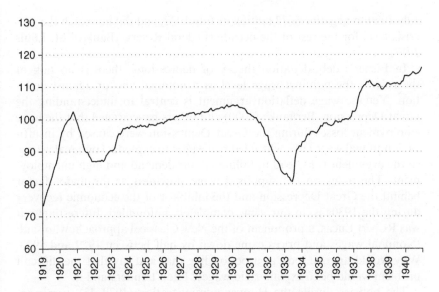

Source: Federal Reserve Bank of St. Louis (2013); own calculations.

Figure 4.8 *Index of composite nominal wages for the USA (1926=100), 1919–40*

cumulative contraction. Irving Fisher (1933) correctly argued that high levels of nominal debt and goods market deflation were the key factors in explaining the destructive power of the financial crisis in the Great Depression. The combination of goods market deflation and high indebtedness leads to an increase of the real debt burden of all the debtors in domestic currency. The more firms are forced or try to pay back loans and increase the pressure on workers to cut nominal wages, the more they owe in real terms. The non-performing loan problem explodes, the coherence of financial markets erodes and the economic boat not only shakes, but it capsizes. Bank failures increase as well, as debtors default and panicked depositors attempt to quickly withdraw their deposits.

The Bank of America failed in December 1930 and, between August 1931 and January 1932, 1860 banks followed suit (Bernanke and James 1991). An even greater number of US banks, roughly 9000 in total, suspended their operations between 1929 and 1933 (Wheelock 1995). In such an environment, surviving banks became much more cautious in their lending policies, but the incentives for productive investment also ceased in the face of low demand and worsening profit expectations. Aggregate net profits of US corporations had fallen dramatically, from $1.7 billion in

July 1929 to negative $677 million in July 1932, and did not reach the pre-crisis level for the rest of the decade (Federal Reserve Bank of St. Louis 2013).

In Fisher's debt-deflation theory of depressions, there is no talk of the role of the nominal wage level as a nominal anchor against deflation. Yet the wage deflation argument is central to understanding the Great Depression. Bernanke (2000) and others have argued that the huge employment losses during the Great Depression were caused by insufficient nominal wage cuts, which led real wages to explode. High real wages, so the argument runs, lead to falling labour demand and high unemployment. The focus on the supposed wage stickiness as the major factor behind the Great Depression and the inhibitor of the economic recovery during the 1930s is, in our view, completely unfounded. Interestingly, it was Robert Lucas, a proponent of the New Classical approach, who said: 'Nominal wages and prices came down by half between 1929 and 1933. Why would anyone look at a period like that and say that the difficult problem would be to explain rigid wages? I don't understand it.'[5]

The policies during the Hoover administration (1929–33) were non-interventionist. Temin (1993, 1994), for example, argues strongly against Hoover's 'deflationary policy' caused by his orthodox adherence to the Gold Standard and belief in neoclassical remedies to solve the crisis. The view which then prevailed was that counter-cyclical fiscal policy would undermine the credibility of the government, whereas monetary easing would damage the value of the dollar (Desai 2011). The Federal Reserve maintained a passive stance initially, but then actually raised interest rates in the fourth quarter of 1931 (Federal Reserve Bank of St. Louis 2013) with the intent of stabilizing the dollar and to not go off the Gold Standard. In the summer of 1931, a series of currency crises hit Europe, and both Germany and Britain went off the Gold Standard, after which the British pound devalued substantially. There was a sentiment in the market that the US dollar would be next, and investors rushed to sell their holdings of dollars. The action of the Fed was thus to preserve the value of the dollar (Temin 1994). There was also no attempt to engage in open-market operations to inject new reserves and/or lend to distressed banks. The function as a lender of last resort was violated by the Fed. Nothing, in sum, was done by the monetary authorities to prevent the wave of bank failures in those years. No fiscal policy was implemented as a remedy either. Moreover, in response to a drop in government revenues given the shrinking tax base during the crisis, the government doubled income tax in 1932.

The Smoot–Hawley Tariff Act of 1930 imposed the highest tariffs on imports yet in the USA in order to encourage the purchase of domestically produced goods. This decision may be understandable from the point of view of a country in a deep recession, but it provoked counter-reactions from other governments, which began increasing their import tariffs as well. This then led to a collapse of world trade and a deeper international recession. Over the next several years, countries worldwide abandoned the Gold Standard and began to devalue their currencies. Overall, the early reactions to the crisis consisted of attempts to balance the budget, not to bail out troubled banks, and introducing protectionism so as to reduce current account deficits under the Gold Standard.

4.2.3 The Great Depression in the USA and the New Deal

After the inauguration of Franklin D. Roosevelt as US president in March 1933, the government decided to introduce a four-day bank holiday (extended for another three days) to analyse banks' balance sheets and restore confidence in the financial sector.[6] This was just one of the immediate measures to tackle the depression. Within the first hundred days, Roosevelt signed major laws that covered all economic sectors, from agriculture to financial services.[7] The Emergency Banking Act, which accompanied the bank holiday, empowered the government to halt bank transactions, investigate the books of banks and determine whether their balance sheets were sound enough to continue business, and to make currency provided by the Federal Reserve System more easily available. The Federal Emergency Relief Act allotted $500 million from the Reconstruction Finance Corporation (RFC) to the states. The Securities Exchange Act created the Securities Exchange Commission, which is still supervising trade of stocks in the USA today. The Banking Act of 1933 – the famous Glass–Steagall Act – separated investment from commercial banks, increased the power of the Federal Reserve Board to oversee transactions in the Federal Reserve System and created the Federal Deposit Insurance Corporation (FDIC). The Banking Act of 1935 made the FDIC a permanent authority in financial markets and shifted power from the regional banks of the Federal Reserve System to the Governors of the Federal Reserve System.

The Thomas Amendment of the Agricultural Adjustment Act from 1933 was the first step towards going off the Gold Standard, which was an important step towards reflation. Gold inflows to the USA increased strongly after leaving the Gold Standard in 1933 and devaluing the dollar in 1933–34. Gold inflows came especially from European countries, where an increasing threat of another war was building up and the pound sterling had lost a lot of its international role. This was described by Friedman and Schwartz (1963, p. 544):

> The money stock grew at a rapid rate in the three successive years from June 1933 to June 1936 . . . The rapid rise was a consequence of the gold inflow produced by the revaluation of gold plus the flight of capital to the United States. It was in no way a consequence of the contemporaneous business expansion.

Production remained meagre and unemployment remained high throughout the first half of the 1930s (Table 4.2). Bank lending remained weak throughout the decade. The deposit–reserve ratio fell between 1933 and 1942 from 8.86 to 4.67 (Romer 1991, p. 21–22), showing that banks did not use their room for manoeuvre to lend.

Roosevelt believed that falling wages and prices were the main factors exacerbating the depression; therefore he attempted – successfully – to prevent a further fall in nominal wages and prices. The National Industrial Recovery Act of 1933 forced employers to agree to 'codes of fair competition' and granted them the suspension of anti-trust legislation. In 1935, the Social Security Act created the first basic social safety net in the USA. The National Labour Relations Act granted workers the right to organize and bargain collectively as well as prevented them from participating in unfair labour practices. The administration also created many programmes to employ the unemployed (e.g. Works Progress Administration). The Fair Labour Standards Act introduced a minimum wage and maximum work hours and finally banned child labour.

Roosevelt's policies were intended to turn a deflationary and contracting economy around, towards expansion. This was also the reason why he decided to devalue the dollar in 1933–34 and why the Federal Reserve made no attempt to sterilize the vast gold inflows throughout the 1930s. By early 1937, the recovery appeared to be under way – with the exception of unemployment, which was still high – and industrial production surpassed its 1929 level (Table 4.2). Eggertson (2008) argues that the recovery was driven by a shift in expectations, which was caused in large part by Roosevelt's policy decisions. But in June 1937 Roosevelt opted for balancing the budget by cutting spending and increasing taxes. Another recession followed in 1938, when industrial production fell by 30 per cent over the course of a few months. In 1938, every fifth person in the USA was still out of work (Galbraith [1954] 2009). In fact, unemployment and real gross national product did not return to their pre-crisis levels until the USA was well into the Second World War.

The New Deal no doubt created the institutional foundation for the long and stable economic expansion after the Second World War, which lasted until the 1970s. However, during the 1930s, despite the benefits of ending wage and price deflation and thus preventing a further downward spiral, nothing was really done to boost aggregate demand. Cary Brown

Table 4.2 *Macroeconomic indicators for the USA, 1929–42*

Year	Gross national product, nominal (in billions of dollars)	Real GNP (in billions of 1939 dollars)	Industrial production (index, August 1929=100)	Dow Jones Industrial Average (index)	Consumer Price Index (August 1929=100)	Un-employ ment rate	Real wages (industrial sector, 1929=100)	Real wages (total, 1929=100)	Govern-ment spending (in billions of dollars)	Govern-ment debt-to-GDP ratio	Govern-ment budget balance (in percen-tage of GDP)
1929	103.6	84.8	95.5	248.5	99.4	3.2	100	100	2.6	16.3	0.7
1930	91.2	79.5	88.7	164.6	93.1	8.7	101.9	98.2	2.7	17.8	0.8
1931	76.5	73.1	69.9	77.9	84.4	15.9	106.0	96.1	4.0	22.0	–0.6
1932	58.7	62.5	57.5	59.9	75.7	23.6	105.3	92.3	3.0	33.2	–4.7
1933	56.4	62.3	51.0	99.9	76.3	24.9	102.5	87.2	3.4	39.9	–4.6
1934	66.0	67.3	64.0	104.0	77.5	21.7	108.8	91.1	5.5	41.1	–5.4
1935	73.3	71.9	74.0	144.1	79.8	20.1	108.3	90.4	5.6	39.2	–3.8
1936	83.8	83.7	83.2	179.9	80.9	16.9	107.2	94.1	7.8	40.3	–5.1
1937	91.9	86.6	102.4	120.8	83.2	14.3	113.0	92.5	6.4	39.6	–2.4
1938	86.1	82.8	75.7	154.8	80.9	19.0	117.4	92.8	7.3	43.2	–0.1
1939	92.2	90.4	89.7	150.2	80.9	17.2	116.4	94.3	8.3	43.8	–3.1
1940	101.4	NA	108.6	131.1	81.5	14.6	NA	NA	8.5	42.3	–2.9
1941	126.7	NA	127.4	111.0	89.6	9.9	NA	NA	12.7	38.6	–3.9
1942	161.9	NA	153.8	119.4	97.7	4.7	NA	NA	31.0	44.7	–12.7

Source: Federal Reserve Bank of St. Louis (2013); own calculations.

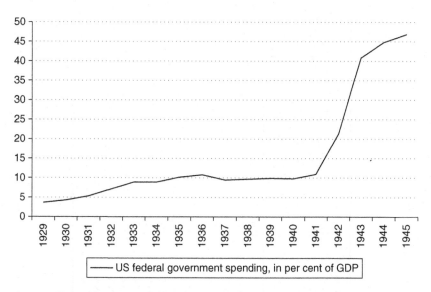

Source: Federal Reserve Bank of St. Louis (2013); own calculations.

Figure 4.9   Government expenditure for the USA, 1929–45

(1956, pp. 863 ff.) famously put it: 'Fiscal policy, then, seems to have been an unsuccessful recovery device in the "thirties" – not because it did not work, but because it was not tried.' During Roosevelt's administration, government spending in relation to GDP (see Figure 4.9) fluctuated between 8 and 11 per cent until 1940. With the military spending for the Second World War, federal expenditures jumped from 12 to 44 per cent of GDP between 1940 and 1943, finally bringing the unemployment rate below 5 per cent and boosting the US GDP.

4.2.4   Concluding Remarks

Although the Great Depression in the USA is usually associated with the stock market crash of 1929, it is important to take a look at prior developments taking place during the 'Roaring Twenties'. In the mid-1920s, a real estate boom took place in the USA, with increasing speculation in the years 1924 and 1925 resulting in strong increases of real estate prices. Leverage was high, and there was an unprecedented mounting up of mortgage debt. In 1926, the real estate bubble came to an end and brought about a long process of foreclosures, with non-performing loans increasing over time and remaining a serious issue throughout the 1930s. In general, real estate bubbles have longer-lasting negative consequences than stock market bubbles, as the former usually involve much more credit, so the process of deleveraging is typically much longer and can last well over a decade. In addition, consumption credits increased sharply, reflecting in part a more unequal income distribution. The stock market bubble and the subsequent October 1929 crash added to the already existing problem of foreclosures and non-performing loans. This led to a first wave of bankruptcies by households, businesses and banks during the 1929–33 recession.

Under the Hoover administration (1929–33) there was no active policy to solve the crisis after it broke out. There was no coordinated bailout of banks from either the government or even the central bank. Fiscal policy focused on the attempt to balance the public budget; however, government debt increased in spite of the efforts at fiscal tightening, because of the recession. There was also no policy to halt disastrous nominal wage cuts, which triggered a deflationary wage–price spiral.

As Irving Fisher (1933) argued, asset price deflation and goods market deflation in a situation of high domestic debt are the worst thing that can happen, as they increase the real debt burden in the whole economy. Deflation also discourages new investment, because it erodes the expected profitability and entrepreneurs abstain from investing. Furthermore, consumption demand is depressed, as households wait to buy durables until prices fall. During deflation, non-performing loans increase and eventually flood the market and lead to the collapse of the financial system. Though Fisher did not discuss the role of the nominal wage level as a nominal anchor against deflation, the wage deflation argument is an important factor in understanding the Great Depression. Many mainstream economists (for instance, Bernanke and James 1991) argued that the huge employment losses during the Great Depression were caused by insufficient nominal wage cuts causing real wages to explode and thus leading to high unemployment. From 1929 to 1933 in the USA, nominal wages fell by more than 20 per cent. In our view, it was in fact the nominal wage cuts that deepened the deflation and led to the explosion of the debt burden and the collapse of the economy.

During Roosevelt's administration (1933–45), *New Deal* policies were aimed at, among other things, strengthening workers' relative bargaining position, consequently preventing further reductions in nominal wages. Other programmes introduced under Roosevelt's leadership such as the Glass–Steagall Act helped in creating an institutional foundation for the *golden age* of capitalism following the Second World War. However, during the 1930s, fiscal stimulus was not used to boost demand and accelerate the recovery. Unemployment remained very high throughout the 1930s, and US output did not return to its pre-crisis levels until the outbreak of the Second World War. Expansionary fiscal policy in the USA was prompted only by the entry of the USA into the Second World War in 1941, soon after which unemployment fell below 10 per cent for the first time in over a decade.

4.3   THE LATIN AMERICAN DEBT CRISIS

4.3.1   The Background

In the period from 1950 to 1980, the weighted average growth rate of the countries of Latin America was around 5.5 per cent annually (see Ocampo 2004), in general under a regime of regulated international capital flows. In the late 1960s and early 1970s, however, Latin American countries deregulated international capital flows. The sweet poison of foreign debt opened up new opportunities of financing for governments and bigger (in many cases state-owned) companies in Latin America. During the 1970s, capital inflows to Latin America came particularly in the form of foreign loans. Long-term foreign debt increased from $68 billion, or 20 per cent of the region's GDP, in 1975 to $238 billion, or 35 per cent of the region's GDP, in 1982: by the end of 1982 the total external debt of Latin America, including short- and long-term debt and IMF credits, was $332 billion, or 49 per cent of the region's GDP (Ramos-Francia et al. 2013). After Mexico's default in 1982, capital inflows stopped abruptly, and the decade thereafter was characterized by large capital outflows because of not only debt servicing obligations but also capital flight. Subsequently, Latin America fell into stagnation for a long period. The 1980s thus became known as a 'lost decade' for Latin America (Dornbusch 1990a, p. 1).

Latin America had suffered from a destructive externally stimulated boom–bust cycle, which led to a long-term stagnation. Figure 4.10 shows net capital flows as a percentage of GDP between 1980 and 1995. The lost decade saw substantial net financial outflows, and only in the 1990s did external private financial inflows, including the repatriation of domestic capital, become positive again. Foreign direct investment as well as portfolio investment did not play a significant role in either the 1970s or the 1980s.

During the 1970s, movements of international capital flows were marked by several external events.

First, capital flows only became possible, as mentioned, as capital controls were dismantled. Most of the countries in this region opened their capital accounts as part of their financial deregulation and liberalization in the late 1960s (Brazil) or during the 1970s (Argentina, Chile, Colombia, Mexico, Peru and Venezuela) (Damill et al. 2013).

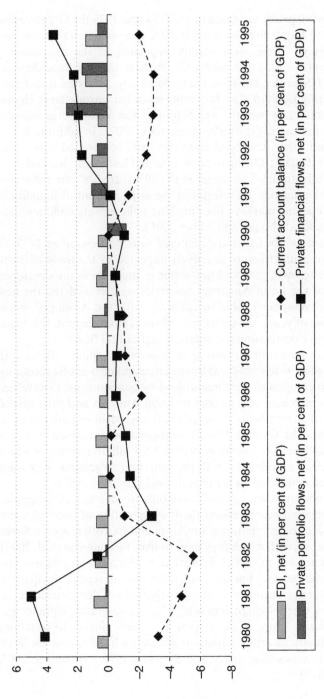

Source: IMF (2014).

Figure 4.10 Current account balance and net capital flows to Latin America, 1980–95

Second, after oil prices increased in 1973–74 and 1979 the Organization of the Petroleum Exporting Countries (OPEC) accumulated high reserves in hard currency.[8] These were mainly deposited in the international banking system (so-called 'petrodollars').[9] At first, most of these deposits were based in US banks, but soon many dollar deposits were transferred to Europe, mainly London, now becoming so-called 'eurodollars'. Hence, international monetary wealth, which looked for attractive investment opportunities, increased drastically (Beenstock 2007). In addition banks in the USA and other developed countries were confronted with lower domestic credit demand. Owing to recessions and low credit demand from oil importing industrialized countries in the 1970s, credits were redirected to Third World countries. As a result of the large amount of liquidity in international financial markets, loan-pushing policies were commonplace (Stallings 1990; Kindleberger and Aliber 2005).

Third, when developed countries entered into a recession in 1973–75 Latin American countries were negatively impacted by the trade channel. However, GDP growth rates did not suffer as much as in the developed world. Some of the Latin American countries were considered the new superstars of development, able to catch up with the developed world within a number of years. Given the now open capital account, this made them an attractive destination for international capital flows.

Fourth, Latin American governments welcomed capital inflows with open arms. Credits were used for infrastructure and also public consumption. Credits to companies were guaranteed by governments. Overvalued exchange rates increased real income in Latin America and safeguarded the legitimacy of governments. Most of the foreign debt in Latin America was government debt. Overall, Third World countries increased their debt to private banks from $11 billion in 1970 to $261 billion in 1982, of which Brazil and Mexico accounted for 43 per cent, and Argentina, Venezuela and Chile for an additional 14 per cent in 1982 (Stallings 1990).

Developing countries are generally able only to get credit denominated in foreign currencies, which reflects the low reputation of their own currencies in the eyes of international investors and has often been referred to as an original sin with which they have to live (Eichengreen et al. 2003). As a result, a currency mismatch is created in which debtors receive revenues in domestic currency but simultaneously have to repay principal and interest in the foreign currency. Consequently, a sharp domestic depreciation in countries where foreign debt is high leads to domestic liquidity and solvency problems. Thus, in developing countries, major depreciations and domestic financial crises actually reinforce each other and are likely to result in twin crises (Kaminsky and Reinhart 1999; Williamson 2005; Damill et al. 2013).

Large capital inflows lead to greater economic fragility, because:

a. High net capital inflows make it easy to finance current account deficits, or even create them.
b. High gross capital inflows increase foreign debt as long as the inflow is not foreign direct investment or portfolio equity investment. Here one has to take into account the fact that some of the gross capital inflows will finance capital outflows in the form of capital flight. Countries caught in a situation of high foreign debt are very vulnerable to small changes in future expectations or any kind of economic shocks that lead to capital flows and/or exchange rate movements and change the real debt burden. Dollarization can be considered as capital flight within the country. It refers to the phenomenon in which part of the domestic monetary wealth is kept in a 'stronger' foreign currency, in particular the US dollar or later also the euro.[10] As a consequence banks with high foreign currency deposits also provide loans to the domestic economy, denominated in foreign currency, and thus create a currency mismatch comparable with foreign credits in foreign currency.
c. Dollarization and capital flight prevent countries from accessing a stable domestically financed credit-investment-income process, because such a process automatically leads to capital exports and depreciation (Herr 2008).[11] For these reasons, central banks often do not have much room to manoeuvre and are constrained to limit domestic credit expansion and growth to lower the risk of triggering a harmful depreciation. Countries can compensate capital outflows by capital inflows and prevent depreciations. For example, capital exports by private households can be compensated by foreign credit taken by the government and the enterprise sector. However, such a constellation leads to ever more fragility.
d. Surges of capital inflows stimulate domestic boom phases. Stock market bubbles especially can be intensified.

When the countries of Latin America relaxed or eliminated controls on capital inflows and outflows, more fragility was brought into their financial systems. They suffered from all elements of a boom–bust cycle. Current account deficits were created, dollarization increased drastically in Latin America, elites kept their monetary wealth abroad, and foreign indebtedness increased substantially. Last, but not least, asset market bubbles were intensified. In Chile, for example, the dollar-denominated value of stocks grew on average 87 per cent annually during the period between 1975 and 1981 (Palma 2013). This was 12 times faster than Chile's GDP growth during the same time.

4.3.2   The Crisis

During the 1970s, Latin America welcomed high foreign inflows of credit, as highlighted above. The mounting debt did not cause any concern for the Latin American governments, nor for the international community.[12] Floating interest rates of foreign debt, which were entirely beyond the control of Latin American governments, were also not seen as a problem.

Both the sharp depreciation of the US dollar in 1979 and the increasing US inflation rate were of great concern for the USA. In 1979 Paul Volcker, the newly appointed president of the Federal Reserve, implemented an extremely restrictive monetary policy to fight inflation and restore the eroding international role of the US dollar. The federal funds rate, already at around 10 per cent by early 1979, peaked at almost 20 per cent in June to July 1981 (Federal Reserve Bank of St. Louis 2013). Higher interest rates combined with the election in 1980 of Ronald Reagan as US president–who advocated a revitalization of the hegemonic position of the USA that had weakened under President Jimmy Carter – strengthened the USA dollar, but also triggered a sharp recession in the USA and most of the other industrialized countries in 1980 and 1981 (Hsu 2013). Commodity and raw material prices fell substantially, and the recession caused demand for imports to decline in many industrialized countries (Ruggiero 1999). At the same time, higher interest rates increased the debt burden for indebted developing countries (the interest on debt rose from around 4–5 per cent to almost 19 per cent in 1980). Furthermore, a reduction in exports made it even harder for developing countries to earn foreign currency to meet their debt obligations. Only in 1982, when the Latin American debt crises broke out and US banks were massively affected by the debt crisis, was this restrictive monetary policy abandoned. Confidence in the US dollar at that time was established, and the inflation rate in the USA was brought down at high economic costs. Thus the cut in US interest rates in 1982 did not lead to a new weakness of the US dollar. The opposite was the case: the US dollar appreciated substantially until 1985, when a new depreciation of the US dollar was triggered (Herr and Kazandziska 2011).

On 12 August 1982, the Mexican finance minister announced that Mexico was unable to meet its debt servicing obligations, after which private banks abruptly stopped lending to Mexico. In the face of the Mexican default, the US Federal Reserve, together with the IMF, arranged a short-term rescue package. Following this, Mexico's government negotiated a longer-term loan with the IMF. However, quickly after Mexico's default, other Latin American countries began to report solvency problems as well. The cessation of new foreign loans led to a general debt crisis in Latin America, and within one year the majority of the countries in this region were negotiating to reschedule their debts. In the first round of negotiations, the interest charged was substantially higher compared to interest for the original loans. Furthermore, the loans provided by the Bretton Woods institutions – at that time especially by the World Bank, which joined the rescue packages – came with attached harsh conditionalities of economic reforms. Initially it was mostly about cuts in public expenditures and fiscal discipline. Later, so-called *Structural Adjustment Programmes* forced countries to privatize state-owned industries, liberalize their domestic financial systems, deregulate protected economic sectors, and so on under the agenda famously known as the Washington Consensus.[13]

The creditors[14] combined were much more organized than the debtor countries (Stallings 1990; Devlin and Ffrench-Davis 1995). The potential insolvency of Latin American countries caused a panic in international financial markets: the Latin American debt crisis was not just a crisis of the Third World, but also threatening the stability and solvency of the international banking system as a whole. Hsu (2013, p. 51) reports that American banks had an exposure of as much as 177 per cent of their equity to the four largest Latin American debtor countries (Argentina, Brazil, Mexico and Venezuela) when the crisis broke out.

Between 1982 and 1988 repeated rounds of rescheduling and debt restructuring took place, including an attempt by the IMF and the World Bank to tackle the international debt crisis via the so-called *Baker Plan*.[15] The Baker Plan was discussed at the annual meeting in Seoul in October 1985, and it consisted of the provision of funds by international financial institutions to the region without involving governments (Ruggiero 1999). However, the Baker Plan was never successfully implemented. When Brazil declared a moratorium on its debt services in February 1987, despite multiple attempts to reschedule and renegotiate its debt, it was widely accepted that the majority of debtor countries were no closer to financial health than in 1982, and that a substantial part of the loans would never be entirely repaid. This led to the *Brady Plan*[16] in March 1989, which involved either a partial debt relief (where debt holders exchanged their loans for so-called 'discount bonds', in which case the debt was immediately reduced by 30 to 50 per cent, with the market-based floating interest rates) or a reduction in interest payments (by exchanging the loans for 'par bonds', which carried the same face value but implied a fixed, below-market interest rate). The negotiations were made on a case-by-case basis, and the first country to restructure under the Brady Plan was Mexico in 1989–90 (EMTA 2014). The adherence to the Brady Plan, of course, was linked to assurances of economic reform in the spirit of the Washington Consensus. Mexico was the first candidate to implement the Brady Plan, and its debt servicing obligations were ultimately reduced by 35 per cent (Devlin and Ffrench-Davis 1995; Ruggiero 1999).[17] Considering the high indebtedness of Latin American countries, a 3 per cent debt relief per year was not enough to sufficiently solve the problem of over-indebtedness. Even more importantly, the fact that the foreign debt problem was not dealt with in a hands-on and timely fashion, but was rather postponed until 1989, prolonged and exacerbated the precarious situation in which much of Latin America found itself, turning the period in fact into a (longer than) lost decade.

4.3.3   The Lost Decade

After 1982, Latin American countries were burdened by big annual net transfers as a consequence of debt servicing obligations.[18] As the Brady Plan was not put in place until 1989, the indebtedness of Latin American countries did not decrease substantially throughout the entire decade. It is widely considered that the external debt problem in Latin America was allowed to persist for too long. The debt problem was not solved in spite of the fact that most foreign debt was public and publicly guaranteed debt (for long-term debt see Figure 4.11).

Furthermore, domestic residents increasingly moved their capital abroad when they saw the crisis developing without hope of a quick solution. In Latin America, capital flight amounted to $151 billion from 1973 to 1987, which was equivalent to 43 per cent of the region's external debt acquired within the same period (Table 4.3). In the extreme case of Venezuela, capital flight was even higher than the external debt attained. Chile, on the other hand, was the only Latin American country which recorded a repatriation of domestic capital during this period. Capital flight was a problem for most of the countries, but it was more pronounced in Mexico, Venezuela and Argentina.

There are several severe consequences of capital flight. Firstly, it weakens productive investments and income generation because part of domestic wealth and credit expansion (either of domestic or of foreign origin) is used to finance capital flight. Secondly, capital flight depletes foreign reserves when countries fight against destabilizing depreciations; fewer reserves are then available to service external debt or to take actions against a currency crisis. Thirdly, capital flight reduces the tax base when the rich hold their assets abroad. Fourthly, the less rich have fewer opportunities to transfer their wealth to foreign countries. They keep hard foreign currency in cash or as deposits in domestic banks. The case of Argentina has especially shown that foreign currency deposits are not safe when the domestic banking system collapses. Fifthly, all the

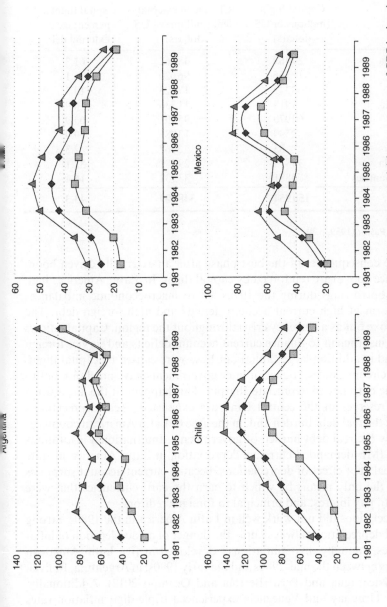

Notes: Total external debt as percentage of GDP is given by the highest line, total long-term external debt as percentage of GDP is given by the middle line, and public debt plus publicly guaranteed debt as percentage of GDP is given by the lowest line.

Source: Ramos-Francia et al. (2013, pp. 120–121); own illustrations.

Figure 4.11 External debt as percentage of GDP for Argentina, Brazil, Chile and Mexico, 1981–89

Table 4.3   Capital flight from Latin America, 1973–87

Country	Capital flight (millions of US dollars)	Change in external debt (millions of US dollars)	Capital flight as percentage of external debt
Argentina	29469	48062	61.3
Brazil	15566	96620	16.1
Chile	−3342	17325	−19.3
Colombia	1913	11336	16.9
Mexico	60970	95401	63.9
Peru	2599	13085	19.9
Uruguay	83	3667	2.3
Venezuela	38815	29381	132.1
Other countries	4881	33932	14.4
Total	**150954**	**348809**	**43.3**

Source: Pastor (1989, p.9).

negative consequences of the bust phase after an externally driven boom phase (see above) are reinforced by capital flight. In Latin America, high foreign borrowings during the 1970s led to macroeconomic imbalances in the form of high current account deficits and high foreign debt. The crisis broke out as a currency crisis throughout the region. Capital inflows became insufficient to finance current account deficits and service foreign debt; and in addition large capital outflows were caused by capital flight. In such circumstances, sooner or later governments have no choice but to allow the currency to depreciate sharply. This happens at the latest when foreign reserves of the central bank are exhausted. Real depreciations increase the real debt burden and, in the case of Latin American countries, primarily the real debt burden of governments. International institutions like the IMF demanded currency depreciation in Latin America in spite of the real debt effect of depreciations, because current account surpluses became the only means by which to earn the hard currencies that were needed to pay interest and principal to foreign creditors.

Depreciations did not work well in Latin America in the 1980s. Strong nominal depreciations always imply the danger of an acceleration of inflation rates. Actually, hyperinflations[19] developed in five Latin American countries between the mid-1980s and the early 1990s: in Argentina, Bolivia, Brazil, Nicaragua and Peru (Bertola and Ocampo 2012). Additionally, Mexico, Uruguay and Venezuela experienced triple-digit inflation rates during the 1980s. Very high inflation rates and hyperinflations developed in the same way as in many other historical examples. As a result of a huge nominal depreciation, real wages for some groups of workers dropped to such low levels that nominal wages had to increase in order to guarantee workers a subsistence wage. Other sectors of the population did not accept the cut in real wages by depreciation and demanded compensating nominal income increases. In such cases, wage inflation adds to the price inflation initially caused by the depreciation, and the economy falls into a depreciation–wage–price spiral. In the case of dollarization, when prices are implicitly indexed with the nominal exchange rate, the depreciation–inflation mechanism is even stronger. Hyperinflation is in these cases not triggered by escalating increases of money supply; money supply follows endogenously the described processes in the economy (Robinson 1938; Fischer et al. 2002; Ramos-Francia et al. 2013).[20]

When countries are not able to create net capital inflows, their current accounts become automatically balanced, whereas large capital flight and net capital outflows make the current accounts positive. After the crisis, Latin American countries quickly reduced their current account deficits, and some even realized substantial surpluses – in particular Mexico, Brazil and later on Argentina (IMF 2014). However, given the relatively weak overall demand during the economic slowdown worldwide in the early 1980s, the surplus was mainly caused by a reduction in imports reflecting a big drop in real GDP. Living standards for the majority of the population dropped substantially as a result of sharply increasing unemployment or underemployment and deteriorating terms of trade.

What happened in Latin America was not a short and sharp recession followed by a recovery (Table 4.4). Compared to 2.7 per cent of annual per capita GDP growth between 1950 and 1980, in the 1980s per capita GDP grew by only 0.9 per cent annually. Per capita GDP growth rates declined to a large extent in the first half of the 1980s, particularly in Bolivia, El Salvador, Venezuela, Argentina, Uruguay and Guatemala (see Table 4.5). Poverty rates increased, reaching 48.3 per cent by the end of the 1980s, which was 8 per cent higher than in 1980 (Ocampo 2004). There is no doubt that the 1980s were a lost decade. During the recovery of the first half of the 1990s, growth was also substantially lower than the region's GDP growth rates before the onset of the debt crisis.

In addition to this, Latin America could not establish financial stability. For example, in 1994 the Mexican 'tequila crisis' affected the entire continent. Again, after the Asian crisis in 1997, most Latin American countries fought to prevent currency crises, of which Argentina's crisis in 2001–02 was the most prominent example.

In the 1980s, first the collapse and later the stagnation of aggregate demand caused the severe economic crisis and the stagnation thereafter. Investment dropped to very low levels.[21] High interest rates on credits,

Table 4.4　Latin America's annual real growth rates, 1950–2002

	1950–80	1980–90	1990–97	1997–2002
GDP growth				
Weighted average	5.5	1.1	3.6	1.3
Simple average	4.8	1.0	3.9	1.7
GDP per capita				
Weighted average	2.7	−0.9	2.0	−0.3
Simple average	2.1	−1.2	1.9	−0.3

Source: Ocampo (2004, p. 70).

Table 4.5　Changes in per capita GDP in Latin America, 1981–85

Country	Cumulative change in per capita GDP, 1981–85 (%)	Country	Cumulative change in per capita GDP, 1981–85 (%)	Country	Cumulative change in per capita GDP, 1981–85 (%)
Argentina	−18.5	Ecuador	−3.9	Panama	0.7
Bolivia	−28.4	El Salvador	−24	Peru	−14.8
Colombia	−0.1	Guatemala	−18.3	Uruguay	−18.6
Costa Rica	−11.2	Mexico	−4.3	Venezuela	−21.6
Chile	−8.7				

Source: Sachs (1986, p. 43); data from the Economic Commission for Latin America and the Caribbean (ECLAC).

cautious behaviour by banks and negative expectations by firms kept investments low. According to Rüdiger Dornbusch, investors in Latin America followed a wait-and-see attitude:

> [They] have an option to postpone the return of flight capital and they will wait until the front loading of investment returns is sufficient to compensate for the risk of relinquishing the liquidity option of a wait-and-see position . . . There is definitely little commitment to a rapid resumption of real investment. The reason for this is residual uncertainty whether stabilisation can in fact be sustained. (Dornbusch 1990b, pp. 17–18)

Consumption demand was depressed because of high unemployment and eroding real incomes. Furthermore, fiscal stimulus was not allowed, because the IMF and other foreign creditors demanded fiscal consolidation as part of the Washington Consensus. Even though positive trade and service balances increased aggregate demand, this component of demand was too small to trigger economic growth.

Economically, socially and politically speaking, development in the 1980s in Latin America was a disaster. Governments either willingly followed or were forced to follow policies in the spirit of the Washington Consensus by international institutions and foreign governments, which privileged the rich and increased profitability while at the same time decreasing the living standard of the majority of people and increasing poverty. Everything seemed to be prepared for investors and a recovery. But investors did not come, which left governments in black despair:

> If the private sector does not respond with investment and capacity expansion, and if confidence and inflation issues bar a public sector expansion, then of course the policy maker becomes the proverbial emperor without clothes: he has sharply increased profitability in the traded goods sector and the profits are taken out as capital flight; there is no growth, there is social injustice and social conflict. (Dornbusch 1990b, p. 13)

4.3.4 Concluding Remarks

A special characteristic of the Latin American externally driven boom–bust cycle of the 1970s and 1980s was that it led to a long-term stagnation. Initially, large capital inflows, mainly advocated by governments, led to overvalued real exchange rates, current account deficits and increased foreign debt denominated in foreign currency. Foreign indebtedness and dollarization created a currency mismatch in these countries. In Latin America, most countries pegged their exchange rate to the US dollar. Current account deficits rose because of relatively high domestic interest rates, relatively high GDP growth rates during the boom phase and easy external means of financing deficits. Flexible exchange rates would probably have increased current account deficits even faster because of nominal currency appreciations. Thus the boom–bust cycle was independent of the exchange rate regime. Domestically, the boom phase was combined with rising asset prices and relatively high economic growth.

In almost all cases a progressive worsening of the current account balance and increasing foreign debt undermine the credibility of exchange rate stability and the country in general. When the possibility of a devaluation of the domestic currency appears more likely, the level of uncertainty increases and risk-averse investors start to reduce their financial commitments to the indebted country. Then, any type of shock can lead to a halt of capital inflows and stimulate cumulative capital outflows. For Latin

America, the boom phase of the 1970s came to an end as a result of the impact that restrictive monetary policies in the USA had on the indebted countries. Capital outflows depleted central bank reserves – as long as the central bank could intervene in foreign exchange markets – and led to very large depreciations, triggering depreciation–inflation spirals which brought very high inflation rates and destructive real-debt effects in Latin America, which suffered from high debt denominated in foreign currency. Governments had to start negotiating with creditors and/or international institutions. According to the policies enforced by external creditors in the spirit of the Washington Consensus, governments had to renounce any possibility of stimulating the economy via fiscal expansion or other measures to stimulate domestic demand.

Latin America suffered from a severe crisis which developed in a long stagnation for two main reasons. Firstly, the external debt problem could not be solved in a quick and efficient manner. The debt crisis broke out in 1982, but the first effective plan to reduce the foreign debt burden was the Brady Plan, which was implemented in 1989. However, this plan reduced the debt burden only moderately. The reduction of the debt burden came too late and was not sufficient to allow a quick recovery of the economy. From a historical perspective, the Latin American debt crisis was remarkable in regard to the strong coordination between creditors and their commitment to reduce the risk of potential illiquidity and insolvency of the international banking system. In response to the crisis they quickly organized a form of international lender of last resort to contain the danger created by the Latin American debt crisis. Yet, as Devlin and Ffrench-Davis (1995) pointed out, a national lender of last resort would usually take action to minimize the overall social costs generated by the financial crisis. But, in this case, the creditor community focused primarily on minimizing the losses of the financial system and did not care about the social situation in the crisis countries.

Secondly, the creditor community forced Washington Consensus policies upon the debtor countries. These policies implied not only balancing the budget, especially through a cut in social expenditure, but also low inflation and currency depreciation. Structural reforms were enforced according to neoclassical beliefs: neoclassical change in institutions – or more general neoclassical 'Ordnungspolitik' – was implemented, including privatization, deregulation, liberalization and the establishment of clear property rights, to name only a few. All of these policies combined do not support economic growth in any active way. Instead, some, like the policy to reduce budget deficits by cutting social spending, even hamper economic growth during an economic crisis. Furthermore, privatization can quickly create an increase in unemployment. There were a number of neoclassical reform policies, but nothing to stimulate demand (Herr and Priewe 2005, 2006).

Because of high external debt and pressure from foreign creditors the countries were not able to throw off the straitjacket of Washington Consensus policies. Moreover, during the crisis and stagnation and all the economic and political uncertainties that came with it, positive expectation could not develop. Wait-and-see attitudes led to low investment. And, last but not least, consumption demand was low because of policies implemented that made the rich richer and the poor poorer. There is no doubt that the over-adjustment imposed upon debtor countries and insistence upon misguided policies prolonged and deepened the Latin American debt crisis, leaving the region mired in a lost decade.

4.4 THE JAPANESE CRISIS

4.4.1 The Background

Until the 1980s Japan was considered one of the Asian miracle countries, experiencing high GDP growth, fast productivity development, successful export orientation and an efficient government which supported economic development (Stiglitz 1996). Japan had been a highly regulated economy with much more government intervention than in developed Western countries. Cooperation between the government and the private sector, combined with successful industrial policy, led to the creation of large Japanese multinational enterprises. The financial system was especially highly regulated (Stiglitz and Uy 1996). For example, international capital flows were regulated, the banking system channelled credits to the industries which were considered important for development, stock market debt securities played an overall unimportant role, and credits to the real estate or household sectors were highly restricted, to name only a few. The Bank of Japan fixed interest rates at low levels and determined the maximum volume of credits commercial banks could grant. This credit rationing system, referred to as 'window guidance', was supported by the rule that enterprises were not allowed to take credit from abroad or to issue debt securities in the domestic market. Within this framework, the Bank of Japan had a substantial control over the developments in the real sector of the economy, including the allocation of credits. Before the 1980s, there was no room for asset market bubbles. Japanese corporate governance had traditionally been characterized by an intense cross-holding system, where the creditor bank was typically among the top five shareholders of a firm (McCauley 2013). Conversely, banks' shares were owned by the bank's borrowers. Such a cross-shareholding system, similar to yet more developed than the one also seen in Germany, was very 'local' by nature, and foreign investors or firms did not play a significant role in Japan's corporate governance of the financial system in general.

To understand the trigger of the Japanese boom phase the international constellation in the 1980s becomes important. Japan has maintained an export-oriented economy since the Second World War, but only started to build up permanent and high current account surpluses in the 1970s (Herr 1990). It became one of the world's major surplus countries, in large part because of its ever-growing bilateral trade imbalance with the USA in the 1980s. The cause of the US current account deficit goes back to the late 1970s. In 1979, in the middle of a severe currency crisis of the US dollar, Paul Volcker was appointed as chairman of the Federal Reserve and implemented a strict anti-inflationary policy which successfully brought down inflation rates, but also created a pronounced recession. One year later, Ronald Reagan was elected as the new US president. Positive expectations about Reagan's policy regime, which it was assumed would implement business-friendly economic policies and revitalize the military, political and economic power of the USA, increased the international reputation of the US dollar. These changes triggered high capital inflows and led to a substantial appreciation of the US dollar. Consequently, this pushed the US current account deficit from a balanced position at the end of the 1970s into a deep deficit, with a large part vis-à-vis Japan. The high current account deficit hampered US industrial development and reduced US employment. In the mid-1980s the strong US dollar became a hot topic in the USA and in the international policy debate. The US government pushed for joint international action to stop a further appreciation of the US dollar and to reduce the US current account deficit.

These developments led to two agreements which had important repercussions for Japan. The Plaza Agreement in 1985 by the (then) G-5 countries[22] attempted to prevent the further appreciation of the US dollar by pushing central banks outside the USA to sell US dollars from their foreign exchange reserves, which were kept almost totally in US dollars. The agreement also required that Japan deregulate its financial system to stimulate more capital inflows to the country and allow an appreciation of the Japanese yen. Over the following two years, the external value of the US dollar lost more than 50 per cent of its value against major currencies, including the Japanese yen, and the US current account deficit was brought down. The danger then became that the US dollar was too weak. This led to the Louvre Accord in 1987, which aimed to stop the depreciation of the US dollar. Moreover, there was the problem that, in spite of a sharp appreciation of the Japanese yen and against the general trend, the high Japanese current account surplus with the USA did not disappear. Among other things, the (then) G-6 governments[23] agreed that Japan should stimulate its economy and cut its interest rates to increase imports via increasing GDP growth. The Japanese government, which was pleased by its new international role, was eager to fulfil its international obligations.

The Bank of Japan in the second half of the 1980s followed a very expansionary monetary policy, including a substantial deregulation of the financial system. These policies stimulated the real economy, but also began to fuel a huge asset price bubble. For the development of the main economic indicators in Japan, see Table 4.6.

4.4.2 The Boom Phase and Its End

The deregulation of the financial system combined with an aggressive expansionary monetary policy led to huge bubbles in the stock and real estate markets during the second half of the 1980s. Between 1985 and 1989, share prices increased by 240 per cent, and property prices by 245 per cent (Werner 2003, p. 89). Figure 4.12 shows the enormous real estate bubble in big cities in Japan at that time.

A huge credit expansion took place in the second half of the 1980s. Financial liberalization was promoted but it was not accompanied by adequate risk management by banks (Ohmi 2010). In addition to this, for the first time enterprises were allowed to finance themselves in the capital market and regulations concerning investment in real estate were loosened. In general, investors took greater risks as a result of higher competition following the deregulation of asset markets (Hsu 2013). Speculative activities increased whereby the real estate sector became the preferred, albeit not the only, target for speculative investment. Werner (2003, p. 95) estimated that loans used for speculation – so-called 'bubble loans' – amounted to about 37 per cent of GDP when the bubble came to an end.

The Bank of Japan did not see any reason to stop the huge credit expansion, because goods market inflation remained low in spite of high GDP growth and the asset bubble (see Table 4.6). On the contrary, the Bank of Japan increased the credit ceiling within the window guidance system and pressured commercial banks to grant more credits to realize the new ceiling in the second half of the 1980s. In former times the central bank had influenced the credit allocation of banks, but this was later abandoned as well (Werner 2003, p. 133).

It was not until 1989 that the Bank of Japan changed its monetary policy, when goods market inflation started to increase moderately. In order to prevent inflation in the goods market the Bank of Japan increased

Table 4.6   Main economic indicators for Japan, 1980–2012

Year	Gross domestic product at constant prices (annual percentage change)	Producer Price Index: total finished goods (2010=100)	Average Consumer Price Index (annual percentage change)	Government net lending/ borrowing (percentage of GDP)	Current account balance (percentage of GDP)
1980	3.2	127.5	7.8	−4.8	−1.0
1981	4.2	130.8	4.9	−4.2	0.4
1982	3.4	132.4	2.7	−4.1	0.6
1983	3.1	132.4	1.9	−4.3	1.7
1984	4.5	133.0	2.3	−2.8	2.7
1985	6.3	133.0	2.0	−1.5	3.7
1986	2.8	130.2	0.6	−1.5	4.2
1987	4.1	127.2	0.1	−0.4	3.4
1988	7.1	125.5	0.7	0.4	2.6
1989	5.4	126.0	2.3	1.2	2.1
1990	5.6	127.3	3.0	1.8	1.4
1991	3.3	127.8	3.3	1.7	1.9
1992	0.8	128.2	1.7	0.6	2.9
1993	0.2	126.6	1.3	−2.5	3.0
1994	0.9	124.9	0.7	−3.9	2.7
1995	1.9	122.8	−0.1	−4.7	2.1
1996	2.6	121.3	0.1	−5.5	1.4
1997	1.6	120.2	1.8	−4.4	2.2
1998	−2.0	118.9	0.7	−5.9	3.0
1999	−0.2	116.9	−0.3	−7.8	2.6
2000	2.3	115.0	−0.7	−8.0	2.5
2001	0.4	112.2	−0.8	−6.0	2.1
2002	0.3	109.5	−0.9	−7.7	2.8
2003	1.7	106.9	−0.3	−7.8	3.2
2004	2.4	105.6	0.0	−5.9	3.7
2005	1.3	104.9	−0.3	−4.8	3.6
2006	1.7	104.6	0.2	−3.7	3.9
2007	2.2	104.5	0.1	−2.1	4.9
2008	−1.0	104.8	1.4	−4.1	3.3
2009	−5.5	101.2	−1.3	−10.4	2.9
2010	4.7	100.0	−0.7	−9.3	3.7
2011	−0.6	99.1	−0.3	−9.9	2.0
2012	2.0	98.1	0.0	−10.1	1.0

Source: Federal Reserve Bank of St. Louis (2013); IMF (2013); own calculations.

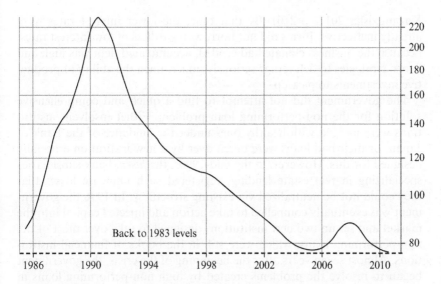

Back to 1983 levels

Note: The index covers the six major Japanese cities (Tokyo, Yokohama, Nagoya, Kyoto, Osaka and Kobe).

Source: Dr. Housing Bubble (2011); data from Japan Real Estate Institute (2012).

Figure 4.12 Japan's residential property index, 1985–2011

the money market interest rate five times between May 1989 and August 1990. More importantly, the window guidance system was used to drastically reduce credit expansion. At the end of 1989, there were signs that asset prices would not increase further. The stock market bubble came to an end, as did the real estate bubble, about one year later. By 1992, stock prices had fallen by half, and they have remained at a low level since. Real estate prices started to fall over a long course of around 15 years and, following a moderate increase after 2006, they fell again to their 1983 levels by 2010 (Figure 4.12).

After the stock market and, especially, the real estate market bubble burst and asset prices began to deflate, many loans defaulted. The problem of non-performing loans remained a grave issue throughout the 1990s, representing 17 per cent of GDP cumulatively from 1992 to 2000 (Hsu 2013). At the same time, real GDP growth dropped to very low levels. By 1992, the government had recognized the impending threat of a severe recession. However, after the crisis began, the Bank of Japan was not quick enough to respond with a suitable monetary policy and took several years – until 1995 – to cut the interest rate to 1 per cent (Herr and

Kazandziska 2011, p.210). By that time, the lower interest rates were already ineffective. Firms did not borrow, regardless of low interest rates, because the business climate had eroded, accumulated debt was high and firms' strategies to deleverage seriously undermined the ability of productive investments to pick up.

The government did not attempt to find a quick and comprehensive solution for the non-performing loan problem. Either insolvent institutions were merged with healthy ones under the guidance of the Bank of Japan, or their bad loans were taken over by a new institution especially designed for this. However, in the mid-1990s, the *jusen*, bank subsidiaries specializing in real estate lending, registered such immense losses that they could not be neutralized via existing structures. In 1996 the government was eventually compelled to take action and injected capital into the market and set up two new institutions designed to take over most of the non-performing loans, which were still in the books of financial institutions. Almost seven years after the beginning of the crisis, the government began to resolve the problems created by high non-performing loans in the financial system that had been left untouched for years (Ohmi 2010). The main explanation that the Japanese government had been reluctant to take decisive political action to solve the non-performing loan problem and restructure the financial system was its concerns about redistributional consequences. It shied away from deciding whether the taxpayer, the owner of financial institutions or the creditors to financial institutions should pay the price for the bubble.

4.4.3   The Lost Decades

The problems of the Japanese economy culminated in the second half of the 1990s and led to a long period of overall poor demand and GDP growth despite consistently high current account surpluses. There were four main issues of concern: 1) the stagnation of the domestic credit expansion and GDP growth during the period after the bubble burst; 2) the spill-overs from the 1997 Asian crisis and the 1998 Russian crisis; 3) deflation in the goods market; and 4) the persistence of non-performing loans. These issues proved particularly destabilizing because of their mutually reinforcing nature:

1.   Companies in Japan followed a strategy to dramatically deleverage. Even with interest rates at zero, the corporate sector did not increase borrowing from banks. Additionally, foreign banks retreated because of the lack of clients. Also corporations did not turn to the capital market for financing. Firms with relatively robust cash flows, especially

those in the export sector, used their surpluses to repair their balance sheets. Richard Koo (2009) refers to this phenomenon as the 'balance sheet recession' and illustrates how Japanese companies focused primarily on repairing their balance sheets by paying down debt after the collapse of asset prices occurred. He also points out that Japan did not suffer from a classical credit crunch because the banking sector did not act as a general bottleneck for the economy. It was the unwillingness of companies to take credit to invest. Even when companies managed to reduce their debt quotas to low levels they did not start to invest again. Obviously, expectations and thus animal spirits were depressed.

Consumption demand remained weak as well. Firstly, low investment demand leads to low income creation, which in turn leads to low consumption demand. This is the essence of a negative goods market multiplier. Secondly, asset prices remained depressed, dampening consumption demand. Thirdly, private households deleveraged and tried to reduce their debt as well. Fourthly, higher unemployment, labour market deregulation following a neoclassical spirit, and higher uncertainty of living conditions of parts of Japanese society also depressed consumption demand. Fifthly, the Gini coefficient for disposable income increased from 0.30 in 1985 to 0.35 in 2005. In comparison with many other OECD countries, Japan still has a relatively equal income distribution, but the change was substantial and reduced the consumption of the poor, who normally have the highest propensity to consume.[24] Last, but not least, Japanese society has been ageing. Such a confluence of forces led to poor consumption demand and also depressed investment.

2. After the bubbles in the 1980s, the fragility of the Japanese financial system became apparent once again when the Asian crisis in 1997 and the Russian crisis broke out one year later. As a consequence of these crises, several large Japanese banks and other financial institutions, which were giving credits to crisis countries, failed and forced the Japanese government to intervene heavily in financial markets. The crisis triggered further radical financial deregulation. In 1997 and 1998, large reforms within the financial sector, often referred to as the 'Big Bang' policies, took place. These abolished among other things all restrictions on international capital flows and on foreign ownership in the domestic financial system (Hsu 2013).

3. Japan began to suffer from goods market deflation. In the period between 1994 and 2008 the Consumer Price Index (CPI) decreased slightly, but the Producer Price Index (PPI) – which is a better indicator to describe the development of the overall inflation rate – decreased more pronouncedly, as shown in Figure 4.13. After the

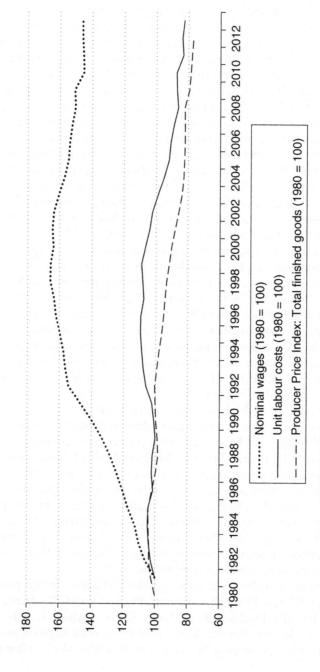

Source: European Commission (2013); Federal Reserve Bank of St. Louis (2013); own calculations.

Figure 4.13 Producer Price Index (PPI), nominal wages and unit-labour costs in Japan, 1980–2012

Asian crisis, deflationary trends worsened and, by the turn of the century, the Bank of Japan had adopted a policy of 'quantitative easing' in addition to the zero-interest-rate policy it had implemented earlier. Investment and GDP slowly picked up in the first half of the 2000s, and the Japanese economy began recovering gradually during this period, albeit at a historically low level. The subprime crisis and the ensuing Great Recession, however, pushed Japan back into stagnation and deflation (Figure 4.13).

4. Goods market deflation substantially aggravated the non-performing loan problem in Japan and made it into a long-term phenomenon (see the debate about deflation in section 4.2). This can be seen when looking at the domestic credit market, which contracted or stagnated, at best, despite the fact that the Bank of Japan wanted to stimulate credit expansion (see Figure 4.14).

This leads to the ultimate question of how to explain deflation in Japan. In section 4.2 it was argued that falling nominal wage costs are the backbone of deflationary processes. This was also the case in Japan. Japanese nominal wage increases were already very low in the early 1990s when the end of the bubble was near. After that, nominal wages stagnated and later even began to decrease. As trend productivity increased further, nominal unit labour costs and, consequently, the price level started to fall over a longer period of time (Figure 4.13). Thus the main explanation for Japanese deflation lies with wage developments. Real wages did not decline, which would be the conclusion drawn from the neoclassical arguments, but rather the contrary took place. Real hourly compensations of employees increased, after productivity increased (Herr and Kazandziska 2011).

The decline in aggregate demand and production after the end of the bubble had serious repercussions for the labour market in Japan. At the peak of the bubble, the unemployment rate stood at around 2 per cent. After the crisis emerged, unemployment continued to rise throughout the 1990s up until 2003, when it reached a high of 6 per cent, a rate which was reached once again in 2009 after some improvements (European Commission 2014). However, real unemployment figures are arguably higher, since many unemployed people are not registered. Decades earlier Japan was used to very low unemployment rates and thus experienced these high rates as a severe shock.

A marked move towards deregulation of the labour market and wage policies in Japan is responsible for the deflationary development. For example, the 1985 Worker Dispatch Law was revised on several occasions to relax the limits – in terms of numbers and sectors – on temporary

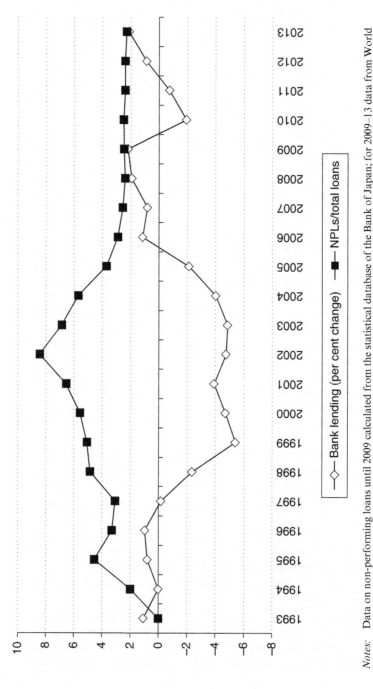

Notes: Data on non-performing loans until 2009 calculated from the statistical database of the Bank of Japan; for 2009–13 data from World Bank.

Source: Bank of Japan (2010); World Bank (2014); authors' calculation.

Figure 4.14   Bank lending (annual percentage change) and non-performing loans (NPLs) as a share of total loans by banks in Japan, 1994–2013

placement of workers (Ohmi 2010). Traditionally, Japan's labour market consisted of regular workers, who have indeterminate contracts and long-term career perspectives, relatively high wages and security, and, in contrast to this, non-regular workers, who get short-term or part-time contracts and can be fired relatively easily. Institutional changes decreased the number of regular workers from 83 per cent of all workers in 1982 to 68 per cent in 2002, and to 66 per cent in 2008 (Nakata and Miyazaki 2010). Deregulation in the labour market caused a bipolarization of the workforce, which had negative repercussions on the Japanese middle class (Hsu 2013).

In order to understand the loss of the nominal wage anchor in Japan, one must also look at the wage bargaining system and the state of labour unions in Japan (Soskice 1990; Herr and Kazandziska 2010). There are thousands of firm unions in Japan which belong to one of the national union federations. Many of these unions organize exclusively regular employees. Thus, on the one hand, non-regular workers were almost entirely excluded from wage bargaining processes. On the other hand, regular workers negotiated wages at the company level. Japanese unions usually linked their wage policy to the interests of companies. During economic hardship, the microeconomic logic of firm-based wage development led to falling nominal wages. Finally, owing to Japan's export-orientated and mercantile strategies, unions were very cautious about demanding nominal wage increases.

Besides deregulating the labour market, the government did not use minimum wages to reduce deflationary pressures. During the deflationary period, the National Council, which recommends annual changes of the statutory minimum wage, nearly froze minimum wage developments completely. Between 1999 and 2006, only very small changes in minimum wages were observed (Herr and Kazandziska 2010).

The question is why, in spite of deflation, Japan did not follow a development comparable to the Great Depression. Of course, the high current account surpluses stabilized demand and production. But the key point is that expansionary fiscal policy prevented a cumulative shrinking of aggregate demand and production. After 1993 Japan experienced high budget deficits – often exceeding 5 per cent of GDP (Table 4.6). Government indebtedness increased remarkably, from around 67 per cent of GDP at the beginning of the crisis in 1990, to around 243 per cent of GDP in 2012, as illustrated in Figure 4.15.

The high budget deficit and in turn the high public debt were only to a small extent the result of active expansionary fiscal policy. The government was preoccupied with budget consolidation as soon as a slight recovery was in sight. When, for example, a slight recovery was observed

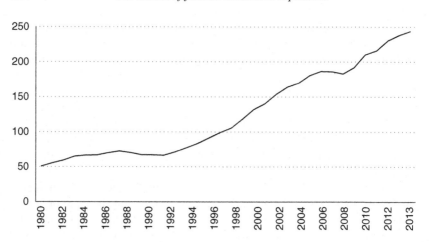

Note: Estimates start after 2011.

Source: IMF (2013).

Figure 4.15 *Japan's general government gross debt as percentage of GDP, 1980–2012*

in 1995 and 1996, social welfare reforms were combined with an attempt at restrictive fiscal policy. The consumption tax was increased from 3 to 5 per cent in 1996, and a programme of public spending cuts was enacted in 1997. This, together with the spill-over of the Asian crisis, led to recession in 1998 and 1999. After 2003 there was another attempt by the Japanese government to gradually consolidate the budget. However, the Great Recession stopped fiscal consolidation (Ohmi 2010). Overall, a more long-term-oriented fiscal policy would have been significantly more helpful at promoting recovery and economic stability in the long run, rather than attempting to reduce budget deficits quickly when the economy showed early signs of recovery. However, Japan allowed the automatic stabilizers to work and did not try to balance the budget in a crisis to the same degree as the Hoover administration during the Great Depression in the USA.

4.4.4 Concluding Remarks

In Japan the bubble was caused by the deregulation of the financial system and an expansionary monetary policy. These policies were mainly implemented because of international pressures, primarily from the United States, which was afflicted by a large current account deficit with Japan during that time. Monetary policy and supervisory institutions completely neglected asset market developments. The huge stock market and real estate bubbles came to a halt when the central bank finally imposed a restrictive monetary policy.

Bubbles of any type are dangerous, but real estate bubbles are particularly problematic, as these usually involve much higher amounts of credit, and are also more closely linked to the consumption behaviour of households. Japan is a prime example of this. The asset price deflation, especially in the real estate sector, created a large volume of non-performing loans and led to a sharp economic downturn. Monetary policy did not respond to this in time. At first, monetary policy had been too loose, culminating in a bubble. Yet, in the aftermath of the bubble's bursting, the Japanese central bank was far too restrictive. Later, the Bank of Japan implemented a zero-interest-rate policy for many years. However, monetary policy was not able to prevent a long-term stagnation due to deflation and the inability to cut nominal interest rates further.[25]

The non-performing loan problem was not handled in an efficient and timely manner in Japan. The problem was allowed to develop for too long, and government intervention was too weak. The government should have acted swiftly and more decisively to clear the balance sheets of financial institutions of non-performing loans. A possible strategy would have been to immediately nationalize unhealthy institutions and eventually re-privatize them after stabilizing them. The government's reluctance to act was likely due to redistributional concerns, namely, the concern of who would bear the costs of restructuring or bailouts. Lobbying is pervasive in Japan and might have been detrimental to the government's decision-making process.

The continuity of the non-performing loan problem was also caused by long-lasting goods market deflation, which increased the real debt burden. The deflation was caused by low demand and GDP growth, combined with increased unemployment, which eventually triggered falling nominal unit labour costs and a wage deflation. The lesson learned from Japan is that weak labour market institutions, which are not able to defend a nominal wage anchor, are extremely dangerous for economic development. The wage bargaining system based on firm-level negotiations followed a microeconomic logic and was not suited to preventing wage deflation. Deregulation of labour markets and an insufficient statutory minimum wage policy added to the weak wage bargaining institutions in Japan.

In retrospect, after the bubble burst, a more expansionary fiscal policy would have been more effective. The Japanese government did provide fiscal stimuli, but as soon as the economy showed some signs of improvement it began to consolidate the budget too soon – without much success. Here, a more decisive action would have been more beneficial.

The Japanese financial crisis and long-term stagnation had no extensive repercussions for the world economy, owing to the local character of the Japanese financial system, which inherited financial institutions unwilling to take credit from abroad. Furthermore, Japanese financial institutions did not sell securitized loans to the rest of the world, as happened in the USA before the outbreak of the subprime crisis.

4.5   LESSONS LEARNED

All three financial crises previously detailed and analysed – the Great Depression in the 1930s, the Latin American crisis in the 1980s and the Japanese crises in the 1990s and 2000s – led to 'lost decades': long periods of low growth and their associated negative economic and social effects. Not all financial crises followed such a pattern. Severe financial crises have also been overcome relatively quickly in the past. Of course, all of these crises involved great economic and social costs. The costs of such shorter crises, however, were far lower in comparison to those of the three crises analysed here.[26] For example, the Asian financial crisis of 1997 lasted relatively shortly in most of the affected countries. Another example is the financial crisis in Sweden in 1991 and 1992, which could be overcome relatively quickly. For the purpose of this analysis, however, we selected financial crises which led to long-term stagnation in order to find out what the crucial factors are that turn financial crises into lost decades.

A summary of the three historical financial crises, analysed in the sections above, is given in Table 4.7. The triggers of all these three crises were different and came, in a narrow sense, from factors outside the economic system. During the Great Depression it was the boom following the end of the First World War, referred to as the 'Roaring Twenties'. In Latin America, it was the relatively good economic development, the deregulation of international capital flows and the availability of foreign credit. In Japan, it was the expansionary monetary policy combined with the deregulation of the domestic financial system. In all of these examples, unsustainable credit expansions played a central role in increasing fragility, eventually leading to a bubble and systemic financial crises. Before the Great Depression and the Japanese crisis real estate bubbles had developed. Also, in both crises, stock market speculation played an important role, though credit-driven speculation in the stock market was especially important before the Great Depression. Latin American countries before the crises accumulated high stocks of foreign debt denominated in foreign

Table 4.7   Summary of the financial crises analysed

	The USA's lost decades in the 1930s/1940s	Latin America's lost decades in the 1980s/1990s	Japan's lost decades in the 1990s/2000s
Trigger of the boom	Extended post-war boom after the end of the First World War.	Deregulation of international capital flows, easy availability of foreign credit, high capital inflows.	Financial deregulation, too expansionary monetary policy.
Type of bubble	Real estate bubble up to 1925, speculation in stock market 1928–29.	International boom–bust cycle; stock market bubble, high capital inflows and current account deficits in the 1970s.	Real estate and stock market bubbles in the second half of the 1980s.
End of the boom	Stock market crash 1929; US banking crisis lasting from 1930 to 1933.	Restrictive US monetary policy; default of Mexico in August 1982; other Latin American countries followed.	Restrictive monetary policy by the Bank of Japan.
Lender of last resort and government action	Insufficient actions as lender of last resort by Federal Reserve.	No lender of last resort, insufficient debt relief.	Ministry of Finance and the Bank of Japan both too slow to react.
Non-performing loans	No debt relief, breakdown of financial institutions, no help for banks.	High foreign indebtedness, no debt relief.	No quick and comprehensive action to clean balance sheets.
Factors for long-term stagnation	Falling nominal wages and goods market deflation; lack of strong fiscal policy; no quick cleaning of balance sheets.	No quick solution to the foreign debt problem, no independence of debtor countries – austerity dictated by foreign creditors.	Falling nominal wages and goods market deflation; however, moderate fiscal stabilization.
Recovery	Start of the war economy in the 1940s.	Unstable development in the 1990s, moderate growth in the 2000s.	Some signs of recovery around the mid-2000s, but slowdown again with the Great Recession.

currency. In all three cases, credit expansion and asset price bubbles were accompanied by a strong real economic expansion, which strengthened the confidence in economic development. In two of the cases, restrictive monetary policy stopped the boom. In Japan, the Bank of Japan started to fight against the slowly developing goods market inflation caused by high GDP growth. In Latin America, the crisis was triggered by the very restrictive US monetary policy at the end of the 1970s. The Great Depression began with the collapse of the stock market bubble in 1929, which was largely independent of monetary policy.

In all three cases, the financial crises that followed the expansions led to prolonged stagnation. The question in our focus is how to explain such lost decades. What went wrong after each of these crises broke out? From the historical analysis four lessons can be drawn.

The *first lesson* is that balance sheets have to be cleaned up very quickly to avoid stagnation after a financial crisis. To clean balance sheets of non-performing loans is extremely important, because the perpetuation of bad loans hinders productive investment and delays a virtuous credit–investment–production–income cycle. Financial institutions will simply not be able or willing to give credit when they suffer from high levels of non-performing loans. Firms with high debt will also be reluctant to take on new credits for investments. In all the three historical cases analysed, balance sheets were not cleaned up quickly. During the Great Depression a large number of banks were allowed to break down, as the central bank and the government did not save them. Breakdowns of banks can be interpreted as a violent method to clean balance sheets. There might be no problem in letting financial institutions of less importance break down when other more healthy and more important institutions are actively supported or even taken over by the government. However, when deposits of the general public are affected and there is no policy in place to protect important institutions and to stimulate new credit expansion after the breakdown of financial institutions, a recovery is almost impossible. Additionally, non-performing loans in the US real estate sector and enterprise sector remained at a high level for many years after the Great Depression. In Japan there is a strikingly similar story to tell. The central bank and government prevented the collapse of part of the financial system, but did not do much to clean balance sheets of financial institutions for a long time. The hope was that the problem would slowly disappear when growth rates recovered. In Latin America, debtors were overburdened with foreign debt, and foreign creditors did not allow balance sheets to be cleaned. The countries were sitting in a trap for a long time.

When we draw the lesson that non-performing loans should be eliminated after a financial crisis breaks out, we are aware that this is very difficult. The difficulty is that each way to clean balance sheets involves deep distributional consequences. When the government takes over non-performing loans from financial institutions, firms or even private households, the taxpayer has to pay in the end. When the government takes over bankrupt financial institutions, the owners and creditors of such institutions suffer. A currency reform privileges holders of real estate and debtors and punishes creditors, including deposit holders in banks. International debt relief implies losses for international creditors. Domestic debt can be taken over to a certain extent by the domestic central bank. However, this may be considered unfair, privileging only some groups in the society.

The *second lesson* is that a severe economic recession and/or a long stagnation increase the danger of deflation. A bad economic situation in combination with weak labour market institutions and wrong beliefs in the benefits of nominal wage cuts can lead to decreasing unit labour costs that stimulate a wage–price downward spiral. The consequences of the erosion of the nominal wage anchor and deflation have been illustrated in the cases of the Great Depression and the Japanese crisis. A real depreciation of the domestic currency in countries that accumulated high debt denominated in foreign currency has a comparable effect to a deflation, because, in this case, the real debt burden also increases for all indebted in foreign currency. Here, the conclusion is that foreign debt in foreign currency is extremely dangerous.

The *third lesson* is that after a systemic financial crisis active governmental policies are needed. Otherwise, the economy might become mired in a prolonged stagnation, and there are no self-adjusting mechanisms through which a recovery will be initiated spontaneously. In the United States, during the Great Depression, monetary policy was not sufficiently expansionary to help to stabilize the crisis. In Japan, monetary policy was too loose while the bubble was developing, and too restrictive during the first years after the bubble burst. A much faster cut of interest rates would have been better directly after the end of the stock market and real estate bubbles. The Latin American countries had no sufficient control over their own interest rates. Firstly, real interest rates for foreign credit exploded after the real depreciation and could not be cut by the indebted countries. Secondly, capital flight prevented the possibility of cutting interest rates to very low levels. Capital controls would have been possible, but to introduce these in a deep financial crisis and against the will of foreign creditors is not easy to do.

As monetary policy becomes less effective, fiscal policy gains in importance. In the 1930s, the lack of fiscal policy led the crisis to snowball out of hand, with catastrophic results. From Japan, we can learn that expansionary fiscal policy can prevent a deflationary collapse of demand, output and employment comparable to the Great Depression. However, during the lost decades after the end of the bubbles, the Japanese government was cautious in its fiscal policy. It did not seem to realize that it was sovereign in its decisions and that there was no limit imposed to its public deficit. A more decisive fiscal policy in Japan probably would have helped to overcome the long stagnation. The Latin American countries had no autonomy to follow an expansionary fiscal policy. Foreign creditors and their adjustment programmes in the spirit of the Washington Consensus simply did not allow an expansionary fiscal policy.

The *fourth lesson* is that an international financial crisis needs international stabilization. When the Latin American debt crisis broke out there was no effective international management to solve it. An international lender of last resort is needed that provides liquidity during a financial crisis and guarantees counter-cyclical long-term lending. A mechanism is also needed to solve an international solvency crisis. In the end an institution has to be established that manages international current account imbalances and unstable international capital flows.

What can we learn from these four lessons for the subprime crisis, the Great Recession and the development thereafter? Looking at the subprime crisis and its management we find mixed results. Banks were comprehensively bailed out in all of the crisis countries involved and, further, many banks were nationalized. This was partly achieved through heavy fiscal interventions and partly by central banks' interventions. A systemic breakdown of commercial banks, as experienced for example during the Great Depression, did not occur. In terms of the distributional effects, the main philosophy of the interventions was to save owners and big creditors of financial institutions at the expense of taxpayers. The crisis of the financial system was not used for radical reforms. President Barack Obama saved Wall Street and did not use the historical window of opportunity to reform the financial system in the way President Roosevelt did in the 1930s.[27] Especially in the European Monetary Union (EMU), the balance sheets of banks are still afflicted with high non-performing loans, to a large extent resulting from the real estate bubbles in Southern European countries. In spite of the bailouts since the beginning of the crisis, non-performing loans doubled in Europe until 2013.[28]

After the Great Recession and a second recession in 2012, which hit a number of Western countries, consumer price inflation, and especially core inflation rates, became very low. The low inflation reflects very low increases in unit labour costs. Any new economic shock can push countries like the USA or currency areas like the EMU into wage deflation. One can learn here from Japan. Seven years after the first shock,

Japan was hit by the Asian crisis in 1997 as a second shock. Based on the fragility created by the first shock, Japan fell into deflation. Since fundamental reforms are missing in the global and national financial systems and the shadow banking system has mainly remained unchanged, future financial crises, which can then lead to deflationary developments, cannot be ruled out.

This has to be seen against the background that labour markets at the beginning of the crisis were already very much deregulated and unions weakened. For example, international institutions have advocated for wage negotiations at the firm level for many years, and recommend wage flexibility according to microeconomic needs (OECD 1994, 2011). In Europe, the Troika (EU Commission, European Central Bank and IMF) pressurizes crisis countries like Spain, Portugal, Greece and Italy (to name only a few) to accept more firm-based wage negotiations and abolish extension mechanisms of sectoral wage bargaining (see Blanchard et al. 2013). The Troika is urging that nominal wages should be reduced in these countries to enhance price competitiveness. In Greece, deflation emerged for the first time since 1968 in March 2013, and other Southern European countries seemed to follow (*Financial Times* 2013b). In October 2013, the *Financial Times* (2013c) stated that Mario Draghi, president of the European Central Bank, was concerned that the EMU was on the edge of deflation. In short, the nominal wage anchor in many Western countries had become so weak that an additional economic shock could lead to a deflationary development.

Although monetary policy after the outbreak of the subprime crisis became very expansionary in many countries, with zero refinancing rates and central banks buying toxic assets in the framework of quantitative easing, it was not able to bring economies back on to a sustainable growth path. Monetary policy helped to stabilize the situation, but, as is well known, its power is asymmetric. It can stop a boom but it cannot create one.[29]

In the USA, as well as in Europe and other countries, the government let automatic stabilizers work and implemented expansionary fiscal policy after the outbreak of the subprime crisis and during the Great Recession, which softened its most disastrous effects substantially. However, further fiscal stimuli would have been needed, since some of the economies recovered only very slowly from the Great Recession and growth rates in general remained very low. Immediately after the end of the worst effects of the Great Recession, consolidation started to dominate fiscal policy. The slowdown of worldwide growth in 2012 and 2013 was caused, to a large extent, by the reduction of fiscal stimuli. Fiscal policy is most problematic in the EMU. The crisis experienced in Southern European countries is similar to the situation experienced in Latin America during the 1980s. The austerity measures imposed by the IMF on the Latin American countries closely resemble those stressed by the Troika in Southern European countries. What we can learn from the Latin American experience is that both the economic and the social costs associated with such austerity are massive. There is a risk that the 'lost decade' of many Southern European countries will turn into a 'lost generation', carrying extremely negative repercussions. In sum, overall monetary and fiscal policy stabilized the first period after the outbreak of the subprime crises. However, fiscal austerity was introduced too early.

Looking at the situation from an international perspective, there is no mechanism established that can handle a global crisis in an efficient way. There is also no mechanism in place that would restrict high current account imbalances or destabilizing international capital flows.

Overall, drawing on the lessons from our historical analysis, we come to the conclusion that the subprime crisis has the potential to lead to a long period of stagnation in Western countries. The financial crisis and the Great Recession were handled in an overall positive way and prevented a development comparable to the Great Depression. However, fiscal stabilization came too early. Balance sheets were only partly cleaned of non-performing loans (as a rule at the cost of the taxpayer). And, finally, no steps were taken to reform the economy in a more fundamental way. The financial system is still the instability centre of a finance-driven type of capitalism. Labour market institutions were further weakened, increasing the danger of deflation. Increasing inequality in income and wealth distribution has not stopped. There is nothing like a Roosevelt-type change in institutions, rules and power relations which could bring a new era of prosperity.

NOTES

1. For the Great Depression, this is true only for the USA.
2. Data on unemployment rates prior to 1929 are not available, nor those on the total workforce during the 1920s.
3. It appears that relatively few households were directly involved in market or speculative activities (Olney 1999).
4. A nominal wage anchor exists when nominal wages increase according to trend productivity development plus the target inflation rate of the central bank (a low inflation rate) (see Herr 2009; Herr and Horn 2012).
5. This statement comes from an interview with Lucas by Arjo Klamer (see Klamer 1983, p. 46).
6. According to Silber (2009) the bank holiday was a remarkable success because of the Emergency Banking Act, which allowed the monetary authorities to provide the amount of currency needed to convince deposit holders of the safety of their assets.

Furthermore, Roosevelt's fireside chat of 12 March 1933 seemed to be successful in achieving a credible regime change (American Presidency Project 2013).

7. We present a very brief summary here. For a more detailed description of the New Deal policies see for instance Rauchway (2008) and Belabed (2011).

8. The price of oil quadrupled in 1973–74 as a result of the oil embargo imposed on the USA by the Arab members of OPEC because of the American support of Israel in the Yom Kippur war. Thus, the rise in oil prices was caused by a sudden shortage of oil in relation to high demand. OPEC decided to establish production quotas amongst its members in order to take a more direct control over world oil prices (Beenstock 2007). In 1979, mainly as a consequence of the weak US dollar, a further doubling of the oil price occurred.

9. In 1974 OPEC current account surpluses amounted to $7.2 billion, and from 1975 to 1979 they were between $20 billion and $40 billion per year (Hsu 2013). An estimated 41 per cent of the oil exporting countries' surplus in foreign currency was deposited in the international banking system in 1974 (Devlin and Ffrench-Davis 1995).

10. This stems from the fact that, given the same amount of monetary wealth in different currencies held, different currencies have different currency premiums; namely, they are perceived to be of different quality. Thus lower-quality currencies suffer from capital flight and dollarization. In developing countries, the degree of dollarization can be extremely high, to the point that domestic currency plays a subordinate role and is used for not much more than domestic transaction purposes (see Herr 2008, 2011).

11. Credit generated by the domestic banking system causes an equivalent increase in monetary wealth. If a substantial proportion of monetary wealth 'leaks' out of the system because the population prefers to keep a large part of its wealth in foreign currency, any domestic credit expansion will lead to capital exports and depreciation of the domestic currency. A depreciation is difficult for developing countries for several reasons. First, it may lead to inflation, in particular when domestic prices and wages are pegged to the exchange rate (which is often the case in developing countries). Second, if the country's debt is denominated in foreign currency, a real depreciation of the domestic currency will increase the real debt burden. Third, real depreciations reduce domestic real income. This might be politically difficult for a government to do. Finally, import–export elasticity may be insufficient, and depreciation may increase a current account deficit.

12. Neither the International Monetary Fund (IMF) nor the World Bank expressed worries; on the contrary, debtor countries were being encouraged to remove capital controls (Devlin and Ffrench-Davis 1995).

13. Williamson (2000, 2004) summarized in ten points the Washington Consensus, 'which most of official Washington thought would be good for Latin American countries' (Williamson 2000, p. 252). The ten points were: 1) fiscal discipline; 2) a redirection of public expenditure priorities toward fields offering both high economic returns and the potential to improve income distribution, such as primary health care, primary education, and infrastructure; 3) tax reform (to lower marginal rates and broaden the tax base); 4) interest-rate liberalization; 5) a competitive exchange rate; 6) trade liberalization; 7) liberalization of FDI inflows; 8) privatization; 9) deregulation (in the sense of abolishing barriers to entry and exit, for example in the field of public utilities); and 10) securing property rights. For a critique on the Washington Consensus see Herr and Priewe (2006).

14. With regard to the origin of creditors, Stallings (1990) reports that US-based banks managed about 42 per cent of the total Latin American debt. Japan, surprisingly, has also played a substantial role in lending to the region, holding almost 16 per cent of the Latin American debt of private banks by 1982. Japanese lending was mostly a result of coordinated national projects, with Latin American private banks working jointly with the Japanese government and trading companies. Other big creditors were European countries, in particular the UK, France and West Germany, and Canada.

15. James Baker was the US Treasury secretary at that time.

16. Bill Brady was a senator from the USA.
17. Other Latin American countries to restructure their debt under the Brady Plan were Argentina, Brazil, Costa Rica, Ecuador, Panama, Uruguay and Venezuela.
18. Devlin and Ffrench-Davis (1995, p. 135) calculated that transfers in total were equivalent to about 4 per cent of the region's GDP, which was even more than the reparation payments faced by Germany after the First World War.
19. Although there is no universally accepted numerical definition of hyperinflation, the one provided by Cagan (1956) is often used, which defines the occurrence of hyperinflation when the monthly inflation rate exceeds 50 per cent. Latin American countries reached the threshold given by Cagan.
20. This explanation is different to Cagan's (1956). He assumed an increase in money supply as the trigger of a high inflation. Then at a certain point velocity of money speeds up and with it the inflation rate.
21. For instance, in Argentina total investment as a percentage of GDP declined from 25 per cent in 1980 to 14 per cent in 1990, and in the case of Mexico there was a 7 per cent decline in this period (for more detailed data, see Bertola and Ocampo 2012; Ramos-Francia et al. 2013).
22. Participants of the Plaza Agreement were France, West Germany, Japan, the United States and the United Kingdom.
23. Participants of the Louvre Accord were France, West Germany, Japan, Canada, the United States and the United Kingdom.
24. The share of wages in national income had shrunk in Japan from over 70 per cent in the 1970s to 57 per cent in 2008 (European Commission 2014). Higher profit shares in national income first of all reflect the increased power of the financial system in Japan after its deregulation and increased rent-seeking behaviour by big Japanese firms.
25. Alan Greenspan and the Federal Reserve learned from this historical period and cut interest rates after the burst of the dot-com bubble in 2000 quickly and substantially.
26. See Kindleberger and Aliber (2005) for a comprehensive overview of historical crises.
27. See for this interpretation Stiglitz (2012).
28. 'European banks' non-performing loans have doubled in just four years to reach close to €1.2tn and are expected to keep rising . . . Rises in the most recent year were driven by deteriorating conditions in Spain, Ireland, Italy and Greece' (*Financial Times* 2013d; see also *Financial Times* 2013a).
29. In the EMU, monetary policy failed to take on the role as a lender of last resort for countries that suffered from sovereign debt crises. Only in July 2012, when Mario Draghi promised to bail out governments in crisis countries provided that they followed the dictates of the Troika, was this function taken over.

REFERENCES

American Presidency Project (2013), Franklin D. Roosevelt, available at: http://www.presidency.ucsb.edu/ws/index.php?pid=14540 (accessed 28 November 2013).
Bank of Japan (2010), Statistical database, available at: http://www.stat-search.boj.or.jp/index_en.html.
Beenstock, M. (2007), 'The rise, fall and rise again of OPEC', in M.J. Oliver and D.H. Aldcroft (eds), *Economic Disasters of the Twentieth Century*, Cheltenham, UK and Northampton, MA, USA: Edward Elgar Publishing.
Belabed, C.A. (2011), *Die Große Depression und der New Deal aus Makroökonomischer Sicht*, Linz: Trauner Verlag.

Bernanke, B.S. (2000), *Essays on the Great Depression*, Princeton, NJ: Princeton University Press.

Bernanke, B.S. and H. James (1991), 'The gold standard, deflation, and financial crisis in the Great Depression: an international comparison', in R. Glenn Hubbard (ed.), *Financial Markets and Financial Crises*, Chicago: University of Chicago Press.

Bertola, L. and J.A. Ocampo (2012), 'Latin America's debt crisis and "lost decade"', Institute for the Study of the Americas conference: Learning from Latin America: Debt Crises, Debt Rescues and When They Work, February.

Blanchard, O., F. Jaumotte and P. Loungani (2013), 'Labour market policies and IMF advice in advanced economies during the Great Recession', IMF Staff Discussion Note 13/02, International Monetary Fund, March.

Brown, C. (1956), 'Fiscal policy in the "thirties": a reappraisal', *American Economic Review*, **46** (5), 857–879.

Cagan, P. (1956), 'The monetary dynamics of hyperinflation', in M. Friedman (ed.), *Studies in the Quantity Theory of Money*, Chicago: University of Chicago Press.

Damill, M., R. Frenkel and M. Rapetti (2013), 'Financial and currency crises in Latin America', in M.H. Wolfson and G.A. Epstein (eds), *The Handbook of the Political Economy of Financial Crises*, Oxford: Oxford University Press.

Desai, P. (2011), *From Financial Crisis to Global Recovery*, New York: Columbia University Press.

Devlin, R. and R. Ffrench-Davis (1995), 'The great Latin American debt crisis: a decade of asymmetric adjustment', *Revista de Economia Politica*, **15** (3), 117–142.

Dornbusch, R. (1990a), 'From stabilisation to growth', NBER Working Paper No. 3302, National Bureau of Economic Research.

Dornbusch, R. (1990b), 'Policies to move from stabilization to growth', CEPR Discussion Paper No. 456, Centre for Economic Policy Research.

Dr. Housing Bubble (2011), 'Looking into the Japanese real estate mirror', available at: http://www.doctorhousingbubble.com/japan-real-estate-bubble-home-prices-back-30-years-zero-percent-mortgage-rates/ (accessed 28 August 2014).

Eggertson, G.B. (2008), 'Great expectations and the end of the depression', *American Economic Review*, September, **98** (4), 1476–1516.

Eichengreen, B., R. Hausmann and U. Panizza (2003), 'Currency mismatches, debt intolerance and original sin: why they are not the same and why it matters', NBER Working Paper No. 10036, National Bureau of Economic Research.

EMTA (2014) Emerging Markets Traders Association, available at: http://www.emta.org/template.aspx?id=35 (accessed 27 August 2014).

European Commission (several years), AMECO database, available at: http://ec.europa.eu/economy_finance/ameco/user/.

Federal Reserve Bank of St. Louis (2013), FRED database, http://research.stlouis-fed.org/fred2/ (accessed 9 September 2013).

Financial Times (2013a), 'The NPL standardization factor', *Financial Times*, 5 November.

Financial Times (2013b), 'Greek deflation accelerates after wages drop', *Financial Times*, 8 November.

Financial Times (2013c), 'Draghi on the edge of deflation', *Financial Times*, 25 October.

Financial Times (2013d), 'Troubled loans at Europe's banks double in value', *Financial Times*, 29 October.

Fischer, S., R. Sahay and C.A. Végh (2002), 'Modern hyper- and high inflations', *Journal of Economic Literature*, **40** (3), 837–880.

Fisher, I. (1929), speech reported by *New York Times*, 17 October.

Fisher, I. (1933), 'The debt-deflation theory of great depressions', *Econometrica*, **1**, 337–357.

Friedman, M. and A. Schwartz (1963), *A Monetary History of the United States, 1867–1960*, Princeton, NJ: Princeton University Press.

Galbraith, J.K. ([1954] 2009), *The Great Crash 1929*, New York: Mariner Books.

Galbraith, J.K. ([1990] 1994), *A Short History of Financial Euphoria*, London: Penguin Books.

Grebler, L., D.M. Blank and L. Winnick (eds) (1956), *Capital Formation in Residential Real Estate: Trends and Prospects*, Princeton, NJ: Princeton University Press.

Herr, H. (1990), 'Der bundesdeutsche und japanische Merkantilismus', in H.-P. Spahn (ed.), *Wirtschaftspolitische Strategien: Probleme ökonomischer Stabilität und Entwicklung in Industrieländern und der Europäischen Gemeinschaft*, Regensburg: Transfer-Verlag.

Herr, H. (2008), 'Financial systems in developing countries and economic development', in E. Hein, T. Niechoj, P. Spahn and A. Truger (eds), *Finance-Led Capitalism? Macroeconomic Effects of Changes in the Financial Sector*, Marburg: Metropolis.

Herr, H. (2009), 'The labour market in a Keynesian economic regime: theoretical debate and empirical findings', *Cambridge Journal of Economics*, **33**, 949–965.

Herr, H. (2011), 'International monetary and financial architecture', in E. Hein and E. Stockhammer (eds), *A Modern Guide to Keynesian Macroeconomics and Economic Policies*, Cheltenham, UK and Northampton, MA, USA: Edward Elgar Publishing.

Herr, H. and G. Horn (2012), 'Wage policy today', GLU Working Paper No. 16, Global Labour University.

Herr, H. and M. Kazandziska (2010), 'The labour market and deflation in Japan', *International Journal of Labour Research, Financial Crises, Deflation and Trade Union Responses: What Are the Lessons?*, **2** (1), 79–98.

Herr, H. and M. Kazandziska (2011), *Macroeconomic Policy Regimes in Western Industrial Countries*, London: Routledge.

Herr, H. and J. Priewe (2005), 'Beyond the Washington Consensus: macroeconomic policies for development', *Internationale Politik und Gesellschaft*, **2**, 72–98.

Herr, H. and J. Priewe (2006), 'The Washington Consensus and (non-)development', in L.R. Wray and M. Forstater (eds), *Money, Financial Instability and Stabilization Policy*, Cheltenham, UK and Northampton, MA, USA: Edward Elgar Publishing.

Holt, C.F. (1977), 'Who benefited from the prosperity of the Twenties?', *Explorations in Economic History*, **14** (3), 277–289.

Hsu, S. (2013), *Financial Crises, 1929 to the Present*, Cheltenham, UK and Northampton, MA, USA: Edward Elgar Publishing.

IMF (2012), 'World Economic Outlook: growth resuming, dangers remain', International Monetary Fund, April.

IMF (2013), World Economic Outlook Database, International Monetary Fund, October.

IMF (2014), World Economic Outlook, Data and Statistics, http://www.imf.org/external/data.htm (accessed 22 August 2014).

Japan Real Estate Institute (2012), http://www.reinet.or.jp/en/.

Kaminsky, G.L. and C.M. Reinhart (1999), 'The twin crises: the causes of banking and balance-of-payment problems', *American Economic Association*, **89** (3), 473–500.

Keynes, J.M. (1930), *A Treatise on Money*, in *Collected Writings*, Vol. V, London: Macmillan.

Keynes, J.M. (1936), *The General Theory of Employment, Interest and Money*, Cambridge, UK: Cambridge University Press.

Kindleberger, C.P. and R.Z. Aliber (2005), *Manias, Panics, and Crashes*, 5th edn, Hoboken, NJ: John Wiley & Sons.

Klamer, A. (1983), *Conversations with Economists*, Totowa, NJ: Rowman & Allanheld.

Koo, R. (2009), *The Holy Grail of Macroeconomics: Lessons from Japan's Great Recession*, Singapore: John Wiley & Sons.

Kuznets, S. (1937), *National Income and Capital Formation, 1919–1935*, NBER Books, Cambridge, MA: National Bureau of Economic Research.

McCauley, R.N. (2013), 'The Japanese boom and bust: "lean" and "clean" lessons', in M.J. Oliver and D.H. Aldcroft (eds), *Economic Disasters of the Twentieth Century*, Cheltenham, UK and Northampton, MA, USA: Edward Elgar Publishing.

Nakata, Y.F. and S. Miyazaki (2010), 'Increasing labour flexibility during the recession in Japan: the role of female workers in manufacturing', in C. Brown, B. Eichengreen and M. Reich (eds), *Labour in the Era of Globalisation*, Cambridge, UK: Cambridge University Press.

Nicholas, T. and A. Scherbina (2011), 'Real estate prices during the Roaring Twenties and the Great Depression', Research Paper No. 18-09, UC Davis Graduate School of Management.

Ocampo, J.A. (2004), 'Latin America's growth and equity frustrations during structural reforms', *Journal of Economic Perspectives*, **18** (2), 67–88.

OECD (1994), *The OECD Jobs Study: Facts, Analysis, Strategies*, Paris: OECD Publishing.

OECD (2011), *Divided We Stand: Why Inequality Keeps Rising*, Paris: OECD Publishing.

Ohmi, N. (2010), 'The Japanese economic crisis of the 1990s', *International Journal of Labour Research, Financial Crises, Deflation and Trade Union Responses: What Are the Lessons?*, **2** (1), 61–77.

Olney, M.L. (1999), 'Avoiding default: the role of credit in the consumption collapse of 1930', *Quarterly Journal of Economics*, **114** (1), 319–335.

Palma, J.G. (2013), 'How the full opening of the capital account to highly liquid and unstable financial markets led Latin America to two and a half cycles of "mania, panic and crash"', in M.H. Wolfson and G.A. Epstein (eds), *The Handbook of the Political Economy of Financial Crises*, Oxford: Oxford University Press.

Pastor, M., Jr (1989), 'Capital flight and the Latin American debt crisis', EPI Study, Economic Policy Institute.

Ramos-Francia, M., A.M. Aguilar-Argaez, S. Garcia-Verdu and G. Cuadra-Garcia

(2013), 'Heading into trouble: a comparison of the Latin American crises and the euro area's current crisis', *Monetaria*, **XXXV** (1), 87–165.

Rauchway, E. (2008), *The Great Depression and the New Deal: A Very Short Introduction*, Oxford: Oxford University Press.

Robinson, J. (1938), 'The economics of inflation', *Economic Journal*, **48** (3), 507–513.

Romer, C.D. (1991), 'What ended the Great Depression?', NBER Working Paper No. 3829, National Bureau of Economic Research.

Ruggiero, G. (1999), 'Latin American debt crisis: what were its causes and is it over?', independent study, available at: http://www.angelfire.com/nj/GregoryRuggiero/latinamericancrisis.html (accessed 25 August 2013).

Sachs, J.D. (1986), 'A new approach to managing the debt crisis', *Columbia Journal of World Business*, **21** (3), 41–49.

Silber, W.L. (2009), 'Why did FDR's bank holiday succeed?', *Economic Policy Review*, **15** (1), 19–30.

Soskice, D. (1990), 'Wage determination: the changing role of institutions in advanced industrialized countries', *Oxford Review of Economic Policy*, **6** (4), 36–61.

Stallings, B. (1990), 'The reluctant giant: Japan and the Latin American debt crisis', *Journal of Latin American Studies*, **22**, 1–30.

Stiglitz, J. (1996), 'Some lessons from the East Asian miracle', *World Bank Research Observer*, **11** (2), 151–177.

Stiglitz, J. (2012), *The Price of Inequality*, London: Norton.

Stiglitz, J.E. and M. Uy (1996), 'Financial markets, public policy, and the East Asian miracle', *World Bank Observer*, **11** (2), 249–276.

Temin, P. (1993), 'Transmission of the Great Depression', *Journal of Economic Perspectives*, **7** (2), 87–102.

Temin, P. (1994), 'The Great Depression', NBER Working Paper No. 62, National Bureau of Economic Research.

Werner, R. (2003), *Princes of the Yen: Japan's Central Bankers and the Transformation of the Economy*, New York: M.E. Sharpe.

Wheelock, D.C. (1995), 'Regulation, market structure, and the bank failures of the Great Depression', *Federal Reserve Bank of St. Louis Review*, March/April, 27–38.

Williamson, J. (2000), 'What should the World Bank think about the Washington Consensus?', *World Bank Research Observer*, **15** (2), 251–264.

Williamson, J. (2004), 'A short history of the Washington Consensus', paper commissioned by Fundacion CUDOB for a conference 'From the Washington Consensus towards a new Global Governance', 24–25 September, Barcelona.

Williamson, J. (2005), *Curbing the Boom–Bust Cycle: Stabilising Capital Flows to Emerging Markets*, Washington, DC: Institute for International Economics.

World Bank (2014), World Development Indicators, available at: http://data.worldbank.org/data-catalog/world-development-indicators.

5. Five explanations for the international financial crisis

Trevor Evans

5.1 INTRODUCTION

The financial crisis which began in the USA in 2007, and which led to the deepest global recession since the Second World War in 2008 and 2009, is only the most recent in a long string of crises and recessions that have afflicted capitalist economies. Breakdowns in economic reproduction did also occur in pre-capitalist societies, but these were primarily due to external factors, such as wars or droughts or the plague. In capitalist economies, by contrast, crises have emerged as a result of developments *within* the economy.[1] This chapter will first briefly explain the background and main features of the current crisis and then examine five of the main approaches to explaining it.

5.2 THE BACKGROUND TO THE CRISIS

5.2.1 Capitalism and Crises

In the nineteenth century, periods of rising prosperity led to investment in expanding production and, encouraged by the profitable opportunities, banks eagerly met increased demands for borrowing. As growth picked up, wages and other prices would begin to rise and erode profits. At the same time, the price of assets (shares, land, even raw materials) would increase and encourage speculative buying, often financed by borrowing, and this would push up prices yet further. At some point the bubble in asset prices would burst and, faced with large losses, bank lending would contract dramatically, causing a major downturn in production, employment and income. The recession, in turn, led to the bankruptcy of the weakest firms, making labour and other resources available to other sectors, so preparing the basis for the next period of expansion. Such crises began in Britain in the early nineteenth century, and cycles of expansion and crises then recurred at approximately ten-year intervals, spreading to include other Western European countries and the USA as industrialization was extended in the second half of the century.

As the scale of industry and finance increased, crises became ever more threatening, and the state began to intervene in an attempt to ameliorate their impact. In the second half of the nineteenth century, the Bank of England developed the function of 'lender of last resort' in order to prevent problems at one bank from setting off a chain of bank failures.[2] This involved making loans available to banks that were basically sound but which were threatened by a sudden lack of short-term funds. Although the USA was the largest capitalist economy by the turn of the twentieth century, because of populist political sentiment it did not have a central bank until the Federal Reserve System was created in 1913.[3]

As is well known, the most serious crisis of all began with the US stock market crash in 1929 and was followed by a wave of bank failures between 1930 and 1932 in which around one-third of USA banks went bankrupt. When the Roosevelt government took office in early 1933, it immediately introduced a series of measures to regulate the financial sector. The Glass–Steagall Act introduced tight controls on the banking sector, including limits on interest rates and a legal separation between commercial banks (which accept deposits and make loans) and investment banks (which advise on and conduct transactions with securities). Shortly after, the Securities and Exchange Commission was set up to regulate the securities markets.

The period that followed the introduction of these controls on the financial system was characterized by an unusual degree of financial stability. From the 1940s until the early 1970s the USA – and the other major capitalist countries, which also had tight regulations on their financial sectors – did not experience any serious financial crises.[4] This period of financial stability was, furthermore, associated with a steady rise in the standard of living of the mass of the population. In the absence of serious recessions, unemployment remained exceptionally low, while real wages increased and the provision of welfare services was expanded.

5.2.2 The Re-Emergence of the Financial Sector

After the Second World War, when US households had built up large savings, US banks initially held substantial reserves of deposits and did not experience the tight regulations as a serious constraint on their activities. By the late 1960s, however, this had begun to change, and the banks began pushing for major changes.

First, the banks initiated a process of financial innovation, developing new instruments that were not explicitly forbidden by the existing regulations. The first of these was the creation of the certificate of deposit in 1966. Because this was, in legal terms, a tradable certificate and not a bank deposit, it enabled banks to attract funds by offering interest rates above the legal maximum set by the government. In subsequent years, the innovations became ever more complex, in part to get round regulations, but also to deliberately obscure the risks involved.

A second important development was the internationalization of the US banking system. In the late 1960s, US banks began to open branches in Europe, predominantly in London, and this expanded rapidly in the course of the 1970s.[5] The big US banks were, in part, following their big US corporate customers, who had begun to invest in Western Europe in the 1960s. But the expansion of US bank branches in London was also strongly motivated by a desire to operate outside the constraints of the US regulatory authorities, in particular to get round restrictions on capital outflows, which had been tightened in the mid-1960s.[6]

The third significant development was a process of financial deregulation. Faced with the processes of innovation and internationalization, the US authorities were faced with a stark choice: either they would have to seriously update the regulatory framework or they would have to accept that banks would increasingly circumvent the existing rules. In fact there was remarkably little discussion. With strong pressure from financial institutions, and a political and ideological climate that had swung towards a belief in the self-regulating capacity of private markets, the US government embarked on a step-by-step process of eliminating the constraints on the financial sector.

5.2.3 Finance-led Capitalism

From around the early 1980s, it is possible to identify a new phase of US capitalism, and because of the central role occupied by the financial sector it is often referred to as finance-led capitalism.[7] Many of the features of this new phase took shape around the same time in Britain under the Thatcher government, and they followed, albeit in a somewhat more moderate form, in France and Germany from the 1990s. The main financial developments included the following.

Firstly, as a result of the process of innovation and deregulation there was an enormous growth of the financial sector. This involved a growth of financial institutions, above all of big banks, but also of non-bank financial institutions, including pension funds and investment funds (known as mutual funds in the USA), and more speculative institutions such as hedge funds and private equity funds; it involved the development of a host of new financial instruments, including complex bonds and speculative instruments such as derivatives; and it included a major expansion of financial markets.

Secondly, the strengthening of the financial sector resulted in pressure on non-financial companies in the industrial and commercial sector to give top priority to achieving the highest possible financial return for shareholders – the pursuit of so-called 'shareholder value'. If companies failed to sustain high dividend payments to shareholders, they were threatened with the risk of big institutional investors selling off their holdings. If share prices then fell significantly, the company was likely to get taken over. To guard against this, companies embarked on repeated rounds of rationalization, outsourcing parts of the work, closing the least efficient plants, and reducing costs – especially wage costs – wherever possible.

Thirdly, non-financial firms – faced with the pressure to raise their own returns – began to engage in financial investments, which appeared to offer a higher return than that obtained from investing in their previous lines of business. In this way, as non-financial companies increased their holdings of financial assets, investment in fixed capital (machinery, equipment and buildings) tended to be weaker than in the earlier post-war period and, as a result, generated fewer jobs.

This new phase of capitalism appeared to be very successful for corporations in the USA. From the early 1980s up until 2007, the share of corporate profits in US national income increased steadily, rising to a level last seen in the mid-1960s.[8] The financial sector benefited in particular, with its share of total pre-tax profits rising from around 15 per cent in the early 1980s to some 35 per cent in the years just before the crisis broke in 2007.[9] However, this was associated with a remorseless pressure on wages and, in practice, economic growth in the USA from the early 1980s was highly dependent on the expansion of credit and the growth of speculative bubbles in asset prices. Despite the government's commitment to free market capitalism, each time the model faltered the Federal Reserve adopted a highly expansive monetary policy so as to forestall a serious recession and crisis.

In the 1980s, the most striking financial development was the extensive use of so-called junk bonds to finance a major wave of corporate takeovers. Compared with the industrial-grade bonds issued by well-known companies, there was a higher risk that these bonds would not be paid back, but they offered a more attractive rate of return and proved highly profitable for the investment banks which managed their issue. In 1989, however, after several years of over-lending, the banks abruptly curtailed the expansion of new loans, and the economic expansion came to an end. The Federal Reserve managed to ameliorate the impact of the downturn by adopting an extremely expansive monetary policy, and interest rates were held down for several years.

In the second half of the 1990s, the US economy experienced its next expansion, which was driven by a boom in information technology. Rising profits and a strong growth of lending fuelled rising investment in new technology and led to a major bubble in share prices. Households with direct or indirect holdings of shares experienced a so-called 'wealth effect', and borrowed to finance higher consumption. This came to an end when the share price bubble burst in early 2000, leading to a collapse in prices that was comparable with that after the famous crash in 1929. However, while this led to a recession in 2001, the Fed was again able to limit the impact of the downturn by adopting a highly expansionary monetary policy, and interest rates were kept exceptionally low for several years.[10]

Between 2002 and 2007, the US economy registered a further expansion, this time driven primarily by a boom in house prices. Financial institutions aggressively expanded their mortgage lending, including lending targeted at low-income households through so-called sub-prime mortgages. As a result of financial deregulation, these were subject to much looser conditions than traditional mortgages, although the interest rates were significantly higher.[11] As increased demand pushed house prices up, many households borrowed money against the increased value of their homes, and this was then used to finance increased consumption. Although wages remained virtually stagnant, the increase in consumption spending was able to drive economic growth in the USA for several years. But, when the bubble in house prices burst in 2007, the whole situation unravelled, detonating the most serious financial crisis since the 1930s.

5.2.4 Securitization

The crisis was set off by the failure of financial instruments created to finance the growth of mortgage lending. In 1988, an international agreement known as the Basel Accord established that banks should hold capital reserves equal to 8 per cent of their lending.[12] This was to ensure that, if loans were not repaid, the capital reserves would provide a bank with a cushion to absorb the losses without driving it into bankruptcy. However, one effect of this regulation was to encourage a process known as securitization, by which the banks would bundle a large number of loans (in the case of mortgages, typically several thousand) and create a security which could be sold on the capital market to a financial investor. In this way, a bank could earn fees and, by removing the loans from its own books, avoid tying up its capital for the life of the mortgages. The investor in turn received the interest and capital payments from the mortgage borrowers.[13]

Mortgage-backed securities were also created by bundling together large numbers of sub-prime mortgages but, because the repayments on these were largely dependent on low-income households, many with irregular employment, they were considered to be riskier than other forms of securities. The big New York investment banks then developed a highly lucrative business, taking the initial securities and creating new, highly complex securities known as collateralized debt obligations in which the rights to repayments were sliced up into *tranches*. The detail of how these instruments were constructed was extremely complicated – indeed, one aim was precisely to obscure the underlying risks involved – but the general principle was as follows. The first or senior tranche had first call on the repayments by mortgage borrowers. Because it was thought that even among low-paid households a certain proportion would always meet their payments, this tranche was considered very safe, but it paid the lowest return. Once repayments to senior tranche holders had been met, holders of the second or mezzanine tranche would receive repayments. These were considered a little more risky, and this tranche therefore offered a slightly higher rate of return. The lowest or equity tranche would receive repayments only when the other tranches had been serviced. If any households failed to meet their repayments, the holders of this tranche would have to carry the loss. Because this tranche carried the most risk, investors had to be offered the highest rate of return.

Securitization was widely hailed by orthodox economists who argued that, by dispersing the risk of losses among a large number of investors, with investors able to select the level of risk they were able to cope with, the financial system as a whole had become more stable. However, many of the big banks themselves held some of the most risky securities, in part attracted by the high returns they paid. Furthermore, these holdings were often financed by borrowing short-term funds at lower rates of interest from other financial institutions. For a time, it was a highly profitable investment. In fact it was so attractive that many European banks – including Germany's publicly owned *Landesbanken* – began to invest in US mortgage-backed securities too. However, when the housing bubble burst and prices began to fall, the value of many mortgage-backed securities and their complex derivatives began to fall precipitously.

5.2.5   The Onset of the Crisis

The crisis broke in August 2007.[14] The immediate cause was that banks did not know to what extent other banks had incurred losses from holding mortgage-related securities and, in order to avoid the risk of not being repaid, banks stopped lending to each other. As a result, the inter-bank money market, where banks borrow and lend short-term funds between themselves, and which is central to the functioning of a modern capitalist banking system, dried up. This occurred almost simultaneously in the USA and in Europe, and both the Federal Reserve and the European Central Bank responded by immediately pumping large amounts of money into the US and euro area inter-bank markets. But, while this prompt response prevented a complete breakdown in the money market, inter-bank lending remained seriously curtailed and, in turn, bank credit to industrial and commercial businesses was reduced markedly. In the following months, the central banks in the USA, the euro area, Britain and Switzerland repeatedly pumped additional funds into their banking systems, but the situation continued to deteriorate as US mortgage-backed securities continued to lose value and the scale of bank losses increased. One signal of the deteriorating situation was the failure of Bear Stearns, one of the leading New York investment banks, in March 2008.

The crisis deepened dramatically in September 2008. At the start of the month, Fannie Mae and Freddie Mac, the two most important semi-public mortgage lending agencies in the USA, ran into serious problems and required major financial support from the government. The key development was the collapse in mid-September of the big New York investment bank Lehman Brothers, which had been deeply involved in the construction of complex mortgage-based securities. The US authorities claimed that, because Lehman was an investment bank (which deals in securities) and not a commercial bank (which accepts deposits and is protected by the central bank), they could not legally intervene. But it is clear that the government had decided to show big financial institutions that they could not count on always being rescued. The way that they did this, however, proved to be a major error of judgement.

The collapse of Lehman Brothers set off a chain of further major financial failures, including that of American International Group, the largest insurer in the world, which had incurred huge liabilities insuring dubious mortgage-backed securities. It also led to an acute sharpening of the crisis in the inter-bank money market, which resulted in an almost complete collapse in bank lending in the USA, even to the most well-known companies. Finally, in early October the crisis hit international stock markets, which lost some 20 per cent of their value in the course of one week in the USA, Europe and even Asia, which had been less touched up to this point.

At the end of the second week in October, amidst a widespread official view that the international financial system was on the edge of collapse, the governments of the USA and the major European countries, including the UK, France and Germany, all announced plans to invest capital directly in banks faced with failure. This amounted, in effect, to a partial nationalization of the banking system, and in the USA the government became the main owner of the two biggest banks, Citibank and Bank of America. At the same time as making capital available, the governments also announced plans to provide guarantees for inter-bank lending in the hope that this would lead to a return to lending.[15] However, while the coordinated state intervention did halt the chain of financial failures, it was unable to prevent a collapse of bank lending, either in the USA or in Europe.

5.2.6   The Global Recession

Several years of strong economic growth in the USA came to an end in 2007 when households were no longer able to finance a further increase in consumer spending by borrowing against rising house prices. When bank lending dried up in October 2008 following the failure of Lehman Brothers, investment abruptly collapsed, and the USA was hit by its most serious slump since the 1930s. In the final quarter of 2008 and the first quarter of 2009, output and employment in the USA dropped abruptly, and the impact of the slump was transmitted to the rest of the world.[16]

The slump was transmitted to Western Europe through two main channels. Firstly, growth in Europe before the crisis had been strongly dependent on exports, largely driven either directly or indirectly by demand from the USA. The slump in US demand, exacerbated by a collapse of trade credit, led to a decline of some 20 per cent in European exports, and Germany, where growth had been especially dependent on exports, was particularly affected. Secondly, as in the USA, the European economy was hit by a sharp reduction in the availability of bank credit as European banks struggled to deal with big losses on holdings in US securities. As a consequence, economic output in the older EU countries fell by 4.4 per cent in the final quarter of 2008 and the first quarter of 2009.[17]

The impact of the crisis in much of Eastern Europe and the Baltic region was even more severe. Many countries had had large current account deficits and, prior to 2007, they had been able to finance these deficits at relatively favourable interest rates by borrowing on the international capital market. However, once the crisis broke in 2007, this financing dried up, leaving the countries with a major problem. Furthermore, most of these countries did not benefit from the protection of being members of the euro area, and were also faced with the danger of a currency crisis. In the event, Hungary and Latvia were forced to turn to the International Monetary

Fund for emergency support, and were required to introduce major cuts in public expenditure, including spending on wages and pensions.[18]

The crisis was transmitted to Asian countries, including Japan and China, primarily through a collapse in the demand for manufactured exports, with Japan's exports falling by 50 per cent, and many smaller Asian exporters suffering from a collapse in the demand for semi-finished products.

As a result of a dramatic decline in industrial output in the USA, Europe and Asia, the demand for energy and other raw materials declined sharply, leading to a notable fall in most primary commodity prices, including that of oil. Consequently, oil exporters such as Russia, the Middle Eastern countries and Venezuela saw a sharp fall in their income, as did the exporters of agricultural and mineral products in Latin America and Africa.

Finally, some of the very poorest in the world were affected by the crisis through a decline in the employment of migrant workers and a fall in the remittances which they were able to send back to their families. This was particularly marked for migrant workers in the USA from Mexico and Central America, but it also affected many other migrant workers from elsewhere in Latin America, Asia and Africa.

5.2.7 Government Responses

The sharp slump in output in the USA and Europe came to an end in spring 2009. In the second half of the year output began to recover slowly, although it remained below the level reached prior to the onset of the crisis. The recovery was aided by significant government stimuli. In the USA, one of the first measures of the Obama government on taking office in early 2009 was to push through a $789 billion programme of increased expenditure and tax cuts, worth about 3 per cent of GDP in 2009 and 2010. In Europe, there were calls for a coordinated fiscal expansion, most notably by the French government. Although Germany opposed this, many countries did subsequently introduce national programmes and, in the event, the programme introduced in Germany, worth around 2.5 per cent of GDP over two years, was one of the largest.

Government programmes have compensated, at least to some extent, for a collapse of spending by private firms. However, these programmes, together with huge sums spent on supporting the financial sector and a big decline in tax revenues, have led to large budget deficits and a dramatic rise in the indebtedness of the major capitalist states. As a result, while output has been stabilized, the focus of the crisis has shifted to the ability of governments to finance their borrowing. The US government has, for some 30 years, relied on large inflows of foreign capital to help finance its budget deficits, but major holders of US debt, such as the Chinese government, have indicated they are uneasy about accumulating ever more US debt. In the euro area, despite unprecedented peace-time indebtedness, the stronger countries are still able to finance substantial borrowing, although countries with large current account deficits in southern Europe have faced greater difficulties. By spring 2010, Greece – although a member of the euro area – was able to borrow only at around twice the rate of interest paid by Germany, and was forced to seek emergency support from other euro area countries and the IMF. Shortly after, the threat that similar problems could spread to other countries, in particular Portugal and Spain, obliged euro area governments to agree to the creation of an unprecedented €440 billion fund to provide support for member states.[19] As a result of the pressure to reduce budget deficits, Ireland, Greece, Spain and Portugal have all been obliged to cut public spending, including spending on wages and pensions. At the time of writing, the ground is also being prepared for cuts in social spending in northern Europe.

Despite expectations at the height of the crisis, governments have been slow to take measures to curb the financial sector. After the threat of financial collapse receded in early 2009, the pressure to introduce major reforms abated. In fact, many of the US banks that survived the crisis began to post large profits again. The market share of the biggest banks had increased, and they were able to benefit from central bank financing at exceptionally low interest rates. More generally, although the model of finance-led capitalism had seemed discredited at the height of the crisis, in both the USA and Europe, governments returned to policies that were in important respects similar to those they had been pursuing before the crisis. In the USA this involves striving to promote a revival of consumer spending, while in Europe – and especially Germany – governments place their hopes in a renewed expansion of exports.

The financial sector has, of course, resolutely opposed the introduction of measures that would seriously restrict their activities, and in the USA the big banks have spent huge sums lobbying Congress to this effect.[20] However, in addition to the pressure which the financial sector can bring to bear, policy responses have also been shaped by the dominant understandings of what went wrong.

5.3 EXPLANATIONS OF THE CRISIS

5.3.1 The Role of Incentives

One of the most widely accepted approaches to explaining the crisis emphasizes the role of perverse incentives. There are numerous instances of this. Firstly, the sales personnel who went from door to door in poor neighbourhoods selling sub-prime mortgages were paid by the number of customers they could get to sign up. They offered very low initial repayment rates (so-called 'teaser rates' that did not even cover the cost of interest) and had no incentive to check people's incomes or to point out that repayments would rise significantly after one or two years (who reads the small print?).

Secondly, the banks which originated the mortgages did not plan to keep these on their own books, but rather to bundle a large number of such loans together and to sell them as a security to a financial investor, such as a pension fund or an investment fund. The banks' aim was therefore to generate as many mortgages as possible, and not to carefully check whether mortgage holders would be able to meet their repayments.

Thirdly, the investment banks which took the initial mortgage-backed securities and then sliced them up to create highly complex collateralized debt obligations generated huge profits from fees. The bankers who put these instruments together were rewarded with lavish bonuses – which could run into millions of dollars a year – that were generally paid in the same year that the instruments were created, irrespective of how they performed in the future.

Finally, the ratings agencies, on whose assessment of risk most investors relied when deciding whether to purchase an unfathomably complex security, were faced with a serious conflict of interest. The agencies are profit-making businesses, and by the height of the housing boom a significant part of their profits was generated from rating complex mortgage-based securities. In fact, only limited data was available to assess the risks (sub-prime mortgages were quite new), and the agencies had an incentive to provide a favourable assessment in order to ensure that the investment banks did not take their profitable business to another agency.

Much of the official discussion of reforms, in both the USA and Europe, has been concerned with how to rectify this pattern of incentives. Bankers have been widely criticized for their greed, which did indeed assume mammoth proportions, and their bonuses have come in for particular scrutiny. However, greed is not something that is entirely new to capitalism, and the significance of individual motivations and perverse incentives can be understood only in the context of broader economic developments.

5.3.2 US Interest-Rate Policy

A second approach to explaining the crisis, put forward by some economists and much repeated in European – and especially German – policy
circles, is the argument that the US central bank kept interest rates too
low and for too long between 2001 and 2004.[21] According to this view the
low interest rates were the key factor which drove the strong growth of
mortgage lending and led to the bubble in house prices which, on bursting,
caused the crisis.

The low interest rate in the USA certainly did make mortgage borrowing more attractive – it actually enabled many poorer households to buy a
house for the first time.[22] However, the criticism of US interest-rate policy
fails to recognize that the whole pattern of growth in the USA since the
1980s has been repeatedly dependent on bouts of highly expansive monetary policy and that without such measures the financial sector would
almost certainly have suffered more serious crises in 1990 and, most especially, in 2001.

Following massive over-lending to finance the wave of takeovers
and mergers in the 1980s, the banks abruptly curtailed further credit in
1989, and the Federal Reserve under its new chairman, Alan Greenspan,
responded by dramatically lowering interest rates, which were kept
low from 1990 to 1994. This relieved pressure on the major banks and,
although many savings banks had to be rescued at this time, a significant
financial crisis was avoided.[23] Furthermore, although the credit crunch
led to a brief recession in 1990, this was remarkably mild. While employment growth was muted for several years, the highly expansive monetary
policy played a key role in creating the conditions for a new period of
expansion.[24]

In the second half of the 1990s, when the US economy registered its
strongest growth for two decades, the stock market soared. At its peak,
it was by most criteria as over-valued as in 1929, but when the bubble
burst in 2000 it did not have such a devastating impact as the earlier
crash, and this was primarily due to the response of the central bank. By
dramatically cutting interest rates from 2001 to 2003, it again relieved the
pressure on key financial institutions and avoided a major financial crisis.
Furthermore, although there was a recession in 2001, as in 1990 it was
brief and mild. When expansion resumed in 2002, it was driven almost
entirely by increased consumption and, with wages stagnant, this was
primarily financed by borrowing – this time against rising house prices.

The fact that European policy makers have harped on about the
supposed errors of US monetary policy also overlooks the fact that
European – and above all German – economic growth in the period from

2002 to 2007 was in important respects dependent on the expansive policy in the USA. In Germany, where wages were at best stagnant, economic growth was largely dependent on increasing exports, while the growth of global demand was driven, primarily, by the credit-financed increase of consumer demand in the USA.

5.3.3 Global Imbalances

A third approach to analysing the crisis identifies the source of the problem not in the USA but rather in developing countries, in particular the Asian exporting countries, which have large current account surpluses.[25] This view has enjoyed considerable resonance in official US circles. The basis for the approach is that a so-called 'global savings glut' led to a large inflow of capital into the USA, and that this contributed to the bubble in share prices in the late 1990s and, following the end of the IT boom, led to low long-term interest rates, which in turn led to the bubble in house prices.

The USA has had a current account deficit since the early 1980s. The size of the deficit increased strongly from the 1990s, and this was only possible because of large offsetting inflows of capital to the USA. The ability of the USA to finance such a deficit was closely related to the role of the US dollar as the principal international reserve currency. Following the Asian financial crisis in 1997–98, countries that had been forced to bow to IMF conditions consciously built up their reserves of foreign currency to avoid such a situation in the future. Meanwhile China, which has built up the largest foreign reserve holdings, has pegged its exchange rate either to the dollar or to a basket of currencies including the dollar, in order to ensure that its export industries remain competitive, and to continue generating jobs for the stream of workers flowing into the cities from the countryside. In addition, oil-exporting countries accumulated substantial surpluses for several years prior to the onset of the crisis, much of which was also invested in US financial assets.

The savings glut hypothesis emphasizes the policy choices made in the developing countries. However, the ability of the Asian countries to achieve large export surpluses was strongly dependent on the demand for their exports, and the most important factor driving this was the credit-financed consumer demand from the USA.[26] Consequently, while the large inflow of capital to the USA did, at least in part, reflect policy choices by Asian governments, those countries faced this choice only because of the demand generated as a result of the strongly expansionary monetary policy in the USA. Furthermore, although speculation played some role in pushing up oil prices, much of the oil-price increase was driven by the strong demand for energy when economic growth was high in both the USA and Asia.

Although the savings glut analysis is primarily applied to developing countries, it should be noted that there have also been strong inflows of capital to the USA from Japan and from Europe, in particular Germany, all of which also had significant export surpluses. Indeed, it was the inflows of private capital from Europe to the USA that led to European banks being hit by such large losses from investments in US mortgage-backed securities.

The USA's dependence on large inflows of capital to finance its current account deficit was widely seen as a problem before the crisis broke. If foreign central banks should cease to invest in dollars, it could set off a crisis of the dollar (referred to in official parlance as 'a disorderly adjustment'). The US authorities have sought to deflect attention from their responsibility for their country's deficit by focusing on China's export surplus, and by making repeated calls for the Chinese authorities to cease intervening in the foreign exchange market and to allow the renminbi to appreciate. In line with its emphasis on eliminating international imbalances, in April 2009 the USA also proposed that the G20 should seek to promote more balanced current accounts, but this was opposed, for one, by Germany.

5.3.4   Deregulation

A fourth approach to explaining the crisis, and one that is much emphasized by critics of the neo-liberal model of capitalism, focuses on the role of policies to deregulate the financial sector.[27] An important step in the process of deregulation was the abandonment of pegged exchange rates in 1973, after which the USA and the other major capitalist states largely left their exchange rates to be determined in the foreign exchange markets. The subsequent volatility of exchange rates was an important impetus for the development of a whole series of so-called derivatives, designed to provide insurance against adverse exchange rate movements. Then, in 1980, as inflation increased in the USA, the legal limit on interest rates was abolished – an important pre-condition for the subsequent introduction of sub-prime mortgages, which charged interest rates some five percentage points higher than standard mortgages.

Following the election of President Reagan in 1980, the process of financial liberalization deepened. A new banking act in 1982 relaxed the regulation of banks, including savings banks, many of which promptly plunged into risky, high-yield business and, after making widespread losses, eventually required a government bail-out costing some $150 billion at the end of the decade. In 1987, the Reagan government replaced Paul Volcker as head of the Federal Reserve with Alan Greenspan, who was seen as more sympathetic to financial deregulation and, under Greenspan, rules on interstate banking and the separation of commercial and investment banks began to be interpreted ever more liberally. The final step, taken in 1999 under the Clinton government, was to repeal the 1933 law that enforced the separation of commercial and investment banks, opening the door for the creation of giant financial conglomerates.

Under Greenspan important decisions were also made *not* to introduce tighter regulation in various areas. The Fed allowed banks to set up subsidiaries, usually in the Caribbean, known as 'structured investment vehicles' which were used to hold financial investments while avoiding the usual rules on minimum capital holdings (which enable banks to absorb losses without going bankrupt).[28] This was where the banks held their investments in the complex mortgage-based securities which, when their value collapsed, set off the crisis. The Fed also decided not to introduce a tighter regulation of financial derivatives, many of which were custom designed (standardization reduced banks' profits) and were sold 'over the counter' or outside organized exchanges. Credit default swaps (CDSs), a derivative which provides insurance against a bond failing, played an important role in the crisis. Such insurance appeared to make investments in mortgage-backed securities even safer. However, many CDSs were sold by investment banks – in particular the investment banking division of AIG – that did not have the resources to meet their obligations if the bonds should fail. Incredibly, prior to the introduction of crisis-induced reforms in 2009, a CDS could be purchased without owning the bond it was insuring, providing the purchaser with a strong interest in the bond failing!

The deregulation of the financial sector, which began in the 1970s, and gained force thanks to the neo-liberal policies of the Reagan and Clinton governments, facilitated the expansion of the financial sector in the USA, the development of new, ever more risky financial instruments, and the enormous build-up of credit which fuelled the stock market bubble in the 1990s and the housing bubble in the next decade. However, while deregulation was certainly a key pillar of neo-liberal philosophy, the actual process of deregulation was introduced step by step in response to pressure from the financial sector, which had found ways of initiating such changes inside the limits of previous laws.[29] The financial sector is still subject to far greater regulation than any other sector of the economy, and the state has attempted to steer the process, most notably by intervening with expansionary policies whenever financial stability appeared to be threatened. It is such intervention to contain crises that has led to the emergence of giant financial institutions which are seen as 'too big to fail'. While the audacity of the big financial institutions' schemes for generating profits beggars belief, they are the instigators of financial deregulation rather than its result. This implies that calls for financial re-regulation will, on their own, not be sufficient to deal with the forces that gave rise to the crisis.

5.3.5   Excess Capital

The fifth and final explanation to be examined here argues that the root cause of the crisis lies in the huge sums of capital which have been accumulated in the USA (and Europe). The incessant drive to obtain the highest possible return on this capital has led to stagnant or at best very low increases in income for large sectors of the population, thereby restricting the growth of their purchasing power in the economy.[30] As a result, in the USA the growth of household consumption and of the economy at large became dependent on many households borrowing more and more, a highly precarious strategy which led to the build-up of an untenable mountain of debt securities that at some stage was doomed to collapse.

In the 1950s and 1960s, capital was quite closely tied to specific industrial and commercial companies. When profitability declined with the end of the post-war boom in the 1970s, the owners of money capital sought greater mobility for their capital so that they could take advantage of whatever opportunities might offer the highest rates of return. This was reflected in the growth of international flows of financial capital. These were predominantly between the developed capitalist countries but, when opportunities presented themselves, capital also flowed into developing countries. Here, with smaller financial markets, this often led to bubbles in share or land prices, and, when these bubbles burst, the capital would rush out, precipitating a major crisis.[31]

From the 1950s to the 1970s, the stock of financial wealth in the USA grew roughly in line with GDP, but this growth then accelerated rapidly. According to a study by McKinsey Global Institute (2009), it rose from 194 per cent of GDP in 1980 to 442 per cent in 2007.[32] This growth could be sustained only so long as the financial assets were able to secure an adequate return. To this end, financial institutions generated a whole range of exotic, complex instruments, for which they charged high fees. As already noted, financial investors also pressured non-financial corporations to give priority to generating higher dividends for shareholders, a process which required a constant process of rationalization and cost cutting, and led to the outsourcing of tasks, including to low-wage countries.[33] At the same time, non-financial corporations began to invest in financial assets, which offered a higher return than they could achieve through productive and commercial projects. Consequently companies tended to invest a smaller proportion of their funds in fixed capital, a development which also had a negative effect on job creation. The overall result was to weaken the growth of employment and to create a sense of insecurity at work – described by mainstream economists as the 'frightened worker' effect. At all events, the growth of real wages for both working- and middle-class employees was seriously constrained.

The problem is demonstrated by the relation between the growth of labour productivity and the growth of wages. Between 1950 and the mid-1970s, productivity and real wages both increased by around 80 per cent. Between 1980 and 2007, however, while productivity again increased by some 80 per cent, real wages increased by slightly less than 40 per cent.[34] In this situation, the number of two-income households increased, and the number of hours worked also increased as workers attempted to compensate for these developments. However, given the increasing gap between the increase in output and the increase in households' purchasing power, the key factor which sustained the growth of consumption was borrowing.

In the 1990s, middle- and upper-middle-class households who felt richer as a result of the increased value of shares they owned, either directly or indirectly through investment and pension funds, began to borrow extensively to finance consumption spending. After the share price bubble burst in 2000, rising house prices enabled many households to borrow, either by refinancing their mortgages or by simply borrowing against the rise in value of their homes (so-called 'home equity withdrawal').

Credit-financed spending not only helped to close the demand deficit; it also provided financial capital with a further means of appropriating interest from a significant segment of the population. However, because such borrowing was dependent on asset-price bubbles it could not be sustained. When house prices ceased to rise, the growth of consumption faltered and the US economy entered a recession. When the edifice of dubious financial instruments folded, the financial system almost collapsed and, with credit virtually unavailable, even to the best-known companies, the US economy entered a slump. The overblown financial sector could for a time reap spectacular profits and enable the US economy to constantly push out the boundaries of growth. But the lurch from one bubble to another built up ever more explosive tensions, which eventually came home to roost.

5.4 CONCLUSION

The model of finance-led capitalism which developed in the USA from the 1980s and in continental Europe from the 1990s provided the basis for a pattern of precarious growth that was very dependent on the growth of credit and the emergence of bubbles in asset prices. Central bank intervention made it possible to sustain growth in the USA each time it faltered, but at the expense of accumulating ever greater contradictions. As European banks invested in apparently high-yielding US securities, they too became entangled in these contradictions. When the crisis broke in 2007–08, governments appeared to accept a need for widespread financial reform, but once the threat of collapse had receded they reverted, essentially, to the same policies that had failed so dramatically.

This response reflects, in part, explanations for the crisis which imply that a recurrence of the near collapse can be avoided without the need for fundamental changes. To this end it is argued, variously, that the pattern of perverse incentives must be modified, that over-expansionary monetary policies must be avoided and that a means of reducing global imbalances must be put in place. But critics of neo-liberalism have questioned this tepid approach and called for a thoroughgoing re-regulation of the financial sector. There is also an even broader critique which argues that the source of the problem lies not only in the financial sector, but with the huge sums of capital that, since the 1970s, have sought the freedom to roam around the world in search of the highest possible return in finance, industry or commerce. This, it is argued, has led to a sustained – and successful – downward pressure on the incomes of large sectors of the population, both in the USA and in Europe, and left economic growth dependent on credit-financed consumption or a striving for export surpluses. According to this view the underlying forces which led to the crisis can be countered only by a fundamental change in the distribution of income, wealth and power.

NOTES

This chapter was first published in *The Perspective of the World Review*, 2011, Vol. 3 (1), 9–28. I am grateful to the Institute for Applied Economic Research – Ipea, Brasilia, for the permission to reprint and to Birgit Mahnkopf and Eckhard Hein for helpful comments.
1. For details of financial crises since the seventeenth century, see Kindleberger (1978).
2. This was first analysed in Bagehot ([1873] 1999).
3. This was prompted by a major crisis in 1907, when the largest private financier, J.P. Morgan, effectively took on the role of central bank, and prevented a financial collapse. For an excellent account, see Mitchell (2007).

4. The only banking crisis during this period was in Brazil in 1962.
5. The number of US banks with overseas branches increased from eight in 1960 to 130 in 1980 (Mizruchi and Davis 2003).
6. The main measures were the interest equalization tax, introduced in 1963 to discourage foreign corporations from raising capital in the US bond market, and the Voluntary Credit Restraint Program, introduced in 1965 to discourage banks in the USA from funding the overseas investments of US corporations.
7. For a discussion of this new phase see the contributions in Epstein (2005).
8. See Lally et al. (2008).
9. US Bureau of Economic Affairs, National Income and Product Accounts, Table 1.14.
10. The Federal Reserve's lead interest rate was reduced in rapid steps from 6.5 per cent in January 2001 to 1 per cent in 2003 and 2004.
11. While the interest rate on a standard 30-year mortgage was 5–6 per cent, that on a sub-prime mortgage could be as much 10 per cent. See Avery et al. (2007).
12. The rate was lower for some forms of lending that were considered to involve a lower risk.
13. For an account of the development of securitization and its role in the crisis, see Tett (2009).
14. For a more detailed account, see Evans (2009).
15. For details, see European Central Bank (2010).
16. US real GDP fell by 3 per cent in the last quarter of 2008 and the first quarter of 2009 (US Bureau of Economic Affairs, National Income and Product Accounts, Table 1.1.1).
17. See Eurostat Table tet20002 for trade and Table teina011 for growth.
18. The Baltic countries were by far the worst hit, with real GDP falling in 2009 by 18 per cent in Latvia, 14.8 per cent in Lithuania and 14.1 per cent in Estonia (Eurostat, Table tsieb020).
19. This was part of a broader package totalling €750 billion, which included an additional €60 billion for an existing programme to provide EU member states with balance of payments support, and €250 billion to be made available by the International Monetary Fund.
20. See, for example, Appelbaum and Lichtblau (2010).
21. For a pithy statement of this view, see Taylor (2009). Taylor was architect of the influential 'Taylor Rule', which proposes a simple formula for guiding central banks' monetary policy. He served as assistant secretary of the Treasury in G.W. Bush's first government, the time when the bubble was developing.
22. The proportion of black, Hispanic and female purchasers was much higher among sub-prime borrowers than among those for standard 'prime' mortgages (see Avery et al. 2007).
23. Many savings and loans associations had made big losses on speculative investments following their deregulation in the early 1980s. Government support, estimated at around $150 billion, was large at the time, but has since been dwarfed in the most recent crisis.
24. The main channel through which this operated was by making the USA less attractive for financial investors so that the dollar weakened, making US exports significantly more competitive.
25. The notion of a 'global savings glut' was put forward before the crisis broke in a series of speeches by Ben Bernanke, Greenspan's successor as chairman of the Federal Reserve. See Bernanke (2005). A more developed analysis, which broadly supports the Bernanke position and was also written before the onset of the crisis, can be found in Wolf (2009).
26. This argument is developed in Duncan (2003/2005).
27. This is mentioned, amongst others, by Baker (2009).
28. In Europe, banks – including the German *Landesbanken* – opened similar subsidiaries, usually in Dublin, to hold their investments in mortgage-based securities. Spain was alone in not allowing its banks to evade minimum capital requirements in this way.

29. This point is stressed in Panitch and Konings (2009).
30. For wage developments in the USA see Lawrence et al. (2009, Table 3.5).
31. The most notable episodes include the crises in Mexico (1994–95), Asia (1997–98) and Russia (1998).
32. The largest increase was in holdings of bonds and shares.
33. For estimates of the gains to US corporations from outsourcing to low-wage countries, see Milberg (2007).
34. Based on figures for hourly output, hourly wages and consumer price inflation from US Bureau of Labour Statistics, Series PRS85006092, PRS85006102 and CUSR0000SA0.

REFERENCES

Appelbaum, B. and E. Lichtblau (2010), 'Banks lobbying against derivatives trading ban', *New York Times*, 9 May.

Avery, R.B., K.P. Brevoort and G.B. Canner (2007), 'The 2006 HMDA data', *Federal Reserve Bulletin*, **93**, 73–109.

Bagehot, W. ([1873] 1999), *Lombard Street: A Description of the Money Market*, New York: John Wiley & Sons.

Baker, D. (2009), *Plunder and Blunder: The Rise and Fall of the Bubble Economy*, Sausalito, CA: PoliPoint Press.

Bernanke, B. (2005), 'The global savings glut and the US current account deficit', Board of Governors of the Federal Reserve System, 10 March.

Duncan, R. (2003/2005), *The Dollar Crisis: Causes, Consequences, Cures*, Singapore: John Wiley & Sons (Asia).

Epstein, G. (ed.) (2005), *Financialisation and the World Economy*, Cheltenham, UK and Northampton, MA, USA: Edward Elgar Publishing.

European Central Bank (2010), 'Measures taken by euro area governments in support of the financial sector', *Monthly Bulletin*, April, 75–90.

Evans, T. (2009), 'The 2002–2007 US economic expansion and the limits of finance-led capitalism', *Studies in Political Economy*, **83**, Spring, 33–59.

Kindleberger, C. (1978), *Manias, Panics and Crashes: A History of Financial Crises*, New York: Macmillan.

Lally, P., A. Hodge and R. Corea (2008), 'Returns of domestic nonfinancial business', Survey of Current Business, US Department of Commerce, May.

Lawrence, M., J. Bernstein and H. Shierholz (2009), *The State of Working America 2008/2009*, Ithaca, NY: Cornell University Press.

McKinsey Global Institute (2009), 'Global financial markets', September.

Milberg, W. (2007), 'Shifting sources and uses of profits: sustaining US financialisation with global value chains', Working Paper 2007-9, Schwartz Centre for Economic Policy Analysis, The New School.

Mitchell, L.E. (2007), *The Speculation Economy: How Finance Triumphed over Industry*, San Francisco: Berrett-Koehler.

Mizruchi, M. and G. Davis (2003), 'The globalization of American banking, 1962 to 1981', in F. Dobbin (ed.), *The Sociology of the Economy*, New York: Russell Sage Foundation.

Panitch, L. and M. Konings (2009), 'Myths of neoliberal deregulation', *New Left Review*, **57**, May–June, 67–83.

Taylor, J.B. (2009), *Getting Off Track: How Government Actions and Interventions*

Caused, Prolonged and Worsened the Financial Crisis, Stanford, CA: Hoover Institution Press.

Tett, G. (2009), *Fool's Gold: How Unrestrained Greed Corrupted a Dream, Shattered Global Markets and Unleashed a Catastrophe*, London: Abacus.

Wolf, Martin (2009), *Fixing Global Finance: How to Curb Financial Crises in the 21st Century*, New Haven, CT: Yale University Press.

6. Income distribution and the financial and economic crisis

Jo Michell

6.1 INTRODUCTION

Analysis of the distribution of income is a far from straightforward matter. For a start, there are a number of ways in which income distribution can be quantified and compared. When it comes to explaining how and why patterns of income distribution evolve over time, the task becomes even more difficult. It is therefore not surprising that there exist a range of views both on the relatively straightforward question of how income distribution has evolved over time and on the more difficult question of what has caused changes in income distribution.

There are two main measures of income distribution. The 'personal distribution' of income describes the relative concentration or dispersion of the income of individuals (or households) drawn from a given population, such as wage-earners. The other measure is the 'functional' income distribution. This is usually defined in marginalist terms as the share of total income accruing to each of the factors of production – labour, land and various types of 'capital' – on the basis of their (marginal) contributions to output. This rather sterile definition obscures the fact that the functional distribution of income actually captures the share of income accruing to each of the social classes identified by the writers in classical political economy.

At the time of these classical writers, social classes – and thus their income streams – were clearly defined: each individual was either a worker, a landlord or a capitalist, and thus the individual's income was likewise clearly defined. With the increasing 'financialization' of households in advanced economies, this is no longer the case. The income of many individuals and households is now composed of a combination of wages, interest and dividend incomes, for example through participation in funded pension schemes.

This introduces important complexities into the relationship between personal and functional income distribution. In a situation in which individuals receive only one type of income, any shift in the functional distribution – from labour to capital, for example – will result in a parallel shift in the personal distribution towards those who receive capital income.[1] However, with a heterogeneous household sector in which the proportions of each income type vary significantly between households, the relationship becomes more complex.

In recent decades, and in sharp contrast with the preoccupations of the classical political economists, income distribution has been off the agenda for the majority of mainstream economists. The collective view was summarized by Nobel prize-winner Robert Lucas in the following statement: 'Of the tendencies that are harmful to sound economics, the most seductive, and in my opinion the most poisonous, is to focus on questions of distribution' (Lucas 2014). This refusal to engage with questions of income distribution is reinforced by the technical apparatus of neoclassical macroeconomics, which has increasingly moved towards the use of techniques which exclude, by assumption, even the possibility of shifts in income distribution.

In the last few years, however, and increasingly in the aftermath of the financial crisis, a number of prominent mainstream economists have begun to resist the myopia of their discipline and have raised the issue of income distribution once more. It is argued that a deepening polarization of income should be seen as a cause for concern both for its own sake and because inequality should be considered one of the deeper causes of the financial and economic crisis.[2] The subject finally emerged from the fringes of the discussion and took centre stage with the watershed publication of the English translation of Piketty's *Capital in the Twenty-First Century* (2014).

This chapter examines the links between widening income inequality and the financial and economic crisis. The chapter is organized as follows. Section 6.2 briefly discusses the data on the changing distribution of income. Section 6.3 considers the explanations put forward to account for these changes. Section 6.4 analyses the links between shifts in the distribution of income and the financial and economic crisis. Section 6.5 concludes.

6.2 CHANGES IN INCOME DISTRIBUTION

Prior to the publication of Piketty's book, the mainstream economics literature – in line with its methodological focus on the individual – almost always focused on measures of personal inequality, such as the distribution of income among different groups of wage-earners or changes in the distribution (and composition) of personal incomes. What emerges from this growing literature on the personal distribution is a picture of a dramatic divergence in income over the last 30 years or so. In many advanced economies, incomes at the top of the distribution have increased enormously, while those close to the median have stagnated, and some groups at the bottom of the distribution have even seen their incomes fall in real terms since the 1970s (Katz and Autor 1998; Feenstra and Hanson 2003; Alvaredo and Piketty 2008).

Piketty's book, with its explicit reference to Marx in the title, brings the categories of political economy – and thus the functional distribution of income – back into the picture. Piketty focuses on the share of income received by 'capital' – essentially everything except labour compensation – and demonstrates that this share has risen significantly since around the 1970s. But, despite being the most prominent contemporary economist to focus on the functional distribution, Piketty is not the first. An important strand of literature exists among those influenced by political economy that has sought to highlight changes in the functional distribution of income. This literature, which focuses in particular on the macroeconomic effects of a falling labour share, can be traced back to the contribution by Bowles and Boyer (1995) and builds on the theoretical framework introduced by Taylor (1983) and Bhaduri and Marglin (1990) to develop empirical estimations of the relative contribution to aggregate demand of spending out of wages and profits and thus classifies countries as either 'wage-led' or 'profit-led'.[3] On this basis, the effects of redistribution from labour to capital can be seen to be either expansionary or stagnationary.

One common measure of the functional distribution of income – the 'adjusted labour share' – is shown for six selected economies in Figure 6.1. In all six, with the exception of the UK, the labour share shows a clear decline from peaks in the mid- to late 1970s to around 2007–08 when the crisis struck. Data for the functional distribution of income in developing countries are less readily available, but the evidence suggests that declines in the labour share of income in less developed countries (LDCs) may be at least as pronounced as in developed countries (Stockhammer 2012).

It should be noted that there are a number of authors who take issue with the claim that the wage share has fallen. One straightforward criticism is that the observed trend decline is a result of the data period selected for analysis: much of the decline since the 1970s is simply a reversal of the sharp increases in the labour share that took place in the 1960s and 1970s (Gordon and Dew-Becker 2008). Others have criticized the data on the basis of calculation methods, particularly in relation to the income of the self-employed.[4] Given that the central mechanism in Piketty (2014) is a rising share of capital income, and thus a falling labour share, it is

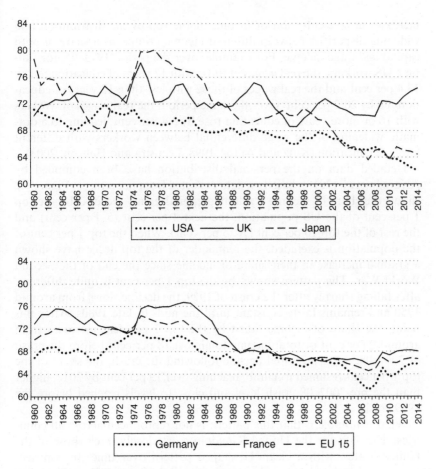

Source: European Commission (2013); own calculation.

Figure 6.1 Adjusted wage share as percentage of GDP at current factor costs, 1960–2012

interesting to note that, based on calculations from the US NIPA tables, Piketty and Saez (2003, p. 19) find that the shares of wages and capital in the US corporate sector have remained close to constant over the long-run period from around 1930 to 2000: 'As is well-known, factor shares in the corporate sector have been fairly flat in the long run with the labor share around 70–75 percent, and the capital share around 25–30 percent.'

The labour share is only one part of a larger story on inequality, however. Measures of the personal distribution of income show significant increases in concentration of income at the top of the distribution and widening disparities between different income groups, as a share of both capital *and* wage income. For example, over the period 1979–95, for full-time US workers, the real wages of those with 12 years of education fell by 13.4 per cent and the real wages of those with less than 12 years of education fell by 20.2 per cent. Over the same period, the real wages of workers with 16 or more years of education rose by 3.4 per cent, leading to a dramatic widening of the wage differential between workers with different levels of education (Katz and Autor, 1998; Feenstra and Hanson, 2003).

Detailed data on the personal distribution have been compiled by Alvaredo et al. (2013), based on data collected from tax returns. Figure 6.2 shows the share of income (excluding capital gains) received by the top 1 per cent of the US population, the next 4 per cent (5–1 per cent) and the rest of the top 10 per cent (10–5 per cent). When the top 1 per cent of the population is excluded, the remainder of the top decile have shown a gradual increase in their share of income since the end of the Second World War. The pattern shown by the top 1 per cent is quite different: after falling sharply after the crash of 1929, the decline slows from around 1950 and remains fairly constant until the mid- to late 1980s. After this point, the share of income taken by the top 1 per cent increases from around 9 per cent of total income to almost 18 per cent before the crash of 2007–08. After an initial decline following the crash, the share of the top 1 per cent resumed its climb, reaching over 19 per cent by 2012, higher than the pre-2007 08 crash level and close to levels reached before the 1929 crash.

What is notable is that this pattern is not reproduced across all countries. The data for the United Kingdom most closely track those of the United States, with a clear 'U'-shaped pattern over time. In contrast, France and Japan show similar patterns until the Second World War, but do not then replicate the remarkable increase in inequality found in the USA and the UK. France and Japan are thus characterized as having an 'L'-shaped pattern of top income shares. Those countries that have seen the sharpest declines in wage shares have seen the least concentration of wage income and vice versa.

Bakija et al. (2008) use tax return data to show that in the US 'executives, managers, supervisors and financial professionals' account for 70 per cent of the increase in the incomes of the top 0.1 per cent between 1979 and 2005 and 60 per cent of the increase going to the top 1 per cent. By 2005, the so-called wages of this group made up over 9 per cent of total national income, up from around 4 per cent in 1979. Despite being classified as wage income in the national accounts, a significant portion of the remuneration of such top executives takes the form of stock options.[5]

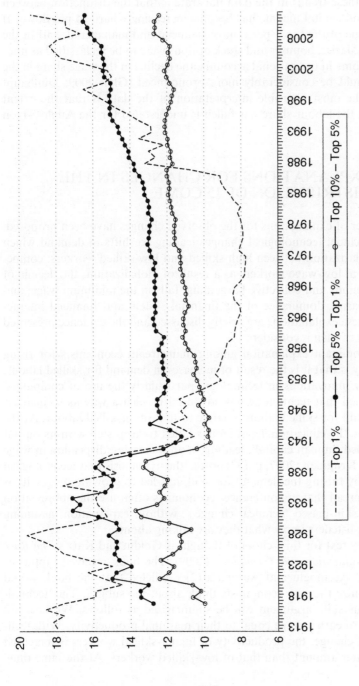

Source: Alvaredo et al. (2013).

Figure 6.2   Personal income distribution in the USA, 1913–2012

What these trends in the data illustrate is that the distinction between labour and capital income has become increasingly hard to pin down. If the income of the top 1 per cent of financial and managerial staff in the form of salaries, bonuses and stock options were to be reclassified as non-wage income in the national accounts, the decline in the wage share in the USA would be considerably more pronounced (Glyn 2009; Dünhaupt 2011). The most plausible interpretation of the data is that the extent to which the labour share has fallen is understated for the Anglo-Saxon countries.

6.3   EXPLANATIONS FOR CHANGES IN THE DISTRIBUTION OF INCOME

A number of explanations for the observed changes have been proposed. These include: technological changes leading to shifts in demand which cause polarization between high-skilled and low-skilled workers; competition from low-wage workers as a result of globalization; the decline of labour unions and collective bargaining; falls in the minimum wage; and the increasing dominance of the financial system and financial interactions. These explanations are briefly discussed and the evidence presented in favour of each is considered.

The dominant explanation among mainstream economists for rising inequality is that it is the result of increases in demand for skilled labour, driven by innovations in technology, particularly the use of computers. It is argued that technology has advanced in such a way as to increase the demand for skilled labour relative to that of unskilled labour. At the same time the educational system has failed to keep step with its output of so-called 'human capital', leading to an increasing dispersion in wage rates. As Krugman (2007, p. 132) notes, 'the hypothesis that technological change, by raising the demand for skill, has led to growing inequality is so widespread that at conferences economists often use the abbreviation SBTC – skill-biased technical change – without explanation, assuming that their listeners know what they are talking about'.

The key text for this school of thought is Goldin and Katz's *The Race between Education and Technology* (2009). The book received rapturous reviews – Acemoglu and Autor (2012) predicted that the book would revolutionize the way economists think about the subject. The 'technology versus skill' argument can be summarized as follows. Workers are assumed to earn a wage equal to their marginal productivity. With technological change, the productivity of higher-skilled workers is increased by a greater amount than that of low-skilled workers. At the same time, it is argued, the educational system has failed to generate enough 'supply' of high-skilled labour, leading to a widening gap between the wages of the two groups.[6]

There are a number of problems with this narrative. Firstly, it cannot explain the absolute fall in real wages that has occurred in some sections of the population – in particular, males without high-school education. Another is raised by Alvaredo et al. (2013): why didn't similar wage dispersion occur in France and Japan? If technological change, rather than political action, were to blame for increasing income inequality, then the same patterns should have been seen equally across the globe. An alternative view is offered by Piketty (2014, pp. 315–321), who argues that, in Anglo-Saxon countries at least, the explosion of wage income at the top of the distribution can be attributed to the rise of 'supermanagers' who extract rents far in excess of their contribution to production.

Those authors who have not subscribed to the deterministic 'supply and demand for skills' view note that the period before the crisis of rising inequality was coincident with a period of deregulation, particularly in the financial sector (Stockhammer 2013), while labour markets were subjected to reforms aimed at increasing 'flexibility' (Palley 1998; Levy and Temin 2007). Supporters of these reforms argued that the reduction in market frictions would lead to increased efficiency and productivity (Greenspan 1998; Blanchard and Giavazzi 2003). Any associated increases in inequality thus resulted from the natural workings of the market once it was allowed free rein to adjust to technological change, changing trade patterns and so on.

In recent years, however, some high-profile mainstream economists have begun to question the notion that political shifts had no role to play in the increasingly apparent divergence in incomes and opportunities in the United States. One author who attributes a substantive role to the conservative political shift is Paul Krugman. Krugman notes the correlation (over the period from around the mid-1970s) between increasing inequality and what he refers to as political 'polarization' arising from a rightward shift of the Republican Party.[7] This leads to the question of causality – the conventional wisdom holds that, with technological change and trade globalization leading to widening inequality, an increase in political 'polarization' between the winners and losers is the outcome: 'That, more or less, is the story I believed when I began working on this book . . . Yet I've become convinced that much of the causation runs the other way – that political change in the form of rising polarization has been a major cause of rising inequality' (Krugman 2007, p. 6). Krugman (2007, p. 7) thus finds himself in the troubling position – '[i]t sounds like economic heresy' – of agreeing with those who put forward the radical proposition that inequality can be affected not only by such 'impersonal' variables as globalization and technical change, but also by the exercise of political power:

> [E]conomists, startled by rising equality . . . discovered to their surprise that the transition from the inequality of the Gilded Age to the relative equality of the postwar era wasn't a gradual evolution. Instead, America's postwar middle-class society was *created*, in just the space of a few years, by the policies of the Roosevelt administration – especially through wartime wage controls. (Krugman 2007, p. 7)[8]

Within mainstream economics, the strengthening view that politics matters is associated in particular with the work of Goldin and Margo (1992) and Levy and Temin (2007). The former authors coined the phrase 'the Great Compression' to refer to the pre-neoliberal period of lower income inequality. They present evidence that, given the shift in 'institutions and norms' – increases in top-bracket income taxes in particular – from the period of what they dub the 'Treaty of Detroit' to that of the Washington Consensus, the conclusion must be drawn that 'technology and trade's impacts are embedded in a larger institutional story' (Levy and Temin 2007, p. 6).[9] The reversal of the Great Compression was thus the result of supply-side policies implemented in reaction to the stagnation and inflation of the late 1970s.

Aside from the political shift, a number of other mechanisms leading to increasing inequality have been identified. Authors have highlighted the decline of the trade union movement in advanced nations as an important explanatory factor in the apparent inability of 'traumatized workers' to resist downward pressures on wages.[10] In the mainstream literature, it is largely taken for granted that greater unionization is associated with greater wage inequality. However, since the publication of Freeman's (1980) seminal study, this view has been substantially weakened. Freeman found that unionization was correlated with a substantial compression of wage incomes. This result has subsequently been confirmed by a number of other more recent studies (e.g. Card et al. 2004).

Alongside the weakening of organized labour and the deregulation of domestic markets, the pre-crisis period was characterized by extensive dismantling of barriers to international trade and capital flows. The effects of globalization and, in particular, the effects of trade competition with developing countries are oft-cited causes of downward pressure on low-skilled wages and 'de-industrialization' in advanced countries. Increased capital mobility, leading to greater potential for foreign outsourcing and international technology transfers, serves to further undermine the bargaining position of workers (Rodrik 1997).

In addition to the wage competition from abroad faced by workers in an increasingly globalized world, the arrival of low-skilled immigrants from overseas is another potential cause of pressure on the wages of the low-skilled. If immigrants mostly take low-paying jobs at the bottom of the income distribution, this will have direct effects on measures of wage dispersion.

A clear divide thus exists between competing interpretations of the rise in inequality that has taken place over the last 30 years. The conventional wisdom holds that the failure of the average worker's wages to keep up with productivity growth is the result of skill-biased technical change and associated changes in the structure of labour demand. This is augmented by the effects of trade and globalization: as markets become more open and competition increases, the polarizing effects of technical change are more powerfully transmitted through otherwise neutral market forces. In this view, the effect of the political drive towards deregulation since the 1980s allows market forces to operate freely and removes the excessive distortions that were put in place in the post-war period.

The alternative view is that the period of deregulation, de-unionization and privatization represents a systematic restructuring of the economic system, undertaken in response to the economic crisis of the late 1970s, and was guided by a conservative policy agenda spearheaded by Friedman's monetarist attack on the Keynesian orthodoxy of the time. The proponents of this policy agenda had been waiting on the sidelines when the economic slowdown and inflationary crisis of the late 1970s gave them the opportunity to impose their policies. Instead of full employment, the control of inflation became the primary goal of macroeconomic policy. The aims of the political class thus became aligned with the interests of an increasingly dominant and 'financialized' corporate sector which had subordinated the goals of long-term investment and productivity growth to short-term gain for shareholders and other financial interests.

6.4   LINKS BETWEEN INEQUALITY AND THE CRISIS

The most obvious connection between rising inequality, falling or stagnant wages and the financial crisis is that the proximate trigger of the crisis was the realization that non-performing mortgage debt, originating in the USA, had spread throughout the financial systems of advanced nations in the form of mortgage-backed securities.

The period preceding the crisis was marked by an enormous increase in private-sector debt in the USA and other advanced nations and, in particular, a significant accumulation of debt in the household sector. In the USA, this debt was, for the most part, accumulated by households occupying a place in the income distribution where incomes had not risen in line with productivity growth, and in many cases had fallen in real terms. At the same time, state provision of services was being scaled back and financial services deregulated. In reaction to stagnating incomes, reduced provision of services by the state and increased access to credit, many households turned to debt in order to maintain living standards. This debt was often obtained by using as collateral housing that was rising in value. Meanwhile, a disproportionate and rising share of income was accruing to wealthy households at the top of the income distribution, setting up an increasing demand for safe, standardized financial assets in which to hold their wealth. Banks responded by securitizing the debt of the poor and selling it to the wealthy.

At the time that these processes were taking place, however, the rapidly rising levels of debt were not seen as cause for concern among most academic economists or policy makers because rising leverage ratios were accompanied by rising asset prices so that the net worth of households was fairly stable:

> In evaluating household debt burdens, one must remember that debt-to-income ratios have been rising for at least a half century. With household assets rising as well, the ratio of net worth to income is currently somewhat higher than its long-run average. So long as financial intermediation continues to expand, both household debt and assets are likely to rise faster than income . . . Overall, the household sector seems to be in good shape, and much of the apparent increase in the household sector's debt ratios over the past decade reflects factors that do not suggest increasing household financial stress. (Greenspan 2004)

Before the crisis struck, the view was widely held that the observed increases in household debt were simply the benign result of efficient financial markets performing their role in allowing households to smooth their consumption expenditures. Along with Greenspan, this view was particularly associated with D. Krueger and Perri (2003, 2006).[11]

While not denying the large increases in income inequality that were taking place, these authors argued that what matters for welfare is consumption outcomes, rather than equality of income *per se*. In well-functioning financial markets, agents faced with a higher volatility of 'transitory components of income' will use financial markets to prevent that volatility feeding through into consumption 'shocks'. Further, greater variance in earnings doesn't matter so long as everyone gets a turn at the top – if the large bonuses and other 'windfalls' go to different households every year, there is no reason to view this as an inequitable outcome.

The Krueger–Perri–Greenspan argument can be summarized as follows. Increased competition as a result of deregulation gave rise to a greater volatility of income. Households mitigate the effects of this volatility on consumption through interaction on the financial markets. The accumulation of debt stocks were the result of the endogenous evolution of the financial system in response to 'demand' from households. Studies by these authors concluded that 'the increase in income inequality for the U.S. in the last 25 years has not been accompanied by a substantial increase in consumption inequality' (D. Krueger and Perri 2006, p. 186).[12]

In these and similar studies, a distinction is drawn between 'within-group' and 'between-group' income and consumption inequality, with the assumption being that 'between-group' inequality – with groups defined in terms of age, sex, ethnicity, education and so on – will be permanent, because it results from fixed characteristics of those groups. On the other hand, 'within-group' inequality is taken as a proxy for transitory changes in income arising from insurable idiosyncratic income shocks.[13] D. Krueger and Perri find that, in both cases, consumption inequality did not rise significantly. They find, however, that income inequality remained fairly stable and closely tracked consumption inequality in the between-group case only. In the case of within-group inequality, however, this increased much more markedly than consumption inequality, leading the authors to conclude that increasing consumer debt was simply the outcome of households insuring themselves against idiosyncratic income shocks.[14]

Aside from the obviously problematic inference that all variance in income of, for example, university-educated middle-aged black males is due to transitory shocks, these studies suffered from a number of other methodological and data-related problems. In particular, the total consumption implied by the survey data used differs significantly from that in NIPA accounts, and the divergence worsens over the period under investigation.[15]

These studies added to an already large literature that attempts to disentangle the complex and simultaneous changes that have occurred in the structure and evolution of wages in the USA. Authors have tried to estimate the relative importance of permanent and transitory wage dispersion in the observed overall increase, the degree to which income mobility has changed over time and the degree to which changes in income feed into changes in consumption.

In an early contribution, Gottschalk and Moffitt (1994) showed that around one-third of the increase in wage inequality of white males was due to higher volatility, while around two-thirds could be attributed to permanent shifts. These results were subsequently updated in Moffitt and

Gottschalk (2008), in which it is shown that volatility increases levelled off after the 1990s, with permanent increases in wage dispersion playing a more significant role subsequently. Cutler and Katz (1992) examined the relationship between changes in income and changes in consumption for different quintiles of the population. They concluded that, in all except the second-highest income quintile, consumption changes were proportional to income changes. In the very lowest quintile, consumption fell *more* than proportionally with income (Cutler and Katz, 1992), and the degree of income volatility was greatest for those in the lowest quintile (Gottschalk and Moffitt, 1994). A more recent study by Cynamon and Fazzari (2013), finds evidence that dissaving increased considerably in the bottom 95 per cent of US households as inequality rose, while saving rates for the top 5 per cent remained stable.

Kopczuk et al. (2010) examined Social Security Administration data and concluded that virtually all of the increase in inequality was due to permanent shifts in the income distribution and, further, that earnings mobility at the top of the distribution had not increased. Overall mobility had increased somewhat, but this was due entirely to a decrease in the gender earnings gap. For men taken separately, income mobility had decreased slightly. Similar results on mobility were found by Bradbury and Katz (2002, p. 5), who concluded: 'Compared to 30 years ago, families at the bottom are poorer relative to families at the top and also a bit more stuck there. Mobility alone has not and is not likely to counteract the hardships caused by increasing inequality.'

The patterns that emerged from these studies can be summarized as follows: 1) permanent shifts in income were of greater significance than transitory effects; 2) the poorest faced the greatest uncertainty and instability in income; 3) the poorest were least likely to use credit to offset transitory changes in income, but were most likely to use credit to offset permanent changes; and 4) for most, the chances of moving into a higher income bracket had not improved.

A number of possible explanations have been put forward as to why households – particularly low-income households – accumulated large volumes of debt in the pre-crisis period. In particular, two key questions need to be addressed: firstly, why did households spend in excess of their income and, secondly, what were the mechanisms that allowed them to do so? Answers to the first question relate directly to rising inequality of income and the falling wage share. While the connection between inequality and the second question is less straightforward, mechanisms have been suggested to explain why increasing the ease of access to credit for households with an increasingly unequal income distribution may have been either politically or macroeconomically convenient – at least in the short term.

In answer to the first of these questions – why did households spend beyond their means? – two main explanations are forthcoming. The first is that, when faced with stagnating or declining real incomes alongside reduced provision of key public services, poor households were pushed into debt (Barba and Pivetti 2009). In this view, some acceptable or minimum standard of living is based on past experience or social norms. It is more difficult to adjust to a lower standard of living than to a higher one. The second explanation relates to the explosion of high incomes at the top. In this view, the attempt by those on lower incomes to emulate the consumption patterns of those further up the income structure led to spending in excess of income. As the distribution of income becomes more dispersed, the lifestyles of those at the top become relatively less affordable for those below them and attempts to keep up thus result in rising indebtedness. While the first of these two mechanisms may explain much of the indebtedness at the bottom of the income distribution, the second can shed light on rising indebtedness in higher income brackets.

The theory of consumption which underpins the already discussed debt-as-insurance view is Friedman's (1957) 'permanent income hypothesis'. Friedman's intervention was an attack on Duesenberry's (1949) 'relative income hypothesis'. Duesenberry had proposed a modified version of the consumption function in which the 'demonstration effects' that occur as individuals experience the higher-quality goods consumed by those on higher incomes affect the consumption decisions of individuals on lower incomes.[16]

Much of the literature on imitative consumption behaviour can ultimately be traced back to Veblen ([1899] 1919), who argued that, in a society in which welfare depends on social status, and social status is gained through 'conspicuous consumption', individuals will make socially determined consumption choices. But, with the advent of increasing mathematical formalization of economic models, such social status models fell out of favour, while those such as Duesenberry who tried to understand the broader determinants of consumption and saving patterns were denounced for 'psychologizing' (Mason 2000).

These debates that led to the abandonment of socially embedded theories of consumption and saving took place during the 'Great Compression'. By the time the 'Great Divergence' got under way in the 1970s, formalized utility theory was in firm control. As economic reality was headed in one direction, theory appeared to have fixed a course in the other:

> Beginning in the 1980s, luxury goods markets expanded dramatically, with both upscaling of goods and services and product innovation at the high end ... Curiously, consumption studies, which were busy rejecting the models

that made sense of this behaviour, had little to say about these developments. Perhaps they had thrown out the proverbial Veblenian baby with the bathwater. (Schor 2007, p. 22)

Nonetheless, a number of authors have returned to the ideas of Veblen and Duesenberry, albeit largely within the framework of optimizing behaviour. In particular, Robert H. Frank has developed the concept of 'positional externalities' in which the utility gained from the possession or consumption of 'positional goods' can be affected by the purchasing behaviour of others. This leads to 'expenditure cascades' as those on lower incomes attempt to imitate the consumption patterns of the better off (Frank 1985, 2005). In a similar vein, Bagwell and Bernheim (1996) present a model in which informational asymmetries that prevent agents from displaying their true relative wealth can be overcome through the 'signalling' effects of conspicuous consumption.

This then leads to the question of what enabled households to accumulate such large and unsustainable debt stocks. On this question, Rajan takes the view that, in order to mitigate the political consequences of declines in the relative incomes of median households, the US government acted to create an environment in which credit extension allowed those families to 'keep up with the Joneses':

> Stripped to its essentials the argument is that if somehow the consumption of middle-class householders keeps up, if they can afford a new car every few years and the occasional exotic holiday, perhaps they will pay less attention to their stagnant monthly paychecks ... [T]he political response ... was to expand lending to households, especially low-income ones ... [E]asy credit has been used as a palliative throughout history by governments that are unable to address the deeper anxieties of the middle class directly. (Rajan 2010, p. 9)

In support of this argument, Rajan emphasizes the role of the government in setting up Fannie Mae and Freddie Mac as a way to enable lower-income households to obtain access to consumption credit. Stiglitz (2010, Chapter 1) takes issue with this view that populist credit expansion was undertaken by a government afraid of the electoral consequences of stagnant incomes. Instead, he points to problems of incentives in the financial system, and in turn to the failure of regulators. Stiglitz points out that, at the time, Fannie and Freddie were not making sub-prime loans, were not involved in commercial real estate and were not dealing in derivatives.

Whether or not credit extension against real estate was a politically motivated phenomenon, an important link emerged between rising house prices and the increasing use of debt by households to finance consumption expenditures. The effects of rising house prices were twofold. Firstly, wealth effects arising as a result of nominal capital gains may have stimulated household consumption demand, increasing debt levels yet further. At the same time, rising nominal wealth provides households with the collateral necessary to obtain credit, by re-mortgaging houses that are rising in value.

An alternative view on the relationship between inequality and debt emphasizes macroeconomic, rather than political, factors in the rising debt levels of households. It is argued that, because the better off tend to save a greater share of their income, rising inequality will tend to reduce the overall level of spending in the economy. Thus, rising inequality tends to reduce aggregate demand and thus output and employment. One way that this tendency towards stagnation can be overcome is the extension of credit to poorer households, allowing them to avoid falling consumption. Thus, financial deregulation provides a mechanism by which the stagnationary tendencies of rising inequality can be overcome: '[T]he economic imbalances that caused the present crisis should be thought of as the outcome of the interaction of the effects of financial deregulation with the macroeconomic effects of rising inequality' (Stockhammer 2013, p. 1).

This argument can be extended to the international sphere. Just as domestic financial deregulation facilitated the build-up of domestic imbalances, the deregulation of international capital flows increased the ease with which countries could run either current account surpluses or deficits. As a result, two growth regimes emerged: a 'debt-led' regime in deficit nations such as the USA and the UK and an 'export-led' regime in surplus nations such as Germany and China. In the first, the extension of credit to households not only supports domestic aggregate demand through consumption expenditures, but also serves to maintain demand in those 'export-led' regimes which operate with an external surplus.

The result of the interaction of these two growth regimes is the accumulation of international financial imbalances. In the case of debt-led economies, those imbalances mostly materialized as the bank debt of households. In the case of export-led regimes, financial imbalances led to the accumulation of external financial assets at the expense of their deficit trade partners. These stocks of financial liabilities may be either public (as in the case of Greece, for example) or private (as in the case of Spain).

In this view, a number of inter-related macroeconomic mechanisms thus combine to generate financial imbalances at both the domestic and the international level. Government policies which weakened the bargaining position of labour resulted in stagnationary tendencies. The solution to the lack of aggregate demand was the emergence of debt-led and export-led regimes. The accumulation of these financial imbalances was made possible by deregulation of both domestic and international banking and finance, allowing for the accumulation of both domestic and cross-border financial positions to cover the rising imbalances (Hein 2012, Chapter 6; Stockhammer 2013).[17]

A related view emphasizes the role of financialization as a contributing factor in the decline in the labour share of income (see, for example, Hein 2011, 2012, 2014). Like 'globalization', 'financialization' is a complex and nebulous concept, and one that has yet to converge on a widely accepted meaning (Michell and Toporowski 2014). For the sake of the current discussion, these issues will be put to one side and, following Hein, the broad definition given in Epstein (2005, p. 3) will serve as a reference point: 'financialisation means the increasing role of financial motives, financial markets, financial actors and financial institutions in the operation of the domestic and international economies'.

It is argued that the financialization of corporations leads to an increase in the power of shareholders, who exert pressure on managers to prioritize dividend income and capital gains. As a result, management decisions will be skewed against expenditure on real capital investment and in favour of activities that will generate returns for financial investors, such as share buy-backs and dividend pay-outs. Shareholders will also exert pressure on firms to 'rationalize' and 'streamline' businesses, so that higher short-term surpluses may be generated. The effects of such reorientation of management priorities may translate into a reduced tolerance of, and willingness to negotiate with, trade unions – resulting in job insecurity and a weakening of the bargaining position of employees.

These changes in incentives directly exert pressure on the labour share of income. But, at the macroeconomic level, the reduced capital investment of firms and the reorientation towards financial profits and operations also reinforce the stagnationary tendencies of the falling wage share. These tendencies may serve to reduce the profitability of the firms sector as a whole if aggregate demand falls sufficiently for the effect to outweigh increased profit margins. The debt-financed expenditures of households provide a mechanism to overcome this tendency and allow firms to realize profits in the face of falling investment expenditures. Thus, the accumulation of household debt serves not only to offset declining aggregate demand, but also to support the profits of non-financial corporations.

The arguments discussed thus far focus on the connection between inequality and crisis almost exclusively in connection with the factors leading to the demand for credit – some have emphasized inequality as a factor increasing the demand for credit, while others have pointed to ineffective regulation and misplaced government action as factors which lay behind the ability of financial institutions to extend this credit. What has not been discussed is the demand for financial *assets*. While the literature engages extensively with the idea that stagnant or falling incomes at the bottom of the income distribution have given rise to increased indebtedness, the implications of rapidly rising incomes at the top of the income distribution are discussed less. In particular, little consideration is given to the macroeconomic effects of the appropriation of an ever greater share of income by those who save the greatest part of their income – a situation that inevitably leads to a rising concentration of wealth among those households.

The tendency of commentators to overlook the role of wealth concentration in the crisis is a puzzling one. As noted by Mishel et al. (2012), wealth inequality in the USA is greater than income inequality: the top 1 per cent, next 9 per cent and bottom 90 per cent shares of income were 16.9 per cent, 25.6 per cent and 57.5 per cent, respectively, in 2004. Shares of wealth were 34.3 per cent, 36.9 per cent and 28.7 per cent, respectively. In a series of papers, Lysandrou (2011a, 2011b, 2011c) and Goda and Lysandrou (2011) argue that the demand for a means by which wealthy households can store this wealth is an aspect of the crisis that has so far been overlooked. In their view, the explosion of financial securities – both in value and in complexity – were the result of a demand arising from the concentration of wealth at the top of the income distribution. Lysandrou (2011a, p. 323) argues that 'toxic assets were created largely in response to external pressures, a principal source of which was global inequality'. With aggregate demand slackening – as a result of falling or stagnant incomes relative to productivity for the great majority – the opportunities for profitable business investment for the wealthy minority were dissipating. At the same time, there was a growth in demand for securities from institutional investors and sovereign wealth managers, in part due to rising global imbalances.

The effects of these dynamics can be seen in the falling yields of securities, even as the supply of such securities increased rapidly. In turn, 'demand for yield' from high-net-worth individuals brought hedge funds into the picture, acting as the conduit between wealthy individuals and the banking system. Feedback between the banking system and the hedge funds, fuelled by the overwhelming demand for investment opportunities, led to ever greater heights of financial 'engineering' and 'innovation', aided and abetted by the drive for financial deregulation. These innovations in turn allowed leverage ratios to rise ever further, stimulating banks to extend credit to poorer, higher-risk borrowers.

6.5 CONCLUSIONS

Over the last 30 years or so, the share of wages in national income has fallen in the majority of countries for which data are available. In the Anglo-Saxon countries in which the labour share has fallen less dramatically, other measures of inequality have increased significantly.

Purely deterministic answers as to why this divergence has taken place, based on technological change and changing trade patterns, are unconvincing. A more compelling explanation is that rising inequality and a falling wage share have been driven by globalization, deregulation and financialization in the context of a policy agenda which has systematically weakened the bargaining power of workers while dismanting social safety nets and reducing public provision of key services. As a result, an increasingly concentrated group of individuals have been able to appropriate a growing share of national incomes, while those at the bottom have been driven into debt.

At the macroeconomic level, this concentration of income has led to inadequate aggregate demand and stagnationary tendencies in advanced economies. Two different and mutually reinforcing mechanisms for maintaining growth rates in the face of falling demand have emerged in response: credit expansion to a household sector faced with stagnant or falling real income, and reliance on exports. The interaction of these two growth regimes in turn gave rise to growing international imbalances. In the face of falling real investment, the rising indebtedness of the household sector served to support the profits of non-financial corporations, as well as generating huge profits for financial corporations.

At the other end of the income distribution, wealth concentration, when combined with changes in institutional investment structures and international imbalances, gave rise to an excess demand for financial assets, especially dollar-denominated securities.

The widely held view that future financial crises can be avoided so long as suitable regulation and reform of the financial system are carried out is therefore incorrect. In addition to such financial reforms, it is essential that policies to combat income inequality take centre stage. This will require significant changes in emphasis, particularly with respect to the focus on 'labour market flexibility' that has weakened trade unions and reduced the bargaining power of labour so substantially in recent decades.

NOTES

1. The opposite extreme is that assumed in neoclassical representative agent models. In these models, all agents are assumed to receive capital and labour income in identical proportions, so a shift from capital income to labour income will have no effect whatsoever on personal income distribution.

2. See, for example, Krugman (2007), Kumhof and Rancière (2010), Rajan (2010) and Stiglitz (2010).

3. See, for example, Bowles and Boyer (1995), Stockhammer and Ederer (2008), Stockhammer et al. (2009), Stockhammer et al. (2011) and Onaran and Galanis (2012).

4. See A. Krueger (1999), Gollin (2002), Feldstein (2008), Rupert (2012) and Elsby et al. (2013) for further discussion on these issues. Gollin (2002, p. 471) concludes that 'estimated labour shares . . . are essentially flat over space and time'.

5. Almost all of the capital gains income which accrues when such options are exercised is treated in the national accounts as wages: 'Nonqualified stock options (NQOs) are not considered income until exercised, at which time the difference between the stock price on the day of exercise and the option price is treated as ordinary wage income . . . [A]bout 95 percent of stock option grants involve NQOs and almost three-fourths are exclusively NQOs' (Goolsbee 2000, pp. 360–361).

6. The conceptual framework can be traced back to Tinbergen (1974, p. 224), who inspired the title of Goldin and Katz's book: 'My approach suggests that it depends on the "race" between demand for third-level manpower due to technological development and the supply of it due to increased schooling, whether the reduction in inequality found for the last century, can be resumed after the stagnant period from 1950 to 1970.' For an early survey of the evolution of this view, see Levy and Murnane (1992). See also Autor et al. (2008).

7. Krugman rejects the view that both parties have shifted substantially to the right.

8. Krugman (2007) repeatedly expresses astonishment that 'Economics 101' fails to provide us with an exhaustive account of the forces that operate to determine the distribution of income and wealth: '[I]nstitutions, norms and the political environment matter a lot more for the distribution of income – and . . . impersonal market forces matter less – than Economics 101 might lead you to believe' (p. 8); 'This persistence makes a strong case that anonymous market forces are less decisive than Economics 101 teaches' (p. 137); 'The idea that rising pay at the top of the scale mainly reflects social and political change . . . strikes some people as . . . too much at odds with Economics 101' (p. 145).

9. The 'institutions and norms' argument is close to the Piketty's 'supermanagers' story: 'this pattern or evolution of income inequality is additional indirect evidence that nonmarket mechanisms such as labor market institutions and social norms regarding inequality may play a role in setting compensation at the top' (Piketty and Saez 2003, p. 34).

10. According to anecdotal evidence, the term originates with Alan Greenspan.

11. Van Treeck and Sturn (2012, p. 11) refer to this position as the 'Krueger–Perri–Greenspan argument'.

12. Gordon and Dew-Becker (2008) go further and argue that the consumption survey data significantly underestimate the actual consumption of poor households because of an in-built bias in the Consumer Price Index which serves to exclude the welfare-enhancing effects of Wal-Mart's pricing behaviour on the consumption basket of those on lower incomes, while simultaneously underestimating the negative effects on those in higher income brackets: 'Both because low-income households shop at Wal-Mart, and because they spend a larger proportion of their household income on food than high-income households, there is a prima-facie case that the retail channel involving Wal-Mart . . . has significantly reduced the cost of living for lower-income households . . . Many high income households have never visited a Wal-Mart. Their expenditures exhibit a higher share of services, particularly high-end services like private secondary schools, college

tuition, high-end spas, massage therapists, landscape gardeners, and other service providers whose relative prices rise steadily relative to the consumer price level' (p. 33). The authors also noted that, 'while the poor may do better when price indexes are corrected, they do much worse when their health outcomes are considered' (p. 45) and, further, that 'lower-income people are more likely to . . . eat unhealthy foods' (p. 35). The possibility that a connection exists between the welfare-enhancing effects of shopping for groceries at Wal-Mart and the welfare-diminishing effects of consuming a less than nutritionally optimal diet appears to have eluded the authors.

13. See also Katz and Autor (1998).
14. A different approach is taken by Bordo and Meissner (2012), who use a panel analysis of 14 countries to argue that, while credit booms do tend to be followed by crises, no evidence can be found of a correlation between inequality and credit booms.
15. For further discussion of the shortcomings of these studies, see van Treeck and Sturn (2012, pp. 12–13).
16. Friedman built upon the 'life-cycle hypothesis' of Modigliani (Modigliani and Blumberg 1954; Ando and Modigliani 1963). Modigliani had previously endorsed, and then rejected, Duesenberry's relative income hypothesis. It has been speculated that the real purpose of Friedman's attack on Duesenberry was to discredit Keynes (Mason 2000).
17. It is interesting that an essentially indistinguishable view was given by Fitoussi and Stiglitz (2009, pp. 3–4), although the authors did not acknowledge any of the preceding authors who had made the same points: 'aggregate demand deficiency preceded the financial crisis and was due to structural changes in income distribution. As the propensity to consume out of low incomes is generally larger, this long-term trend in income redistribution by itself would have had the macroeconomic effect of depressing aggregate demand. In the USA the compression of low incomes was compensated by the reduction of household savings and by mounting indebtedness that allowed spending patterns to be kept virtually unchanged . . . Most European countries tread a different path. The redistribution to higher incomes resulted in an increase in national savings and depressed growth . . . These two paths were mutually reinforcing because the savings from the EU zone contributed to the financing of US borrowing, along with surpluses of other regions . . . Thus, the combination of structural disequilibria that goes by the name of global imbalances resulted in a fragile equilibrium that temporarily solved the aggregate demand problem on a global scale at the expense of future growth.'

REFERENCES

Acemoglu, D. and D. Autor (2012), 'What does human capital do? A review of Goldin and Katz's "The Race between Education and Technology"', *Journal of Economic Literature*, **50**, 426–463.

Alvaredo, F. and T. Piketty (2008), 'The dynamics of income concentration over the twentieth century: the case of advanced economies', http://www.jourdan.ens.fr/piketty/fichiers/public/PIK2008DYNalvaredo.pdf.

Alvaredo, F., A.B. Atkinson, T. Piketty and E. Saez (2013), The World Top Incomes Database, accessed October 2013.

Ando, A. and F. Modigliani (1963), 'The "life cycle" hypothesis of saving: aggregate implications and tests', *American Economic Review*, **53**, 55–84.

Autor, D.H., L.F. Katz and M.S. Kearney (2008), 'Trends in U.S. wage inequality: revising the revisionists', *Review of Economics and Statistics*, **90**, 300–323.

Bagwell, L.S. and B.D. Bernheim (1996), 'Veblen effects in a theory of conspicuous consumption', *American Economic Review*, **86**, 349–373.

Bakija, J., A. Cole and B. Heim (2008), 'Jobs and income growth of top earners and the causes of changing income inequality: evidence from U.S. tax return data', Department of Economics Working Papers 2010-22, Department of Economics, Williams College, available at: http://web.williams.edu/Economics/wp/BakijaColeHeimJobsIncomeGrowthTopEarners.pdf.

Barba, A. and M. Pivetti (2009), 'Rising household debt: its causes and macroeconomic implications – a long-period analysis', *Cambridge Journal of Economics*, **33**, 113–137.

Bhaduri, A. and S. Marglin (1990), 'Unemployment and the real wage: the economic basis for contesting political ideologies', *Cambridge Journal of Economics*, **14**, 375–393.

Blanchard, O. and F. Giavazzi (2003), 'Macroeconomic effects of regulation and deregulation in goods and labor markets', *Quarterly Journal of Economics*, **118**, 879–907.

Bordo, M.D. and C.M. Meissner (2012), 'Does inequality lead to a financial crisis?', *Journal of International Money and Finance*, **31**, 2147–2161.

Bowles, S. and R. Boyer (1995), 'Wages, aggregate demand and unemployment in an open economy: an empirical investigation', in G. Epstein and H. Gintis (eds), *Macroeconomic Policy after the Conservative Era: Studies in Investment, Saving and Finance*, Cambridge, UK: Cambridge University Press.

Bradbury, K. and J. Katz (2002), 'Are lifetime incomes growing more unequal? Looking at new evidence on family income mobility', *Regional Review*, **12** (4), 2–5.

Card, D., T. Lemieux and W.C. Riddell (2004), 'Unions and wage inequality', *Journal of Labor Research*, **25** (4), 519–562.

Cutler, D.M. and L.F. Katz (1992), 'Rising inequality? Changes in the distribution of income and consumption in the 1980's', *American Economic Review*, **82**, 546–551.

Cynamon, B. and S. Fazzari (2013), 'Inequality and household finance during the consumer age', Working Paper No. 752, Levy Economics Institute.

Duesenberry, J.S. (1949), *Income, Saving and the Theory of Consumer Behaviour*, Cambridge, MA: Harvard University Press.

Dünhaupt, P. (2011), 'Financialization, corporate governance and income distribution in the USA and Germany: introducing an adjusted wage share indicator', in T. Niechoj, Ö. Onaran, E. Stockhammer, A. Truger and T. van Treeck (eds), *Stabilising an Unequal Economy? Public Debt, Financial Regulation, and Income Distribution*, Marburg: Metropolis.

Elsby, M.W.L., B. Hobijn and A. Şahin (2013), 'The decline of the U.S. labor share', conference draft, presented at Autumn 2003 Brookings Panel on Economic Activity.

Epstein, G.E. (2005), *Financialisation and the World Economy*, Cheltenham, UK and Northampton, MA, USA: Edward Elgar Publishing.

European Commission (2013), AMECO database, accessed October 2013.

Feenstra, R.C. and G.H. Hanson (2003), 'Global production sharing and rising inequality: a survey of trade and wages', in K. Choi and J. Harrigan (eds), *Handbook of International Trade*, Oxford: Basil Blackwell.

Feldstein, M.S. (2008), 'Did wages reflect growth in productivity?', NBER Working Paper No. 13953, National Bureau of Economic Research.

Fitoussi, J.-P. and J. Stiglitz (2009), 'The ways out of the crisis and the building of a more cohesive world', Document de travail 2009-17, OFCE Centre de recherche en économie de Sciences Po.

Frank, R.H. (1985), *Choosing the Right Pond: Human Behaviour and the Quest for Status*, New York: Oxford University Press.

Frank, R.H. (2005), 'Positional externalities cause large and preventable welfare losses', *American Economic Review*, **95** (2), 137–141. Papers and proceedings of the 117th annual meeting of the American Economic Association, 7–9 January 2005, Philadelphia, PA.

Freeman, R.B. (1980), 'Unionism and the dispersion of wages', *Industrial and Labor Relations Review*, **34** (1), 3–23.

Friedman, M. (1957), 'The permanent income hypothesis', in M. Friedman, *A Theory of the Consumption Function*, Princeton, NJ: Princeton University Press.

Glyn, A. (2009), 'Functional distribution and inequality', in W. Salverda, B. Nolan and T.M. Smeeding (eds), *The Oxford Handbook of Economy Inequality*, Oxford: Oxford University Press.

Goda, T. and P. Lysandrou (2011), 'The contribution of wealth concentration to the subprime crisis: a quantitative estimation', Documentos de Trabajo Economía y Finanzas 11-14, CIEF, Universidad EAFIT.

Goldin, C. and L.F. Katz (2009), *The Race between Education and Technology*, Cambridge, MA: Harvard University Press.

Goldin, C. and R.A. Margo (1992), 'The great compression: the wage structure in the United States at mid-century', *Quarterly Journal of Economics*, **107**, 1–34.

Gollin, D. (2002), 'Getting income shares right', *Journal of Political Economy*, **110**, 458–474.

Goolsbee, A. (2000), 'What happens when you tax the rich? Evidence from executive compensation', *Journal of Political Economy*, **108**, 352–378.

Gordon, R.J. and I. Dew-Becker (2008), 'Controversies about the rise of American inequality: a survey', NBER Working Paper No. 13982, National Bureau of Economic Research.

Gottschalk, P. and R. Moffitt (1994), 'The growth of earnings instability in the U.S. labor market', *Brookings Papers on Economic Activity*, **2**, 217–254.

Greenspan, A. (1998), 'The globalization of finance', *Cato Journal*, **17** (3), 243–250.

Greenspan, A. (2004), 'Understanding household debt obligations', remarks made at the Credit Union National Association 2004 Governmental Affairs Conference, 23 February, Washington, DC, available at: http://www.federal reserve.gov/boardDocs/speeches/2004/20040223/default.htm.

Hein, E. (2011), 'Distribution, "financialisation" and the financial and economic crisis – implications for post-crisis economic policies', MPRA Paper 31180, Munich Personal RePEc Archive.

Hein, E. (2012), *The Macroeconomics of Finance-dominated Capitalism – And Its Crisis*, Cheltenham, UK and Northampton, MA, USA: Edward Elgar Publishing.

Hein, E. (2014), 'Finance-dominated capitalism and redistribution of income: a Kaleckian perspective', *Cambridge Journal of Economics*, advance access, doi:10.1093/cje/bet038.

Katz, L.F. and D.H. Autor (1998), 'Changes in the wage structure and earnings inequality', in O. Ashenfelter and D. Card (eds), *Handbook of Labor Economics*, Amsterdam: North-Holland.

Kopczuk, W., E. Saez and S. Jae (2010), 'Earnings inequality and mobility in the United States: evidence from social security data since 1937', *Quarterly Journal of Economics*, **125**, 91–128.

Krueger, A.B. (1999), 'Measuring labor's share', *American Economic Review, Papers and Proceedings*, **89** (2), 45–51.

Krueger, D. and F. Perri (2003), 'On the welfare consequences of the increase in inequality in the United States', NBER Working Paper No. 9993, National Bureau of Economic Research.

Krueger, D. and F. Perri (2006), 'Does income inequality lead to consumption inequality? Evidence and theory', *Review of Economic Studies*, **73**, 163–193.

Krugman, P. (2007), *The Conscience of a Liberal*, New York: W.W. Norton & Company.

Kumhof, M. and R. Rancière (2010), 'Inequality, leverage and crises', IMF Working Paper WP/10/268, International Monetary Fund.

Levy, F. and R.J. Murnane (1992), 'U.S. earnings levels and earnings inequality: a review of recent trends and proposed explanations', *Journal of Economic Literature*, **30**, 1333–1381.

Levy, F. and P. Temin (2007), 'Inequality and institutions in 20th century America', NBER Working Paper No. 13106, National Bureau of Economic Research.

Lucas, R.E. (2014), 'The industrial revolution: past and future', Federal Reserve Bank of Minneapolis Annual Report Essay.

Lysandrou, P. (2011a), 'Global inequality as one of the root causes of the financial crisis: a suggested explanation', *Economy and Society*, **40**, 323–344.

Lysandrou, P. (2011b), 'Global inequality, wealth concentration and the subprime crisis: a Marxian commodity theory analysis', *Development and Change*, **42**, 183–208.

Lysandrou, P. (2011c), 'The primacy of hedge funds in the subprime crisis', *Journal of Post-Keynesian Economics*, **34** (2), 225–253.

Mason, R. (2000), 'The social significance of consumption: James Duesenberry's contribution to consumer theory', *Journal of Economic Issues*, **34**, 553–572.

Michell, J. and J. Toporowski (2014), 'Critical observations on financialization and the financial process', *International Journal of Political Economy*, **42** (4), 67–82.

Mishel, L., J. Bivens, E. Gould and H. Shierholz (2012), *The State of Working America*, 12th edn, Ithaca, NY: Cornell University Press.

Modigliani, F. and R. Blumberg (1954), 'Utility analysis and the consumption function: an interpretation of cross-section data', in K. Kurihara (ed.), *Post Keynesian Economics*, New Brunswick, NJ: Rutgers University Press.

Moffitt, R. and P. Gottschalk (2008), 'Trends in the transitory variance of male earnings in the U.S., 1970–2004', Boston College Working Papers in Economics 697, Boston College Department of Economics, available at: http://ideas.repec.org/p/boc/bocoec/697.html.

Onaran, Ö. and G. Galanis (2012), 'Is aggregate demand wage-led or profit-led? National and global effects', ILO Conditions of Work and Employment Series No. 40, International Labour Organization.

Palley, T.I. (1998), *Plenty of Nothing: The Downsizing of the American Dream and the Case for Structural Keynesianism*, Princeton, NJ: Princeton University Press.

Piketty, T. (2014), *Capital in the Twenty-First Century*, Cambridge, MA: Harvard University Press.

Piketty, T. and E. Saez (2003), 'Income inequality in the United States', *Quarterly Journal of Economics*, **118**, 1–39.

Rajan, R.G. (2010), *Fault Lines: How Hidden Fractures Still Threaten the World Economy*, Princeton, NJ: Princeton University Press.

Rodrik, D. (1997), *Has International Integration Gone Too Far?*, Washington, DC: Institute for International Economics.

Rupert, P. (2012), 'Is labor's share of income declining?', blog entry, available at: http://econsnapshot.com/2012/10/16/is-labors-share-of-income-declining/.

Schor, J.B. (2007), 'In defense of consumer critique: revisiting the consumption debates of the twentieth century', *Annals of the American Academy of Political and Social Science*, **611**, 16–30.

Stiglitz, J.E. (2010), *Freefall: America, Free Markets, and the Sinking of the World Economy*, New York: W.W. Norton & Company.

Stockhammer, E. (2012), 'Why have wage shares fallen? A panel analysis of the determinants of functional income distribution', ILO Conditions of Work and Employment Series, International Labour Organization.

Stockhammer, E. (2013), 'Rising inequality as a cause of the present crisis', *Cambridge Journal of Economics*, advance access, doi: 10.1093/cje/bet052.

Stockhammer, E. and S. Ederer (2008), 'Demand effects of a falling wage share in Austria', *Empirica*, **35**, 481–502.

Stockhammer, E., Ö. Onaran and S. Ederer (2009), 'Functional income distribution and aggregate demand in the euro area', *Cambridge Journal of Economics*, **33**, 139–159.

Stockhammer, E., E. Hein and L. Grafl (2011), 'Globalization and the effects of changes in functional income distribution on aggregate demand in Germany', *International Review of Applied Economics*, **25**, 1–23.

Taylor, L. (1983), *Structuralist Macroeconomics: Applicable Models for the Third World*, New York: Basic Books.

Tinbergen, J. (1974), 'Substitution of graduate by other labour', *Kyklos*, **27**, 217–226.

van Treeck, T. and S. Sturn (2012), 'Income inequality as a cause of the Great Recession? A survey of current debates', ILO Conditions of Work and Employment Series No. 39, International Labour Organization.

Veblen, T. ([1899] 1919), *The Theory of the Leisure Class: An Economic Study of Institutions*, New York: B.W. Huebsch.

7. Global and European imbalances and the crisis: a critical review

Carlos A. Carrasco and Felipe Serrano

7.1 INTRODUCTION

The wave of *global imbalances* generated since the turn of the twenty-first century between the US economy and those of the South-East Asian emerging economies and oil-exporting countries were identified early on as a fundamental cause of the global financial crisis. The argument linking the crisis to these imbalances, in broad strokes, was that current account surpluses generated by emerging economies were placed in US financial assets. These flows, in the form of asset demand, pushed down long-term interest rates, which encouraged a credit boom that fuelled a real estate market bubble. In other words, the US financial system came under strong pressure to receive and recycle capital flows from abroad.

Until the outbreak of the crisis, global imbalances were perceived, at least by some researchers, as a signal of a new global equilibrium that might persist over time. However, another group of researchers argued that these imbalances should be corrected by appropriate fiscal and monetary policies in the USA and by exchange rate adjustments in China to avoid a radical adjustment induced by a *sudden stop* of foreign capital flows into the US economy, an event with a high probability of dragging the global economy into crisis. The financial crisis, however, revealed that both hypotheses were wrong. The chain broke in what was seen as the stronger link: the supposedly solvent US financial system.

Moreover, research conducted after the start of the crisis pointed to two important developments that contributed to a weakening of the initial relationship between the financial crisis and global imbalances. This research showed, first, that net capital flows into the US economy from emerging markets were a relatively small part of overall flows and, second, that, although European countries on the whole manifested equilibrium in their external balances during the years preceding the crisis, their banking systems were active players in the US financial system. The basic conclusion of the new research is that the roots of the crisis can be found in the fragility of the international monetary and financial system rather than in current account imbalances.

Nevertheless, current account imbalances demand attention, especially if we take European countries as a benchmark. While it is accepted that these imbalances are not the source of the crisis, they must be considered a *symptom* of a grander problem, which requires a solution to avoid similar crises in the future. Southern European economies, running large external deficits during the years before the crisis, faced sudden stops of external flows, which forced these countries to make intensive internal adjustments and appeal for help from international aid programmes to avoid default.

In this chapter, we survey and analyse the economic literature on global and European imbalances and their connection to the global financial crisis, with the aim of clarifying this relationship. The chapter is organized as follows: in section 7.2, we show how the research related to global imbalances evolved; in section 7.3, we focus on the relationship between current account imbalances and the crisis in the European Union; in section 7.4, we summarize and conclude.

We highlight some of our conclusions presently. First, to better understand the crisis, deeper analysis of gross rather than net capital flows is needed. Second, owing to the fragility of the international financial system, we recommend constant monitoring of credit levels as preventive indicators of future financial crises. Finally, given the European experience with current account imbalances, we argue that these imbalances must be addressed in the medium term to prevent future financial crises.

7.2   THE FINANCIAL CRISIS AND GLOBAL IMBALANCES

In 2005, the International Monetary Fund (IMF), in its annual report, drew attention to the risk to global economic and financial stability posed by increasing current account imbalances, chiefly involving the US economy and those of the emerging economies of Asia and the oil-exporting countries, where the former demanded exports from the latter, accumulating large deficits in its current account equivalent to the other economies' surpluses. From a financial perspective, the US deficits were financed by capital flows into the US capital market from emerging economies.[1]

Risk to global economic and financial stability, observed at the beginning of the century, arose from the size of the economies involved in global imbalances, as a severe correction (e.g. a sudden stop) could negatively affect the global economy. However, in the years leading up to the crisis, there was no widespread consensus on the nature, origin and potential risks associated with these imbalances. Some argued that global imbalances reflected a new type of global equilibrium that could be maintained over time without necessarily ending in crisis. The notion of a *saving glut*, proposed by Bernanke (2005), and the idea that a *Bretton Woods II system* had taken form (Dooley et al. 2003, 2004) are paradigmatic examples of this view. On the other hand, for authors such as Obstfeld and Rogoff (2000, 2004), Blanchard et al. (2005) and Cline (2005), these global imbalances represented a dangerous situation that posed serious risks to international economic and financial stability. In a survey of the pre-crisis period, Xafa (2007) referred to the first group as representative of the *new paradigm* and the latter as representative of the *traditional view*.

For the traditional view, the source of the problem lay in the decline of savings rates in the USA, which led to large and prolonged current account deficits. This decline resulted from overly lax fiscal and monetary policies (Blanchard 2007) that needed to be corrected urgently, or financial markets could otherwise experience a loss of confidence. A sudden stop of capital flows into the USA would trigger an adjustment process and a general crisis for the USA and global economy, with massive sell-offs of dollar-denominated assets and an increase in US interest rates.

For the new paradigm advocates, global imbalances were explained as a product of structural changes and economic policies implemented in other countries, changes that caused savings rates in emerging market economies to increase. These savings accumulated in the form of financial assets issued in the USA. While these changes and policies remained in force, global imbalances, these observers argued, would persist. Nonetheless, from this point of view, global imbalances did not involve serious risk to the global economy.

The economic crisis did not materialize in the way the advocates of the traditional view expected. A loss of confidence of international investors in the US economy did not occur, and hence there was no sudden stop of capital flows into the US economy, inducing a devaluation of the dollar along with an internal adjustment in the US economy that would drag the global economy into crisis.

The causal relationship between the financial crisis and the problem of global imbalances created a rupture in the equilibrium described by the new paradigm. However, the break came in the presumably stronger component of the new global equilibrium: the US financial system. The Economic Report of the President (2009, pp. 62–73) presents the following diagnosis of the origin of the crisis:

> The roots of the current global financial crisis began in the late 1990s. A rapid increase in saving by developing countries ... resulted in a large influx of capital to the United States ... driving down the return on safe assets. The relatively low yield on safe assets likely encouraged investors to look for higher yields from riskier assets ... What turned out to be an underpricing of risk across a number of markets ... and an uncertainty about how this risk was distributed throughout the global financial system, set the stage for subsequent financial distress.

Ultimately, foreign capital flows into the USA from emerging economies pushed down long-term interest rates (Warnock and Warnock 2009), forcing the US financial system to recycle large amounts of capital through financial innovation. This innovation encouraged the growth of a speculative bubble that ended up dragging the entire financial system into an unprecedented crisis.

This interpretation of the origin of the crisis becomes paradoxical when we examine discussions of the global imbalances at the beginning of the century. It is possible to say that both paradigms, the traditional view and the new paradigm, failed to properly assess where the real problem was located, that is, in the inability of the US financial system to intermediate *responsibly* (Portes 2009) the large amount of capital arriving in the USA. With the notable exception of the Bank for International Settlements, no observer appeared to recognize the weaknesses of the US financial system. Instead, the dominant view was the opposite: capital flows were placed on US assets because of the quality and solvency of US financial institutions (Forbes 2008).

At present, there is no broad consensus on the role played in the crisis by global imbalances. Initial differences in diagnosis, noted in the Economic Report of the President (2009), arose from difficulties in explaining the extent of the crisis based on considerations of net capital inflows received by the US economy from emerging and oil-exporting countries. In a financially liberalized world economy, the relevant capital flows are the gross flows. Furthermore, saving glut economies were not the only ones involved in buying US assets. The banking system of the European Monetary Union (EMU) was an active player in purchases of these assets. Consideration of this evidence has led some authors (Acharya and Schnabl 2010; Borio and Disyatat 2011) to deny a connection between the financial crisis and global imbalances. According to these authors, the origin of the crisis is found in the weakness of the US financial system resulting from liberalization and deregulation. However, other authors (Blanchard 2007; Bernanke et al. 2011; Obstfeld 2012a) take a less radical view. Accepting the analytical relevance of the weakness of the financial system, they still consider current account imbalances to be a policy-relevant issue in maintaining financial and economic stability.

Nevertheless, recent empirical evidence (Bertaut et al. 2012) does appear to indicate the existence of a relationship between capital inflows into the US financial market (coming from both emerging markets and European countries) and the decrease in the US interest rates. This evidence would accept some part of the initial diagnosis noted in the Economic Report of the President (2009). However, an accurate understanding of the factors leading the capital inflows into the US economy remains an unsolved problem: were these capital inflows endogenously induced by financial innovation developed in the USA, or was it the arrival of these capital inflows which brought about innovation as a way to recycle the excess liquidity in the US market? The answer to this problem is relevant, since, if the innovation precedes capital influx, capital flows are independent of the current account balances and the origin of the crisis can be found in the liberalization of the financial system. Otherwise, the saving glut hypothesis (supplemented in terms proposed by Bernanke at al. 2011) would be a relevant explanation of the origin of the crisis: it was excess of liquidity which *broke* the US financial system. Regardless of the conclusion one reaches, it is clear that there is a need to regulate the financial system to prevent credit booms from encouraging bubble creation.

7.2.1 The Equilibrium Approach

As noted above, under the saving glut approach, global imbalances originated as a result of structural factors and policies implemented by economic authorities in emerging and oil-exporting countries, policies that led to a steady accumulation of US assets by the rest of the world. The prevailing central thesis before the burst of the crisis argued that current account imbalances represented an equilibrium situation that could be sustained over time, as noted by Mendoza et al. (2007, p. 36): 'The large negative net foreign asset position of the USA is fully sustainable and does not lead to a worldwide financial crisis.'[2] To understand the basis for this opinion, it is necessary to answer the following three questions:

1. What factors explain the increase in savings in emerging market and commodity-export-oriented economies?
2. Why were these savings not held in the financial systems of these countries and instead exported abroad?
3. Why was the US financial market the main recipient of these flows of savings?

7.2.1.1   Savings in emerging market economies

Theoretical and empirical research has proposed different but complementary hypotheses to explain the growth of the savings rate observed since the late 1990s in most emerging market economies. The first explanation (Dooley et al. 2003, 2004; Cline and Williamson 2008; Herr 2008; Rodrik 2008; Herrerias and Orts 2010; Catte et al. 2011; King 2011) focuses on the growth model selected by some emerging market economies, especially in East Asia, with China in the lead. These economies have opted for a model of export-led growth, which requires depressed domestic consumption to maintain a devalued exchange rate. The maintenance of the exchange rate at competitive levels requires holding sufficient reserves to enable intervention in currency markets to maintain the desired parity.

A second argument connects foreign currency reserve accumulation with precautionary savings. The economic literature highlights three reasons for reserve accumulation associated with the precautionary savings motive:

1. There may be a fear of external shocks that could induce sudden capital outflows or inflows (Calvo and Reinhart 2002; Aizenman et al. 2011; King 2011; Porcile et al. 2011; Taguchi 2011; Dominguez et al. 2012; Menkhoff 2013). Since the liberalization of capital markets, emerging economies have been subject to recurrent currency tensions caused by capital flows. The costs of these tensions have been high, leading authorities in these countries to protect themselves by accumulating reserves.
2. Another reason relates to the ageing of the population (Ferrucci and Miralles 2007; Horioka and Wan 2007) and the lack of social protection schemes (public pensions and health care) that address the needs associated with an ageing population (Carroll and Jeanne 2009).
3. In the case of commodity-exporting countries, reserve accumulation has been used by the monetary authorities to hedge against fluctuations in commodity prices. Through such accumulation, these countries have been able to control variations in domestic demand, preventing fluctuations in commodity prices from causing domestic demand fluctuations (Kilian et al. 2009; Bems and Carvalho-Filho 2011; Le and Chang 2013).

A third explanation identifies the problem not in excess savings of emerging markets but in an *investment drought* that arose in the aftermath of the financial crises in southern Asia in 1997 (Felipe et al. 2006; Chinn and Ito 2008). The crisis, for these authors, led to a decrease in domestic credit levels along with the creation of excess capacity and a relative fall in profit rates, all of which combined contributed to a decline in investment across emerging economies in Asia, leading them to implement export-led growth strategies.

A fourth reason relates the savings excess with underdevelopment of the financial and legal systems in emerging markets (Ferrucci and Miralles 2007; King 2011). There are several reasons for this connection (Prasad 2009). On the one hand, in fast-growing economies, such as the Asian emerging economies, desired consumption bundles shifted toward durable goods like cars and houses. Owing to the impossibility of borrowing against future income in the context of an underdeveloped financial system, households increased savings to self-finance purchases. From this perspective, savings arise because of a lack of diversification opportunities. In addition, low or negative interest rates due to financial repression could lead to higher savings abroad. However, available empirical evidence does not find a clear relationship between savings rates and the degree of financial development (Chinn and Ito 2007). Chinn and Ito (2007) show that, for some key Asian countries, there is a positive relationship between financial development and savings rates. Furthermore, economies with more developed financial markets exhibit smaller current account imbalances if they also have highly developed legal systems and open financial markets.

7.2.1.2 Savings exports to the US financial market

In the years preceding the crisis, capital exports from emerging markets, especially to the US financial market, were viewed as a logical consequence of an inter-temporal optimization process. Global financial trade allowed countries to share and diversify risk. In this perspective, current account imbalances resulted from firms' and households' inter-temporal optimization activities, leading to the efficient allocation of resources, and would thus not raise policy concerns. Papers by Mendoza et al. (2007) and Caballero et al. (2008) are especially clear exponents of this point of view. In both papers, capital exports from emerging markets arise as a result of the heterogeneity of financial systems that are integrated as a consequence of the liberalization of financial markets. In Caballero et al. (2008), the ability to supply assets is captured as financial imperfections. Given financial underdevelopment, emerging economies are unable to generate sufficiently attractive financial assets to absorb domestic savings. Therefore, international savers re-direct their capital towards assets of countries with more developed financial systems. In Mendoza et al. (2007), financial imperfections directly affect savings via the demand for assets. Countries with developed financial systems tend to reduce savings and increase their accumulation of net foreign liabilities. From this perspective, financial heterogeneity results in changes in the portfolio composition of net foreign assets. Therefore, countries with deeper financial markets tend to increase borrowing from abroad and allocate their resources to risky assets.

The selection of the US financial market as the main recipient of savings from emerging market economies and oil-exporting countries was based, according to this view, on the characteristic quality and efficiency of the US financial system. Perhaps the clearest expression of this perspective was provided some months before the outbreak of the crisis, in the concluding section of an NBER working paper by Forbes (2008, p. 32, emphasis added):[3]

> Although foreigners investing in U.S. equity and bond markets have earned lower returns over the past five years ... there are still several reasons why they might choose to continue investing in the United States and financing the large U.S. current account deficit. More specifically, foreign investors may choose to purchase U.S. portfolio investments *in order to benefit from the highly developed, liquid, and efficient U.S. financial markets, from the strong corporate governance and institutions in the United States, and/or to diversify risk.*

7.2.2 Beyond the Saving Glut Hypothesis: The Financial Fragility Hypothesis

The speed and intensity with which the crisis spread through the financial systems of developed economies highlighted the degree of financial connectedness between these countries, interconnections that had not been accounted for in the saving glut hypothesis. On the one hand, European Union (EU) countries (with a relatively balanced current account) had been active agents, especially through their banks, in the US financial markets, taking positions in both financial assets and liabilities. On the other hand, it was demonstrated that the portfolios' compositions differed, depending on the origins of the capital flows.

Bernanke et al. (2011) present empirical evidence showing that emerging economies accumulated mainly safe and liquid assets, even when the profitability of such assets was declining. This marked preference for safe assets was related to foreign currency reserve management and accumulation undertaken in these countries. Regarding European banking, empirical evidence suggests a clear preference for risky assets financed through borrowing in the US financial markets (McGuire and von Peter 2009). Hence, the crisis of the US financial system spread and expanded to various European countries' financial systems through the positions investors in these countries had taken in these assets. Moreover, the situation worsened as a result of a mismatch between maturity terms and the currency structure of assets and liabilities accumulated by European banks. Taking into account the important role played by European banks in US financial markets in the years preceding the crisis undermines the notion that global imbalances played a causal role in the crisis. The extent of the fall in long-term interest rates in the USA cannot be explained by the volumes of capital flows coming from emerging and oil-exporting countries. Only when considering flows from EU countries is it possible to sustain the view that external capital flows affected interest rates (Bertaut et al. 2012).

New empirical evidence reveals the weakness of the relationship between current account imbalances and the crisis and turns analytical attention toward the fragility of the financial and monetary system as the fundamental cause of the crisis (Acharya and Schnabl 2010; Borio and Disyatat 2011; Taylor 2012). In this new view, net capital flows, a key variable for saving glut advocates, have lost explanatory relevance, while gross capital flows have gained analytical importance. Net capital flows account for only a small part of all capital movements in global capital flows (Lane and Milesi-Ferretti 2008; Obstfeld 2012b). Moreover, the boom and bust capital flows cycle must be analysed in the context of changing global financial conditions and not exclusively in the context of the domestic destination economies (Forbes and Warnock 2012).

As information about developments in the years preceding the crisis has been accumulated, the view that global imbalances were not the trigger of the crisis has gained increasing attraction. The US financial market was stressed by large inflows of foreign capital. However, the management of such capital flows could have been avoided if the system had been subjected to strict controls. The same is true of European financial systems. The main lesson to be drawn from the new research is that, to prevent future financial crises, new regulations that limit expansions of credit are required. As shown by various empirical studies in recent years (Jordà et al. 2011; Taylor 2012; Drehmann 2013), the dominant predictors of financial crises are not current account imbalances but credit growth.

7.2.3 Rebalancing an Unbalanced World

The role of financial fragility in the crisis and the need for regulatory reform to address this fragility are widely recognized. However, views regarding the need to correct global imbalances to overcome the current crisis remain divergent. For most critical observers of the saving glut hypothesis (Borio and Disyatat 2011), current account imbalances are irrelevant in the current economic context. Efforts, they argue, should instead focus on reforming the financial system. However, this view is not widely shared. In general, current account imbalances are considered relevant (Blanchard 2007; Obstfeld and Rogoff 2009; Obstfeld 2012a; Ferreiro et al. 2013), and it is generally seen as necessary to take appropriate action to correct them, at least in the medium term, a view also held by some international organizations, such as the IMF. Among the reasons advanced for correcting global imbalances are the intersectoral changes that often accompany current account imbalances. These changes, which are mainly manifested as excessive growth of non-tradable goods sectors, have had costs in terms of reduced productivity growth. Furthermore, deficit financing still creates potential problems with respect to the credibility of capital markets. The various balance of payments crises that have been observed in past decades show that the possibility of *sudden stops* must be borne in mind. The latest paradigmatic example is provided by EMU countries. After accumulating large external deficits in the years preceding the crisis, southern European economies have faced serious difficulties in financing their deficits in recent years.

In correcting these imbalances, both the US economy and emerging market economies should be involved. In the case of the USA, the financial crisis has already helped to correct some of the internal imbalances with effects on the current account balance. The rates of growth of internal consumption have slowed, and it has contributed to improving the US external position. In the case of the latter, emerging economies should implement economic policies and industrial changes that re-orient their economic growth models from export-led growth toward domestic demand-led growth (Blanchard and Milesi-Ferretti 2009). The expansion of domestic demand would decrease savings rates in such countries, which would help contain current account surpluses while stimulating the exports of developed economies. To move in this direction, various actions must be taken. First, and most immediately, governments in these countries should implement economic policies intended to reduce the rate of savings as a step toward stimulating domestic demand. A decline in the savings rate could be affected, for example, by addressing any of the precautionary savings motives noted above, especially that related to the absence of social protections in these countries, notably in China. Second, these economies should seek to improve their institutional frameworks, especially that of the financial system. More efficient financial systems would achieve several objectives. On the one hand, an improvement in access to credit, for both consumption and investment, would help to reduce the savings rate. On the other hand, it would reduce the need to export capital abroad because of an increased supply of attractive assets for domestic savers. Finally, as emphasized by Prasad et al. (2007), the development of financial markets in these countries would improve the absorptive capacity of foreign capital flows, leading to improvements in productivity and thus in economic growth.

7.3 INTERNAL EUROPEAN IMBALANCES

As mentioned above, the EU, as a whole, had a balanced current account in the years leading up to the crisis. However, within the EU, countries had widely divergent balance of payments positions (Lane and Milesi-Ferretti 2007a). Current account imbalances within the EU have characteristics substantially different from those identified by the saving glut hypothesis. In the case of the EU, these imbalances correspond to what economic theory predicts when economies with differing levels of development enter into a process of economic integration. Relatively less developed countries should shed their current account deficits, which are financed by capital imports from more developed economies (with current account surpluses). Theoretically, these imbalances should stop when the catching-up process ends, as a result of real convergence between countries. Figure 7.1 shows the pattern described above for the EU-28 and thus for Eurozone countries. The countries with low levels of per capita income relative to Germany have run external deficits throughout the period. By contrast, countries with high per capita income relative to Germany have run current account surpluses throughout the period.

However, this evidence does not necessarily imply that these imbalances are part of a process of real convergence between European economies. A lack of sectorial studies of the behaviour of the various components of the current account makes it impossible to conclude that imports of less developed economies have helped improve their productive assets and thus their overall productivity. Observed imbalances might respond, for instance, to expansionary policies in the southern economies that do not relate directly to the process of convergence. These imbalances could also result from a loss of competitiveness of the economies of southern Europe, owing to changes in real exchange rates or other factors, for instance diverging demographic paths. A combination of all these factors appears to be at the origin of the current account imbalances observed within the EU.

7.3.1 Determinants of European Imbalances

The few studies that have examined the nature of these European imbalances, especially in deficit countries, point to a combination of the above factors. Campa and Gavilán (2011) note that, in the cases of Portugal

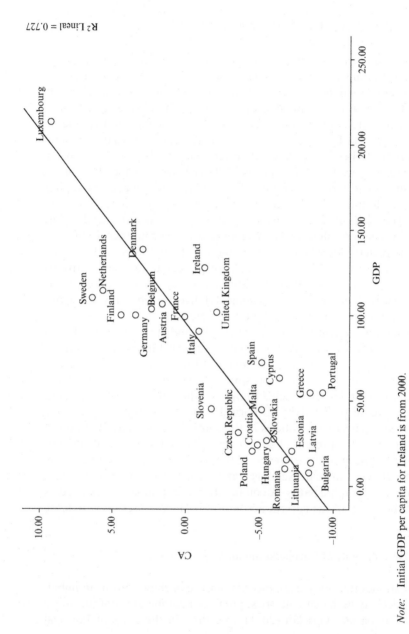

R2 Líneal = 0.727

Note: Initial GDP per capita for Ireland is from 2000.

Source: Data from Eurostat and the World Development Indicators.

Figure 7.1 Initial (1999) GDP per capita (relative to Germany) versus current account average (1999–2012) for EU-28

and Spain, deficits appear to be determined by expectations of future growth, which suggests that these deficits are part of a process of real convergence. In Belke and Dreger (2013), this conclusion is extended to all the deficit countries in the EU, although these authors maintain that the catching-up process does not fully explain the current account imbalances in the deficit countries. Loss of competitiveness is, for these authors, the key determinant of the deficits incurred by the countries at the centre of the crisis.

The competitiveness problem of southern European economies is, in part, related to the growth model implemented by Germany following German reunification, as argued by Schnabl and Freitag (2012). These authors note that the gains in competitiveness of the German economy were obtained through a reduction in unit labour costs that resulted from relative stagnation in public and private wages and an erosion of union bargaining power. The containment of German unit labour costs, along with an opposite movement of this variable in the deficit countries, helped reduce the competitiveness of the latter countries (Belke and Dreger 2013). Table 7.1 shows period average data for key variables in a selection of Eurozone countries. In part 1A of Table 7.1, we show data for unit labour costs. In relative terms, the increase in unit labour costs was significantly higher in deficit countries (Spain, Portugal, Greece, Ireland and Italy). In Germany, meanwhile, unit labour costs remained constant or even decreased just before the onset of the crisis. In the remainder of the core countries, the observed growth of unit labour costs is lower than in the southern countries.

A second factor that may have contributed to weakening competitiveness of the deficit economies has been the differential evolution of inflation rates. Southern economies as a whole benefited from entry into the single currency by importing price stability from northern economies. However, price stability coexisted with higher inflation in the southern countries, reflected in positive inflation differentials relative to core countries (see part 1B of Table 7.1). These differentials are explained by two factors: on the one hand, the relative slowness of some structural reforms in the southern countries and, on the other hand, the differences in their labour market institutions, with higher increases in wages than in productivity (see part 1C of Table 7.1).

The combined effects of the different trends in unit labour costs and inflation rates helped worsen the real exchange rates of the deficit countries. As shown in part 1D of Table 7.1, the real effective exchange rate evolution shows significant differences between countries. Since the establishment of the EMU, Germany has managed to keep its real exchange rate at levels below those that prevailed before the formation of the EMU.

Table 7.1 *Key macroeconomic variables for selected Eurozone countries, 1996–2012*

	Austria	Belgium	Finland	France	Germany	Greece	Ireland	Italy	Netherlands	Portugal	Spain
1A. Nominal unit labour costs* (average annual growth rate)											
1996–1998	−0.60	0.57	0.27	0.43	−0.27			1.97	1.47	3.73	
1999–2007	0.56	1.59	1.04	1.81	−0.12	2.79	3.51	2.23	2.06	2.70	3.14
2008–2011	2.56	2.96	4.10	2.20	2.18	0.86	−1.30	2.30	2.30	0.26	0.24
1B. Inflation* (average annual rate of Harmonized Index of Consumer Prices)											
1997–1998	1.00	1.20	1.25	1.00	1.05	4.95	1.70	1.95	1.85	2.05	1.85
1999–2007	1.76	1.98	1.56	1.78	1.57	3.20	3.40	2.30	2.41	2.93	3.12
2008–2012	2.30	2.56	2.74	1.90	1.76	2.86	0.58	2.42	1.88	1.92	2.28
1C. Real labour productivity per person employed* (average annual growth rate)											
1996–1998	2.13	1.47	2.63	1.20	1.17	2.47	3.90	0.87	1.17	2.00	0.37
1999–2007	1.53	1.20	2.13	1.06	1.14	2.66	2.31	0.17	1.30	1.18	0.02
2008–2011	−0.42	−0.34	−0.94	0.14	−0.06	−1.28	1.60	−0.96	−0.34	0.80	2.12
1D. Real effective exchange rate* (vs EA-17, average percentage change, based on unit labour costs)											
1996–1998	−1.92	−1.16	−1.43	−0.22	−2.89	3.21	1.87	6.04	−0.05	2.81	1.02
1999–2007	−0.63	0.27	−0.31	0.37	−2.11	0.81	2.14	0.96	1.00	1.06	1.54
2008–2012	0.30	0.76	1.92	0.16	0.01	−1.50	−3.46	0.50	0.21	−1.47	−1.75

1E. Average annual rate of assets accumulation**

1996–1998	11.83	9.51	15.03	17.35	15.53	7.28	37.73	18.04	15.89	20.61	14.81
1999–2007	14.12	7.75	15.53	8.21	9.20	8.14	11.71	4.16	8.38	7.45	8.33
2008–2011	−3.20	−2.80	11.54	−0.17	2.25	1.35	5.93	−2.42	−0.72	−3.21	−2.66

1F. Average annual rate of liabilities accumulation**

1996–1998	11.95	6.74	20.44	13.46	18.75	10.46	26.27	16.66	20.17	20.85	11.38
1999–2007	12.29	8.87	9.31	8.98	7.81	12.82	12.67	5.38	8.32	9.60	11.13
2008–2011	−4.60	−4.60	7.30	2.04	2.46	−1.37	6.88	−2.51	−2.80	−1.16	−1.00

1G. Private credit flow (percentage of GDP, annual period average)

1996–1998	5.53	7.33	1.07	3.23	6.47	6.03		3.10	14.93	14.93	8.50
1999–2007	7.83	6.12	9.32	8.18	2.28	12.17	26.83	8.98	14.41	15.26	21.29
2008–2012	4.00	8.64	7.32	5.62	0.58	2.16	5.68	3.00	4.44	3.96	−0.50

Notes:
EA-17: euro area when it consisted of 17 member states (i.e. excluding Latvia).
Nominal unit labour cost data start in 2001 for Greece and Spain and 1999 for Ireland.
Real effective exchange rate positive increase means a loss of competitiveness.
Private credit flow data for Ireland start in 2002.

Source: * Own calculation based on Eurostat; and ** own calculation based on the extended version of Lane and Milesi-Ferretti (2007b).

The countries in the poorest position are Spain and Italy, while the loss of competitiveness in Portugal was relatively less severe.

Empirical studies have also pointed to other possible factors that may have influenced the differing trajectories of the balance of payments among different countries of the EMU. Among these, demographic factors have received special attention. Empirical evidence (Hassan et al. 2011) has shown that the age structure of a population affects savings rates and thus current account balances. Contrary to what theory predicts, countries with relatively pronounced ageing show rising savings rates and accordingly surpluses in their current account balances, while countries with younger populations, as predicted by theory, tend to take on greater indebtedness. Some studies have suggested (Barnes et al. 2010; Aizenman and Sengupta 2011) that the current account imbalances within the EU[4] can be related to demographic differences between the northern European countries (with older populations) and southern European deficit countries (with population structures characterized by less negative dependency ratios). This would be particularly relevant for Ireland and, with some variations, Spain.

Finally, some studies have examined the potential connection between public sector deficits and current account deficits, especially in the deficit countries. However, conclusions reached have ranged from no relationship (Blanchard 2007) to a positive relationship that is less than one to one (Barnes et al. 2010). These results are to be expected in view of the differing conditions that characterize the deficit countries. While, in the Spanish case, excess borrowing has been primarily private, in the cases of Italy and Greece (Brissimis et al. 2010) public sector borrowing has been the predominant source of financial difficulties. The connection between public sector deficits and current account deficits, therefore, cannot be generalized across countries.

7.3.2 Financial Integration and Internal Imbalances

The process of financial and monetary integration that has occurred in the EU is critical to understanding how European countries have been able to maintain current account imbalances over time. In this regard, there are also differences between the direction of the flows observed in the EU and the financial flows that have led to global imbalances.

In section 7.2, we noted that one reason for the seemingly contradictory direction of financial flows from emerging economies to the US economy was the underdevelopment of financial markets in emerging economies (Caballero et al. 2008), a problem that did not exist in the European case. Financial systems in EMU countries were relatively homogeneous at the time that the process of integration intensified, that is, with a high degree of financial development and, in principle, high institutional quality in the field of regulation and supervision. Therefore, economic and financial integration helped to reduce transaction costs (Spiegel 2008) and created conditions for free capital flows in response to *market signals*. The market signals to which we refer are numerous. First, capital began to flow from surplus countries in the core of Europe to southern countries, encouraged by expectations generated by the process of European integration into a monetary union. As noted in this section, economic integration should in theory lead, through a process of real convergence, to a gradual reduction of differences in income levels across countries. Therefore, expectations of high relative yields, due to catching-up, encouraged capital to flow to peripheral countries (Spain, Portugal, Ireland and Greece). Second, the demand for capital from the southern economies was further incentivized. On the one hand, capital demand was incentivized by the lower interest rates (Schnabl and Freitag 2012) that accompanied the process of monetary integration. In some years, real interest rates in convergence countries became negative, leading to significant increases in the demand for credit. On the other hand, the disappearance of transaction costs associated with adoption of the single currency (Lane and Milesi-Ferretti 2007a; Lane 2013) also spurred capital demand. Ultimately, increased credit demand from convergence countries could be accommodated without serious difficulty by national banks in these countries through borrowing in European capital markets.

However, capital flows into these countries cannot be explained solely by current account imbalances. As noted above, it is necessary to differentiate between net capital flows (those associated with current account balances) and gross capital flows. For instance, the accumulation of financial assets and liabilities is much higher in each country than what can be accounted for by the accumulation of current account deficits and surpluses (see parts 1E and 1F of Table 7.1). Countries characterized by high degrees of financialization within the group of rescued countries include Ireland, Portugal and Spain. With respect to northern countries, relatively high intensity financialization is seen in the Netherlands.

In addition, there was a turning point in the mid-1990s in the rate of assets and liabilities accumulation, a period in which the southern economies had not incurred current account deficits of magnitudes similar to the levels that would be observed later. Capital movements from outside and inside the EU did not follow the logic of economic integration but a broader process of financial globalization. Monetary and financial integration made the EMU a geographical space in which gross capital flows were more intense than in other parts of the world economy. The flows within the EMU responded to the levels of expected volatility and profitability in global financial markets.

7.3.3   The Financial Crisis and the European Crisis

The fragility of the financial system can be identified as one of the main causes of the European crisis. Capital inflows into southern European economies allowed for an unprecedented credit expansion (see part 1G of Table 7.1), which encouraged and maintained over time speculative bubbles in housing markets, especially in Spain and Ireland. Banks in these countries financed the credit expansion by borrowing in European capital markets. The ease of access to credit for southern European banks, in addition to low prices, can only be understood as partly a result of the formation of the European Financial System that accompanied the creation of the single currency and partly a result of the state of future profitability expectations. The large-scale borrowing had both positive aspects and significant potential risks. Among the positive aspects was, of course, access to the funds necessary to finance the process of real convergence in the southern countries. One of the most obvious risks arose from the temporal dimension of most of the credits. These were short-term loans, which heightened the vulnerability of the national banking systems to capital flow reversals.

The US financial crisis created the necessary conditions to end the indebtedness process.[5] The crisis led to liquidity shortages, which hampered the ability of the southern European banks to continue refinancing their loans in the European capital markets. The suppliers of capital in these markets, mainly banks from Germany, France and the Netherlands, found that their balance sheets were contaminated with toxic assets issued in the USA, forcing them to cut credit lines that they had with the economies of southern Europe. The banking systems of these countries, which were not heavily contaminated with these toxic assets (the Spanish case is the most significant), then had trouble refinancing their loans, which forced them to cut domestic credit. Without credit, the housing bubble burst, and the financial crisis morphed into an economic crisis. Banks then began to add to their problems with new liabilities, as they experienced new problems with assets.

This mutation entailed a dramatic revision in expected growth rates of these economies from those that were calculated when the single currency was introduced. International investors began to incorporate information regarding macroeconomic fundamentals of the countries into their expectations formation process (Ca'Zorzi et al. 2012; Gibson et al. 2012; Beirne and Fratzscher 2013), which translated into a sudden stop of external capital for some of these countries. Bailouts of Ireland, Greece and Portugal and the opening of a credit line to stabilize the banking system in Spain were the chosen alternatives to default in these economies.

Hence, the European experience also shows that, indeed, the financial system has played an important role in the creation and transmission of the crisis among financially integrated countries (Kollmann et al. 2011; Kalemli-Ozcan et al. 2013). However, countries with current account imbalances have faced funding problems that have aggravated the already delicate situation. Hence, these imbalances matter (Boissay 2011).

Recovery of growth in the southern European economies is proving to be a long and complex process. There are several forces delaying recovery. The most obvious, of course, is the lack of a flexible nominal exchange rate that could correct balance of payments problems. This lack is forcing a restoration of external balances through harsh reductions in real wages (internal devaluation) and excessively restrictive fiscal policies in the context of depressed economies. Thus, the external sector has become the only potential source of renewed growth.

However, this solution is not exempt from difficulties. The housing bubble, fuelled by credit expansion in the years preceding the crisis, caused distortions in the allocation of resources between non-tradable and tradable sectors (Jaumotte and Sodsriwiboon 2010). Non-tradable sectors grew more in relative terms than tradable sectors, with consequent negative effects on the productivity and competitiveness of the southern economies. Reallocation of resources, especially of employment, from non-tradable to tradable sectors is an inherently slow process, which has in addition been hampered, first, by a lack of credit and, second, by competition between southern European economies and non-European emerging market economies. This is especially important for economies whose distinctive advantage is cost competition.[6] These economies thus face tough adjustment processes that are likely to be extended over time.

7.4 FINAL REMARKS

Research in the aftermath of the financial crisis has emphasized that the connection between global imbalances and the crisis is weak. This conclusion follows logically from the recognition that, in a globalized world economy, it is gross flows rather than net flows that matter. Moreover, capital flows have not responded to macroeconomic fundamentals in either host or surplus countries but to the level of expected volatility and profitability in global financial markets. The roots of the crisis lie in the fragility of the international monetary and financial system. Therefore, stricter control and supervision of the international monetary and financial system are needed to avoid similar crises in the future.

However, the conclusion that the roots of the crisis lie in the fragility of the international monetary and financial system does not mean that current account imbalances have no relevance to an understanding of the crisis. This is especially evident in the case of European economies. Deficit countries in southern Europe faced sudden stops of capital inflows, forcing them to implement harsh adjustment policies in addition to resorting to international aid. It is not desirable to ignore current account imbalances, as they are a symptom of what can be triggered through an indebtedness process that ends in crisis.

NOTES

The research leading to these results has received funding from the European Union Seventh Framework Programme (FP7/2007–2013) under Grant Agreement No. 266800 and from Basque Government Consolidated Research Group (IT712–13). The views expressed during the execution of the FESSUD project, in whatever form and/or by whatever medium, are the sole responsibility of the authors. The European Union is not liable for any use that may be made of the information contained therein. We are very grateful for comments from participants in the 2013 FESSUD Conference, which was held in Amsterdam. Remaining errors are the responsibility of the authors.

1. For further information about data regarding these imbalances see Ferreiro et al. (2013).
2. This work was subsequently published in the *Journal of Political Economy* (**117** (3), 2009, pp. 371–416), but with the citation noted above omitted. The crisis had already begun and this conclusion, extracted from a sophisticated model, could not be sustained. The idea that global imbalances represented a new kind of equilibrium, as proposed in many papers in the pre-crisis period, was simply a conviction lacking any scientific basis. This, however, did not prevent it from being accepted as an implication of sophisticated models.
3. This work was published in the *Journal of International Economics* in 2010. However, the conclusion presented in the working paper and reproduced in these pages had disappeared.
4. The relationship between current account imbalances and population age structure was initially investigated as an explanatory factor in the current account imbalances between the USA and Japan in the 1980s by Feroli (2006), who shows a positive relationship.
5. It is possible that the indebtedness process would have become exhausted without the financial crisis. Capacity for indebtedness, for both private and public players, may be limited, especially in the private sector. Those limits are set by the rate of growth of the economy, which ultimately defines the bounds of debt sustainability. However, it is conceivable that the deleveraging process in the southern economies, in that hypothetical scenario, would be less traumatic than the current deleveraging process, as instruments exist to affect the process and smooth out its negative effects.
6. There have been suggestions of alternative adjustment policies in the southern European countries, including expansionary policies in northern countries, especially Germany. An increase in aggregate demand in northern economies would generate an increase in demand for imports in those countries and thus increased demand for southern economies' exports. However, the effects of such expansionary policies in northern Europe are likely to be limited as a result of competition faced by southern European economies

from emerging market economies. This is especially important for economies whose distinctive leadership is via cost competition.

REFERENCES

Acharya, V. and P. Schnabl (2010), 'Do global imbalances spread global imbalances? The case of asset-backed commercial paper during the financial crisis of 2007–09', *IMF Economic Review*, **58** (1), 37–73.

Aizenman, J. and R. Sengupta (2011), 'Global imbalances: is Germany the new China? A sceptical view', *Open Economies Review*, **22**, 387–400.

Aizenman, J., M. Hutchison and I. Noy (2011), 'Inflation targeting and real exchange rates in emerging markets', *World Development*, **39** (5), 712–724.

Barnes, S., J. Lawson and A. Radziwill (2010), 'Current account imbalances in the euro area: a comparative perspective', OECD Economics Department Working Papers No. 826, OECD.

Beirne, J. and M. Fratzscher (2013), 'The pricing of sovereign risk and contagion during the European sovereign debt crisis', *Journal of International Money and Finance*, **34**, 60–82.

Belke, A. and C. Dreger (2013), 'Current account imbalances in the euro area: does catching-up explain the development?', *Review of International Economics*, **21** (1), 6–17.

Bems, R. and I. Carvalho-Filho (2011), 'The current account and precautionary savings for exporters of exhaustible resources', *Journal of International Economics*, **84**, 48–64.

Bernanke, B.S. (2005), 'The global saving glut and the U.S. current account deficit', remarks at Sandridge Lecture, 10 March, Richmond, VA.

Bernanke, B.S., C. Bertaut, L.P. DeMarco and S. Kamin (2011), 'International capital flows and the returns to safe assets in the United States, 2003–2007', International Finance Discussion Papers, Federal Reserve.

Bertaut, C., L.P. DeMarco, S. Kamin and R. Tryon (2012), 'ABS inflows to the United States and the global financial crisis', *Journal of International Economics*, **88**, 219–234.

Blanchard, O. (2007), 'Current account deficits in rich countries', *IMF Staff Papers*, **54** (2), 191–219.

Blanchard, O. and G.M. Milesi-Ferretti (2009), 'Global imbalances: in midstream?', IMF Staff Position Notes No. 29, International Monetary Fund.

Blanchard, O., F. Giavazzi and F. Sa (2005), 'International investors, the U.S. current account and the dollar', *Brookings Papers on Economic Activity*, **36** (1), 1–66.

Boissay, F. (2011), 'Financial imbalances and financial fragility', ECB Working Paper Series No. 1317, European Central Bank.

Borio, C. and P. Disyatat (2011), 'Global imbalances and the financial crisis: link or no link?', BIS Working Paper No. 346, Bank for International Settlements.

Brissimis, S.N., G. Hondroyiannis, C. Papazoglou, N.T. Tsaveas and M.A. Vasardani (2010), 'Current account determinants and external sustainability in periods of structural change', ECB Working Paper Series No. 1243, European Central Bank.

Caballero, R., E. Farhi and P. Gourinchas (2008), 'An equilibrium model of "global imbalances" and low interest rates', *American Economic Review*, **98** (1), 358–393.

Calvo, G. and C. Reinhart (2002), 'Fear of floating', *Quarterly Journal of Economics*, **117** (2), 379–408.

Campa, J.M. and A. Gavilán (2011), 'Current accounts in the euro area: an intertemporal approach', *Journal of International Money and Finance*, **30** (1), 205–228.

Carroll, C.D. and O. Jeanne (2009), 'A tractable model of precautionary reserves, net foreign assets, or sovereign wealth funds', NBER Working Paper No. 15228, National Bureau of Economic Research.

Catte, P., P. Cova, P. Pagano and I. Visco (2011), 'The role of macroeconomic policies in the global crisis', *Journal of Policy Modeling*, **33** (6), 787–803.

Ca'Zorzi, M., A. Chudik and A. Dieppe (2012), 'Thousands of models, one story: current account imbalances in the global economy', ECB Working Paper Series No. 1441, European Central Bank, June.

Chinn, M.D. and H. Ito (2007), 'Current account balances, financial development and institutions: assaying the world "saving glut"', *Journal of International Money and Finance*, **26**, 546–569.

Chinn, M.D. and H. Ito (2008), 'Global current account imbalances: American fiscal policy vs. East Asian savings', *Review of International Economics*, **16** (3), 479–498.

Cline, W. (2005), *The United States as a Debtor Nation*, Washington, DC: Institute for International Economics.

Cline, W.R. and J. Williamson (2008), 'New estimates of fundamental equilibrium exchange rates', Policy Briefs PB08-7, Peterson Institute.

Dominguez, K.M.E., Y. Hashimoto and T. Ito (2012), 'International reserves and global financial crisis', *Journal of International Economics*, **88** (2), 388–406.

Dooley, M., D. Folkerts-Landau and P. Garber (2003), 'An essay on the revived Bretton Woods system', NBER Working Paper No. 9971, National Bureau of Economic Research.

Dooley, M., D. Folkerts-Landau and P. Garber (2004), 'The U.S. current account deficit and economic development: collateral for a total return swap', NBER Working Paper No. 10727, National Bureau of Economic Research.

Drehmann, M. (2013), 'Total credit as an early warning indicator for systemic banking crises', *BIS Quarterly Review*, June, 41–45.

Economic Report of the President (2009), Executive Office of the President and the Council of Economic Advisers, United States of America.

Felipe, J., K. Kintanar and J.A. Lim (2006), 'Asia's current account surplus: savings glut or investment drought?', *Asian Development Review*, **23** (1), 16–54.

Feroli, M. (2006), 'Demography and the US current account deficits', *North American Journal of Economics and Finance*, **17** (1), 1–16.

Ferreiro, J., P. Peinado and F. Serrano (2013), 'Global imbalances and capital movements as constraints to the international economy recovery', in P. Arestis and M. Sawyer (eds), *Economic Policies, Governance and the New Economics*, London: Palgrave Macmillan.

Ferrucci, G. and C. Miralles (2007), 'Saving behaviour and global imbalances: the role of emerging market economies', ECB Working Papers Series No. 842, European Central Bank.

Forbes, K. (2008), 'Why do foreigners invest in the United States?', NBER Working Paper No. 13908, National Bureau of Economic Research.

Forbes, K. and F. Warnock (2012), 'Capital flow waves: surges, stops, flight and retrenchment', *Journal of International Economics*, **88** (2), 235–251.

Gibson, H.D., S.G. Hall and G.S. Tavlas (2012), 'The Greek financial crisis: growing imbalances and sovereign spreads', *Journal of International Money and Finance*, **32**, 498–516.

Hassan, A., R. Salim and H. Bloch (2011), 'Population age structure, saving, capital flows and the real exchange rate: a survey of the literature', *Journal of Economic Surveys*, **25** (4), 708–736.

Herr, H. (2008), 'Financial systems in developing countries and economic development', in E. Hein, T. Niechoj, P. Spahn and A. Truger (eds), *Finance-Led Capitalism? Macroeconomic Effects of Changes in the Financial Sector*, Marburg: Metropolis.

Herrerias, M.J. and V. Orts (2010), 'Is the export-led growth hypothesis enough to account for China's growth?', *China and the World Economy*, **18** (4), 34–51.

Horioka, C.Y. and J. Wan (2007), 'The determinants of household saving in China: a dynamic panel analysis of provincial data', *Journal of Money, Credit and Banking*, **39** (8), 2077–2096.

Jaumotte, F. and P. Sodsriwiboon (2010), 'Current account imbalances in the Southern Euro Area', IMF Working Papers WP/10/139, International Monetary Fund.

Jordà, O., M. Schularick and A.M. Taylor (2011), 'Financial crisis, credit booms, and external imbalances: 140 years of lessons', *IMF Economic Review*, **59** (2), 340–378.

Kalemli-Ozcan, S., E. Papaioannou and F. Perri (2013), 'Global banks and crisis transmission', *Journal of International Economics*, **89** (2), 495–510.

Kilian, L., A. Rebucci and N. Spatafora (2009), 'Oil shocks and external balances', *Journal of International Economics*, **77**, 181–194.

King, M. (2011), 'Global imbalances and the perspective of the Bank of England', *Bank of England Quarterly Bulletin*, Q1, 43–48.

Kollmann, R., Z. Enders and G.J. Müller (2011), 'Global banking and international business cycle', *European Economic Review*, **55**, 407–426.

Lane, P. (2013), 'Capital flows in the euro area', European Economy: Economic Papers No. 497, European Commission.

Lane, P. and G.M. Milesi-Ferretti (2007a), 'Europe and global imbalances', IMF Working Papers 07/144, International Monetary Fund.

Lane, P. and G.M. Milesi-Ferretti (2007b), 'The external wealth of nations mark II', *Journal of International Economics*, **73**, 223–250.

Lane, P. and G.M. Milesi-Ferretti (2008), 'The drivers of financial globalization', *American Economic Review*, **98** (2), 327–332.

Le, T. and Y. Chang (2013), 'Oil prices shocks and trade imbalances', *Energy Economics*, **36**, 78–96.

McGuire, P. and G. von Peter (2009), 'The US dollar shortage in global banking', *BIS Quarterly Review*, March, 47–63.

Mendoza, E., V. Quadrini and J. Ríos-Rull (2007), 'Financial integration, financial deepness and global imbalances', NBER Working Paper No. 12909, National Bureau of Economic Research.

Menkhoff, L. (2013), 'Foreign exchange intervention in emerging markets: a survey of empirical studies', *World Economy*, **36** (9), 1187–1208.

Obstfeld, M. (2012a), 'Does the current account still matter?', *American Economic Review: Papers and Proceedings*, **102** (3), 1–23.

Obstfeld, M. (2012b), 'Financial flows, financial crises, and global imbalances', *Journal of International Money and Finance*, **31**, 469–480.

Obstfeld, M. and K. Rogoff (2000), 'The six major puzzles in international macroeconomics: is there a common cause?', in B.S. Bernanke and K. Rogoff (eds), *NBER Macroeconomics Annual*, Cambridge, MA: MIT Press.

Obstfeld, M. and K. Rogoff (2004), 'The unsustainable U.S. current account position revisited', NBER Working Paper No. 10869, National Bureau of Economic Research.

Obstfeld, M. and K. Rogoff (2009), 'Global imbalances and the financial crisis: products and common causes', *Proceedings, Federal Reserve Bank of San Francisco*, 131–172.

Porcile, G., A. Gomes de Souza and R. Viana (2011), 'External debt sustainability and policy rules in a small globalised economy', *Structural Change and Economic Dynamics*, **22**, 269–276.

Portes, R. (2009), 'Global imbalances', in M. Dewatripont, X. Freixas and R.Portes (eds), *Macroeconomic Stability and Financial Regulation: Key Issues for the G-20*, London: Centre for Economic Policy Research.

Prasad, E. (2009), 'Rebalancing growth in Asia', IZA Discussion Papers Series No. 4298, Institute for the Study of Labor.

Prasad, E., R. Rajan and A. Subramanian (2007), 'Foreign capital and economic growth', *Brookings Papers on Economic Activity*, **38** (1), 153–230.

Rodrik, D. (2008), 'The real exchange rate and economic growth', *Brookings Papers on Economic Activity*, Fall, 365–412.

Schnabl, G. and S. Freitag (2012), 'Reverse causality in global and intra-European imbalances', *Review of International Economics*, **20** (4), 674–690.

Spiegel, M. (2008), 'Monetary and financial integration in the EMU: push or pull?', *Review of International Economics*, **17** (4), 751–776.

Taguchi, H. (2011), 'Monetary autonomy in emerging market economies: the role of foreign reserves', *Emerging Markets Review*, **12**, 371–388.

Taylor, A. (2012), 'The great leveraging', BIS Working Paper No. 398, Bank for International Settlements.

Warnock, F. and V. Warnock (2009), 'International capital flows and U.S. interest rates', *Journal of International Money and Finance*, **28**, 903–919.

Xafa, M. (2007), 'Global imbalances and financial stability', IMF Working Paper No. 111, international Monetary Fund.

8. Financial deregulation and the 2007–08 US financial crisis

Özgür Orhangazi

8.1 INTRODUCTION

Following the Great Depression of the 1930s, a series of financial regulations were introduced in the United States. The main aims of these regulations were to ensure the stability of the financial sector and enhance its role in supporting investment and production by the non-financial corporate sector. In addition to these regulations, the state's involvement in active macroeconomic management increased, especially after the Second World War, and international trade and finance regulations were introduced following the Bretton Woods conference. Keynesian policies were used to generate demand and to tackle business cycles, while the state carried out heavy infrastructural investment and regulated key industries. Social expenditure programmes were established, together with a redistributive taxation system. This configuration provided high rates of economic growth, and hence the era is usually referred to as the 'golden age' of capitalism. While, on the labour side, membership ratios in unions were increasing and real wages were going up in this period, corporations were taking advantage of an environment in which domestic product markets had an oligopolistic character and foreign competition was limited. However, a serious crisis emerged in the 1970s. At the international level, the fixed exchange rate regime of the Bretton Woods system collapsed. The US economy entered into a period of stagnation, accompanied by high rates of inflation. Profitability of the US non-financial corporate sector declined significantly. This decline in the rate of profit and the associated problems created the dynamics that led to the dismantling of the regulatory framework of the era. Two dynamics were central in determining the path of economic transformation in the coming decades: the corporations' search for ways to increase profitability and the rise of finance in a gradually deregulated system (Orhangazi 2011).

Financial deregulation (and the reluctance to introduce regulation on new financial products) was a significant factor in preparing the conditions for the 2007–08 financial crisis. In the run-up to the crisis, deregulation created an environment in which mortgage lending expanded and speculation in other financial markets was heightened, even though riskiness was steadily increasing. The end result was, first, the failure of mortgage firms, banks and a major insurance company, followed by the collapse of the market for short-term loans. This initially led to a liquidity crisis and then to insolvencies and a debt deflation, and the whole economy sank into a deep recession. In this chapter, I review the history of regulation and deregulation in the USA and discuss the channels through which financial deregulation contributed to the 2007–08 crisis.

It is important to underline that financial deregulation was not the only reason behind the financial crisis and the ensuing 'Great Recession'. In fact, as Epstein and Wolfson (2013, p. 2) note, 'financial crises are not caused by finance alone and certainly have impacts that go way beyond finance'. The financial deregulation process should be understood within the context of the broader structural changes that took place in the US economy, as well as in the global economy, within the last few decades. Financial deregulation was not simply a change in policy preferences but an important part of a broader structural transformation. As the regulations were declared inefficient and the Keynesian regime of accumulation was dismantled, trade and finance were liberalized in a process in which privatization and deregulation became the policy principles. The attempts to recover profitability included breaking up labour's power with the help of anti-labour policies and globally relocating production to lower-cost sites. Labour incomes were curtailed, real wages stagnated and inequality increased to historical heights. This process was accompanied by intensified international competition among large corporations, excess capacity and increased financialization of non-financial corporations (Crotty 2003; Stockhammer 2004; Orhangazi 2008a, 2008b).

Keeping these in mind, I begin in section 8.2 with a brief overview of the history of regulation and deregulation in the US economy. In section 8.3, I discuss the channels through which financial deregulation contributed to the financial crisis. I review the policy suggestions of those who see financial deregulation as the main contributor of the financial crisis in section 8.4. In section 8.5, I provide a critical assessment of these, while broadly situating financial deregulation within the context of the broader changes in capitalism since the early 1980s.

8.2 REGULATION AND DEREGULATION IN HISTORICAL PERSPECTIVE

US financial markets in the early twentieth century were largely unregulated, and high volumes of speculative activity prevailed, culminating in the stock market crash of 1929. Many banks failed, and significant misconduct was revealed in Wall Street. The 1929 stock market crash and the ensuing Great Depression led to a series of regulatory acts. The main objectives of these regulations were to ensure financial stability and to support growth and capital accumulation. A stable financial sector was to provide low-cost credit to the non-financial corporate sector and support production and investment. Hence, a new financial structure emerged, based on the following key features. First, the Federal Deposit Insurance Corporation (FDIC) was formed to provide deposit insurance and ward off bank runs. Second, 'firewalls' were created between capital markets and depository institutions in order to isolate the money markets from the riskier activities of capital markets. The intermediary function of dealing with corporate shares and bonds was reserved solely for investment banks. Deposit banks were prohibited from underwriting and placing corporate stocks and bonds and from holding speculative assets. Commercial bank loans were to meet mainly short-term financing needs, while investment banks managed long-term financing needs. Third, Regulation Q put limits on deposit interest rates to limit excessive competition among banks and to ensure low loan rates. Fourth, the FDIC and the Comptroller of the Currency were given powers to ensure the prudence of the banking sector and limit competition in and entry to the sector. Fifth, the Securities Act of 1933 regulated the securities markets, and the Securities and Exchange Commission (SEC) was established to regulate secondary trading. Sixth, the Commodity Exchange Act of 1936 regulated the exchanges for commodities and futures trading. Furthermore, other pieces of regulation were established for different parts of the financial system. Savings and loans associations were to be overseen by the Federal Home Loan Banks created in 1933, and credit unions by the Bureau of Federal Credit Unions. The regulation of insurance companies was left to individual states. The international financial system was also regulated, a fixed exchange rate system was based on a dollar standard tied to gold, and capital controls were introduced (Isenberg 2000, 2003; Sherman 2009).

This configuration, combined with a series of regulations in key sectors and an active macroeconomic management by the state, contributed to the high rates of economic growth during the 'golden age' of capitalism. Nevertheless, a serious crisis emerged in the 1970s. The economy entered into a period of stagnation with an increasing rate of inflation.

This coincided with the collapse of the fixed exchange rate regime of the Bretton Woods international financial system.

The significant decline in the profitability of non-financial corporations and the associated problems created the dynamics that led to the transformation from the regulated system to neoliberalism. Two dynamics were central in this regard: the corporations' search for ways to increase profitability and the rise of finance in a gradually deregulated system (Orhangazi 2011). Keynesian macroeconomic management policies were renounced, and deregulation in key industries was gradually put in motion. Starting with the Airline Deregulation Act of 1978, regulated industries were subjected to a process of deregulation and regulated monopolies such as AT&T were broken up. At the same time, cutbacks in social programmes were put in motion, together with tax cuts for corporations (Kotz 2013). Paul Volcker was appointed to the Federal Reserve in 1979, and he quickly increased the interest rates. The end result was a significant increase in the unemployment rate and hence an undermining of the bargaining power of labour. The Reagan administration signalled that this shift in policy was permanent by introducing a direct attack on labour, beginning with the break-up of the air traffic controllers' strike in 1981. Once highly regulated industries such as transportation, communications and electricity were later deregulated.

The financial sector had tried to eliminate or undermine regulations since it began taking shape in the 1930s and 1940s, but it was the 1970s that marked the beginning of a long process of deregulation for the sector. The 1970s witnessed a tendency towards liberalizing finance, accompanied by financial innovations aimed at circumventing financial regulations as well as responding to adverse macroeconomic conditions (Orhangazi 2008a). The end of the fixed exchange rate regime and then of capital controls led to subsequent volatility of exchange rates, which provided a major impetus for the development of financial derivatives. The first wave of financial deregulation included the Depository Institutions Deregulation and Monetary Control Act of 1980 and the Garn–St. Germain Act of 1982. Interest rate controls were abolished in 1980. The second wave began with the US Financial Modernization Act of 1999, which allowed increased diversification of financial activities that could be undertaken by financial institutions. The 1933 Glass–Steagall Act, imposing a separation between commercial and investment banks, was repealed in 1999. The Commodity Futures Modernization Act of 2000 left credit default swaps (CDS) and equity default swaps (EDS) unregulated. The amendment to the Employee Retirement Income Security Act in 2000 permitted pensions to buy mortgage-backed securities (MBS) and asset-backed securities (ABS), which increased the demand for securitized assets. In addition to the removal of existing regulations, in this era there was a reluctance to impose tighter regulation on financial innovations. Kregel (2010) describes this reluctance as follows: 'There was no lack of regulation governing the financial institutions that engaged in the buildup of financial layering and pyramiding on an ever-declining cushion of cash' (p. 12) and 'many of the difficulties stemmed not from lack of regulation but from a failure to fully implement existing regulations . . . [A]ll that was necessary was the appropriate application of existing regulations, and nothing more needed to be done' (p. 1).

While the crisis of the 1970s and the collapse of the fixed exchange rate regime provided the general conditions for financial deregulation, a number of specific developments in the 1960s and 1970s had already paved the road to financial deregulation and liberalization (Orhangazi 2008a). To begin with, accelerating inflation in the 1970s pushed the regulated system to its limits. The regulated financial system depended on a stable rate of inflation, as banks could tolerate low interest rates and finance long-term loans with short-term deposits without a high risk of maturity mismatch as long as inflation stayed in check. Increasing inflation pushed real interest rates down, especially after 1973, and lowered the profitability of commercial banks. Around the same time, large corporate borrowers began turning towards the commercial paper market (short-term money market securities issued by private firms), exacerbating commercial banks' problems and expanding the commercial paper market. The decline in corporate loans in banks' portfolios was going to be a major factor in the banks' expansion into the consumer credit and mortgage markets in the following decades. Banks responded with a series of innovations that were devised to keep their market share by working around regulations. An earlier example of these innovations was the introduction of the negotiable certificate of deposit. These innovations contributed to the dismantling of the regulatory framework by making the existing regulations obsolete and, at the same time, contributed to the expansion of the financial sector in general. Later on, rapid progress in information and communication technologies enabled further financial innovations.

A wave of US mergers was accompanied by a move overseas of these merged corporations at the end of the 1960s. The internationalization of production had created a change in the financial needs of the non-financial corporations by the 1970s, and this contributed to the deregulatory drive. The Glass–Steagall Act kept commercial banks away from this merger wave, and they were not involved in the financing of the mergers. When the large conglomerates increasingly looked abroad in search of markets, the US commercial banks started to move out in order to meet these corporations' financial needs. However, they were constrained by the interest equalization tax, which was introduced in 1963 and aimed to stop the movement of US dollars abroad. This led banks to open foreign branches to meet the borrowing needs of these multinational corporations. As industrial firms reached their national limits and intensified their pursuit of opening up to cross-border operations, the predominant business and economic theories of the era began to claim that regulations and restrictions were barriers to development, employment, profitability and survival. Hence, the success of industrial and productive firms created a powerful push to get rid of the regulatory restrictions to allow them to spread to new markets, areas and lines of business.

The increasing power of financial institutions over time was another significant factor in the push towards further deregulation. After the oil price hikes of the 1970s, oil producing countries recycled their vast amounts of 'petrodollars' through banks in Europe and New York. Banks began searching for profitable investment opportunities after suddenly acquiring these large amounts of funds. As the rates of return in the USA and in Europe were not high in the slow growth years of the 1970s, they began pushing for an opening up of international investment opportunities. The need for international financial opening required by these banks and their increased power contributed to the pressures towards financial liberalization and deregulation. The banks acquired a significant amount of influence through the command of these large funds and began a process of 'loan pushing'. The key event was the Mexican default in 1982, which threatened the solvency of most New York banks. What the decade of the 1980s showed to the world after the default of Mexico was that the creditors were protected (financial power indeed won), while the Washington Consensus policies – shaped in response to this crisis (or seizing this opportunity) by the IMF, World Bank and US Treasury, and surely influenced by the financial lobby in Washington and elsewhere – were now the new way of thinking, doing business and governing.

Among these financial institutions, the share of institutional investors' asset holdings in total financial assets began increasing, especially in the 1990s. Investment funds attracted savings that had previously been held in fixed term bank deposits. The introduction of funded pension schemes created a huge rise in the flow of money into the securities market to buy corporate stocks, as well as corporate and government bonds. Taxes on finance capital were also reduced, especially on the new pension and investment funds, in order to create incentives for small investors' participation. While institutional investors benefited from deregulation, technological advances enabled them to increase their size by driving their costs down.

8.3 THE ROLE OF FINANCIAL DEREGULATION IN THE CRISIS

8.3.1 Theoretical Background

As these developments contributed to the impetus towards deregulation, 'free market' theories in economics and finance slowly gained predominance and provided a theoretical support for the structural transformations. According to the mainstream economic and financial theory, the financial sector simply serves the needs of the economy and improves its efficiency. The standard models portray markets and economies as inherently stable and macroeconomic models study only stable states that are affected by external shocks. Financial markets provide essential services such as providing liquidity, mobilizing and pooling savings and allocating them to investment. They gather, process and disseminate information possessed by different agents in the economy and hence provide services of screening and monitoring, risk management, diversification and hedging. According to these models, as financial markets provide these functions, the prices of financial assets are supposed to reflect their fundamental values in the real economy. Financial markets, therefore, increase the allocative efficiency of the system. These models conclude that financial markets do their job best in an environment of minimum regulation. Regulation distorts the system. Investors seeking to achieve maximum return for a certain risk level will choose the optimal risk for them and, in the process, allocate resources to their most productive use. Left on their own, without any regulation, financial market actors will behave in their own interest, and this will create outcomes that are efficient (Dowd 1996).

As financial economists developed these models with strong unrealistic assumptions, individuals and businesses built on these models. Crotty (2013), who provides a thorough critique of the deregulated financial system and the theories that support it, argues that the theory of 'efficient financial markets' is a fairy tale based on grossly unrealistic assumptions. This theory was a significant contributor to the crisis, as it helped justify the financial deregulation process. It gained predominance in economics partly because of the flawed methodological argument that the realism of the assumptions did not matter. However, this theory could not be empirically validated for a number of reasons. Crotty (2013) concludes that an analysis of the financial markets should be based on the Keynes–Minsky approach, which has affinities with the Marxian approach. These approaches see capitalist financial markets as inherently unstable. The basic dynamics of a financial crisis originate in the fundamental features of the capitalist system, while variations in each crisis appear as a result of institutional changes over time (Wolfson 2013). Keynesian and Marxian approaches attribute a dual role to finance, where finance is at the same time a significant accelerator of accumulation and a major source of instability (Orhangazi 2011). Keynes had argued that investment under capitalism is fundamentally unstable, and financial markets further contribute to this instability. Minsky (1982, 1986) developed this argument and concluded that only big government institutions can bring a certain level of stability to the fundamentally unstable capitalist economy. In the Minskian version of the argument, where investment spending is seen as the main force in the economy, a financially robust environment (low levels of debt, low interest rates, and liquid conditions for businesses and households) encourages higher levels of investment spending. Increased investment generates an increase in profits and encourages even further investment and increased confidence in the economy. As confidence increases, banks make more and riskier loans, leading eventually to increases in debt ratios as coverage ratios fall. This process creates financial fragility in the sense that an unexpected downturn in the economy would lead to payment difficulties for the fragile units. Furthermore, speculation in financial markets can create euphoria, and an initial increase in asset prices can lead to further increases through the expectations channel. As the demand for these assets and their prices increase, risks associated with these assets are underestimated and asset bubbles are formed. Such a bubble in financial markets has significant effects on the real economy, as it could lead to an increase in consumption through wealth effects or in investment expenditures. However, a reversal leads to serious problems by deflating aggregate demand as well.

Marxian approaches, while mostly emphasizing the real sector roots of capitalist instability, also point out the potentially destabilizing role of finance. Financial institutions support capital accumulation by mobilizing large amounts of money capital and allow accumulation to take place at a faster rate and a larger scale than would otherwise be possible. However, finance also contributes to capitalist instability, which can originate either in the financial realm or in the real sector and be exacerbated by finance. When there are favourable conditions for accumulation, investment expands rapidly, leading firms to use more credit. The pace and scale of expansion at this stage depend on the amount of financial capital invested in capital accumulation. These expansions endogenously create disturbances in the financial or real side of the economy. An adverse development in the real side of the economy could be turned into a crisis and collapse if it leads to or is accompanied by troubles in the financial markets. Likewise, a disturbance originating in the financial sector can spread to the real side of the economy by disrupting the accumulation process. An overextended and fragile system can turn what might have been a mild downturn into a financial crisis (Orhangazi 2011).

8.3.2 From Deregulation to Crisis: Channels

The 2007–08 financial crisis erupted at the end of a long process of financial deregulation. Securitization was widespread, and the originate-and-distribute model in mortgage lending was prevalent, as risks spread through the system with little accountability. When housing prices began declining and adjustable mortgage rates were raised to higher levels, a number of borrowers began defaulting on their mortgage loans. Asset-backed securities linked to the mortgage market began losing value. As the mortgage-backed securities were spread across all financial institutions, the crisis spread to other assets based on short-term debt. Repo markets, asset-backed commercial paper markets, and money market mutual funds were at the centre of this crisis. Securitization loosened the link between creditors and borrowers and created the possibility for illiquidity as concerns about marketability rose.

Financial deregulation prepared the conditions for the crisis through five different but closely related channels: 1) rapid expansion of financial innovations, including complex financial derivatives, and the accompanying excessive leverage; 2) increased securitization; 3) emergence and expansion of shadow banking with minimum regulation and a concomitant banking concentration; 4) increased risk taking by financial institutions; and 5) flawed decisions based on flawed financial models. Each one increased the fragility of the financial system in different ways. Let's look at them briefly.

8.3.2.1 Financial innovations and leverage

Financial innovations contributed to the increase in leverage by allowing financial institutions to offload risky assets and thus reduce capital requirements. Lack of regulation encouraged excessive leverage. Unregulated financial innovations contributed to risky credit expansion and financial investments. In the housing market, the appearance of ever-increasing prices led households to borrow up to the full market value of their houses and borrow more through refinancing arrangements, encouraged by banks, as the market value of houses went up. In this process, little, if any at all, attention was paid to the ability of these households to service the debt.

On the other hand, a major problem with the derivatives is that even small losses on derivative holdings have the potential to destroy bank capital, as they are not included in capital ratios. While derivatives could allow banks to hedge risks, they also increased risk-taking activity and allowed banks to increase their leverage. After the collapse and bailout of AIG, it was revealed that it used bailout funds to pay off bad bets made by banks on CDOs. These bets were essentially pure gambling schemes used by banks, as they placed bets on securities they did not even hold (Nersiyan and Wray 2010, p. 18).

8.3.2.2   Securitization

Financial deregulation and liberalization enabled increased securitization. Securitization refers to the process where traditionally illiquid loans are packaged into different types of securities and sold in financial markets. In the process, the original lender brings together a portfolio of loans – a method known as pooling of loans – and sells it to a special purpose vehicle (SPV). The SPV sells rated securities in order to finance these. At the end, securitization turns a loan that would have traditionally been held on the balance sheet of the originating bank into a marketable security and moves it off the balance sheet. Securitization led to higher levels of risk and fragility, because it encouraged the reduction of standards for procedures and inadequate evaluation of the loans, since each party began relying on others for a thorough investigation of the loans. The subprime mortgage market was a case in point. While investors who bought mortgage-backed securities did not thoroughly investigate them, financial institutions failed to understand and disclose their risks, and the credit-rating agencies failed in evaluating the complex securities.

Securitization also loosened the link between the creditors and borrowers and created the possibility for illiquidity as concerns about marketability rose. Furthermore, securitization created the illusion that subprime mortgage lending had become much safer and led to a rapid inflow of money into the market (Pollin 2008, p. 120). However, when asset prices started to decline, complex interconnections in the financial markets began working in reverse and bringing financial institutions down, and uncontrolled securitization and high leverage led to spreading panic. For example, credit default swaps made securitized loans appear safe. CDSs were marketed as a tool to hedge against risks, and it was argued that they helped distribute risks to those who were most willing and able to bear them. Banks used them to hide risks on their balance sheets. While they were engaged in risky activities, they bought CDSs to 'hedge' and managed to maintain a risk-free appearance (Nersiyan and Wray 2010, p. 15). For example, a bank could hold risky financial assets and then buy 'insurance' from AIG on these securities. On top of this, it could make a bet that AIG would fail and not honour this insurance. All this was supposed to protect the bank from any risk. However, for these bets there was always a counterparty, which brought the whole structure into a crisis in the end (Nersiyan and Wray 2010, pp. 15–16).

Complex techniques of pooling and tranching different types of financial instruments with different levels of risk led to the creation of more and more complex securitized pools of loans that were supposed to bring high returns with low risk. Flawed mathematical models were used for their evaluation. In the mortgage market, this meant an expansion of mortgage loans to riskier borrowers, and it provided the basis for what can be called an inverted pyramid of structured products. Moreover, lack of regulation led to a decline in underwriting standards as well as consumer protection. In addition, securitization contributed to financial institutions becoming interconnected through an intricate web of financing, investment and securitization operations, which further made it increasingly more difficult to assess risk independently.

8.3.2.3 Shadow banking

Shadow banking, in its broadest definition, refers to institutions such as 'investment banks, money-market mutual funds, and mortgage brokers; rather old contracts, such as sale and repurchase agreements ("repo"); and more esoteric instruments such as asset-backed securities (ABS), collateralized-debt obligations (CDOs), and asset-backed commercial paper (ABCP)' (Gorton and Metrick 2010, p. 1). Financial deregulation, together with financial innovations, caused an expansion of these instruments of shadow banking. Money market mutual funds, securitization and repurchase transactions played a central role in the crisis, as they are key elements of off-balance-sheet activity. Financial deregulation opened up the way for banks to engage in an array of risky activities. These activities were mostly incompatible with traditional banking roles. In fact, '[m]any of the larger banks have changed so much that it is unclear whether they can be called banks – since they did little underwriting, and tried to shift risks off balance sheets – either by packaging and selling assets or by purchasing "insurance" in the form of CDSs' (Nersiyan and Wray 2010, pp. 9–10). The ABS were issued by SPVs, which were established to hold assets as well as debt obligations backed by these assets. However, these were not actual institutions but were entities created for bookkeeping purposes. Banks used these to move securitized assets off their balance sheets on to the SPVs, which then would issue bonds and commercial paper that was backed by the pooled assets. In this way, banks could avoid capital and reserve requirements and increase their leverage, as well as their return on equity (Nersiyan and Wray 2010, p. 8). Furthermore, financial deregulation has contributed to increased concentration in the banking sector through the repeal of the Glass–Steagall Act. This made the financial system more fragile, as it created only a few institutions, which dominated most of the sector. Deregulation also turned these giant banks into 'universal banks' that engage in diverse financial activities, in addition to commercial banking, investment banking and insurance activities.

8.3.2.4 Risk

Financial deregulation and complicated financial innovations created incentives for the financial institutions to undertake risky investments. The high degree of competition among financial institutions created further incentives for them to take risky actions in order to protect their market share and profitability. A long period of economic expansion with low default rates contributed to these by increasing the level of confidence in the economy in general and especially within the financial sector. On top of this, the pay structure in financial institutions favoured and encouraged excessive risk taking while not paying enough attention to long-term risks. For example, in the subprime market, loan officers were earning large commissions as they brought new customers to the banks. When loans began underperforming, later on, loan officers did not have to return these commissions (Pollin 2008, p. 120).

8.3.2.5 Flawed models, flawed decisions

Part of the rhetoric on financial deregulation included an emphasis on self-surveillance and self-policing of the financial sector. For example, assessment and regulation of sophisticated financial instruments such as derivatives, collateralized debt obligations and structured investment vehicles were mostly left to financial market institutions, and they used highly sophisticated quantitative models of risk assessment for this purpose. This led to an underestimation of the real risks and created a situation where it became increasingly more difficult to distinguish poor judgement from fraudulent behaviour. The belief that market mechanisms and the profit motive bring socially optimum outcomes created an environment in which both complicated financial innovations and risky decisions made by the financial institutions went unchecked. Government intervention in markets has been considered to be counter-productive, and the belief in the self-regulation of markets has slowly gained sufficient support since the 1980s. This belief presupposed that financial market decision makers are in a better position to understand what they are doing than government officials, who have no expertise in banking and finance, and, since these financial market decision makers are sophisticated people, they will not take actions that could undermine their own interests and create fragility. Tymoigne (2010), however, has argued that risk management techniques encouraged unsound financial practices and high leverage, while self-regulation only created dangerous and at times even fraudulent business practices. While emphasis was put on short-term profitability, lending standards were loosened in a 'race to the bottom'.

8.3.2.6 Greed, irrationality and other factors

Those who attribute a central role to financial deregulation in creating the financial crisis see other arguments putting factors such as subprime lending, greed, speculation and so on at the centre as having little explanatory power. In fact, the greedy actions of market participants are explained by the requirements of market mechanisms. While some, such as Blundell-Wignall et al. (2008), point out four regulatory changes regarding homeownership strategies,[1] these were not necessarily causal factors but rather compounding factors. Subprime lending itself can explain only a small part of the entire story of financial collapse, and may not even have had such deleterious effects if its financial terms had been carefully adapted and related to the core incomes of the borrowers, enabling them to meet their payment obligations. Moreover:

> most market participants behave rationally in the sense that stiff competition and short-term incentives to reach money-return targets push them to do *whatever* is legally (and sometimes illegally) possible to maintain their market shares ... [T]his exclusive concern for individual financial accumulation pushes aside the long-term and indirect feedback effects that lead to financial fragility and increased systemic risk ... Market participants have no patience for those indirect effects, even if these indirect effects make them directly worse off, because they are too complex to include in the decision-making process or because it does not look like that market participants will be affected by them. (Tymoigne 2009, p. 16, emphasis in the original)

8.3.2.7 International transmission

International transmission mechanisms included investments of banks outside the USA in assets tied to US mortgage lending. The financial crisis in the USA quickly turned into a global financial crisis as a result of the unregulated nature of international finance. Initially, increased uncertainty over the creditworthiness of counterparties, both in the USA and in Europe, created a liquidity crisis. Banks began preferring to remain liquid and were unwilling to lend. As a result of this, short-term spreads quickly rose to record levels (Kregel 2008, pp. 2–3). Deregulated and interconnected financial markets, together with increased securitization and leverage, spread the risk around the world. Yet some of the contagion of the US financial crisis was controlled by the liquidity injections of the central banks and the efforts of the G20 together with the IMF (Singh 2013).

8.4   REGULATION, DEREGULATION, RE-REGULATION?

Given the size and significance of the financial crisis, it is not surprising that a large number of policy proposals were put forward. While after the crisis there was general agreement about the need for new regulation (for example, the Basel Committee on Banking Supervision (2010) focused on liquidity requirements, flexible capital requirements, maximum leverage ratios, etc.), there were more fundamental calls for reform as well. The basic idea in these proposals is that unregulated competition and the profit motive create short-termism in the economy and the prioritization of individual interest over social interest. The general argument is that the stability of the financial system is in the interest of society at large and should take priority over private financial interests. The suggested reforms have the general aim of detecting and preventing financial fragility and hence protecting against financial crises. A more general and fundamental policy proposal, and a general idea looming behind most of the proposals above, is that the financial sector has grown too big and needs to be downsized. A number of more concrete policy proposals include the following.

A financial transactions tax has been proposed in order to raise the cost of speculative trading and hence to discourage excessive speculation in the financial markets. For example, Pollin (2008) argues that a small sales tax on all financial transactions would be a measure that would promote both financial stability and fairness. An asset-based reserve requirement is another proposal to discourage financial institutions from holding excessive amounts of risky assets and, at the same time, to provide a cushion when market downturns occur. This kind of regulation would require financial institutions to keep a certain amount of cash in a reserve fund in proportion to the risky assets that they hold. On the other hand, excessive competition is seen as one of the reasons behind excessive risk taking. Therefore, it is proposed that new regulations should protect banks from competition and provide them with a reliable and cheap source of financing through the central bank. (Wray 2007; Tymoigne 2010).

Given the role of financial innovations in the run-up to the financial crisis, it is argued that each and every financial innovation should be regulated and supervised. Tymoigne (2010) argues that a one-time regulation is not sufficient and there should be regulatory follow-ups after financial innovations are permitted to exist for a certain period of time.

Rating agencies were seen as partly responsible for the financial crisis, as financial assets that received high ratings from these agencies turned out to be quite risky. It was highly improbable that rating agencies would have performed large amounts of credit assessments with the required diligence and accuracy, and when their ratings turned out to be inadequate they were not held accountable. A more fundamental problem was that an issuer of a structured financial product would usually shop around the rating agencies to find the one that would give a high rating with the lowest cost. Therefore, conservative risk assessments would never make it to the market and, over time, conservative rating agencies also began conforming to the practice of the others to protect their market shares. Therefore, a new structure for rating agencies is proposed by some (Kregel 2008; Diomande et al. 2009).

Another regulation proposal is the introduction of different ways of evaluating creditworthiness and different measures of financial robustness. According to Tymoigne (2010), evaluating creditworthiness only by the value of the collateral asset is not sufficient. What matters is the capacity to generate incomes that are sufficient to cover debt commitments. Hence, for individual institutions as well as the economy, regulators should focus on these cash flows. This is different from the probability of default, credit ratings and FICO scores, as financial fragility is measured based on an analysis of not only balance sheets and cash flow but also the underlying assets. In this type of evaluation, the essential questions include whether continuous refinancing is needed and, if so, whether this need is growing in relation to outstanding debt. These questions can be explored by key financial indicators such as the ratio of refinancing loans and their growth rate, the dynamics of debt and asset prices, and the structure of net cash inflows versus cash outflows.

Especially in the case of the USA, the high number of regulators with limited mandates over different segments of the financial system is seen as part of the problem by some. For example, Edgar (2009) argues that, in the USA, having a number of regulatory agencies with limited mandates over particular segments of the financial system creates both confusion and room for regulatory arbitrage. Therefore, a unified regulatory structure is envisioned in order to prevent the financial sector from engaging in regulatory arbitrage.

While this brief overview gives an idea about some of the regulatory proposals that were put forward after the financial crisis, D'Arista (2009b) provides a succinct overview of financial reform proposals and Ash et al. (2009) provide a detailed programme of both financial regulation and economic reform under the title 'A Progressive Program for Economic Recovery and Financial Reconstruction'.

8.5 DEREGULATION AND STRUCTURAL PROBLEMS OF THE ECONOMY

Analyses that focus on financial market deregulation as one of the main causes of the crisis are based on the theoretical premise that left to their own workings financial markets are inherently unstable. We see that, in the past decades, financial deregulation created an environment in which financial fragility steadily increased and resulted in a deep financial crisis. However, it is important to underline that financial deregulation was not the only reason behind the financial crisis and the prolonged economic stagnation that followed it. In the previous sections, the financial deregulation process was situated within the context of the broader structural changes that took place in the US economy, as well as in the global economy. The growing financialization of the economy and financial deregulation were directly related to other problems in the rest of the economy. In the post-1980s era, structural problems such as slow growth of aggregate demand, cut-throat industrial competition, global restructuring of production and global imbalances accompanied the financial deregulation and liberalization trends (Crotty 2003; Orhangazi 2008a, 2008b). In fact, finance has both contributed to some of these problems and, at the same time, provided temporary solutions to the same problems (Orhangazi 2011). For example, asset bubbles in the 1990s and 2000s largely drove the US economy and created a strong source of demand (Baker 2013).

Another important issue that needs to be considered is that the discussion on financial regulation often leaves aside the issue of power. In the USA, the political problem is the excessive power of the financial industry (Dymski 2010a, 2010b). For example, a significant part of the literature on deregulation seems to ignore the power of the financial sector and its capacity to affect legislation regarding the financial sector. Much reference is made to the first wave of financial regulation in the USA in the 1930s. However, this was also a period when labour was successful in organizing and increasing its power vis-à-vis capital. Wolfson (2013, p. 181) notes that:

> the 1930s and 1940s saw a relative balance of power between labor and capital rather than the dominance of either one. Workers were able to influence government and use the power of government to promote their interests – to encourage the formation of unions, to create a social safety net, and, most relevant for our purposes here, to restrain the destructive competitive tendencies of an unrestrained market and to provide government support for depositors through deposit insurance.

Furthermore, the issue of power needs to be considered at the global level as well.[2]

Finally, most policy suggestions generally aim to constrain finance and seek to bring it back to its original function, subservient to the needs of the economy. They are built on the understanding that a more managed capitalism is required in order to sustain stability and growth. This is clearly a very radical position given the state of the economics discipline. The aftermath of the financial crisis showed that this is also significantly more radical than the majority of politicians can accept. However, both the Keynes–Minsky tradition and the Marxian tradition remind us that even stability under capitalism is destabilizing and, in the absence of a change in the main economic structures, relations and incentives, fixing the system will prepare the ground for future crises (Seda and Orhangazi 2010). Furthermore, the global financial and economic crisis is only one among many crises, including the crises related to the environment, energy and food. Yet, the 2007–08 financial crisis and the ensuing economic stagnation, increased unemployment and poverty, and general deterioration in living standards remind us that radical alternatives to the current economic order must be found.

NOTES

1. These changes comprised the following: '(1) [T]he Bush administration['s] "American Dream" zero equity mortgage proposals became operative, helping low-income families to obtain mortgages; (2) [...] the Office of Federal Housing Enterprise Oversight (OFHEO), [which was the regulator of Fannie Mae and Freddie Mac at the time,] imposed greater capital requirements and balance-sheet controls on those two government-sponsored mortgage securitisation monoliths, opening the way for banks to move in on their "patch" with plenty of low-income mortgages coming on-stream; (3) the Basel II accord on international bank regulation was published and opened an arbitrage opportunity for banks that caused them to accelerate off-balance-sheet activity; and (4) the SEC agreed to allow investment banks [...] voluntarily to benefit from regulation changes to manage risk using capital calculations under the "consolidated supervised entities program".' (Blundell–Wignall et al. 2008, p. 3).
2. In this regard, the privileged position of the USA, especially its capital account surplus, needs to be considered as well. D'Arista (2009a) suggests thinking about the international monetary system.

REFERENCES

Ash, M. et al. (2009), 'A progressive program for economic recovery and financial reconstruction', Political Economy Research Institute and Schwartz Center for Economic Policy Analysis, January.
Baker, D. (2013), 'Speculation and asset bubbles', in G. Epstein and M. Wolfson (eds), *The Handbook of the Political Economy of Financial Crises*, Oxford: Oxford University Press.

Basel Committee on Banking Supervision (2010), 'The Group of Governors and Heads of Supervision reach broad agreement on Basel Committee capital and liquidity reform package', press release, 26 July.

Blundell-Wignall, A., P. Atkinson and S.H. Lee (2008), 'The current financial crisis: causes and policy issues', *OECD Financial Market Trends*, **95** (2), 1–21.

Crotty, J. (2003), 'The neoliberal paradox: the impact of destructive product market competition and impatient finance on nonfinancial corporations in the neoliberal era', *Review of Radical Political Economics*, **35** (3), 271–279.

Crotty, J. (2013), 'The realism of assumptions does matter: why Keynes–Minsky theory must replace efficient market theory as the guide to financial regulation policy', in G. Epstein and M. Wolfson (eds), *The Handbook of the Political Economy of Financial Crises*, Oxford: Oxford University Press.

D'Arista, J. (2009a), 'The evolving international monetary system', *Cambridge Journal of Economics*, **33**, 633–652.

D'Arista, J. (2009b), 'Rebuilding the framework for financial regulation', EPI Briefing Paper No. 231, Economic Policy Institute.

Diomande, M.A., J.S. Heintz and R.N. Pollin (2009), 'Why U.S. financial markets need a public credit rating agency', *Economists' Voice*, **6** (6), 1–4.

Dowd, K. (1996), 'The case for financial laissez-faire', *Economic Journal*, **106**, 679–687.

Dymski, G. (2010a), 'Three futures of postcrisis banking in the Americas: the financial trilemma and the Wall Street complex', Working Paper No. 604, Levy Economics Institute.

Dymski, G. (2010b), 'The global crisis and the governance of power in finance', in P. Arestis, R. Sobreira and J.L. Oreiro (eds), *The Financial Crisis: Origins and Implications*, Houndmills, Basingstoke: Palgrave Macmillan.

Edgar, R.J. (2009), 'The future of financial regulation: lessons from the global financial crisis', *Australian Economic Review*, **42** (4), 470–476.

Epstein, G. and M. Wolfson (2013), 'Introduction: the political economy of financial crises', in G. Epstein and M. Wolfson (eds), *The Handbook of the Political Economy of Financial Crises*, Oxford: Oxford University Press.

Gorton, G. and A. Metrick (2010), 'Regulating the shadow banking system', *Brookings Papers on Economic Activity*, **41** (2), 261–312.

Isenberg, D. (2000), 'The political economy of financial reform: the origins of the US deregulation of 1980 and 1982', in R. Pollin (ed.), *Capitalism, Socialism, and Radical Political Economy*, Cheltenham, UK and Northampton, MA, USA: Edward Elgar Publishing.

Isenberg, D. (2003), 'The national origin of financial liberalization: the case of the United States', in P. Arestis, M. Baddeley and J. McCombie (eds), *Globalisation, Regionalism and Economic Activity*, Cheltenham, UK and Northampton, MA, USA: Edward Elgar Publishing.

Kotz, D. (2013), 'Changes in the postwar global economy and the roots of the financial crisis', in G. Epstein and M. Wolfson (eds), *The Handbook of the Political Economy of Financial Crises*, Oxford: Oxford University Press.

Kregel, J. (2008), 'Changes in the US financial system and the subprime crisis', Working Paper No. 530, Levy Economics Institute.

Kregel, J. (2010), 'Is reregulation of the financial system an oxymoron?', Working Paper No. 585, Levy Economics Institute.

Minsky, H.P. (1982), *Can 'It' Happen Again?*, Armonk, NY: M.E. Sharpe.

Minsky, H.P. (1986), *Stabilizing an Unstable Economy*, New Haven, CT: Yale University Press.

Nersiyan, Y. and R.L. Wray (2010), 'The global crisis and the shift to shadow banking', Working Paper No. 587, Levy Economics Institute.

Orhangazi, Ö. (2008a), *Financialization of the U.S. Economy*, Cheltenham, UK and Northampton, MA, USA: Edward Elgar Publishing.

Orhangazi, Ö. (2008b), 'Financialization and capital accumulation in the non-financial corporate sector: a theoretical and empirical investigation on the U.S. economy, 1973–2003', *Cambridge Journal of Economics*, **32** (6), 863–886.

Orhangazi, Ö. (2011), '"Financial" vs. "Real": an overview of the contradictory role and place of finance in the modern economy', in P. Zarembka and R. Desai (eds), *Research in Political Economy*, Vol. 27, Bingley, UK: Emerald Group.

Pollin, R. (2008), 'The housing bubble and financial deregulation: isn't enough enough?', *New Labor Forum*, **17** (2), 118–121.

Seda, I. and Ö. Orhangazi (2010), 'The role of finance in the latest capitalist downturn', in E. Kawano, T.N. Masterson and J. Teller-Elsberg (eds), *Solidarity Economy I: Building Alternatives for People and Planet*, Amherst, MA: Center for Popular Economics.

Sherman, M. (2009), 'A short history of financial deregulation in the United States', report, Center for Economic and Policy Research, July.

Singh, A. (2013), 'The economic and financial crisis of 2008–2010: the international dimension', in G. Epstein and M. Wolfson (eds), *The Handbook of the Political Economy of Financial Crises*, Oxford: Oxford University Press.

Stockhammer, E. (2004), 'Financialization and the slowdown of accumulation', *Cambridge Journal of Economics*, **28** (5), 719–741.

Tymoigne, E. (2009), 'Securitization, deregulation, economic stability, and financial crisis, part II: deregulation, financial crisis, and policy implications', Working Paper No. 573.2, Levy Economics Institute.

Tymoigne, E. (2010), 'Financial stability, regulatory buffers, and economic growth: some postrecession regulatory implications', Working Paper No. 637, Levy Economics Institute.

Wolfson, M. (2013), 'An institutional theory of financial crises', in G. Epstein and M. Wolfson (eds), *The Handbook of the Political Economy of Financial Crises*, Oxford: Oxford University Press.

Wray, L.R. (2007), 'A post Keynesian view of central bank independence, policy targets, and the rules versus discretion debate', *Journal of Post Keynesian Economics*, **30** (1), 119–141.

9. The role of incentives for the Great Recession: securitization and contagion

Giampaolo Gabbi, Alesia Kalbaska and Alessandro Vercelli

9.1 INTRODUCTION

Most causes and consequences of the financial crisis and the subsequent Great Recession may be investigated from the point of view of incentives. We apply this point of view exclusively to securitization and contagion. Our analysis, however, is not restricted to the role of incentives, but surveys and discusses different aspects of the process of securitization, and of the related financial contagion between countries and economic units, that may be relevant for understanding the Great Recession.

The reason to connect the literature on contagion with that on securitization in this chapter is because there is a wide consensus on the observation that the process of securitization has deeply modified the process of propagation of financial distress, although there are different ideas on its determinants and implications. Financial and real contagion can be sparked by fundamental factors affecting price co-movements. Although these propagation mechanisms could be considered normal interconnections, rather than contagion processes in the strict sense of the term, these factors can be triggered by either global or local shocks. Contagion can also be interpreted, in another way, as a result of the behaviour of investors and changes in their attitude towards risk. This kind of contagion, also defined as irrational, could be associated with panic, herd behaviour, loss of confidence and increases in risk aversion. These two ways to describe contagion processes are usually based on separate contributions, but empirically irrational events are more likely to occur when fundamentals are weak. A promising approach helping to describe the contagion features and, eventually, to define early warning systems and critical factors is the network approach that allows a systematic investigation of the structural conditions and implications of contagion processes.

This methodology is based on accounting interactions between economic units. When applied to the banking system, it normally uses information about mutual interbank payment systems exposures. This approach has significant policy implications that may help in guiding the choice of policy rules and interventions on the basis of the network topology, degree and strength of interconnections between relevant economic units.

Most of the financial innovations developed during the last few decades, and often quoted as responsible for their contributions to the contagion which occurred during the 2007 crisis, initiated a set of interconnections among the agents involved, with several accounting linkages. Particularly, credit risk transfer processes, such as loan sales, credit derivatives, and securitizations, can be analysed as network facilitators aimed at transferring the credit and financial exposure to third parties. Securitization has had a significant impact as a catalyst of the financial crisis process by pushing the excessive indebtedness of many players, including households, while contributing to the rapidity and intensity of its transmission. The growing importance of securitization-based structured finance in the balance sheets of economic units increased the rapidity and strength of contagion, originating a generalized balance sheet recession.

The literature on contagion addresses the issues related to the strength and nature of the propagation of financial distress in the light of the empirical evidence. We thus begin the chapter with a survey of this literature in the hope of finding important clues on the subject matter of the chapter. This is the transformation of the propagation process, as a consequence of the process of financialization, in particular of securitization, which has greatly reduced the incentives of the units securitizing assets to review their value and the risk involved by holding them. The systemic consequences of securitization, considered benign ex ante by the supervisory authorities ('the market knows better'), proved to be devastating ex post ('no one knows'). In particular, the ensuing discharge of banks' responsibilities encouraged their excessive leverage, which was a crucial precondition of the crisis. The securitization process has also consequently increased banks' regulatory arbitrage to reduce the capital absorbed by credit risk, transferring the loan or mortgage exposure from the banking book to the trading book.

At the moment, the two strands of literature (contagion and securitization) remain surprisingly detached from one another, although the recent contributions to the structural approach raise concrete hopes of a constructive integration in the future.

In section 9.2 we briefly recall the basic principles of the asymmetric information approach (from now on AIA), its mainstream version (from now on A1) and the main alternative branch of the AIA (from now on A2), focusing on the emergence and evolution of a parallel banking system often called the 'shadow banking system', and we discuss the role of securitization in changing the financial system environment. In section 9.3 we explore the state of the art on financial contagion. The role of contagion in the Great Recession is briefly reconstructed in section 9.4. We discuss the policy implications of the two main branches of the AIA, particularly for securitization and shadow banking, in section 9.5. Section 9.6 concludes.

9.2 SECURITIZATION, CONTAGION AND THE IMPACT ON THE GREAT RECESSION

Orthodox theories aim to explain economic and financial behaviour as a rational response to market signals. Nevertheless, if we look at the economic system in this way, the very existence of banks becomes a puzzle. In a perfectly competitive market, where all agents are fully rational and their information is complete, why should banks exist? The supply of loanable funds should match the demand of credit directly in the market, guaranteeing the smooth and efficient working of the system without requiring any need of financial intermediation. Therefore, in this view, the explanation of banks' role and behaviour must be found in some significant deviation from the general equilibrium (GE) assumptions. In recent decades (since the early 1970s), the crucial deviation from the GE model, introduced to justify the prominent role of banks and to explain their behaviour, is the ubiquitous existence of asymmetric information (AI) in financial markets. This assumption has been used to explain many stylized facts observed in financial markets under physiological conditions and also to account for some of their pathologies.

The asymmetric information approach constructs the interconnections between financial and real sectors by focusing on the different quality and quantity of information available to counterparties in financial contracts. In particular, borrowers are assumed to have better information than lenders about their investment projects and capacity to pay back their obligations (Akerlof 1970). The structural nature of AI is likely to produce significant deviations from optimal equilibrium (Mishkin 1991). The higher interest rate results in greater adverse selection, as well as in credit rationing (Stiglitz and Weiss 1981). Under these circumstances, the higher interest rate does not equilibrate the market even in the case of an excess demand for loans but, on the contrary, further increases disequilibrium. This cumulative out-of-equilibrium process may easily lead to a credit crunch and possibly to a collapse of financial markets (Mankiw 1986).

Coming to the subprime financial crisis, the AIA splits into two alternative explanations, having radically different policy implications. The crucial divergences between them are rooted in a different understanding of the evolution of banking since the early 1980s, and the role played by securitization in recent years.

Securitization is the creation and issuance of debt securities, or bonds, whose payments of principal and interest derive from cash flows generated by separate pools of assets. Financial institutions and businesses of all kinds use securitization to immediately realize the value of a cash-producing asset. These are typically financial assets, such as loans, but can also be trade receivables or leases. In most cases, the originator of the asset anticipates a regular stream of payments. By pooling the assets together, the payment streams can be used to support interest and principal payments on debt securities. When assets are securitized, the originator receives the payment stream as a lump sum rather than spread out over time. Securitized mortgages are known as mortgage-backed securities (MBS), while securitized assets (non-mortgage loans or assets with expected payment streams) are known as asset-backed securities (ABS).

The mortgage-backed securities arose from the secondary mortgage market in 1970. Investors had traded whole loans, or un-securitized mortgages, for some time before the US Government National Mortgage Association (GNMA) guaranteed the first mortgage pass-through securities, which pass the principal and interest payments on mortgages through to investors. Pass-throughs were an innovation in the secondary mortgage market. The whole-loan market, the buying and selling of mortgages, was relatively illiquid. This presented a risk to mortgage lenders, who could find themselves unable to find buyers if they wanted to sell their loan portfolios both quickly and at an acceptable price. Holding the loans also meant exposure to the risk that rising interest rates could drive a lender's interest cost higher than its interest income. Trading whole loans meant a raft of details and paperwork that made the business relatively costly. MBS changed that. By combining similar loans into pools, the government agencies were able to pass the mortgage payments through to the certificate holders or investors. This change made the secondary mortgage market more attractive to investors and lenders alike. Investors now had a liquid instrument, and lenders had the option to move any interest rate risk associated with mortgages off their balance sheet.

Growth in the pass-through market inevitably led to innovations, such as collateralized mortgage obligations (CMO), ABS and collateralized debt obligations (CDO). Fannie Mae issued the first CMO in 1983 and redirected the cash flows to create securities with several different payment features. The central goal with CMOs was to address prepayment risk.

ABS emerged in 1985 when the Sperry Lease Finance Corporation created securities backed by its computer equipment leases. Sperry sold its rights to the lease payments to a special purpose vehicle (SPV). Interests in the SPV were, in turn, sold to investors through an underwriter. Since then, the market has grown and evolved to include the securitization of a variety of asset types, including car loans, credit card receivables, home equity loans, manufactured housing loans, student loans and even future entertainment royalties. Credit card receivables, car and home equity loans make up about 60 per cent of all ABS. Manufactured housing loans, student loans and equipment leases constitute most of the other ABS.

From the end of the 1980s, in order to improve the liquidity and tradability of securitizations, a new kind of structured asset-backed security, the CDO, was issued. A CDO is an asset-backed security whose underlying collateral is typically a portfolio of bonds or bank loans. The typical collateral for these assets is structured finance securities (such as mortgage-backed securities, home equity asset-backed securities or commercial mortgage-backed securities), leveraged loans, corporate bonds, real estate investment trust (REIT) debt and commercial real estate mortgage debt. For the number and complexity of underlying assets, the fair pricing of CDOs has always been a puzzle. According to Rajan (2008), rather than reducing risk through diversification, CDOs and other derivatives spread risk and uncertainty about the value of the underlying assets more widely.

According to the A1 view, the process of securitization progressively transformed the traditional model of banking (originate-to-hold), where banks have strong incentives to reduce the problems raised by AI, contributing to a beneficial reduction of systemic risk. In the newly developed model (originate-to-distribute), the credit originated by banks is typically securitized and sold to the market. A bank draws significant advantages from this new strategy, but produces negative externalities for the system as a whole at the same time, as it shifts the risk to the market, eventually increasing systemic risk. The incentives of banks to accurately assess the reliability of borrowers, the soundness of their investment projects, and the risks involved in lending are significantly weakened, since they are not residual claimants on these loans (Gorton 2008). According to Gorton (2008, p. 28), 'all the major bank regulators and central bankers appear to subscribe to this view, though their views have differences and nuances'.

A different approach (A2) focuses on the relationship between securitization and contagion in the shadow banking system (Gorton 2008), whose basic idea is that the financial crisis that started in 2007 in the USA originated within the shadow banking system when an unexpected exogenous shock (the slowdown of housing prices in mid-2006) first affected the

MBS market and then the whole banking system. In this view, the essence of banking (Gorton 2008) is that of creating an information-insensitive debt that tends to retain its value when new information becomes available (Gorton and Pennacchi 1990; Gorton 2009). This kind of debt is immune to adverse selection and is very liquid exactly because 'its value rarely changes and so it can be traded without fear that some people have secret information about the value of debt' (Gorton 2009, pp. 2–3). Information-insensitive debt was originally limited to demand deposits, but 'demand deposits are of no use to large firms, banks, hedge funds, and corporate treasuries, which may need to deposit large amounts of money for a short period of time' (Gorton 2009, pp. 3–4). Firms deposit their short-term liquidity in the sale and repurchase ('repo') market. These deposits are 'insured' by posting bonds as collateral, including, increasingly, securitized products. The collateral may be re-hypothecated with multiplicative effects. Collateral is a sort of currency for firms, since it not only mitigates default risk but may also be reused or spent. Repo is thus a form of banking, as it creates 'deposits' of money on call. The progressive growth of the repo market stimulated the parallel growth of securitization to satisfy the increasing need of collateral for derivative positions and settlement purposes. Securitization itself is seen by Gorton as a form of banking, since SPVs hold loans financed with high-grade debt, which is largely information-insensitive. Securitized debt is also in demand as collateral, because SPVs are 'bankruptcy remote', since the failure of the originator of loans does not affect the investors in securitized bonds.

In the decade preceding the subprime crisis, securitization and repo banking became organic parts of an alternative banking system, parallel to the regulated banking system, that came to be called 'shadow banking'. The main trouble with shadow banking was the fact that its peculiar 'deposits' gave the illusion of being information-insensitive and thus 'insured' by the market through the process of collateralization mentioned above. However, the 2007 crisis revealed that such a belief was just an illusion. The collaterals suddenly became information-sensitive as soon as the crisis burst. What is worse, much of the required information was not available, in particular about where the exposures to the shock were located. The ensuing panic paralysed the entire interbank market, because no one knew which bank was particularly exposed to the shock.

9.3   FINANCIAL CONTAGION AND ITS PROPAGATION: THEORIES AND EMPIRICAL EVIDENCE

The recent global financial crisis that was triggered by the bubble in the US housing market has again demonstrated how an initially country-specific shock could spread quickly around the globe like a contagious disease. Indeed, a medical metaphor such as contagion became a common feature of the functioning of financial markets.

Although there is no general agreement on the definition of contagion in economics and finance, the standard approach to contagion has traditionally focused on the correlation between relevant time series (Sell 2001; Panizza et al. 2009). Within this approach we may identify different research streams that strongly disagree on the theoretical assumptions, the econometric methods and the implications of empirical evidence. Thus, part of the literature defines contagion as the co-movements between relevant time series that take place after a bad shock (Kaminsky and Reinhart 2000). Another part considers only the 'excess' co-movements (relative to the norm) as the evidence for contagion (Forbes and Rigobon 2002; Caporin et al. 2012).

The classification suggested by the World Bank (2014) distinguishes between three definitions of contagion on the basis of the nature of its occurrence. According to a broad definition, contagion is referred to as the cross-country transmission of shocks or the general spill-over effects. This definition assumes that contagion can be caused by any type of linkages between countries (fundamental and non-fundamental). According to a more restrictive definition, contagion is referred to as the transmission of shocks to other countries that occurs beyond any fundamental links or common shocks. Contagion in this sense can be caused by 'irrational' phenomena (financial panic, herd behaviour). According to a very restrictive definition, contagion also occurs beyond fundamental linkages but only when cross-country correlations increase during 'crisis times' relative to correlations during 'tranquil times'. This definition allows a feasible econometric measurement of contagion.

Thus, there are different theories proposed as an explanation for the occurrence of contagion effects. According to Dornbusch et al. (2000) it is possible to distinguish two main types of contagion. The first type is so-called 'fundamentals-based contagion', which refers to co-movements in time series as a result of normal interdependencies between markets. Among fundamental factors there can be common global shocks, which can trigger crises in several countries simultaneously, and a local economic shock that can transmit across borders through trade and financial linkages. However, most of the literature distinguishes fundamental linkages from contagion (Masson 1998; Dornbusch et al. 2000; Kaminsky and Reinhart 2000).

The second type of contagion is often called 'irrational' and implies the transmission of financial crises as a result of the behaviour of investors and changes in their attitudes towards risk rather than macroeconomic fundamentals. Thus, 'irrational contagion' is normally associated with panic, herd behaviour, loss of confidence and increases in risk aversion, even though these events are more likely to occur when fundamentals are weak.

Nevertheless, there are at least three reasons for which investors' behaviour should not necessarily be considered irrational but rather individually rational. First, Calvo and Mendoza (2000) show that information asymmetries and the high fixed costs required for gathering and processing country-specific information make investors imitate the behaviour of other investors instead of collecting country-specific information on their own. Besides, highly diversified investors have lower incentives to learn about individual countries than investors with few diversification opportunities. Therefore, diversification may exacerbate herd behaviour by making investors more sensitive to market news or rumours. Similarly, Pasquariello (2007) examines how heterogeneity of private information may induce financial contagion. The author shows that contagion can still be an equilibrium outcome when speculators receive heterogeneous fundamental information. Second, investors' behaviour can be determined by changes in their expectations of what others would do (Diamond and Dybvig 1983). Thus, it is rational for investors to withdraw funds if the funding pool is limited and if it is expected that other depositors will do the same. In a similar vein, after hitting one country the liquidity crisis can hit another country if investors see it as being the last eligible for support from a limited fund sponsored by the international lenders of last resort. The third explanation for investors' behaviour lies in the high reputation costs they incur. Sometimes investors may refrain from acting first and thus prefer to follow the 'crowd' in order to avoid the risk of making a wrong decision, which can damage their reputation.

9.3.1 Empirical Measurement of Contagion

In the literature there is also ambiguity concerning the empirical measurement of financial contagion. However, broadly speaking, it is possible to distinguish two different approaches: statistical and structural. The statistical approach studies changes in the co-movements of asset prices, sovereign spreads, capital flows, rates of return and so on. Under this approach, contagion is often said to be caused by 'irrational' phenomena (financial panic, herd behaviour) and usually measured as a marked increase in correlations between selected time series during 'crisis times' relative to some 'tranquil period'. This approach may provide some useful insights on the strength and nature of contagion processes, but clouds the structure of the effective causal links between increasingly interconnected economic units.

In contrast, the structural approach focuses on the structural characteristics of the system that are represented by the structure of linkages between economic units. However, some researchers argue that the transmission of shocks via real or financial links constitutes normal interdependence rather than contagion (Masson 1998). They believe that 'pure' contagion should refer only to changes in the perception of market players and their attitudes towards risk.

These two approaches to financial contagion address different issues and carry with them distinctive policy implications. Therefore, they are not necessarily mutually exclusive.

9.3.1.1   Statistical approach to contagion

The literature on statistical tests for the existence of financial contagion is very broad (Pericoli and Sbracia 2003; Dungey et al. 2005; Pesaran and Pick 2007). In order to measure contagion, researchers often used data on stock market returns, interest rates, exchange rates, and bond and credit default swap (CDS) spreads. However, there is no unifying framework of testing for contagion during financial crises. Instead, a broad range of different methodologies has been developed. This by no means makes the assessment of contagion easier.

Empirical tests based on the correlation coefficients of asset prices are the most popular. In this category, evidence of contagion is confirmed by a marked increase in correlations between selected time series. The main advantage of the correlation approach is that it provides a straightforward framework to test for contagion by simply comparing cross-market correlation coefficients after a shock or crisis with coefficients during a relatively stable period. However, Forbes and Rigobon (2002) suggest that, in order to measure financial contagion correctly, it is necessary to control for general volatility arising during financial crises, since its simultaneous rise could be due just to normal interdependencies between markets.

Based on the approach of Forbes and Rigobon (2002), Andenmatten and Brill (2011) conclude that European countries experienced both contagion and interdependence. Bhanot et al. (2012) examine whether the sovereign debt crisis in Greece led to contagion to the sovereign bond markets of Portugal, Ireland, Italy and Spain. The authors reveal a significant increase in unconditional correlations between the yield spreads of

Greece and other markets during the crisis. However, after they account for time-varying volatility and changes in fundamental factors, they find no evidence of contagion from Greece to other peripheral countries. Other interesting papers on the early developments of the European sovereign debt crisis are surveyed in Kalbaska and Gatkowski (2012).

A considerable amount of empirical literature is also devoted to the study of causal relationships between selected time series by means of vector autoregressive (VAR) and vector error correction (VEC) models. The key advantage of this framework is that it allows direct identification of spill-overs, since estimated parameters indicate the extent to which one variable causes (in a Granger sense) another variable. O'Kane (2012) studies the relationship between the price of the Eurozone sovereign CDS and bond market, finding evidence for a Granger causal relationship with a one-day lag from CDSs to bonds for Greece and Spain, the reverse relationship for France and Italy, and a feedback relationship for Ireland and Portugal. Using a three-step Granger causality/VEC model applied to sovereign bond spreads and stock returns, Gentile and Giordano (2013) find that causality patterns have changed during the 'crisis' period compared to the pre-crisis period. Their results highlight that Germany and Spain have a leading role in spreading contagion in the sovereign bond market, whereas Italy shows a high degree of vulnerability. The results of Kalbaska and Gatkowski (2012) also indicate that the causality relationships between CDS spreads of peripheral Eurozone countries have been significantly reinforced during the crisis in sovereign debt markets.

There are also other tests for financial contagion. Mink and Haan (2012) use an event study approach to examine the impact of news about the economic situation in Greece and news about its bailout on bank stock prices in 2010. The authors find that only news about the Greek bailout has a significant effect on bank stock prices, whereas news about the situation in Greece does not lead to abnormal returns. Caporin et al. (2012) evaluate the extent of contagion in the Eurozone CDSs by using a reduced-form approach based on quantile regressions. The authors show that the propagation of shocks in Europe's CDSs has been remarkably constant for the period 2008–11, even though a significant part of the peripheral countries has been extremely affected by their sovereign debt and fiscal situations.

Metiu (2012) elaborates on a canonical model of contagion proposed by Pesaran and Pick (2007) and investigates sovereign risk contagion in the Eurozone between 2008 and 2012. The author finds significant cross-border contagion since the outbreak of the global financial crisis. Manasse and Zavalloni (2013) study European sovereign CDS spreads by estimating an econometric model with time-varying parameters. They find that, unlike the US subprime crisis, which affected many European sovereigns, the Greek crisis is largely a matter concerning the Eurozone. Their findings also state that core Eurozone members are less vulnerable to contagion, possibly because of a safe-haven effect, than peripheral countries.

There also exists a vast empirical literature on systemic risk, which is closely related to contagion, since systemic risk usually refers to situations where multiple financial institutions fail as a result of a common shock or a contagion process (Allen et al. 2010). Thus, Adrian and Brunnermeier (2011) developed a co-risk approach that allows for the value at risk of one institution in distress to be measured, conditional on another institution (or the whole financial system) being in distress. Segoviano and Goodhart (2009) developed a distress dependence matrix approach. The authors generate a multivariate distribution describing asset price movements of different institutions. From this multivariate distribution, they derive pairwise conditional probabilities of distress. Thus, the approach permits the probability of one institution falling into distress to be calculated, conditional on the probability of another institution being in distress (International Monetary Fund 2009).

Thus, the statistical approach is normally applied to market data available at high frequency. However, although market data allow the co-movements of risk to be captured and investors' behaviour distinguished from alternative explanations of contagion, often market participants overestimate risk during periods of crisis and underestimate it during tranquil periods.

9.3.1.2 Structural approach to contagion

In our opinion, in order to measure financial contagion, it would be more promising to adopt a network approach that allows a systematic investigation of the structural conditions and implications of contagion processes (Markose et al. 2010; Giansante et al. 2012; Markose 2012). This methodology is in principle rigorous, as it is based on accounting interactions between economic units. This does not exclude the study of behavioural factors, because the reaction of decision makers to accounting changes may be affected by expectations, risk aversion and irrational factors. Indeed, the main causal mechanism of contagion is rooted in the strict interaction between the balance sheets of economic units. An unexpected reduction of financial inflows of a unit typically translates into a reduction of the financial outflows of the same unit, which immediately brings about an identical reduction of financial inflows of one or more interconnected units. At the same time, an unexpected reduction of expected inflows reduces the net worth of the unit altering its decision strategies. In particular, when net worth breaches the perceived safety threshold, units try to recover the safety margin by deleveraging and fire-selling, greatly accelerating the vicious circle of contagion (Minsky 1982; Vercelli 2011). Therefore, the contagion process crucially depends on the structure and strength of the interrelations between the balance sheets of economic units.

A considerable amount of literature has been published on contagion in financial networks. A large part of the theoretical contributions focuses on the effects of various parameters and network structures on the resilience of the network to contagion. Allen and Gale (2000) model contagion in the network formed by four banks and find that the likelihood of the propagation of financial distress between network players is mainly determined by the nature of their interconnectedness. Thus, complete network structures, where all entities are connected to each other, are more resilient to contagion, as each entity bears a small share of the shock. Nier et al. (2007) apply network theory to capture the generic relationship between the level of systemic risk in the banking system and its key characteristics, such as the size of exposures, capital buffers, degree of connectivity and degree of concentration. The authors conclude that the higher the interbank exposures and the lower the banks' capital buffers, the more susceptible the banking system is to contagion effects. Besides, more concentrated banking systems are exposed to larger systemic risks. Another important finding is that the degree of connectivity has a non-monotonic effect on the resilience of a banking system to contagion. Thus, at first, a small increase in connectivity causes large contagion effects; however, when connectivity reaches a certain point, the resilience to contagion improves. Gai and Kapadia (2010) examine how the likelihood of contagion and its potential impact vary with aggregate and idiosyncratic shocks, changes in network structure and liquidity of the asset market. The authors suggest that the financial market can be characterized by a robust-yet-fragile nature; that is, contagion is rather an unlikely event, but can have devastating effects once it occurs.

Along with numerous theoretical contributions on systemic risk and financial contagion, a large body of empirical literature has emerged on the topic. In some empirical studies, researchers compute network measures and track the evolution of network properties over time. Von Peter (2007) shows how network measures can be used to identify the most important banking centres in the international banking network. Garratt et al. (2011) apply a network clustering technique to estimate how the interconnectedness of international banking groups affects the spread of systemic risk in the network in 1985–2009, finding that the contagious capacity of the international banking network was increasing during that period and peaked at the time of the Lehman Brothers collapse. Minoiu and Reyes (2011) study the evolution of the global banking network of 184 countries over the period 1978–2009 and document that the network was relatively unstable.

In recent years, there has been an increasing amount of literature that has focused on monitoring systemic risk within the banking systems of individual countries (Müller 2006, for Switzerland; Furfine 2009, for the USA; Mistrulli 2011, for Italy). Most papers in this strand have access to the data on interbank exposures only on the aggregate basis. In order to know the actual structure of bilateral exposures, the authors apply statistical methods (e.g. the maximum entropy technique) assuming that bank lending is spread as evenly as possible. The majority of papers finds that contagion appears to be a possible, but rather an unlikely, event. Upper (2011) provides a critical overview of this literature and argues that it needs to incorporate behavioural foundations in order to be more suitable for policy making.

Several attempts have also been undertaken to analyse cross-border linkages. Thus, Chan-Lau (2010) and Espinosa-Vega and Solé (2010) illustrate how financial surveillance across borders can be analysed with network methods. The authors consider not only credit but also funding shocks and their joint realization at a particular point in time. Degryse et al. (2010) study cross-border contagion from triggering countries to the banking systems of recipient countries in a multi-period context (1999–2006). Kalbaska (2013) tracks changes in the banking system sensitivity to cross-border contagion in 2006–11. The author finds that a single failure among Eurozone peripheral countries could be absorbed by the network, whereas multiple initial failures could be more dangerous.

The network approach usually uses information about mutual exposures between banks and/or other economic units. Although it accounts for only direct financial inter-linkages between units, its main advantage is that results can be clearly assigned to one specific channel of shock transmission. Besides, the network approach has significant policy implications that may help in guiding the choice of policy rules and interventions on the basis of the network topology, degree and strength of interconnections between relevant economic units.

We wish to emphasize that in both statistical and structural approaches the contagion process is by definition a crucial component of the propagation process. However, it also plays the role of triggering a critical financial process within units, sectors and countries not yet hit by the crisis. The statistical approach may thus help to explain the origin of a critical financial process in a country when it is triggered by the spill-over of financial instability developing in another country. The structural approach is significant in studying the propagation of financial instability from one unit to other units interconnected with it, providing microeconomic foundations to the analysis of contagion processes. In both cases, the process of contagion forwards changes in incentives of other agents and hence pushes most economic units towards similar decision strategies (herd behaviour), for example inducing a generalized process of deleveraging and fire selling.

The potential role of securitization to explain contagion can be adequately found out within the structural approach. As a matter of fact, securitizations require a complex network of interconnections among agents who play different roles, with heterogeneous contributions to risk allocation and, consequently, to contagion. There are six fundamental steps in a securitization. 1) An SPV is created to hold title to the assets underlying securities. 2) The originator or holder of the assets sells the assets (existing or future) to the SPV. The administrator collects the payment due from the obligor and passes it to the SPV. 3) The agent and trustee accept the responsibility for overseeing that all the parties to the securitization deal perform in accordance with the securitization trust agreement. 4) The SPV, with the assistance of an investment banker, issues securities, which are distributed to investors. Dealers play an important role once an issue is initially distributed, especially to enhance liquidity. 5) Since the investors take on the risk of the asset pool rather than the originator, credit rating agencies play an important role. The rating process assesses the strength of the cash flow and the mechanism designed to ensure full and timely payment by the process of selection of loans of appropriate credit quality, the extent of credit and liquidity support provided, and the strength of the legal framework. 6) Finally, the SPV pays the originator for the assets with the proceeds from the sale of securities.

The strong interconnection of all these agents shows how a single securitization could be seen as a network of responsibilities, obligations and risks, whose strength and clustering explain the systemic impact of the failure of any single node or hub involved. For many investors, information on the risk retained by a securitizing bank may be difficult and costly to obtain, leading to imprecise estimates of the bank's overall credit risk. As the subprime mortgage crisis has made clear, uncertainty on the true degree of risk of bank assets can lead to severe funding problems. These problems are likely to be more pronounced for banks with a larger share of short-term liabilities and wholesale liabilities, which are subject to frequent rollover on markets that tend to be highly sensitive to issuers' conditions. Hence, under this hypothesis, the probability of using credit transfer techniques should be negatively correlated with the share of short-term liabilities and interbank liabilities. The lower transparency of the bank's assets due to the securitization should increase the cost of funding sources, with a bank policy more unlikely to benefit from credit transfer solutions, such as securitizations.

9.4 CONTAGION AND THE GREAT RECESSION

Combining the contributions of the two main branches of the AIA we get useful insights into the processes of contagion that have characterized the propagation of the financial turmoil triggered by the subprime crisis. Focusing on the USA, we can distinguish four main contagion processes. The first is the effect of the bust of the housing bubble on the value of MBS. When, after an unprecedented boom, the price index of houses started to decline, this was promptly reflected in the value of mortgages and therefore also in the value of the derivatives (MBS) directly based on their value. At first, this shock affected only the subprime asset classes, whose value significantly declined.

A second devastating process of contagion followed: a bank run in the repo market, as analysed by the A2. In the preceding years, since Treasury bills happened to be more and more in short supply, AAA-rated MBS had been increasingly used as collateral for loans in the repo market in the belief that they were information-insensitive debt. This produced a vicious circle between increasing 'haircuts' and reducing the supply of high-quality collateral, drying up the main source of liquidity of the units operating in the repo market.

The third contagion process (deleveraging) rapidly transferred the growing financial distress from shadow banking to the regulated market. Finding it increasingly difficult to refinance their debt because of evaporating liquidity, highly leveraged banks started a process of fire sale of assets to recover as soon as possible a sufficient margin of financial safety, but this triggered an updated form of the debt-deflation vicious circle (Fisher 1933). The collapse in the value of assets produced by the herd behaviour of financial units increased the indebtedness and illiquidity of most units, eventually producing the virtual insolvency of many of them.

Finally, the fourth process of contagion transferred the crisis from the financial system to the real economy: the generalized reduction of income and wealth produced by the financial crisis and the severe credit crunch produced by the illiquidity and mutual mistrust of banks brought about a deep and persistent recession, soon called the 'Great Recession'.

This reconstruction of the sequence and interaction of the main contagion channels in the USA (in Europe, the crisis echoed a similar process along with a sovereign debt contagion) may contribute to a more complete assessment of the strength and shortcomings of the literature surveyed in this chapter as far as the Great Recession is concerned. The AIA focuses on the changes to the structure of incentives to explain the propagation of the crisis. Its two main branches provide insights into the contribution of financial contagion to the process of rapid propagation and amplification of financial distress. In both cases the vector of the pathologic structural change underlying the crisis is identified in the process of securitization, starting in the 1970s, whose progressive growth and generalization have deeply affected the functioning of the financial system. The A2 focuses on its role in the emergence of shadow banking, while the A1 focuses more on its impact on the prevailing model of regulated banking. The integration of the insights provided by the two main branches of the AIA is thus useful in understanding the structural changes in the financial markets underlying the Great Recession, but is limited by its theoretical assumptions, as will be argued in the concluding remarks of our chapter.

9.5 REGULATORY IMPLICATIONS

The securitization process and its link with the contagion risk allow us to find out how the two main branches of the AIA draw regulatory implications, particularly after the beginning of the crisis. Both approaches agree that the distortions of securitization and shadow banking should be mended; the policy measures go in the direction of an effective downsizing of securitization and the request that all the operations, including those that are currently off balance sheet, be rigorously registered in the balance sheets of banks. Though the policy authorities seem to endorse the A1 analysis, they have been so far reluctant, or unable, to push with the necessary energy towards the implementation of these measures. Strong opposition by powerful financial lobbies makes operationalizing such regulations even more difficult.

The treatment of securitization within the Basel II framework suffered from the idea that the process was able to transform credit risk exposures into a portfolio exposed to market risk able to originate liquidity useful for financial institutions. Moreover, financial rules were apt to introduce arbitrage opportunity both for banks adopting standardized methodologies and for those validated with their internal models.

The key issues that made securitizations a difficult area for the Basel Committee were the inherent level of complexity existing in securitization transactions and the fact that there is little standardization. It is worth noting that, albeit in an implicit way, Basel II analyses securitization as either a risk transfer tool or a funding tool, and tends to disregard the other potential drivers. In order to accommodate transactions which are neither risk transfer nor funding, Pillar 2 provides certain level of discretion to supervisory authorities in the application of the rules. This discretion was biased by the incapacity to model the risk within a macro-prudential framework.

The regulatory framework is not considered, by AIA supporters, as the crucial cause of the bank panic of 2008 for three basic reasons. First, it is claimed that the process of securitization, contrary to the intentions of some advocates, did not succeed in transferring all the risk of loans from the originators (banks) to the buyers (investors). In particular, originators retained a number of direct risks. Loans are warehoused before they are securitized; then they are transferred to the underwriters, while dealer bankers underwriting the CDOs also have to warehouse securitization tranches. Second, originators of loans and mortgages keep a participation in returns or losses that may accrue from the loans originated as a result of servicing rates and retained interests, in particular in the case of interest-only securities, principal-only securities and residual securities. In addition, some banks keep the most senior portions of CDOs on their balance sheets. Third, the existence of implicit contractual arrangements between buyers of tranches and the structured investment vehicle (SIV) sponsor that guarantees them has been empirically documented (Gorton 2008) and has led some SIV sponsors to take these items back on to their balance sheets.

In summary, the effective practice of securitization shows that the transfer of risk from the banks originating loans to investors is only partial. Systemic risk and AI increase as risk is spread in an opaque way over much larger categories of subjects participating in the chain of loans securitization. None of the subjects involved in the securitization chain retains significant incentives to assess the risk of securitized loans but, according to the second point of view, this is by itself insufficient to explain the banking panic triggered by the subprime crisis. In this view, in order to understand the latter we have to remember that the process of securitization has become a crucial component of the shadow banking system interacting with the traditional one but having a certain degree of autonomy.

The deregulation of financial markets introduced in the 1980s caused bank charter values to decline. The growing competition also from non-banks induced banks to reduce capital, to increase risk and to rely on financial innovation. Both the systematic process of securitization and shadow banking can be seen as responses of the banking system to the new policy environment to preserve the returns on equity in banking. Unfortunately, shadow banking was profitable for banks and other financial agents, but vulnerable to panic, since the system of market insurance through collateral believed to be information-insensitive turned out not to be panic-proof at all.

The best regulatory solution is the adoption of a series of measures meant to create charter value and information-insensitive debt, following the conclusions embedded within the A2 approach. This is possible only through a strict regulation of whatever subject plays the role of banking (including the emission of securitized products and the creation of repo deposits). This could be obtained by introducing the following measures (Gorton 2009):

1. The senior tranches of securitization products should be insured by the state.
2. The government must supervise and examine banks directly, including the processes of securitization, rather than relying on the loose and questionable control of rating agencies.
3. Securitization should be limited with entry barriers, and any firm that enters should be deemed a 'bank' and subject to supervision.

Points 1 and 2 are instrumental to the creation of reliable information-insensitive debt, while point 3 creates value for the production of information-insensitive debt. The previous choices would not encourage moral hazard because of the fear of compromising a valuable charter. On the contrary, as shown by the history of banking in the USA, moral hazard develops in a climate of unfettered competition as a way to defeat competitors by any means.

Both AI branches capture some significant features of the recent evolution of the banking system and, in particular, of the 2007–08 bank panic. The main difference between them derives from an alternative view of the role of securitization in financial markets. The A1 sees securitization mainly as a factor of distortion of the traditional model of commercial banking, while the A2 sees securitization as a crucial component of a parallel banking system identifiable as 'shadow banking system'. If taken seriously, the A1 should lead to a policy of 'financial repression' focused on the elimination (or heavy mitigation) of securitization and shadow banking, while according to the A2 shadow banking should not be repressed but strictly regulated. In our opinion, these policy prescriptions do not exclude each other and should be strictly coordinated. The policy prescriptions of A1, however, are greatly weakened by the illusion that the necessary financial repression may be implemented by self-regulation, while the policy prescriptions of A2 are not credible unless the shadow dimension of the parallel banking system is made transparent by the necessary accounting rigour.

The reason why both branches of the AIA appear to be limited in facing the drawbacks of securitization is to be found in the limitations of general equilibrium theory underlying AI. In our opinion financial behaviour and distress depend not only on AI but more in general on the nature and degree of uncertainty – whether it is asymmetric or not. In particular, the case of 'symmetric ignorance' and 'symmetric disinformation' should be taken into account. AI is a significant and ubiquitous source of systemic uncertainty, but it is not the only one. The spreading of risk across a plurality of unknown and unknowable subjects emphasized by both branches of the AIA implies by itself that uncertainty over the value and risk of securitized assets is strong or radical. In addition, information and uncertainty do not exhaust the causes of financial crises and their propagation.

More specifically, the A1 approach suffers from a basic internal contradiction. While the theory shows that an apparently small deviation from the axioms of general equilibrium theory is sufficient to question the properties of efficiency and optimality of a competitive equilibrium, many supporters of this approach are not willing to abandon the idea that self-regulation of markets is superior to regulation by law, even in the extreme circumstances of a great crisis. The exponents of the A1 seem thus convinced that a supervised self-regulation will be sufficient to restore the right incentives to optimizing behaviour.

This wishful thinking is explicitly rejected by the A2. An accurate reconstruction of the history of banking clearly shows that financial stability requires strict rules of public regulation and supervision. Gorton's arguments are liable to the criticism of implicit theorizing, since the relationship between the basic concepts and the subsequent steps of the claim are insufficiently clarified. The crucial concept that banking is in its essence about creation of information-insensitive debt goes a long way towards the understanding of recent banking practices, but the concept is too narrow. This provides a sharp focus to the argument but clouds the relations with other broader theoretical approaches.

9.6 CONCLUSIONS

A crucial role of banking has always been the creation of secure debt in the broad sense of shock-insensitive debt; however, its meaning and implications are not fully analysed. In particular, the A2 mentions the relationship between the shock insensitivity of an asset, its liquidity and the risk of holding it, but their crucial relations are not analysed in depth. In addition, although new information is an important category of potential shocks, there are other important shocks that have a different nature: particularly those triggered by the interaction between the balance sheets of the units that implicitly play an important role in both branches of the AIA. The latter are not information shocks, but the consequence of market interaction necessarily reflected by accounting figures.

Information and shock sensitivity is a similar concept to financial fragility: in both cases a small perturbation is sufficient to change the qualitative behaviour of economic units (Minsky 1982, 1986; Vercelli 1991, 2011). Both branches of the AIA aim to provide a theory of the propagation of financial crises, not of their ultimate causes. The triggering factors are perceived to be exogenous, as is typical of mainstream business cycle theory. However, while in the equilibrium business cycle the exogeneity of shocks is a logical necessity, given the assumption of persisting equilibrium, the AI deviation from general equilibrium theory implies the existence of disequilibrium processes. The A1 particularly contributes to clarify that the new model of banking (originate-to-distribute) is conducive to a more rapid and self-reinforcing process of propagation of financial distress through units, sectors and countries. The A2 shows that the parallel banking system (shadow banking as synthesis of securitization and repo market) provides a devastating mechanism of financial distress propagation under the existing institutional arrangements. This interaction may be understood only by delving into the processes of contagion, focusing on the propagation of the financial crisis from mortgage-related assets to the rest of finance and then to the whole economy.

It is therefore surprising that the literature on the recent crisis springing from the AIA is so weakly connected with the literature on contagion. We speculate that this may depend on the fact that the traditional statistical approach is too macro-oriented to combine with the AIA, which is intrinsically micro-based, or at least requires a disaggregation between categories of decision makers having a different degree and quality of information. As for the structural literature on contagion, there is an obvious potential of integration that may lead to a useful interaction between the two approaches in the future, since both are about the propagation of financial distress through economic units, taking into account the balance sheet interaction between them. To the best of our knowledge, however, this integration has not yet progressed extensively, most probably because of the complexity of the models that study structural contagion.

REFERENCES

Adrian, T. and M. Brunnermeier (2011), 'CoVar', NBER Working Paper No. 17454, National Bureau of Economic Research.
Akerlof, G. (1970), 'The market for "lemons": quality uncertainty and market mechanism', *Quarterly Journal of Economics*, **84** (3), 488–500.
Allen, F. and D. Gale (2000), 'Financial contagion', *Journal of Political Economy*, **108** (1), 1–33.
Allen, F., A. Babus and E. Carletti (2010), 'Financial connections and systemic risk', NBER Working Paper No. 16177, National Bureau of Economic Research.

Andenmatten, S. and F. Brill (2011), 'Measuring co-movements of CDS premia during the Greek debt crisis', Discussion Papers 11-04, University of Bern.

Bhanot, K., N. Burns, D. Hunter and M. Williams (2012), 'Was there contagion in Eurozone sovereign bond markets during the Greek debt crisis?', Working Paper Series No. 006FIN-73-2012, University of Texas at San Antonio.

Calvo, G. and E. Mendoza (2000), 'Rational contagion and the globalization of securities markets', *Journal of International Economics*, **51** (1), 79–113.

Caporin, M., L. Pelizzon, F. Ravazzolo and R. Rigobon (2012), 'Measuring sovereign contagion in Europe', CAMP Working Paper Series No. 4/2012, Centre for Applied Macro- and Petroleum Economics.

Chan-Lau, J. (2010), 'Balance sheet network analysis of too-connected-to-fail risk in global and domestic banking systems', IMF Working Paper No. 10/107, International Monetary Fund.

Degryse, H., M. Elahi and M. Penas (2010), 'Cross-border exposures and financial contagion', *International Review of Finance*, **10** (2), 209–240.

Diamond, D. and P. Dybvig (1983), 'Bank runs, deposit insurance and liquidity', *Journal of Political Economy*, **91** (3), 401–419.

Dornbusch, R., Y. Park and S. Claessens (2000), 'Contagion: understanding how it spreads', *World Bank Research Observer*, **15** (2), 177–197.

Dungey, M., R. Fry, B. González-Hermosillo and V. Martin (2005), 'Empirical modelling of contagion: a review of methodologies', *Quantitative Finance*, **5** (1), 9–24.

Espinosa-Vega, M. and J. Solé (2010), 'Cross-border financial surveillance: a network perspective', IMF Working Paper No. 10/105, International Monetary Fund.

Fisher, I. (1933), 'The debt deflation theory of great depressions', *Econometrica*, **1** (4), 337–357.

Forbes, K. and R. Rigobon (2002), 'No contagion, only interdependence: measuring stock market comovements', *Journal of Finance*, **57**, 2223–2261.

Furfine, C. (2009), 'Interbank exposures: quantifying the risk of contagion', *Journal of Money, Credit and Banking*, **35** (1), 111–128.

Gai, P. and S. Kapadia (2010), 'Contagion in financial networks', *Proceedings of the Royal Society A*, **466**, 2401–2423.

Garratt, R., L. Mahadeva and K. Svirydzenka (2011), 'Mapping systemic risk in the international banking network', Working Paper No. 413, Bank of England.

Gentile, M. and L. Giordano (2013), 'Financial contagion during Lehman default and sovereign debt crisis: an empirical analysis on euro area bond and equity markets', *Journal of Financial Management, Markets and Institutions*, **1** (2), 197–224.

Giansante, S., C. Chiarella, S. Sordi and A. Vercelli (2012), 'Structural contagion and vulnerability to unexpected liquidity shortfalls', *Journal of Economic Behavior and Organization*, **83** (3), 558–569.

Gorton, G. (2008), 'The panic of 2007', in *Maintaining Stability in a Changing Financial System*, Proceedings of the 2008 Jackson Hole Conference, Federal Reserve Bank of Kansas City.

Gorton, G. (2009), 'Information, liquidity and the (ongoing) panic of 2007', *American Economic Review, Papers and Proceedings*, **99** (2), 567–572.

Gorton, G. and G. Pennacchi (1990), 'Financial intermediaries and liquidity creation', *Journal of Finance*, **45** (1), 49–72.

International Monetary Fund (2009), 'Responding to the financial crisis and measuring systemic risks', *Global Financial Stability Report*, April.

Kalbaska, A. (2013), 'From sovereigns to banks: evidence on cross-border contagion (2006–2011)', DEPS Working Paper No. 680, University of Siena.

Kalbaska, A. and M. Gatkowski (2012), 'Eurozone sovereign contagion: evidence from the CDS market (2005–2010)', *Journal of Economic Behavior and Organization*, **83** (3), 657–673.

Kaminsky, G. and C. Reinhart (2000), 'On crises, contagion and confusion', *Journal of International Economics*, **51** (1), 145–168.

Manasse, P. and L. Zavalloni (2013), 'Sovereign contagion in Europe: evidence from the CDS market', Working Paper DSE No. 863, Università di Bologna, Department of Economics.

Mankiw, N. (1986), 'The allocation of credit and financial collapse', *Quarterly Journal of Economics*, **101** (3), 455–470.

Markose, S. (2012), 'Systemic risk from global financial derivatives: a network analysis of contagion and its mitigation with super-spreader tax', IMF Working Paper No. 12/282, International Monetary Fund.

Markose, S., S. Giansante, M. Gatkowski and A. Shaghaghi (2010), 'Too interconnected to fail: financial contagion and systemic risk in network model of CDS and other credit enhancement obligations of US banks', Discussion Paper Series No. 683, University of Essex.

Masson, P. (1998), 'Contagion: monsoonal effects, spillovers and jumps between multiple equilibria', IMF Working Paper No. 98/142, International Monetary Fund.

Metiu, N. (2012), 'Sovereign risk contagion in the Eurozone', *Economics Letters*, **117**, 35–38.

Mink, M. and J. Haan (2012), 'Contagion during the Greek sovereign debt crisis', DNB Working Paper No. 335, De Nederlansche Bank.

Minoiu, C. and J. Reyes (2011), 'A network analysis of global banking: 1978–2009', IMF Working Paper No. 11/74, International Monetary Fund.

Minsky, H. (1982), *Can 'It' Happen Again? Essays on Instability and Finance*, Armonk, NY: M.E. Sharpe.

Minsky, H. (1986), *Stabilizing an Unstable Economy*, New Haven, CT: Yale University Press.

Mishkin, F. (1991), 'Asymmetric information and financial crises: a historical perspective', in R. Hubbard (ed.), *Financial Markets and Financial Crises*, Chicago: University of Chicago Press.

Mistrulli, P. (2011), 'Assessing financial contagion in the interbank market: maximum entropy versus observed interbank lending patterns', *Journal of Banking and Finance*, **35**, 1114–1127.

Müller, J. (2006), 'Interbank credit lines as a channel of contagion', *Journal of Financial Services Research*, **29** (1), 37–60.

Nier, E., J. Yang, T. Yorulmazer and A. Alentorn (2007), 'Network models and financial stability', *Journal of Economic Dynamics and Control*, **31**, 2033–2060.

O'Kane, D. (2012), 'The link between Eurozone sovereign debt and CDS prices', working paper, EDHEC-Risk Institute, January.

Panizza, U., F. Sturzenegger and J. Zettelmayer (2009), 'The economics and law of sovereign debt and default', *Journal of Economic Literature*, **47**, 651–698.

Pasquariello, P. (2007), 'Imperfect competition, information heterogeneity and financial contagion', *Review of Financial Studies*, **20** (2), 391–426.

Pericoli, M. and M. Sbracia (2003), 'A primer on financial contagion', *Journal of Economic Surveys*, **17** (4), 571–608.

Pesaran, M. and A. Pick (2007), 'Econometric issues in the analysis of contagion', *Journal of Economic Dynamics and Control*, **31** (4), 1245–1277.

Rajan R. (2008), 'Bankers' pay is deeply flawed', *Financial Times*, 9 January.

Segoviano, M. and C. Goodhart (2009), 'Banking stability measures', IMF Working Paper No. 09/4, International Monetary Fund.

Sell, F. (2001), *Contagion in Financial Markets*, Cheltenham, UK and Northampton, MA, USA: Edward Elgar Publishing.

Stiglitz, J. and A. Weiss (1981), 'Credit rationing in markets with imperfect information', *American Economic Review*, **71** (3), 393–410.

Upper, C. (2011), 'Simulation methods to assess the danger of contagion in interbank markets', *Journal of Financial Stability*, **7** (3), 111–125.

Vercelli, A. (1991), *Methodological Foundations of Macroeconomics: Keynes and Lucas*, Cambridge, UK: Cambridge University Press.

Vercelli, A. (2011), 'A perspective on Minsky moments: revisiting the core of the financial instability hypothesis', *Review of Political Economy*, **23** (1), 49–67.

von Peter, G. (2007), 'International banking centres: a network perspective', *BIS Quarterly Review*, December, 33–45.

World Bank (2014), 'Definitions of contagion', http://econ.worldbank.org/WBSITE/EXTERNAL/EXTDEC/EXTRESEARCH/EXTPROGRAMS/EXTMACROECO/0,,contentMDK:20889756~pagePK:64168182~piPK:64168060~theSitePK:477872,00.html.

10. Risk management, the subprime crisis and finance-dominated capitalism: what went wrong? A systematic literature review

Sérgio Lagoa, Emanuel Leão and Ricardo Barradas

10.1 INTRODUCTION

In most developed countries, the financial sector has seen a growth in employment, value added, visibility and power. Some authors call this phenomenon financialization (Epstein 2005) or financed-dominated capitalism, which is characterized by features such as: 1) enormous growth of financial markets; 2) deregulation of the financial system and of the economy in general; (3) the emergence of new financial institutions and markets; and 4) the appearance of a culture oriented to the individual, the market and rationality.

Some authors see the growth of finance and financial deregulation as essentially beneficial, believing that a well-developed financial sector stimulates economic growth and financial markets guide the efficient allocation of resources (e.g. IMF 2006, p. 51). Securitization, for example, allows risk to be spread to institutions that are better equipped to deal with it.

There is, however, a large body of literature on financialization highlighting the negative consequences of that phenomenon, such as: firms aim to maximize their short-run financial value at the cost of sustainable productive investments; economic and social public policies are pushed into accepting market mechanisms in all areas, sometimes with deleterious consequences for efficiency and equity; and growing areas of economic and social life are exposed to the volatility and crises that often characterize financial markets.

This chapter is concerned with the implications of both visions of finance for risk management. The mainstream view argues that, as finance grows, risk management becomes more efficient and therefore ensures the diversification and control of risk. For example, when mortgage debts are divided and packaged into securities, risk is diversified and reduced.

In contrast, the financialization approach is sceptical about the financial sector's capacity to manage risk effectively. As finance expands and new financial institutions and markets emerge in a context of financial deregulation, the pressure for short-run profit and growth leads to more risk and ultimately to crises. Firms tend to ignore their long-run survival and other social values.

We review the literature to assess the role of risk management in the subprime crisis in order to evaluate which of the two aforementioned visions prevails and which is more persuasive. It should be noted that the simple fact that a crisis has occurred does not mean necessarily that the mainstream view is wrong. Even if risk management is perfectly executed, great losses may be incurred as a result of bad luck or unforeseeable risks.

The financial literature provides no single definition of risk management. In one of the broadest definitions, risk management is defined as the identification and management of a corporation's exposure to financial risk (Kaen 2005).

In general, efficient risk management is key if financial organizations are to survive crises, and this was particularly true during the subprime crisis. The literature has described many factors that contributed to this crisis. One of the most salient factors is the poorly designed incentives of the players in the collateralized debt obligations (CDO)[1] market (Kashyap 2010; Rötheli 2010), including bank managers (Nelson and Katzenstein 2014) and credit rating agencies (Gupta et al. 2010; Lang and Jagtiani 2010). The production of excessively complex and opaque CDOs was facilitated by the bubble in the real estate market (Voinea and Anton 2009; Nelson and Katzenstein 2014). Other factors commonly mentioned include the excessive leverage of households and banks (Hellwig 2008), US monetary policy (Foo 2008; Rötheli 2010), deregulation, international imbalances related to a high US current account deficit, and the enormously increased amount of funds seeking high returns (with this growth ultimately linked to increased income and wealth inequality).

The excessive amount of credit granted to households was linked to the financialization of the mortgage market, and it progressively facilitated global financial investments (Aalbers 2008). Banks excessively increased leverage to boost shareholders' returns (Palley 2007) by using short-term funds to finance long-term investments, thereby raising systemic risk (Hellwig 2008). This risk was also heightened by the pro-cyclicality introduced into the system by credit ratings, margin calls and credit default swap (CDS) spreads (Turner 2009).

Whereas hedging strategies based on CDS made individual investors feel safer, they increased risk for the financial system as a whole (Crotty 2009). Derivatives in general, and CDS in particular, take the separation between asset ownership and direct ownership of a tangible or intangible asset to an unprecedented extreme, and simultaneously give the wrong impression that risk can be controlled scientifically (Wigan 2009).

Increased income inequality created the conditions that allowed the financial crisis, working through both the supply side and mostly the demand side of financial assets (Lysandrou 2011). The supply of CDOs depended on subprime mortgages to poor households. These households had difficulties in meeting their obligations towards banks because of lower wages and higher living costs, but this was also true of relatively wealthy households in periods of increasing interest rates and falling asset prices (Langley 2008).

The remainder of the chapter is organized as follows. Section 10.2 addresses the main risk management failures during the crisis, and section 10.3 sets out the lessons and recommendations that can be drawn from the analysis of these failures. Section 10.4 concludes.

10.2 RISK MANAGEMENT FAILURES

Haubrich (2001), Stulz (2008) and Jorion (2009) note that even when risk management is flawlessly executed it does not guarantee that major losses will not occur. There can be an unlucky one-in-a-hundred event or an overly risky business decision. Haubrich (2001) adds that risk management may break down when optimal private levels of risk are not socially optimal. The question that we would like to address is whether there was a failure of risk management during the subprime crisis or if it was simply a case of bad luck or poor business decisions.

Stulz (2008) states that the risk management process involves five stages: identification, measurement, communication, monitoring and management of risks. As we shall see, problems have arisen in each of these stages. We have organized the weaknesses of risk management identified in the subprime crisis literature into three categories: methodology and technique; governance and strategy; and regulation and external factors (Box 10.1).

**BOX 10.1   MAJOR RISK MANAGEMENT FAILURES
              IDENTIFIED IN THE LITERATURE**

Methodology and technique:

- ill-suited risk metrics, namely value at risk (VaR) measures;
- overconfidence in quantitative models and lack of qualitative analysis;
- neglected risks (e.g. liquidity, reputational and concentration risks, and contagion);
- rapid evolution of financial products, characterized by high complexity and low transparency.

Governance and strategy:

- disaggregated vision of risk;
- lack of a capital allocation strategy;
- little importance given to risk management;
- failures in internal communication, risk control and auditing;
- flaws in the design of compensation arrangements;
- cultural weaknesses.

Regulation and external factors:

- excessive reliance on external ratings that were performed incorrectly;
- poor regulatory framework, namely capital regulation;
- gaps in accounting standards and regulatory requirements;
- the 'too big to fail' problem;
- monetary policy preventing the market from reassessing the importance of risk.

10.2.1   Methodology and Technique

To begin with, the first type of failure results from using inappropriate risk metrics. During the subprime crisis, banks, credit rating agencies and international regulators employed sophisticated risk management metrics, and VaR was the most widely adopted model (Stulz 2008; Nelson and Katzenstein 2014). Since VaR models are not meant to reveal the distribution of the losses that exceed the VaR limit, they are of little use if risk managers want to understand potentially catastrophic losses with a low probability of occurring (Stulz 2008).

Crotty (2009) and Nelson and Katzenstein (2014) argue that VaR systematically underestimates low-probability events because it is based on the Gaussian distribution, which under-represents these high-cost events in distribution tails. Extreme and unlikely events with serious consequences, or 'black swans', make the distribution more skewed (Taleb 2007).

Stulz (2008) notes that top risk management should not focus primarily on daily VaR but on long-run indicators of risk. Moreover, daily VaR implicitly assumes that assets can be sold quickly or hedged and, therefore, a corporation can essentially limit its losses within a day. But this may not be feasible at a time of low liquidity, as observed in the subprime crisis.

Nelson and Katzenstein (2014) advocate that the failures of the VaR methodology were fundamental in creating and exacerbating the subprime collapse. Firstly, VaR was calculated on the basis of very short time series data (often less than 12 months), which did not include any serious crises. The reason for this procedure is that the structured debt products were new, and it was believed that old ABS data were not relevant given the changes in the mortgage market in the previous two decades. Given the lack of historical data to assess risk, firms had to use proxies (e.g. corporate bonds rated AAA), which proved incorrect. Therefore, there was an under-valuation of risk, and VaR models did not capture well the behaviour of new structured debt products when severe shocks hit the markets and liquidity decreased (SSG 2008).

The risk of structured subprime products (CDO and MBS) was assessed assuming that house prices would not fall. In general, there was an underestimation of the possible losses on those products (SSG 2008). Indeed, based on the available historical data, it was difficult for risk managers to estimate the losses arising from a wide housing market collapse, as this had occurred only in the 1930s (Crotty 2009; Nelson and Katzenstein 2014). This is a good illustration of the fact that statistical techniques of risk management are useful tools when there are a lot of data and when it is reasonable to expect future returns to have the same distribution as past returns, but that in other cases using historical data is of little use because the risk has never manifested itself in the observed time period (Stulz 2008).

The Turner Report also mentions that the wide adoption of VaR models amplified the crisis by inducing 'similar and simultaneous behaviour by numerous players' (Turner 2009, p.45). Risk measured by VaR models rises at times of increased volatility and, in an attempt to reduce risk, investors start selling, thus amplifying the crisis (*Economist* 2008).

In fact, VaR has difficulty in capturing systemic risk, since it assumes that each firm's actions do not affect the market outcome (Stiglitz 2009; Turner 2009). However, in a situation where all firms behave in a similar way, the risk will be much higher than the model predicts. It is equally disturbing that the VaR assessment of risk may be lowest precisely when systemic risk is at its highest level, as in the spring of 2007.

Hellwig (2008), Crotty (2009) and Jackson (2010) also criticize the VaR hypothesis that future asset price correlations will be similar to those of the past. Crotty (2009) and Jackson (2010) add that securities kept off the balance sheet were not included in VaR estimations, ignoring the possibility that the risk from these securities may come back on to the balance sheet.

Lang and Jagtiani (2010) and Beyhaghi and Hawley (2013) agree that the use of sophisticated but untested models of risk management was a key element of the crisis and led to many corporations underestimating risks and engaging in excessive risk taking. Ashby (2010) demonstrates that many financial institutions showed an excessive reliance on quantitative tools and failed to adopt adequate stress and scenario testing. Banks that made stress tests used very weak assumptions; they never considered a full freezing of the money market (Larosière 2009) and overestimated the advantages of diversification in a crisis (SSG 2008).

Several reasons are advanced for the overconfidence in quantitative risk models and under-utilization of qualitative approaches. Firstly, a culture had emerged that focused on market mechanisms and quantification. Another factor was the need to use rules of thumb in the presence of uncertainty (Nelson and Katzenstein 2014). Finally, Lapavitsas (2011) shows that, as banks increased credit to households, they started to use sophisticated statistical techniques of credit scoring to assess households' risks because of the large number of households and the relatively small size of each transaction.

A side effect of quantitative risk models is that they give the impression that organizations are protected against risk, ultimately leading to professionals being overconfident (Hellwig 2008; Nelson and Katzenstein 2014). Nelson and Katzenstein (2014) argue that this confidence in risk models is illusory and that the mathematical treatment of risk does not make sense in a world of irreducible and unquantifiable uncertainty.

The subprime crisis was one that required a more qualitative approach to risk (Voinea and Anton 2009; Nelson and Katzenstein 2014). Sophisticated statistical models could not substitute for qualitative judgements on the nature of the housing market boom, the presence of irrational exuberance and the problems of moral hazard and adverse selection in the subprime credit market and securitization process (Lang and Jagtiani 2010). These judgements should have taken into account that the economy becomes unstable at times of economic growth as a result of the excess of optimism (Lakonishok et al. 1994) and the emergence of speculators (Minsky 1994). Additionally, the SSG (2008) reports that traditional tools of credit risk management, such as industry analysis, were not in place in several firms that invested in the CDO market.

Another important failure in the subprime crisis was that some risks were overlooked. Jorion (2009) notes that the crisis exposed serious flaws in risk models, namely in the risk category 'known unknowns', that is, risks identified but measured inaccurately (model risk and liquidity risk), and also in the category 'unknown unknowns', which are risks that are not covered by most analyses, such as structural and regulatory changes in capital markets and contagion. In the category of known unknowns, he mentions the importance of model risk. This includes, firstly, the ignorance or wilful neglect of known risk factors. He notes that during the financial crisis it became obvious that many firms had ignored the so-called basis risk for their hedges, a problem well known since the LTCM crisis. It includes, secondly, the inaccurate measurement of risk factor distributions (including volatilities and correlations). In the subprime crisis this was manifested for example in rating agencies assuming too low correlations for the rating of different tranches of asset-backed pools. It includes, thirdly, problems with the risk mapping process.[2] UBS, for example, reports that it had mapped AAA-rated tranches from structured credit to the yield curve of AAA corporate bonds, which ignores important differences in the involved risks. More generally, the mapping process involves approximations, which are particularly problematic for new products. This is highly dangerous, since those products are more profitable and therefore more actively traded among banks.

In relation to liquidity risk, Jorion (2009) argues that management does not usually account for this owing to its complexity and the difficulty of reducing it to simple quantitative rules. Consequently, financial corporations generally did not anticipate the liquidity constraints that arose during the subprime crisis (Voinea and Anton 2009), or that credit risk problems could turn into liquidity problems (Larosière 2009).

Reputational risk was also underestimated. During the financial turmoil, banks felt obliged to supply liquidity to conduits and structured investment vehicles (SIVs) in order to maintain their reputation (SSG 2008). Conduits and SIVs proved to be a source of systemic risk that was largely ignored because of their lack of transparency (Hellwig 2008).

Similarly, Jorion (2009) claims that it is difficult to account fully for counterparty risk, and consequently most scenarios failed to consider it. He stresses that we need to know not only our counterparties, but also our counterparty's counterparties. This risk became increasingly important owing to the use of derivatives to invest and hedge positions.

Concentration risk was also largely disregarded, with financial corporations taking extremely concentrated positions in the mortgage market despite the basic principle of diversification. The reasons for such behaviour can be found in principal–agent problems, internal to firms, that were not addressed by the corporate governance structure (Lang and Jagtiani 2010) and the lack of an integrated capital allocation strategy (Sabato 2009), issues that we will turn to below.

A more fundamental problem with risk management is that it rested on unrealistic theoretical assumptions, such as the efficient market hypothesis (Williams 2011; Beyhaghi and Hawley 2013). The generalized use of these assumptions led to feedback loops and deceived practitioners, which paradoxically made risk management contribute to the increase of risk. González-Páramo (2011) stresses that banks were overconfident about the efficiency of markets and the ability of financial innovations to spread risk. Crotty (2009) notes that, in some cases, risks were transferred to clients who were not able to understand them fully, thereby increasing systemic risk in financial markets.

An interesting aspect is that the evolution of financial products outpaced the evolution of risk management (Voinea and Anton 2009) and the regulators' capacity to adapt (González-Páramo 2011). Structured financial products were extremely complex, with several layers of MBS making risk evaluation difficult (Larosière 2009), and thus firms were not able to anticipate that losses could affect even the super-senior tranches of CDOs (SSG 2008).

This complexity contributed to the lack of transparency of the MBS and CDO markets (Crotty 2009), which was amplified by the securitization process (Stiglitz 2009). Moreover, the lack of transparency in financial markets and within certain financial institutions raised doubts about the dimension and location of credit risk and undermined confidence in the system (Larosière 2009).

10.2.2   Governance and Strategy

Another strand of explanation for the subprime crisis is based on failures in corporate governance, which did not safeguard against excessive risk taking. Some authors emphasize that the lack of implementation of enterprise risk management (ERM) made it difficult to prevent risks (Kirkpatrick 2009). In the ERM approach, all risks are assembled in a strategic and coordinated framework, and a specific entity has an overview of the company's risk. Three main weaknesses in the insufficient implementation of such a strategy have been reported.

Firstly, the disaggregated vision of risk was a key problem (Sabato 2009; Lang and Jagtiani 2010). By trying to create an independent risk management function, organizations isolated it from the overall investment process and thus limited its ability to influence the main decisions (Flaherty et al. 2013). Moreover, financial innovations associated with the subprime market were developed by isolated departments, and they were not integrated in the general business model, which implied that firms had no perception of their aggregate risk (*Economist* 2008). The disaggregated vision of risk also resulted from an inadequate and fragmented infrastructure that made effective risk identification and measurement difficult (SSG 2009). In some cases, this problem was clearly associated with the poor integration of data that had resulted from corporations' multiple mergers and acquisitions.

Secondly, Kirkpatrick (2009), Sabato (2009) and SSG (2009) argue that the failure of risk management in most banks was in part due to the lack of a capital allocation strategy by the board, with the delineation and imposition of a level of acceptable risk and suitable risk metrics.

Thirdly and finally, the figure of chief risk officer (CRO) did not play a sufficiently important role at the board level (Lang and Jagtiani 2010), and risk management was considered a support function (KPMG 2009).

Some authors argue that failures in reporting risk and communication between risk management staff and senior management were also common in financial institutions and information was not provided with sufficient regularity (Ashby 2010; Lang and Jagtiani 2010). KPMG (2009), however, reports that communication across units of the organization did not play a major role in the crisis.

Therefore, a lack of communication, but also the fact that the board and the senior management did not always fully understand the new structured products, meant that they had no overview of their firms' overall exposure to risk (Larosière 2009; Turner 2009). The board also failed to have proper control over business line managers owing to inadequate internal risk control and auditing (Larosière 2009; SSG 2009; Lang and Jagtiani 2010). This includes, in particular, delays in the identification, limitation and treatment of losses and frauds (Jawadi 2010).

Excessive risk taking by traders was also facilitated by internal institutional arrangements that favoured risk takers at the expense of control personnel and so led to a lack of internal supervision (SSG 2009), and complicity between managers and traders that led to fraud in many cases (Jawadi 2010). The complicity between managers and traders to take excessive risk has to be understood in the context of an irrationally exuberant market.

It should also be noted that compensation arrangements were not associated with strategy, risk appetite and long-term interests of corporations (Kirkpatrick 2009; KPMG 2009). They were skewed to maximize same-year results, disconnected from risk, as they did not take into account the true economic profits with the deduction of all appropriate costs (SSG 2009). Remuneration schemes favoured high-risk, high-return investments (Acharya and Richardson 2009; Crotty 2009; Kashyap 2010). Lang and Jagtiani (2010) focus on the fact that managers were given incentives to increase the profitability of their business lines rather than to consider the corporation's overall risk position.

According to the SSG (2009), another central problem associated with compensation practices was that they were driven by the need to attract and retain talent and often were not integrated with the corporation's risk control. Hellwig (2008) adds that employees were naturally concerned with their careers and remuneration, which led to enormous peer pressure, so that anyone who doubted a new and profitable business like MBOs would not be well regarded by colleagues.

According to Freeman (2010), the huge monetary rewards given to high-level managers in financial institutions, instead of leading them to improve products offered, made them redistribute rents from consumers to firms, make high-risk investments and misreport financial returns. In particular, the top management of commercial banks was interested in increasing assets and profits, which meant they had to increase credit. Since good borrowers already had credit, the only alternative was to increase credit to less creditworthy clients: the subprime segment (Adrian and Shin 2010).

Finally, Ashby (2010)'s survey stresses human and cultural weaknesses such as ego, greed and 'disaster myopia'. It can be concluded from KPMG (2009)'s survey that risk culture was one of the elements of risk management that most contributed to the crisis.

10.2.3   Regulation and External Factors

External conditions also made risk management more difficult and created incentives for excessive risk taking. The assignment of incorrect ratings by rating agencies led banks towards excessive risk. More generally, the incentives of all agents in the securitization chain were misaligned. Banks also did not perform appropriate due diligences and relied excessively on external ratings (González-Páramo 2011).

Hellwig (2008) and Ashby (2010) found that competitive pressures prevented financial institutions from staying out of the most profitable risky activities.

Sabato (2009) points out that the poor regulatory framework based on the belief that banks could be trusted to regulate themselves was one of the main flaws causing the subprime crisis. Freeman (2010) claims that governments experimented with laissez-faire capitalism by deregulating financial markets. The lack of regulation can also be explained by regulatory capture of supervisors by the financial sector.

Indeed, Basel II trusted in banks' own models to assess some important risks like market and credit risks. Ashby (2010)'s interviewees (risk managers from a range of financial institutions) indicate the presence of significant regulatory failures in design (for instance, Basel II and its focus on capital requirements) and implementation (namely, supervisors' capacity to make effective judgements). One of the main criticisms of Basel II was the incentive to use credit securitization and shadow banking organizations to reduce regulatory capital, as the regulatory framework was lax and almost non-existent in the shadow banking system (Crotty 2009). Hellwig (2008) highlights other perverse effects of capital regulation. Banks were able to use quantitative risk management models to economize on regulatory capital, thus exacerbating the insufficiency of capital that amplified the crisis. Since regulators were trusting in capital regulation, they had not efficiently monitored risk management functions and did not prevent highly concentrated risk.

In addition, monitoring was hampered by gaps in accounting standards and regulatory requirements, for example the absence of commonly accepted accounting principles for risky products that would ensure a clear and comparable disclosure in annual reports (Kirkpatrick 2009). Better accounting standards and greater transparency about risks and products would have facilitated the working of market discipline, which did not play a major role in limiting risk taking by banks (Turner 2009). Contrarily, Best (2010) doubts that other financial crises will be avoided by providing the market with better and more information about financial instruments, because the true risk of some instruments is impossible to calculate and it is unclear whether the market has the ability or interest to make appropriate use of this information. Dowd (2009) and Lang and Jagtiani (2010) for example emphasize that large financial corporations were not given appropriate incentives to worry about 'tail-risk' owing to the government's 'too big to fail' policy. The largest banks were financed at lower rates than their true risk justified, allowing them to expand risky activities even further (Moss 2009). Panageas (2010) develops a model where the possibility of bailout by outside stakeholders allows firms to choose high-volatility investments while net worth is high.

Finally, monetary policy also played a role by mitigating the fall in asset prices, especially after the burst of the internet bubble, which prevented the market from reassessing the importance of risk (González-Páramo 2011).

10.3   RISK MANAGEMENT RECOMMENDATIONS

By identifying the faults in risk management many lessons can be learned and, based on this, a range of recommendations can be made. Once again we group these into three broad areas: methodology and technique; governance and strategy; and regulation and external factors (Box 10.2).

BOX 10.2   MAJOR RECOMMENDATIONS OF IMPROVEMENT TO RISK MANAGEMENT IDENTIFIED IN THE LITERATURE

Methodology and technique:

- more dynamic and systematic attention to certain risks and adoption of capital buffers to account for them;
- complementing quantitative models with qualitative approaches;
- improving technical aspects of quantitative analysis.

Governance and strategy:

- adoption of an ERM approach: involvement of all employees and creation of limits on risk taking in accordance with organization culture;
- increasing the importance of risk-related matters, namely the introduction of an independent CRO;
- improving the effectiveness of risk control frameworks and internal communication;
- long-term investment in high-quality professionals and technology to obtain in-house credit analysis capabilities;
- remuneration systems linked to long-term return and risk.

Regulation and external factors:

- rethinking capital regulation;
- greater transparency and better regulation of off-balance-sheet securities;
- greater harmonization and coordination of national liquidity regimes and supervision practices;
- monetary policy that focuses more on bubbles and financial stability;
- change in the treatment of large banks;
- reform of credit rating agencies;
- improvement in the structure of markets of complex financial products.

10.3.1 Methodology and Technique

One main lesson from the crisis is that some types of risks cannot be overlooked and others must be taken more seriously. Even though liquidity, counterparty and regulatory risks[3] are difficult to measure, banks should be aware of them; capital buffers should exist to account for them, and they should not grow to the extent that they can cause a bankruptcy (Jorion 2009). Nevertheless, since banks cannot have enough capital to service a systemic collapse of the financial system, the role of 'risk manager of last resort' rests on the regulator (Jorion 2009).

In particular, Golub and Crum (2010) stress the increasing importance of policy or regulatory risk, as changes in policy often result in a structural break in the covariance of economic variables. In many markets, policy risk surpasses the risk arising from economic fundamentals.

Concentration risk also warrants a watchful eye. This is of particular importance when new financial products, such as subprime securities, for which there is little prior experience, are involved (CRMPG 2008; Foo 2008; Jackson 2010).

Golub and Crum (2010) argue that corporations should acknowledge that market risk can change dramatically, and they should be very vigilant about investments that require continuity in risk appetite or the ability to foresee risk appetite and volatilities. Foo (2008) claims that investors should take into account that excessive demand for financial products may lead prices to move away from fundamentals. Another important message of the crisis is that risk cannot be seen in a static environment (*Economist* 2008). In the presence of a systemic event, things hitherto taken for granted disappear when all investors start selling and panic sets in.

A comprehensive view of all risks must be adopted to capture the interaction between different types of risks leading to compounding effects (González-Páramo 2011). For example, liquidity risk during the crisis interacted with market risk, and each reinforced the other.

The use of a less quantitative approach to risk is also commonly recommended. Risk management is a task for experienced professionals and not machines (Jorion 2009), and risk models should support and not drive decision making (KPMG 2009). Golub and Crum (2010) stress that investors in securitized products should look beyond data in order to develop a deeper and direct understanding of the underlying assets; this includes the behaviour, incentives and practices of all players involved in the securitization process.

Other tools of risk analysis are suggested to complement quantitative models. Stulz (2008) concludes that the probabilities of large losses cannot be measured very precisely, and corporations should therefore rely less on these estimates and pay more attention to the implications of such losses on their profitability and survival. Instead of depending on traditional measures of risk, based on stable returns and correlations, they should construct forward-looking scenarios that make more use of expert views (SSG 2008; Jorion 2009) and stress tests (Ashby 2010; Jackson 2010), especially to assess situations of contagion (CRMPG 2008) and policy risk (Golub and Crum 2010). Institutions are required to consider new types of risk that emerge; notably, risk plans should lead and not lag behind business development (Accenture 2013). A more critical and deeper approach that goes beyond the available technology is also necessary when analysing risk (CRMPG 2008).

The very nature of extreme events, or 'black swans', means they cannot be predicted, but their impact can be minimized if, for example, potential areas in which extreme events may occur or where failure is highly costly are identified (Taleb 2007). The most important lesson of the subprime crisis is that financial crises are more common than previously thought, and they may be different from past crises (González-Páramo 2011).

Improvements should be made to some technical aspects of quantitative analysis used by banks and regulators that failed during the crisis (Stiglitz 2009). For example, risk models should be flexible enough to adapt to changes in market conditions, use more suitable distributions than the normal distribution, be aware that correlations may change in crises, use longer samples that include serious crises (or use qualitative analysis when this is not possible), include off-balance-sheet securities in the models' estimates of risk, and not over-rely on untested models.

In short, we can conclude that, although quantitative models are an important tool for banks and regulators in assessing risk, their application needs to be improved, and they should be complemented with qualitative tools, analyses and expert views. González-Páramo (2011) indicates that the problem is not the risk measures and models used *per se*, but the lack of understanding of their limitations. Unlike natural sciences, which have fundamental laws, economics and finance study a system composed of human interactions.

Banks that did well in the 2008 crisis avoided many of the above-mentioned mistakes (SSG 2008). Resilient banks had a firm-wide risk perspective and a cooperative organizational structure of risk management, shared information across departments, and developed in-house expertise. This leads us to the importance of governance issues.

10.3.2 Governance and Strategy

The technical and methodological issues in risk management are undoubtedly important, but even the best techniques will be misused in the absence of adequate governance and appropriate incentives. KPMG (2009) and Ashby (2010) suggest the need to improve risk governance and create a risk culture through the widespread adoption of the ERM approach to ensure that all employees understand and are proactively involved in the risk management process. The board of directors needs to set realistic limits on risks that fit the institution's culture and risk aversion and which serve as a foundation of an organization's system of controls (see also SSG 2008). Ashby (2010) recommends that firms should aim at the creation of a culture of prudence and security.

Risk governance also implies the need to increase the importance that organizations give to risk-related matters. Managers should become more risk aware, give careful consideration to the risks associated with their strategic decisions, manage risk for longer horizons, take a comprehensive view of all risks, and be prepared to react rapidly and determinedly when they believe firms are exposed to excessive risk (Stulz 2008; Ashby 2010). Thus, risk managers should build contingency hedging plans that can be implemented quickly if the corporation wants to reduce its risk in a short period.

It is necessary to build stronger relations between all levels of the organization, including the business lines, audit committee, internal audit and board of directors (KPMG 2009). Reliable quantitative and qualitative information should move between them in a timely manner.

Walker (2009) and Jackson (2010) propose the introduction of a board of risk, separate from the board of directors and independent from the audit committee; its role would be to oversee and guide the directors on current and future risk exposures. The Walker Report also recommends having a CRO who participates in risk management and control with a firm-wide perspective and independence from business units. In this regard, Aebi et al. (2012) conclude that banks with the best performance during the subprime crisis were those where the CRO reported directly to the board of directors and not to the CEO.

According to the Accenture (2013) survey of 446 financial and non-financial organizations around the world, some progress has already been made, as nearly all surveyed organizations have a CRO (though some may not have a formal title); it also reports that nowadays risk management plays a much bigger role in business decisions.

Even though several authors propose that financial firms should adopt an ERM of risk, this approach is not free from criticism. Power (2009) suggests that ERM uses a control-based approach and cannot appreciate the risk of the organization's interconnectedness with the economy. Instead, he argues in favour of business continuity management (BCM), which is a recently developed hybrid approach to risk management, and includes IT and emergency management professionals among others. BCM uses non-accounting knowledge to shed light on the interconnectedness characteristic of economic life.

Risk can become more relevant in an organization only if the effectiveness of risk control frameworks is improved, namely through more accurate and timely risk reports (Ashby 2010) and greater independence between traders and risk controllers (Jawadi 2010). Risk limits are especially important in new lines of business, where the measurement of risk is more imprecise (*Economist* 2008). In support of this recommendation, Ellul and Yerramilli (2013) show that more effective risk controls reduced the risk of US bank holding companies during the subprime crisis.

The improvement in risk management is also fundamentally related to a stronger long-term investment in high-quality professionals and technology (Golub and Crum 2010; Accenture 2013). Each corporation should ensure it has a team of professional risk managers with substantial subject matter expertise, practical experience and strong communication skills, as well as the appropriate technology and infrastructures to develop suitable risk metrics. KPMG (2009) adds that banks need to improve risk expertise at senior levels, because this is crucial for more robust and informed business decisions.

Regarding in-house knowledge on credit risk, Golub and Crum (2010) add that corporations should recognize that financial certification is useless during systemic shocks. Instead, they must rely more upon their own credit analysis, surveillance and due-diligence capabilities to understand investments, or avoid investing in certain classes of risky assets (González-Páramo 2011).

Given that good professionals can still make extremely risky decisions when faced with the wrong incentives, changes in the remuneration system are often recommended. Crotty and Epstein (2009) indicate that it is vital to eliminate the widespread faults in incentive structures and moral hazard in the financial system in order to avoid a future crisis. In particular, the top management of bailed-out institutions should also be strongly penalized. Incentives should be based on long-term shareholder interests (Crotty and Epstein 2009; KPMG 2009; Walker 2009; Ashby 2010; Jackson 2010), without asymmetries in the treatment of gains and losses (Stiglitz 2009). Walker (2009) and Rötheli (2010) suggest that compensations should take into account the risk assumed, with salaries and bonuses linked to risk measures and not only to profitability.

10.3.3 Regulation and External Factors

A change in regulation is also essential to promote a safer financial system. Gualandri et al. (2009) note that it is necessary to rethink the Basel Accord in order to take the relation between solvency and liquidity into account. They agree that proper liquidity risk management helps to lower the probability of insolvency and that a bank's capacity to obtain liquidity in severe market conditions depends directly on the adequacy of its capital. Therefore, the proposal to develop a more robust, standardized and rigorous stress testing and contingency funding plans to minimize the losses when financial strains occur enjoys wide support (SSG 2008; González-Páramo 2011).

The maximum leverage ratios of investment banks should also be reduced to make them less vulnerable to changes in market risk. More generally, regulators should be aware of the risk of rising leverage in the financial system during booms (Stiglitz 2009). The creation of counter-cyclical capital requirements to restrict the growth of financial assets in good times has been proposed by Crotty and Epstein (2009). These proposals have already been addressed in Basel III. In Canada, a strong regulatory control of capital implied that Canadian banks were better capitalized than their US counterparts before and during the subprime crisis, thus contributing to a better performance of banks in Canada during this crisis (Seccareccia 2013).

The shadow banking system and investment banks must also be adequately regulated, and off-balance-sheet vehicles should be subject to adequate capital requirements that eliminate regulatory arbitrage (Crotty and Epstein 2009). Similarly, increases in the capital required for some securitized assets should be placed on the agenda, and reputational risk (associated with conduits and SIVs) should be addressed (SSG 2008).

In addition, Rötheli (2010) defends more transparency and greater regulation of off-balance-sheet products. The accounting and disclosure of off-balance-sheet vehicles and products should be clearer; during the recent financial crisis, knowing which banks held the so-called 'toxic assets' was a major problem (SSG 2008; Kirkpatrick 2009). Shareholders and risk managers must also collaborate to improve the functioning of financial markets by producing better information (Rötheli 2010).

However, Stiglitz (2009) and Ashby (2010) stress that capital rules naturally lead to regulatory arbitrage in banks, and therefore these rules cannot replace close supervision of bank practices. Ashby (2010) recalls that capital regulation may have negative effects on the quality of risk management and financial innovation, and that regulators should find a balance between hard rules and flexible practices.

Gualandri et al. (2009) also recommend greater harmonization and coordination of national liquidity regimes and supervision practices, especially for the large banks and financial conglomerates. The global financial infrastructure and policy response should be changed to better address counterparty risk, avoid contagion effects (González-Páramo 2011) and maintain public trust in banks by reacting in a timely fashion to crises (Foo 2008). The rescue of problematic banks by the authorities is defendable to avoid public panic and social turmoil.

Stiglitz (2009) and Rötheli (2010) add that central banks should be more concerned with financial market stability (including asset bubbles) and its impact on growth and employment, and make use of other tools to guarantee it. The formation of a financial markets stability authority to monitor the stability of the entire financial system is crucial (Stiglitz 2009).

Changing the treatment of large banks is another topic on the reform agenda, not only because bailouts have proven extremely expensive for the taxpayer (Rötheli 2010), but also because of the moral hazard caused by the existence of 'too big to fail' banks (González-Páramo 2011). Rötheli (2010) proposes introducing limits on the size of individual banks or the practice of special supervision for large banks. In our view, the former option must take into account that, up to a certain size, large banks play a significant role in innovation and cost reduction. But Stiglitz (2009) supports the break-up of large banks because of both the 'too big to fail' issue and competition problems. Such proposals have to take into consideration that more competition may imply banks have greater incentives to undertake risky activities. Canada's case study shows that low competition between banks may promote more financial stability (Seccareccia 2013).

Any future bailouts of banks should be funded by financial institutions (Crotty and Epstein 2009). A structure similar to the insurance deposit scheme for commercial banks should be created for other financial institutions.

Rötheli (2010) also recommends a reform of credit rating agencies in order to eliminate the tendency towards the underestimation of risks due to conflicts of interests. Measuring the accuracy of ratings would be a good solution. Stiglitz (2009) argues that rating agencies should be carefully regulated and that the government should create a rating agency.

Crotty and Epstein (2009) defend the prohibition of any financial product that is too complex to be sold in an exchange. Regulatory agencies should also monitor the creation of new financial products closely and apply a 'regulatory precautionary principle' to assess whether a new product should be allowed in the market in light of its systemic impact (Crotty and Epstein 2009). Moreover, confining financial products to exchanges would increase transparency and efficiency of the economy, reduce counterparty risk, and limit the size of the market of these products (Stiglitz 2009).

Jackson (2010) advocates that the lack of standardized structures or documentation in mortgage securitization made search costs very high, which increased the reliance on ratings. At the same time, the standards of due diligence declined over time. According to Crotty and Epstein (2009), banks that create complex structured products should be required to undertake due diligence to evaluate the risk of each underlying mortgage; the ultimate ownership of the mortgage should be clear, and it should be impossible for this to be done externally by rating agencies. This would clarify the risk of complex products and make their production less profitable. Moreover, the bank originating the mortgage should retain at least a 20 per cent equity share (Stiglitz 2009).

Price setting in the MBS market should also be made clearer (Voinea and Anton 2009). Accordingly, the European Central Bank and market participants have already promoted an initiative to disclose information on each loan on the European ABS market (González-Páramo 2011). At the bottom of the chain, predatory credit and usury practices should also be banned by regulation and supervision. Variable rates in mortgages, where the interest rate can increase substantially after an initial period of low interest, should also be prohibited, especially for low-income individuals (Stiglitz 2009).

10.4 CONCLUDING REMARKS

This chapter discussed the role of risk management in the context of the subprime financial crisis. There is no doubt that several macroeconomic factors have to be taken into account in order to understand the crisis; these include the increase in house prices, the high demand for financial products from international investors, the Fed's low interest rate policy, and regulation errors. However, the behaviour of financial corporations was at the core of the crisis; not only were they too optimistic and not only did they take excessive risk without making a correct appraisal of risk across the subprime securitization chain, but they also created complex financial products with little transparency and used CDS that only exacerbated existing risks within the financial system.

The reasons for financial institutions' failure to manage risk appropriately are striking, since this is supposedly one of their main roles in the economy. We organized the explanations for this failure into three main groups: technique and methodology; corporate governance and strategy;

and regulation and external factors. At the technical level, risk models showed several limitations; when dealing with new and complex products in particular, qualitative judgements were largely ignored and several important risks were overlooked (namely liquidity, counterparty and systemic risks). Another major shortcoming was the inappropriate risk governance structure, which gave little importance to risk matters and was characterized by a fragmented vision of risk, poor monitoring and auditing, improperly designed incentives, and cultural weaknesses. Regulators and external forces also failed to fulfil their role correctly owing to a lack of efficient monitoring by regulators, the incorrect design of Basel II on some key aspects, the 'too big to fail' problem, poor accounting standards, and insufficient market discipline.

Given the shortcomings identified, the literature proposes several remedies to improve risk management. From the methodological and technical perspective, it is important to pay more attention to certain risks. Quantitative analysis should be improved and complemented by qualitative models, scenario analysis and stress tests. Regarding governance, institutions should have a strategic approach to risk, be concerned with their long-term survival and align their remuneration schemes accordingly; the risk governance structure should be strengthened. Finally, regulation must be changed to avoid a future crisis. The Basel Agreement and prudential regulation must be reassessed, credit rating agencies have to be reformed, transparency and regulation of off-balance-sheet products and vehicles must be increased, the 'too big to fail' problem needs to be addressed, and improvements must also be made to the structure of markets. Finally, monetary policy should take into account its effect on asset price bubbles.

Even though much still needs to be done, many of the aforementioned recommendations have already been taken up by regulators around the world. Basel III is probably the most relevant step towards stronger regulation, with the reinforcement of capital requirements, and the introduction of new liquidity requirements. The Basel Committee on Banking Supervision also issued new regulations in 2013 on risk data aggregation and risk reporting that were applicable to systemically important banks at the global and domestic levels. Measures have also been taken to increase the trade of derivatives in organized and transparent markets. Furthermore, the EU started debating a proposal to limit bankers' bonuses in 2012 (Leão and Leão 2012). Other important measures are the introduction of a resolution framework for international financial firms, and procedures to deal with banks of systemic importance (Giustiniani and Thornton 2011).

Our discussion supports the financialization perspective of risk management in the crisis. Large non-financial firms, previously a major source of profit for banks, have started to raise funds directly on the markets

(Lapavitsas 2011). As a result, and in a context of deregulation of the financial system, the banking system has gone through a deep restructuring process with the growth of the shadow banking system and the move from traditional banking to fee-generating banking, grounded on the originate-and-distribute model, and the increase of lending to households rather than to firms (Stockhammer 2010).

One of the most prominent channels of financialization is the alignment between corporate and financial market interests (Palley 2007). This is done by making managers' remuneration dependent on corporations' stock price evolution, and through the encouragement of debt. This has negative implications for risk management, since managers focus on the short-run behaviour of the share price and take excessive leverage. More generally, the rise of short-termism is related to the growth of institutional investors, changes in governance control, and the prominence of finance in the economy (Orhangazi 2008, p. 74).

Increasing inequality in functional and personal income distribution has led to a growing volume of capital flooding financial markets, in search of high returns. Faced with this pressure and abundant capital, banks paid less attention to risk and were more concerned about obtaining high returns.

The need to increase profits in the short run led to the creation of complex mortgage-backed securities, without proper risk assessment, which ultimately gave rise to the crisis. The fact that regulators trusted in the self-regulation and market discipline of financial institutions also proved to be misguided, as neither of the mechanisms was sufficient to foster a sustainable approach to risk. Simultaneously, risk taking by financial institutions increased systemic risk and volatility in the economy. Cultural aspects associated with ego, greed and overconfidence in both markets and quantitative tools also play a part in explaining the crisis.

We can therefore conclude that the shortcomings in risk management identified during the subprime crisis should be interpreted by using the broad concept of financialization, as this will foster the design of more effective regulations to prevent further crises.

NOTES

We thank the editors, in particular Daniel Detzer and Eckhard Hein, and also Trevor Evans, Ricardo Mamede, Vladimiro Oliveira, and the participants in the conference 'Financialisation and the Financial Crisis' (Amsterdam, October 2013) for their valuable comments. The usual disclaimer applies.

1. CDOs are part of the wider asset-backed securities (ABS) market, which also includes residential and commercial mortgage-backed securities (MBS).

2. A process that facilitates risk measurement of complex products by decomposing them into simpler, standardized instruments and assigning risk factors to each of the instruments.
3. Regulatory risk is the risk deriving from changes in government intervention.

REFERENCES

Aalbers, M.B. (2008), 'The financialisation of home and the mortgage market crisis', *Competition and Change*, **12** (2), 148–166.

Accenture (2013), 'Risk management for an era of greater uncertainty', Accenture 2013 Global Risk Management Study, Accenture.

Acharya, V.V. and M.P. Richardson (2009), 'Causes of the financial crisis', *Critical Review*, **21** (2–3), 195–210.

Adrian, T. and H.S. Shin (2010), 'The changing nature of financial intermediation and the financial crisis of 2007–2009', *Annual Review of Economics*, **2** (1), 603–618.

Aebi, V., G. Sabato and M. Schmid (2012), 'Risk management, corporate governance, and bank performance in the financial crisis', *Journal of Banking and Finance*, **36** (12), 3213–3226.

Ashby, S. (2010), 'The 2007–09 financial crisis: learning the risk management lessons', mimeo, Nottingham Business School, January.

Best, J. (2010), 'The limits of financial risk management: or what we didn't learn from the Asian crisis', *New Political Economy*, **15** (1), 29–49.

Beyhaghi, M. and J.P. Hawley (2013), 'Modern portfolio theory and risk management: assumptions and unintended consequences', *Journal of Sustainable Finance and Investment*, **3** (1), 17–37.

CRMPG (Counterparty Risk Management Policy Group) (2008), 'Containing systemic risk: the road to reform', report of the CRMPG III, August.

Crotty, J. (2009), 'Structural causes of the global financial crisis: a critical assessment of the "new financial architecture"', *Cambridge Journal of Economics*, **33** (4), 563–580.

Crotty, J. and G. Epstein (2009), 'Regulating the U.S. financial system to avoid another meltdown', *Economic and Political Weekly*, **XLIV** (13).

Dowd, K. (2009), 'Moral hazard and the financial crisis', *Cato Journal*, **29** (1), 141–166.

Economist (2008), 'Professionally gloomy', Special Report on International Banking, 15 May.

Ellul, A. and V. Yerramilli (2013), 'Stronger risk controls, lower risk: evidence from US bank holding companies', *Journal of Finance*, **68** (5), 1757–1803.

Epstein, Gerald A. (2005), *Financialization and the World Economy*, Cheltenham, UK and Northampton, MA, USA: Edward Elgar Publishing.

Flaherty, J.C., Jr, G. Gourgey and S. Natarajan (2013), 'Five lessons learned: risk management after the crisis', *European Financial Review*, 30 April.

Foo, C. (2008), 'Conceptual lessons on financial strategy following the US subprime crisis', *Journal of Risk Finance*, **9** (3), 292–302.

Freeman, R.B. (2010), 'It's financialisation!', *International Labour Review*, **149** (2), 163–183.

Giustiniani, A. and J. Thornton (2011), 'Post-crisis financial reform: where do we stand?', *Journal of Financial Regulation and Compliance*, **19** (4), 323–336.

Golub, B.W. and C.C. Crum (2010), 'Risk management lessons worth remembering from the credit crisis of 2007–2009', *Journal of Portfolio Management*, **36** (3), 21–44.

González-Páramo, J.M. (2011), 'Rethinking risk management: from lessons learned to taking action', speech at the Risk and Return South Africa Conference, 4 March, Cape Town.

Gualandri, E., A. Landi and V. Venturelli (2009), 'Financial crisis and new dimensions of liquidity risk: rethinking prudential regulation and supervision', *Bancaria Editrice*, **7** (1), 24–42.

Gupta, V., R.K. Mittal and V.K. Bhalla (2010), 'Role of the credit rating agencies in the financial market crisis', *Journal of Development and Agricultural Economics*, **2** (7), 268–276.

Haubrich, J.G. (2001), 'Risk management and financial crises', Federal Reserve Bank of Cleveland, 1 February.

Hellwig, M. (2008), 'Systemic risk in the financial sector: an analysis of the subprime-mortgage financial crisis', preprints of the Max Planck Institute for Research on Collective Goods 2008/43, Bonn, November.

IMF (2006), *Global Financial Stability Report*, Washington, DC: International Monetary Fund.

Jackson, P. (2010), 'A false sense of security: lessons for bank risk management from the crisis', paper presented at the SUERF/Central Bank and Financial Services Authority of Ireland Conference on Regulation and Banking after the Crisis, 20 September.

Jawadi, F. (2010), 'Financial crises, bank losses, risk management and audit: what happened?', *Applied Economics Letters*, **17** (10), 1019–1022.

Jorion, P. (2009), 'Risk management lessons from the credit crisis', *European Financial Management*, **15** (5), 923–933.

Kaen, F. (2005), 'Risk management, corporate governance and the public corporation', in M. Frenkel, U. Hommel and M. Rodolf (eds), *Risk Management: Challenge and Opportunity*, Berlin: Springer.

Kashyap, A.K. (2010), 'Lessons from the financial crisis for risk management', paper prepared for the Financial Crisis Inquiry Commission, 27 February.

Kirkpatrick, G. (2009), 'The corporate governance lessons from the financial crisis', *OECD Journal: Financial Market Trends*, **2009** (1), 61–87.

KPMG (2009), 'Never again? Risk management in banking beyond the credit crisis', KPMG International.

Lakonishok, J., A. Shleifer and R.W. Vishney (1994), 'Contrarian investment, extrapolation, and risk', *Journal of Finance*, **49** (5), 1541–1578.

Lang, W.W. and J. Jagtiani (2010), 'The mortgage and financial crises: the role of credit risk management and corporate governance', *Atlantic Economic Journal*, **38** (2), 123–144.

Langley, P. (2008), 'Financialization and the consumer credit boom', *Competition and Change*, **12** (2), 133–147.

Lapavitsas, C. (2011), 'Theorizing financialisation', *Work, Employment and Society*, **25** (4), 611–626.

Larosière, J. de (2009), 'The de Larosière Group report', High-Level Group on Financial Supervision in the EU, 25 February, Brussels.

Leão, E.R. and P.R. Leão (2012), 'The subprime crisis and the global public policy response', Working Paper No. 2012/16, Dinâmia'CET – IUL, Lisbon.

Lysandrou, P. (2011), 'Global inequality and the global financial crisis: the new transmission mechanism', in J. Michie (ed.), *The Handbook of Globalisation*, Cheltenham, UK and Northampton, MA, USA: Edward Elgar Publishing.

Minsky, H.P. (1994), 'The instability hypothesis', in P. Arestis and M. Sawyer (eds), *The Elgar Companion to Radical Political Economy*, Aldershot, UK and Brookfield, VT, USA: Edward Elgar Publishing.

Moss, D. (2009), 'An ounce of prevention: financial regulation, moral hazard, and the end of "too big to fail"', *Harvard Magazine*, September–October.

Nelson, S.C. and P.J. Katzenstein (2014), 'Uncertainty, risk, and the financial crisis of 2008', *International Organization*, **68** (02), 361–392.

Orhangazi, Ö. (2008), *Financialization and the US Economy*, Cheltenham, UK and Northampton, MA, USA: Edward Elgar Publishing.

Palley, T.I. (2007), 'Financialization: what it is and why it matters', Working Paper No. 525, Levy Economics Institute.

Panageas, S. (2010), 'Bailouts, the incentive to manage risk, and financial crises', *Journal of Financial Economics*, **95** (3), 296–311.

Power, M. (2009), 'The risk management of nothing', *Accounting, Organizations and Society*, **34** (6–7), 849–855.

Rötheli, T.F. (2010), 'Causes of the financial crisis: risk misperception, policy mistakes, and banks' bounded rationality', *Journal of Socio-Economics*, **39** (2), 119–126.

Sabato, G. (2009), 'Financial crisis: where did risk management fail?', mimeo, Royal Bank of Scotland, 24 August.

Seccareccia, M. (2013), 'Financialization and the transformation of commercial banking: understanding the recent Canadian experience before and during the international financial crisis', *Journal of Post Keynesian Economics*, **35** (2), 277–300.

SSG (Senior Supervisors Group) (2008), 'Observations on risk management practices during the recent market turbulence', 6 March.

SSG (Senior Supervisors Group) (2009), 'Risk management lessons from the global banking crisis of 2008', 21 October.

Stiglitz, J. (2009), 'Principles for a new financial architecture', reference document by the Chairman of the Commission of Experts of the President of the UN General Assembly on Reforms of the International Monetary and Financial System.

Stockhammer, E. (2010), 'Financialization and the global economy', Working Paper No. 240, Levy Economics Institute.

Stulz, R.M. (2008), 'Risk management failures: what are they and when do they happen?', Working Paper No. 2008-03-017, Fisher College of Business.

Taleb, N.N. (2007), *The Black Swan: The Impact of the Highly Improbable*, New York: Random House.

Turner, A. (2009), *The Turner Review: A Regulatory Response to the Global Banking Crisis*, March, London: Financial Services Authority.

Voinea, G. and S.G. Anton (2009), 'Lessons from the current financial crisis: a risk management approach', *Review of Economic and Business Studies*, **1** (3), 139–147.

Walker, D. (2009), *A Review of Corporate Governance in UK Banks and Other*

Financial Industry Entities: Final Recommendations, 26 November, London: HM Treasury.

Wigan, D. (2009), 'Financialisation and derivatives: constructing an artifice of indifference', *Competition and Change*, **13** (2), 157–172.

Williams, E.E. (2011), 'In the land of the blind the one-eyed are king: how financial economics contributed to the collapse of 2008–2009', *Journal of Post Keynesian Economics*, **34** (1), 3–24.

Index